BRECHT

Ronald Hayman

BRECHT

A BIOGRAPHY

Weidenfeld & Nicolson
London

All rights reserved. No part of this publication
may be reproduced, stored in a retrieval system, or
transmitted, in any form or by any means, electronic,
mechanical, photocopying, recording or otherwise,
without the prior permission of the copyright holder.

First published in Great Britain by
George Weidenfeld & Nicolson Ltd
91 Clapham High Street
London sw4

ISBN 0 297 78198 7 cased

ISBN 0 297 78206 1 paperback

Printed in Great Britain by
Butler & Tanner Ltd
Frome and London

For Ute

Contents

PART FOUR – BRECHT IN HOLLYWOOD

PART FIVE – TOWARDS THE SCHIFFBAUERDAMM

Illustrations

Brecht with his brother and mother, 1908
Brecht with Otto Müller and Georg Pfanzelt
Brecht with Paula Banholzer, 1918 (*Bilderdienst Süddeutscher Verlag*)
Marianne Zoff and Hanne, 1923
Baal at the Deutches Theater, Berlin, 1926 (*Bilderdienst Süddeutscher Verlag*)
Brecht with Elisabeth Hauptmann, 1927 (*Ullstein Bilderdienst*)
Helene Weigel at her make-up mirror, *c.* 1929
Brecht with Stefan, 1931
Brecht in London, 1936
Brecht with Helene Weigel, *c.* 1939
Brecht with Margarete Steffin, 1941
Ruth Berlau, *c.* 1945 (*Johannes Hoffman*)
Brecht with Caspar Neher, 1948 (*Berliner Ensemble*)
Helene Weigel in *Mutter Courage*, Berlin (*Hainer Hill*)
Helene Weigel in *Mutter Courage*, Berlin (*Vera Tenschert*)
Brecht in Buckow (*Author's photo*)

(Unless otherwise indicated, the pictures were provided by the Bertolt-Brecht-Erben, East Berlin.)

Acknowledgements

I am grateful to the Arts Council of Great Britain and the Crompton Bequest for awarding me grants during the years 1980-2, when I was working on this book, and to the British Council for help with the travelling expenses on my trips to Germany.

I must thank Frau Barbara Brecht-Schall for meeting me in London and Berlin to talk about her father, for allowing me access to the material in the Brecht Archive and for letting me read the unpublished poems. I am grateful to Brecht's brother, Professor Walter Brecht, for receiving me in Darmstadt and talking about their childhood. I am also indebted to Dr Hans Bunge for showing me the typescript of his book on Ruth Berlau, *Brechts Lai-Tu: Ruth Berlau erzählt*.

For advice on how to approach the subject I am indebted to Eric Bentley, Martin Esslin and John Willett; for talking to me about their memories of Brecht to Elizabeth Bergner, Hans Bunge, Ernst Kahler, Isot Kilian, Heinz Kuckhahn, Joseph Losey, Käthe Rülicke-Weiler, Ekkehard Schall, Heinz Schubert, Ernst Schumacher and Manfred Wekwerth; and for corresponding helpfully, to John Fuegi, Jack Lindsay, David Pike, George Rylands and James Stern.

While I was working at the archive Hertha Ramthun and Günter Glaese were helpful; and I have also received help from American librarians who sent me photocopies: Louisa Bowen of the Morris Library, Southern University at Carbondale, Elisabeth Ann Falsey of the Houghton Library, Harvard, and David Schoonover of the Beinecke Collection, Yale.

For help in organizing the footnotes and for commenting on the first draft I am grateful to Catharine Carver, and for hospitality in Berlin to Klaus Peter Steiger. I was also given advice - and books - by Dr Willi Lange of the GDR Embassy.

I am indebted for more help than I can describe to Linden Lawson, who edited this book, to Jane Cary, her assistant, and to Tanya Schmoller, who copy-edited.

It is too late to thank Otto Zarek for introducing me to Brecht, but I remember him - and all he did for me when I was living in Berlin - with gratitude.

The translations are my own.

Chronology

p. 140 **1929** **April** Marries Weigel. Publication of *Lindbergh* (radio version) in *Uhu*.

p. 145 **June** Works on *Happy End*.

Aug. Rehearsals.

Winter Works on *Daniel Drew, Fatzer, Joe Fleischhacker* and *Der Brotladen* (*The Bread Shop*).

p. 147 **1930** **Feb.–March** Rehearsals of *Mahagonny* opera in Leipzig.

p. 152 **Spring** Works on *Die Massnahme* (*The Remedial Measure*).

p. 149 **May–July** Works in Le Lavandou on *Die heilige Johanna der Schlachthöfe* (*St Joan of the Slaughterhouses*) and *Die Ausnahme und die Regel* (*The Exception and the Rule*).

Aug. Submits screenplay for *Dreigroschenoper* film. Nero Films rejects it but proceeds with the filming. Brecht sues.

Oct. Weigel gives birth to Barbara.

p. 155 **1931** **Jan.–Feb.** Brecht directs *Mann ist Mann* in Berlin.

p. 160 **May–June** Holiday in Switzerland and France.

p. 161 **June** Joins Weigel and children in Ammersee.

August Screenplay for the film *Kuhle Wampe* completed. Shooting begins.

Autumn Adapts *Die Mutter* (*The Mother*) from Gorki.

p. 164 **Dec.** Simultaneous rehearsals for *Mahagonny* and *Die Mutter*.

Winter Completes *Die heilige Johanna der Schlachthöfe*.

p. 165 **1932** **Jan.** Relationship with Margarete Steffin.

p. 166 **Feb.** Police ban agitprop performances of *Die Mutter*.

p. 168 **May** Travels to Moscow for première of *Kuhle Wampe*.

Aug. Holiday in Unterschondorf. Buys house in Utting.

Nov. Attends Karl Korsch's lectures.

p. 170 **1933** **Feb.** In a clinic. When Reichstag is burnt escapes to Prague with Weigel and Stefan. (Barbara is with grandparents.)

March To Vienna.

p. 173 **April** To Switzerland.

p. 174 **May** To Paris for ballet *Die sieben Todsünden* (*The Seven Deadly Sins*).

p. 175 **June** Settles in Denmark.

Aug. Buys house in Skovbostrand.

p. 177 **Sept.** Back to Paris.

1939 May   Stays on island of Lidingö. His father dies.

Sept.   Begins *Mutter Courage*.

Nov.   Completes *Mutter Courage* and radio play *Das*
Verhör des Lukullus (*The Trial of Lucullus*).

Dec.   Works on Julius Caesar novel.

1940   Jan.   Writes story 'Der Augsburger Kreidekreis' (The Augsburg Chalk Circle). Writes *Esskultur* (*Culinary Culture*), a miniature detective novel.

March   In bed for three weeks with flu.

April   Sails with family and Margarete Steffin to Helsinki. Moves into a house in Tölö.

May   Resumes work on *Der gute Mensch von Sezuan*.

July   Invited by Hella Wuolijoki to stay on her estate in Kausala.

Aug.–Sept.   Converts her comedy *The Sawdust Princess* into *Herr Puntila und sein Knecht Matti* (*Herr Puntila and his Man Matti*).

Oct.   Starts *Flüchtlingsgespräche* (*Refugee Conversations*). Moves back to Helsinki.

1941   March–April   Writes *Der aufhaltsame Aufstieg des Arturo Ui* (*The Resistible Rise of Arturo Ui*).

May   With Ruth Berlau, Margarete Steffin and family, he leaves for Moscow, where Margarete Steffin dies.

July   Arrives in Los Angeles. Settles in Santa Monica, near Hollywood.

Dec.   Works on Joan of Arc play.

1942   Feb.   Registered for military service.

July–Oct.   Works on screenplay for Fritz Lang. Brecht wants to call it *Trust the People*.

Aug.   Moves to a bigger house. Works on *Messingkauf*.

Oct.–Jan. 1943   Works with Feuchtwanger on *Die Gesichte der Simone Machard* (*The Visions of Simone Machard*).

Nov.–Dec.   Shooting of film, now titled *Hangmen Also Die*.

1943   Feb.   Goes to New York. Stays with Berlau.

March–May   Collaborates with H.R. Hays on an adaptation of Webster's *The Duchess of Malfi*. Later involves
W.H. Auden. Commits himself to working with Piscator

p. 320   **July–Aug.**   Works on *Kleines Organon für das Theater*.

p. 324   **Oct.**   Brecht and Weigel go to Salzburg and then, via Prague, to East Berlin.

p. 328   **Nov.**   Auditions for *Mutter Courage*. Erich Engel arrives to co-direct.

p. 330   **Dec.**   Negotiations for a studio theatre within the Deutsches Theater.

p. 333 **1949**   **Jan.**   Berliner Ensemble created.

           Feb.   Weigel is appointed as artistic director. Brecht goes to Zürich.

p. 337   **April**   Brecht negotiates for Austrian citizenship. Completes draft of *Die Tage der Commune* (*The Days of the Commune*).

p. 338   **May**   Back to Berlin, via Salzburg. Arrangements for *Puntila* as new company's opening production.

           June–July   In St Hedwig's hospital with kidney trouble.

           Aug.   To Salzburg.

           Sept.   To Munich and, on 4 September, back to Berlin.

p. 341   **Nov.**   New company's opening production.

p. 342   **Dec.**   Adapts Lenz's *Der Hofmeister* (*The Private Tutor*).

p. 344 **1950**   **April**   Brecht and Weigel granted Austrian citizenship.

p. 345   **Aug.**   Holiday in Ahrenshoop.

p. 348   **Dec.**   Rehearsals for *Die Mutter*. Works with Neher on a play for Salzburg Festival.

p. 354 **1951**   **Jan.**   Preparations for production of *Das Verhör des Lukullus* (*The Trial of Lucullus*) at the opera house. Brecht goes into hospital for a check-up.

p. 355   **March**   Opera received unfavourably by Party leaders.

p. 356   **May**   Works on adaptation of Shakespeare's *Coriolanus*.

p. 358   **June**   Works on text for *Der Herrnburger Bericht* (*The Herrnburg Report*), a cantata.

           July–Aug.   In Ahrenshoop.

p. 360   **Oct.**   Awarded National Prize, first class. Revised version of opera, *Die Verurteilung des Lukullus* (*The Condemnation of Lucullus*), is staged.

           Nov.–Dec.   Works on *Coriolanus*.

      1952   **Jan.**   Original version of opera successfully premièred in Frankfurt.

Performances

29 Sept. 1922 *Trommeln in der Nacht* (*Drums in the Night*) at the Kammerspiele, Munich, directed by Otto Falckenberg, designed by Otto Reigbert, with Erwin Faber (Kragler).

9 May 1923 *Im Dickicht* (later called *Im Dickicht der Städte – In the Jungle of the Cities*) at the Residenztheater, Munich, directed by Erich Engel, designed by Caspar Neher, with Erwin Faber (Garga) and Otto Wernicke (Shlink).

8 Dec. 1923 *Baal* at the Altes Theater, Leipzig, directed by Alwin Kronacher, designed by Paul Thiersch with Lothar Körner (Baal).

18 March 1924 *Leben Eduards des Zweiten von England* (*Life of Edward II of England*) at the Kammerspiele, Munich, directed by Brecht, designed by Neher, with Erwin Faber (Edward II), Erich Riewe (Gaveston) and Oskar Homolka (Mortimer).

14 Feb. 1926 *Lebenslauf des Mannes Baal* (*Career of the Man Baal*) at the Deutsches Theater, Berlin (a matinée presented by the Junge Bühne) co-directed by Brecht, with Oskar Homolka (Baal) and Paul Bildt (Ekart).

25 Sept. 1926 *Mann ist Mann* (*Man is Man*) premièred simultaneously at the Landestheater, Darmstadt, directed by Jacob Geis, designed by Neher, with Ernst Legal (Galy Gay); and in the small auditorium of the Städtisches Theater, Düsseldorf, directed by Josef Münch, designed by Harry Breuer, with Ewald Balser (Galy Gay).

11 Dec. 1926 *Die Hochzeit* (*The Wedding*) at the Schauspielhaus, Frankfurt, directed by Melchior Vischer, designed by Ludwig Sievert.

17 July 1927 *Mahagonny*, with music by Kurt Weill, in the Stadttheater, Baden-Baden, directed by Brecht and designed by Neher, with Irene Eden (Bessie), Lotte Lenya (Jessie) and Erik Wirl (Charlie).

5 Jan. 1982 *Mann ist Mann* at the Volksbühne, Berlin, directed by Engel, designed by Neher, with Heinrich George (Galy Gay).

31 Aug. 1928 *Die Dreigroschenoper* (*The Threepenny Opera*), with music by Weill, at the Theater am Schiffbauerdamm, Berlin, directed by Engel, designed by Neher, with Roma Bahn (Polly), Harald Paulsen (Macheath), Kurt Gerron (Brown) and Erich Ponto (Peachum).

July 1929 *Der Lindberghflug* (later re-titled *Der Ozeanflug – The Flight Across the Ocean*), with music by Paul Hindemith and Kurt Weill, directed on radio by Ernst Hardt, and then staged by Brecht on 27 July at the Stadthalle, Baden-Baden, conducted by Hermann Scherchen.

28 July 1929 *Das Badener Lehrstück vom Einverständnis* (*The Baden Didactic Play about Acquiescence*), with music by Hindemith, directed by Brecht at the Stadthalle, Baden-Baden, with Joseph Witt.

31 Aug. 1929 *Happy End*, with music by Weill, at the Theater am Schiffbauerdamm, Berlin, directed by Brecht and Engel, designed by Neher, with Carola Neher (Lilian), Helene Weigel (the Fly), Oskar Homolka and Peter Lorre.

9 March 1930 *Aufstieg und Fall der Stadt Mahagonny* (*Rise and Fall of the City of Mahagonny*), with music by Weill, at the Opernhaus, Leipzig, directed by Walther Brugmann, designed by Neher, conducted by Gustav Brecher, with Paul Beinert (Paul).

23 June 1930 *Der Jasager* (*The Yes-Sayer*) at the Zentralinstitut für Erziehung und Unterricht, Berlin, directed by Brecht and Weill, conducted by Kurt Drabek, with Otto Hopf (Teacher).

13 Dec. 1930 *Die Massnahme* (*The Remedial Measure*), with music by Hanns Eisler, at the Philharmonie, Berlin, directed by Slatan Dudow, conducted by Karl Rankl, with Helene Weigel, Ernst Busch and Alexander Granach.

6 Feb. 1931 *Mann ist Mann* at the Staatstheater, Berlin, directed by Brecht, designed by Neher, with Peter Lorre (Galy Gay).

17 Jan. 1932 *Die Mutter* (*The Mother*), with music by Eisler, at the Wallner Theater, Berlin, and then from 17 Jan. at the Theater am Schiffbauerdamm, Berlin, directed by Emil Burri and Brecht, designed by Neher, with Weigel (Vlassova) and Ernst Busch (Pavel).

11 April 1932 Shortened version of *Die heilige Johanna der Schlachthöfe* (*St Joan of the Slaughterhouses*) broadcast on Radio Berlin, directed by Alfred Braun, with Carola Neher (Joan) and Fritz Kortner (Mauler).

14 May 1932 *Kuhle Wampe*, a screenplay by Brecht and Ernst Ottwalt, premièred in Moscow, directed by Slatan Dudow, with Ernst Busch (Fritz) and Herta Thiele (Anni).

30 May 1932 *Kuhle Wampe* premièred in Berlin at the Atrium Cinema.

7 June 1933 *Anna-Anna ou les sept péchés capitaux* (*Anna-Anna or the Seven Deadly Sins*) (in French), with music by Weill, at the Théâtre des Champs-Elysées, Paris, staged by George Balanchine and Boris Koch-no, designed by Neher, conducted by Maurice d'Abravanel with Tilly Losch and Lotte Lenya.

Spring 1935 Scenes from *Die Rundköpfe und die Spitzköpfe (Roundheads and Sharpheads)* at the Thälmann-Klub, Moscow, directed by Alexander Granach, with Alexander Granach and amateurs.

19 Nov. 1935 *The Mother* (in English), translated by Paul Peters, with music by Hanns Eisler, at the Civic Repertory Theatre, New York, directed by Victor Wolfson, designed by Mordecai Gorelik.

4 Nov. 1936 *Die Rundköpfe und die Spitzköpfe* (in Danish) at the Riddersalen Theatre, Copenhagen, directed by Per Knutzon, with Asbjorn Andersen (Iberin) and Lulu Ziegler (Nanna).

16 Oct. 1937 *Die Gewehre der Frau Carrar (Señora Carrar's Rifles)* at the Salle Adyar, Paris, directed by Slatan Dudow, designed by Heinz Lohmar, with Weigel (Carrar).

1 May 1938 *Die Ausnahme und die Regel (The Exception and the Rule)* (in Hebrew) at a Kibbutz at Givat Chaim, Palestine, directed by Alfred Wolf.

21 May 1938 *Furcht und Elend des Dritten Reiches (Fear and Suffering in the Third Reich)* under the title 99% at the Salle d'Iéna, Paris, directed by Slatan Dudow, designed by Heinz Lohmar, with music by Paul Dessau, with Weigel and Ernst Busch.

Aug. 1939 *Dansen (Dance)* (in Swedish, under the pseudonym John Kent). Two one-act plays *Was kostet das Eisen? (What Price Iron?)* and a variant on it at the Tollare People's School, Stockholm.

12 May 1940 *Das Verhör des Lukullus (The Trial of Lucullus)* broadcast by Radio Beromünster, Berne, Switzerland, directed by Ernst Bringolf.

19 April 1940 *Mutter Courage und ihre Kinder (Mother Courage and her Children)* at the Schauspielhaus, Zürich, directed by Leopold Lindtberg, designed by Teo Otto, with music by Paul Burkhard, with Therese Giehse (Mother Courage).

5 Jan. 1942 *Furcht und Elend des Dritten Reiches* at the Fraternal Clubhouse, New York, directed by Berthold Viertel.

4 Feb. 1943 *Der gute Mensch von Sezuan (The Good Woman of Setzuan)* at the Schauspielhaus, Zürich, directed by Leonard Steckel, designed by Teo Otto with Maria Becker (Shen Te).

26 March 1943 *Hangmen Also Die* premièred in Hollywood, directed by Fritz Lang, with Brian Donlevy, Walter Brennan and Anna Lee.

9 Sept. 1943 *Leben des Galilei (Life of Galileo)* at the Schauspielhaus, Zürich, directed by Leonard Steckel, designed by Teo Otto, with music by Hanns Eisler, with Leonard Steckel (Galileo).

23 Sept. 1946   John Webster's *The Duchess of Malfi* at the Shubert Theatre, Boston, directed by George Rylands, with Elisabeth Bergner (Duchess) and John Carradine (Cardinal).

31 July 1947   *Life of Galileo* (translated by Brecht and Charles Laughton) at the Coronet Theatre, Hollywood, directed by Joseph Losey, designed by Robert Davison, music by Hanns Eisler, with Charles Laughton (Galileo).

15 Feb. 1948   *Antigone* at the Stadttheater, Chur, Switzerland, directed by Brecht, designed by Neher, with Weigel (Antigone) and Hans Gaugler (Kreon).

4 May 1948   *The Caucasian Chalk Circle* (English translation by Eric and Maja Bentley). Amateur production at the Nourse Little Theatre, Northfield, Minnesota, directed by Henry Goodman.

5 June 1948   *Herr Puntila und sein Knecht Matti* (*Herr Puntila and his Man Matti*) at the Schauspielhaus, Zürich, directed by Kurt Hirschfeld, designed by Teo Otto, with Leonard Steckel (Puntila) and Gustav Knuth (Matti).

11 Jan. 1949   *Mutter Courage* at the Deutsches Theater, East Berlin, directed by Brecht and Engel, designed by Heinrich Kilger with Weigel (Courage), Angelika Hurwicz (Kattrin), Paul Bildt (cook), Werner Hinz (chaplain) and Ernst Kahler (Eilif).

15 April 1950   *Der Hofmeister* (*The Private Tutor*) (adapted from the play by J.M.R. Lenz) at the Deutsches Theater, East Berlin, directed by Brecht, designed by Neher, with Hans Gaugler (Läuffer).

17 March 1951   *Das Verhör des Lukullus* (*The Trial of Lucullus*) at the Deutsche Staatsoper, East Berlin, with music by Paul Dessau, directed by Wolf Völker, designed by Neher, conducted by Hermann Scherchen.

5 Aug. 1951   *Der Herrnburger Bericht* (*The Herrnburg Report*) at the Deutsches Theater, East Berlin, directed by Egon Monk, designed by Neher, music by Paul Dessau, conducted by Hans Sandig.

12 Oct. 1951   *Die Verurteilung des Lukullus* (*The Condemnation of Lucullus*) at the Deutsche Staatsoper, East Berlin, with music by Paul Dessau, directed by Wolf Völker, designed by Neher, conducted by Hermann Scherchen with Alfred Hülgert (Lukullus).

7 Oct. 1954   *Der kaukasische Kreidekreis* at the Theater am Schiffbauerdamm, East Berlin, designed by Karl von Appen with Angelika Hurwicz (Grusche) and Ernst Busch (Azdak).

Part One

BAVARIAN BEGINNINGS

1 / The One and the Many

At the age of fifteen Brecht was already showing that he could put his knowledge of the Bible to good literary use. He had one gift in common with Jesus: they both knew how to state a complex truth about human behaviour in a provocative story with the resonance of a riddle.

A sick old man was walking through the country. Four young lads overpowered him and took away his possessions. Sadly the old man went on. But at the next crossroads he saw to his astonishment that three of the robbers were overpowering the fourth, to take his loot away from him. But it fell into the roadway during the fight. Joyfully the old man picked it up and hurried away. But in the next town he was arrested and taken before the judge. The four lads were standing there and, in unity again, they indicted him. The judge, however, decided as follows: the old man must give back the last of his possessions to the young boys. 'Since', said the wise and just judge, 'otherwise the four fellows could cause trouble in the country.'

Titled 'The Balkan War' and signed Berthold Eugen, this parable appeared in the Augsburg school magazine *Die Ernte* (*The Harvest*) in August 1913. The author – also co-founder and co-editor of the magazine – was taking cynical pleasure in the premiss that society cannot afford justice. The rights of the one must be sacrificed to the interests of the many.

In 1913 the old man would have been identifiable as Turkey, 'the sick old man of the Bosphorus'. In the first Balkan War (1912–13) the old Turkish empire had been dispossessed of nearly all its European territories by four allies – Serbia, Bulgaria, Greece and Montenegro – but in the second war (May–August 1913) Bulgaria fought against the other three. Serbia benefited most, and the Austrian empire might have been at risk if Russia had supported Serbian expansionism. By the end of 1912 the German Kaiser, Wilhelm II, was already in favour of declaring war on Russia and France. In the schools teachers tried to encourage patriotism, and the boys were subjected to inflammatory lectures from pioneer pilots and captains of submarines.[1] To the precocious author of the political parable, it was clear that the great powers were motivated by expediency, not by morality or respect for historical precedent. Though Brecht's parents had done their best to inculcate traditional moral values, the boy was already aware that in private life, as in politics, the most profitable course was the ruthless pursuit of self-interest.

Would it be possible to live in accordance with biblical precepts? The question is central to Brecht's first play. Titled *Die Bibel* (*The Bible*), the play, which is six and a half pages long, was also written in 1913 and published in the January 1914 issue of *Die Ernte*. The Catholics are advancing on a Dutch Protestant city, which can be saved only by the immolation of an innocent girl. Should the mayor's daughter sacrifice herself? Her brother urges her to save thousands of people; her grandfather argues that one soul is more valuable than a thousand bodies. Once again conflict centres on the opposition of interests between the one and the many. Now, as later, Brecht is interested in differences of attitude and in historical context, not in motivation. The girl is distraught as she rushes from the room: fire is beating on the windows, bells are clanging and cannon thundering.

Though Brecht was not yet adept at translating historical images into theatrical pictures, his imagination moved easily between the present and the past. Not that he ever acknowledged any indebtedness to history teachers or any other teachers: 'In nine years of being marinated in an Augsburg Gymnasium, I didn't succeed in helping my teachers to make any real progress. They were indefatigable in developing my taste for leisure and independence.'[2] The joke rests on a bedrock of truth. As a boy Brecht could make rapid headway with any task, mental or physical, that he set himself, but once it was no longer a challenge he lost interest in it. At different times he was given lessons in piano, violin, guitar and recorder, but he persevered with none of them. What purpose was there in playing an instrument? Brecht was not lazy, but his taste for independence encouraged him to resist all pressure from above: to be what he wanted to be, he must have leisure for doing whatever he liked.

Augsburg, when Brecht was born there on 10 February 1898, was no longer a great mercantile city. Forty miles to the north-west of Munich, it was provincial in comparison, with a population of about 80,000, a textile industry, some papermills and a growing engineering industry.

Brecht would later try to detach himself from his childhood, rejecting the name, Eugen, by which he was known in it, and hardening his other name, Berthold, into Bertholt or Bert. Early childhood memories seldom feature in his work and he hardly ever spoke about his parents or his past. Nor did he want to think of himself as Bavarian, though in 1806 Augsburg had been incorporated into Bavaria. A Bavarian accent was prevalent there, but it was a Swabian accent that was noticeable in Brecht's speech. He even felt entitled to rewrite personal history. According to his ballad 'Vom armen B.B.' ('Of poor B.B.') he was carried 'from the black forests' into the city while in his mother's womb. In fact his parents both came from the small Black Forest town of Achern, in Baden, but his mother moved to Augsburg before she married and his father had been living there since 1893. He was working as a clerk for the Haindl paper factory, a Catholic family business which had been founded in 1849 with seven workers and, fifty years later, had three hundred.

Brecht's father was a mild, cheerful, pleasant-looking man of medium height, lightly built, with a lively gait. On 14 May 1897, the day before he married, he moved into the house where his son was to be born nine months later: 7 Auf dem Rain. On their wedding day, 15 May 1897, Berthold Friedrich Brecht was twenty-eight and Wilhelmine Friederike Sophie Brezing twenty-five. Far from being of peasant descent on both sides of the family, as early biographies have it, Brecht stemmed from two families that can both be traced back to the sixteenth century. His father's ancestors were solidly middle-class. One was a tenant farmer of Götz von Berlichingen's; later in the line came a headmaster, a carter's man, a fisherman, two teachers, and two surgeons (one in the army).[3] Brecht's maternal grandfather was a stationmaster, the son of a stocking weaver descended from five generations of bucket makers. Sophie had grown up in an Upper Swabian village, Rossberg, but her parents spent their last years in Augsburg. Because of the file-cutters' workshop on the ground floor, the house at 7 Auf dem Rain was noisy, and when the baby was only seven months old the Brechts moved to 1 Bei den 7 Kindeln, where their second son, Walter, was born on 29 June 1900.

Ten weeks later they moved again, to one of the houses which had been built in the suburb of Klaucke, near the papermill, for disabled workers, pensioners and paupers. It was in Bleichstrasse at the corner of Frühlingstrasse, overlooking the Oblatter wall. 'Past my father's house an avenue of chestnut trees flanked the old city moat; on the other side was the old city wall with the remains of ancient fortifications. Swans swam in the pond-like water.' Near by was a balloon factory, and the rows of identical two-storey houses were typical of those built in the 1890s for industrial workers. 'The courtyard of the house in which the Brechts lived, narrowed by concrete walls, emphasized this coldness and lovelessness, but it was still one of the pleasantest in this drab environment, with its south side jutting out towards the avenue of ancient chestnut trees and the town moat, behind the dark-red ivy-clad scenery provided by the old fortress.'[4]

In 1899, while still a clerk, Berthold Friedrich Brecht had written a history of the fifty-year-old paper factory and, in January 1901, on being promoted to the post of Chief Clerk, had been put in charge of the house in Bleichstrasse. His family occupied the first floor and had the use of two attic rooms. One was for the maid, who had to work all round the clock and earned only 12 marks a year; the other attic room was shared by the boys until the elder brother ousted the younger. Being more delicate, Eugen gave his mother the impression of needing a room to himself.

Though the boys were allowed to play in the street with other children, these were hardly ever allowed inside the flat, and in the warfare between gangs of boys in neighbouring houses Eugen did not fight bravely. Under pressure he would run indoors, calling for his mother, but he was often beaten up by the others. Sometimes the children played on top of the city walls and around the remains of the old fortifications. When it rained they would play in the entrance hall.[5] Unlike some of the others, the Brecht boys were never allowed to run about with bare feet.

Though sixteen years were to elapse before Berthold Brecht was promoted to sales director, he worked conscientiously. He was a keen fisherman, and he sang in a choral society. He loved animals and the family kept pets. He was a Catholic and his wife was a Protestant, but his younger son has no memory of any family arguments about religion. The boys were brought up as Protestants, and it was their mother who made all the arrangements about schooling. Their father gave opinions, took decisions, signed documents and paid bills, but he was too busy at work to spend much time with the boys.[6]

Sophie Brecht was a simple but sensitive woman who soon formed the impression that there was something special about her older son, a frail, nervous, difficult child who did not take much pleasure in eating. Cardiac trouble had asserted itself before he was nine, and twice he was taken to a sanatorium in the Black Forest. Physical debility gave him an extra affinity with his mother, whose health was poor. She had to spend a lot of time resting, and enjoyed reading. Her taste for poetry was unsophisticated, but a notebook she used for recipes also contains poems, some copied out in ink, one (a humorous love poem in dialect) cut out from a newspaper and pasted in.

When Eugen was five and going to a kindergarten run by barefoot friars – Augsburg was 75 per cent Catholic – he had to spend extra time there because his mother was too ill to look after him. In June 1905, while she was taking a cure at Bad Rain, the two boys stayed with her sister. Her husband was less literary in his inclinations. He called Eugen 'my little poet', would shake his head, tolerantly amused, saying: 'If only I knew where he got it from.' He also made cracks about it: 'Do you know the difference between me and my son? I'm a poet's dad and he's a dud poet.'[7] Walter was the happier and more extrovert of the two boys; Eugen was dreamy, thoughtful, and temperamentally disinclined, from the beginning, to invest effort in activities that brought no gratification. He hated washing, and it was impossible to train him in hygienic habits. He could quickly learn a new technique – in playing an instrument or a game – but he was immune to the bourgeois mania for self-improvement, and he discovered that grown-ups had only limited means at their disposal for imposing their will on him, for punishing him when he did something generally considered 'bad', or for making him persevere with something 'good' but strenuous. He was also liable to be brutally impatient if his brother was slow to learn something he found easy. At the age of six or seven Walter had to dog-paddle his way to safety in the deep water of the swimming-pool while Eugen and the friends who had helped him to throw the younger boy in watched from the side laughing. Sometimes the brothers would attack each other, using forks as weapons, but on the whole there was not much fighting, if only because Eugen took little pleasure in sitting astride a younger boy, pinning his shoulder-blades to the ground: it was more fun to play with older boys.

From the age of six Eugen attended a Protestant elementary school. There were only two classes, with boys and girls taught together in both, and the two classrooms had low doors and small windows. He claimed afterwards to have been bored throughout his four years there, but lessons featured the book his mother was always quoting and reading from – the Lutheran Bible. Later he would not only write plays in parable form but often think in parable terms: the biblical influence ran deep.

Playing games with his brother and with his friends – all boys from respectable middle-class families – he had found it easy to dominate. 'His nature was always to boss others about, to impose his will on them', and at school, too, he tried to be the ringleader. When he was about ten he liked organizing his friends and their lead soldiers. 'We positioned the figures exactly according to Eugen's battle plans. He was the only one to control the game, whether as Napoleon or Frederick the Great. We were his generals and did what he told us.'⁸

As his mother's health deteriorated, her absences and indispositions may have inflicted psychological damage on this already nervous boy. In the summer of 1908 he missed six weeks of school: having contracted a facial twitch, he was sent to recover in Bad Dürrheim, though his mother's illness was already straining his father's financial resources.

In September 1908, at the age of ten, Eugen was sent to the Royal Bavarian Realgymnasium, which gave Latin precedence over Greek, and the humanities over the sciences. His form master was Franz Xaver Herrenreiter, who taught German, Latin, history and geography – 'a large, astonishingly ugly man, who in his youth, it was said, had wanted to become a professor, but failed'. He often sprang unexpected tests on his pupils, and did not conceal his pleasure when his questions defeated them. He was in the habit of 'going behind the blackboard two or three times in each lesson to extricate from his pocket a piece of cheese which wasn't wrapped up and which he'd proceed to munch as he talked'.⁹

During his second year at the school Brecht had a new form master, Dr Philip Hofmann, but the following year he was again under Herrenreiter, who now taught him German and Latin, but not history or geography. Though he would remember Herrenreiter as the best of his teachers, nothing seemed more useful than the unintentional instruction in how to exploit an adversary's weaknesses. Once a year the school inspector sat in on a lesson, ostensibly to see how the boys were getting on, but actually to check on the teacher. On one of these visits the boys responded to each of Herr Herrenreiter's questions with a dull silence. 'This time the man took no pleasure in our failure. He contracted jaundice, stayed in bed for a long time and, when he came back, was never again the voluptuous old cheese-chewer he'd been.'¹⁰ The many had power over the one, however superior his position.

The young Brecht got high marks for German composition, but in other subjects showed only average ability. Generally he was reluctant to take part in escapades, but he had already discovered the value of guile, and he was resourceful in protecting his interests. The French teacher marked according to a rigid point system in which each mistake counted, and promotion to a senior class depended on a high score. When a friend of Brecht's tried to cheat by rubbing out some of the red underlinings, the teacher could easily spot the erasing. Brecht was more cunning. Needing a higher mark for his essay on Molière's comedies, he drew additional red lines under sentences that had no mistakes in them and then complained. Outwitted, the teacher improved Brecht's mark.[11]

In 1910 a new housekeeper, the ladylike Marie Roecker, joined the household. Someone was needed to take over the duties that illness was forcing Sophie Brecht to neglect. Fräulein Roecker had cooked for a hotel in Ulm, could speak French, could make clothes and could devote her whole life to the family's welfare. She gave Eugen and Walter extra French lessons and made most of their clothes, including the suits they wore to school.[12]

Instead of following Eugen to the Realgymnasium, Walter was sent to the Realschule. More practical than his older brother, he was to be prepared for a more scientific career.

Eugen was twelve when he had a serious heart attack; later he would claim that he had 'achieved through temerity a demonstrable heart seizure'.[13] The joke masks an overriding need to be in control of each situation, and though his strong competitive instinct made him a bad loser, he was finding it so easy to dominate his peers that there was more fun to be had from making friends with older boys and matching his wits against those of his teachers. If a man lets himself be provoked, he is vulnerable, and in the Lower Third (1911–12) Brecht teased the form master, Dr Richard Ledermann, by taking essay questions too literally. To 'What draws us to mountain peaks?' his answer was 'Funicular railways'.[14]

In so far as he was rebelling, quietly, against the teachers' authority, he was also rebelling against current moral assumptions. If the French master had paid elaborate lip-service to the idea of justice, this only meant he had 'sworn allegiance to a malevolent goddess ... who demanded fearful sacrifices'. The cynical schoolboy could see how a teacher would use his power and authority to inculcate in his victims the same vicious virtues that had given him power.

Equipped with pedagogical skills and years of experience, he teaches his pupil to be a replica of himself. The pupil learns everything he needs to succeed in life. It's the same as what's needed to make progress in the school – deceit, a semblance of knowledge, the ability to revenge oneself with impunity, speedy mastery of commonplaces, obsequiousness, servility, willingness to betray one's equals to the higher authorities etc. etc. Most important of all is knowledge of humanity. This can be acquired by understanding the teacher.[15]

Though Brecht did not formulate it like this until much later, he would not have been able to write the Balkan War parable if he had not been precociously aware of the double standard in morality. Most children have a strong inclination to model themselves on the teachers they admire; admiration did not come easily to Eugen. This is not to say that he was anti-bourgeois. Later he would reject middle-class values and develop a violent antipathy towards buying and selling, but as a boy, though sympathetic towards the maid who had such a long working day, Eugen was generally contemptuous of those who owned nothing and, with Walter, he earned money by collecting chestnuts and selling them in the town on market days. They used nets to catch chestnuts floating down the River Lech but, having got soft, these were harder to sell. More fun was to be had out of making money than out of games like Halma, which were so easy to win; chess, however, was more interesting. By the age of thirteen Eugen was playing chess regularly with friends who came to his home. Together with some schoolfriends, he founded a chess club called 'Amicitia'. It had only seven members, but he helped to edit a duplicated journal for it. Neither the club nor the journal were authorized by the headmaster, and when they were discovered members were punished with two hours of detention.[16]

His mother, always distressed when he was in trouble, was hoping that his confirmation, which was to be on 29 March 1912, would help to reform him. He took the preparatory work seriously and had no difficulty in learning the words he had to say. The ceremony was held in the Barfüsser Church, and at the meal afterwards he asked permission to take off his stiff collar. His mother refused this at first, but soon relented: vacillation appears to have been as characteristic of her as ambivalence was of him. She doted and disapproved, feeling ashamed if he took a long time in the lavatory. 'The drones will be eaten by the bees', he was often told, and, no less often, that God loved innocence. He was given the Bible to read as if it were medicine, and she recoiled from boyish sexuality. In an early poem, 'Die Bekenntnisse eines Erst-Kommunikanten' (Confessions of a First Communicant), the mother finds out by smelling her son's nightshirt that the ritual has failed to reform him.[17]

From the age of ten he had been a rapid and voracious reader, held up as an example to the other boys in the class for his knowledge of literature. He inflamed his friends with his passion for Karl May's books, and he could write essays in half the time allocated. When a second-hand puppet theatre was installed in the house of his classmate, Rudolf Hartmann, with papier mâché puppets about 7 centimetres in height, it was Eugen who directed the productions. The repertory included scenes from *Faust*,

Hamlet and Büchner's *Leonce und Lena*. Eugen's ambition was to be like the Berlin theatre critic Alfred Kerr.[18]

By the time he had moved up to the Lower Second (1913–14) he was reading Verlaine, Rimbaud, Villon, Hauptmann and Tagore, as well as thrillers.[19] In August 1913, when the first issue of *Die Ernte* appeared, he had contributed not only the Balkan War parable but a critique of Wagner, and the first part of a 'satire' called 'Die Geschichte von einem, der nie zu spät kam' ('The Story of One Who Never Came Too Late'), the second part being published in the following issue. A boy is so clever and such a stickler for punctuality that nothing seems impossible for him. Perhaps he will become a prince of poets, perhaps a soldier-emperor. Or perhaps a king of the Stock Exchange. After protracted indecision he becomes a salesman in a warehouse. When, at the age of fifteen, he falls in love, he writes an inordinately long poem to the girl, who starts going out, before she receives it, with another boy. Literature has failed where action might have succeeded.

In the February 1914 issue of *Die Ernte*, under the title 'Märchen' ('Fairy-tale') Brecht wrote an eight-line story of a prince who lies in a flowery meadow, dreaming about white castles until, becoming king, and moving into a white castle, he dreams about flowery meadows. In both stories the young author was apparently directing his primitive didacticism mainly at himself. If his behaviour towards girls was already alternating, as it did four years later, between 'rather touching reticence and ... outright impudence',[20] he was warning himself that in relationships, as in everything else, nothing was more dangerous than the fantasies which led to indecision and inaction.

In 'Die Mutter und der Tod' ('The Mother and Death'), which appeared in the same issue of *Die Ernte*, the covert subject was his mother. While her husband, the locksmith, goes to fetch the midwife, the mother-to-be dreams that her husband is with a fair-haired boy who resembles him. When the locksmith returns, he finds his wife dead and the new-born son weeping on her breast. Eugen was terrified that his ailing mother would die young. It was she, more than anyone else, who had given him the licence he had to go his own way. Convinced that he was 'quite different from us', she had encouraged the growth of his self-confidence, while her absences and indispositions had helped him to become emotionally self-supporting.[21] He had learned that to be loved is to have power, and though he would come to relish the power he gained from women's love, he would never need, after his mother's death, to be as dependent as most men are on female reassurance.

His self-sufficiency made it easier for him to consolidate his successes, which came early. Most tyro writers are excited by the possibility of exploring their identity on paper; Brecht was more excited by the prospect of increasing his power over adults and contemporaries, and he was not held back by any notion of duty to tell the truth. After publishing the two stories, together with three essays, in the final issue of *Die Ernte*, which appeared in February 1914, he made himself known to Wilhelm Brüstle, editor of the local paper, *Augsburger Neueste Nachrichten*, who describes him as 'a timid, retiring young man, who spoke only when one wound him up. He was full of genuine feeling for life, inspired with hunger for life, which he pursued with alert senses. ... He was devoid of sentimentality. He seemed to be searching for both happiness and truth. ... He was very gregarious, especially among his young friends.' After reading some of this precocious schoolboy's verse, Brüstle gave him a book of poems to review – Karl Lieblich's *Trautelse*. Improvising on the basis of the power games he had played with teachers, Brecht wrote an insincerely enthusiastic review, comparing the rhythm with Verlaine's. The object was to please his editor, who had been corresponding with the poet.

What secured Brecht's foothold on journalism was his dexterity in expressing patriotic feelings after war broke out in August 1914. Herrenreiter was recruiting schoolboy volunteers to help with the harvest, while another teacher, Herr Weber, trained boys as cadets. At the beginning of the month, when Eugen had to do a spell of duty as an aeroplane lookout on the Berlach Tower, he lost no time in using the newspaper as a platform for a public appeal that others should follow his example: 'Admittedly, your bed won't march up with you for the two hours, but you'll be performing a small service in our dear fatherland's common cause, and you will enjoy, free of charge, the pleasures of being on guard at the tower.'[22]

Nine days later his 'Notizen über unsere Zeit' ('Notes on Our Time') appeared in the newspaper. Clearly, this was no time and the newspaper no place for unpatriotic scepticism about values and motives. 'Loyally, the whole nation stands united. ... We are armed, morally armed. The steadfast German character, moulded by German poets and thinkers over two centuries, is now proving itself. Calm and composed, with steely discipline but burning with enthusiasm, not so much exultantly as with gritted teeth, our men have gone into battle. ... All of us, all Germans, fear God and nothing else in the world.'[23] Writing for *Die Ernte* he had instinctively denuded his prose of rhetorical *appassionato*, but the virtue of simplicity had become a luxury he was willing to renounce. Like a village preacher put into uniform as an army chaplain, he saw the opportunity of exciting a large audience; he was not going to waste his opportunity by indulging himself in good prose. If the moment called for windy rhetoric, he would produce windy rhetoric, and, according to Brüstle, he was 'no doubt vastly encouraged' by reactions to it. But 'in spite of his early literary successes, he lost none of his reticence, he merely became more self-assured in his gait'.[24]

According to his brother, the reticence was in evidence only when he wished to preserve distance. Mostly he wanted to assert himself, to have his authority accepted, and mostly he succeeded. He had enough self-confidence to believe, in almost any situation, that he knew what ought to be done and how best to do it. As a young child, watching cows being milked, he gave the milkmaid his advice: 'Just pull the stopper out of the cow and then the milk will come out by itself.' He was almost compulsive about offering practical suggestions, even when he had no specialist knowledge of the subject, and by the age of fifteen he was getting his advice taken seriously by his friends, even when they were older than he was. Caspar Neher was a year older – a good-looking boy, the son of a schoolteacher. Quick to recognize the talent in Neher's paintings, Eugen advised him to cultivate the same Zolaesque virtues he was himself trying to cultivate as a writer: 'the post of great Naturalist (painter) is still waiting to be filled. The soul of the people hasn't yet been explored.' Neher had sent him a Faust painting. 'Window and light are very beautiful', he responded, but it would be better to avoid 'coarse and improbable lighting effects'. The treatment of light could convey a poetic mood, 'but the poet (and painter in my opinion) is dependent on reality. To combine truth to nature *with* idealism is art.' He went on to quote: 'Reality is the bed on which the great poet dreams his dreams.' You don't need material 'that's outstanding because of its external beauty. You don't need kings as heroes, or poets, or philosophers. (No Antigone, no Faust.) The story of a washerwoman (Mutter Wolff in *Der Biberpelz* [Hauptmann's *The Fur Coat*]) can also be tragic (and therefore (?) beautiful). What matters is the spirit *of the artist*, who transforms the object, permeates it with his being. ... A modern painter must read Zola.'[25]

The style of this letter is quite different from the style of the newspaper articles, but the young Brecht was not totally immune to patriotic idealism. For the gymnastic society to which his father belonged he wrote a chauvinistic four-line verse 'on the occasion of the start of hostilities'. In his story 'Der Freiwillige' ('The Volunteer'), which was published in the newspaper a few days later, a father enlists to redeem the honour of his son, who is in prison.[26] The idea for the story may have come from an experience Brecht described in the first of his seven 'Augsburger Kriegsbriefe' (war letters): he had seen a father standing at the barrier, gazing out at his three sons, who were about to march away. 'He neither shouted nor waved. He looked on in silence, as his sons marched by, calling to him. . . . I saw no tears in the great wise eyes. But this coarse face was a prayer.'[27] Long before he opted to live in the German Democratic Republic, Brecht showed a talent for writing literary propaganda. Now, as later, rhetoric in his writing is a tell-tale symptom but, at the age of sixteen, he could not have been unambivalently cynical about the war effort, when it was not only teachers but the country's leading intellectuals who were uncritically raising their voices in support of the General Staff. Brecht was not alone in feeling ambivalent: what was unique, now as later, was his clear-minded realization that ambivalences do not have to be straddled. Both sides can be exploited, either separately or simultaneously. In a review he praised *Krieg: ein Te Deum*, a play by Hauptmann's brother Carl, who equated war with 'wholesale murder', portraying the imperial powers as beasts and birds of prey casually filling the earth with cripples. But Brecht went on writing jingoistic verse. For a year after 'Der Freiwillige' he published no prose, and ambivalence is visible in some of the verse. But one of his 1915 poems, 'Der belgische Acker' ('The Belgian Field', published on 12 July), celebrates 'the plough that the German fist pushed on its iron way' and 'the songs, strong as iron, of Germany's victorious greatness'.[28]

The ambivalence had become more uncomfortable by the time he wrote 'Dankgottesdienst' ('Thanksgiving Service'), a story published on 12 August 1915. After hearing the news of his son's 'heroic death', an organist improvises a voluntary expressing grief for the boy who behaved badly before joining up. Like 'Der Freiwillige', the story is about redeeming a reputation, but the predominant mood is more depressed.

Brecht's local prestige as a writer boosted both his self-confidence and his superiors' indulgence, even if this nocturnal dialogue with his form master corresponds only loosely with an actual conversation:

So, where have you been, Herr Brecht? Why are you out at this late hour?

I've just been to see my uncle, Herr Studienrat.

Aha! Ha! So what are you carrying in that bag, Brecht?

My guitar, Herr Studienrat.

Aha! Ha! Your guitar. And for what purpose, Brecht, do you take your guitar when you go to see your uncle?

Yes, I had to play to him, Herr Studienrat.

Aha! Ha! So you had to play to him. But I saw you coming out of that pub, Brecht.

I had to relieve nature there, Herr Studienrat.

Aha! Ha! So you had to relieve nature, Brecht, in that pub with your guitar. Aha! Now go straight home.

Certainly, Herr Studienrat, but first I have to go and play to my grandfather.[29]

The man who would later make such a good impression on the House Committee on Un-American Activities had an early training in how to conceal feelings of superiority when subjected to cross-questioning.

He was only seventeen when he had his first sexual experience. He went skating with a girl who was not content just to be kissed on the way home. 'She was fifteen but very mature.' He confided in a friend, who told him there were dangers in making love without knowing the technique: one couple, unable to disengage, had been taken to hospital in an ambulance. Anxious to avoid this predicament, Brecht consulted a local prostitute, who explained what he should do.[30]

When the new term started on 16 September 1915, there were only fifteen boys in the class: eleven of his former classmates were in the army, as were ten of the teachers, and some of the Lower First's lessons were held jointly with the Upper First. According to Dr Ledermann, who was now teaching him German, 'Brecht was one of those highly gifted and original pupils whom one never forgets, even if he was not among the most pleasing boys in his class.' Unlike colleagues who complained that he was 'impudent, boisterous and arrogant', Ledermann was 'quite satisfied with his behaviour and also with his achievements, and I often turned a blind eye to something, or helped him out of trouble. ... Among his fellow-pupils there were only a few he deemed worthy of befriending.'[31] According to a former friend, he was always feuding with Ledermann, 'But that must certainly have been on account of the wretched teaching that kept pushing nationalistic war propaganda at us.' The boys, especially the seniors, were often bored and irritated by the teachers' attempts to drum up patriotic sentiment by means of rhetorical speeches and militaristic songs.

Ledermann was particularly incensed by Brecht's lack of respect for Schiller's *Wallensteins Lager*: in comparison with the current war, he wrote, Wallenstein's was a 'beer-tent idyll', and Schiller's style was schoolteacherish.[32] Brecht may have been more interested in provoking Ledermann than in evaluating Schiller's play, but his low opinion of the teachers prejudiced him against the literature they revered, while his attitude to romantic lyrics was coloured by experiences of love-making gleaned at an age when most boys of his generation had to be content with reading about it.

Surrounded by admiring friends, he found it easy to seduce girls, and his bad reputation was helpful. He was rumoured to have burnt a Bible and a catechism. From the beginning of his richly rewarding sexual career, he carried on several relationships simultaneously. At Steinicke's bookshop in Heiligkreuz Gasse, he made advances to all three assistants – one of them later married his friend Georg Pfanzelt. Through another friend, Otto Müller (whom he dubbed Müllereisert), he met (when still only seventeen) a pale, pretty girl called Paula Banholzer, a doctor's daughter. Müller was out walking with her one day when he saw Brecht on the other side of the road, beckoning him. Crossing, Müller was told to introduce Paula and then leave them alone together. After routing his rival, Brecht tried to meet her every day. At first she tried to avoid him, but he was relentless, often appearing outside her window, accompanied by friends, to serenade her, and eventually her resistance crumbled. Another rival, Heiner Hagg, records: 'He was an artist in persuasion, and, with women, witty and gallant, always at their service, with a kiss on the hand.'[33] Paula was a Catholic, and he often accompanied her to Mass in the Cathedral. 'The compulsion to obey and the force of belief in Catholicism', she remembers, 'strongly impressed him. He told me Catholicism was more consistent.'

She was not allowed to go out in the evenings, except to the theatre, and then she was collected at the end of the show by either her parents or the maid.[34] He gave her a male nickname, Paul Bittersüss (bitter-sweet), or 'Bi' for short. Instinctively he knew that by giving people names which stuck to them – Müller adopted the name Müllereisert – he was establishing a proprietorial right. But he did not become closely attached to her until he was nineteen, and by then he had been through a good deal of painful adolescent frustration, lusting in particular after a dairywoman's daughter, Sophie Renner, and Rose Maria Aman, the attractive daughter of a hairdresser. After meeting her in an ice-cream parlour, he slipped her a note, complimenting her on her long hair and asking for a date. The first time he kissed her she recoiled in terror, pushing him away. When she explained that she did not know whether a kiss had consequences, he did not reassure her. 'My dear child, you must go to your mother and let her explain.'[35]

Like many young lovers, Brecht found his girls most adorable when inaccessible, and least interesting when most affectionate. The more rapid the turnover was, the more violent the oscillations between rapture and intolerance. Rose Maria soon became suspect: 'But she goes all out to seduce, like a bitch on heat.' Surely the motive was 'lust for procreation'.[36]

During his last year at school he became infatuated with Therese Ostheimer, who belonged to a strict Catholic family. He walked home with her several times and wrote a long love-letter, which her father confiscated. But Ernestine Müller, a cousin of his classmate Rudolf Hartmann, did not so consistently rebuff him. To his male classmates he seemed to cut an unromantic figure. Hans Werner Sorgel, a classmate in the Upper First, remembers him as usually having a dirty shirt collar and being 'in the habit of pushing his head, which looked as if it was too big for his body, slightly forward, as if he were short-sighted'.

His sexual successes may have helped him to consolidate the courage he needed to make an unequivocal statement of negative feelings towards the war. While he was in the Lower First he had to write an essay on the stock theme cued by Horace's line *Dulce et decorum est pro patria mori* (It is sweet and proper to die for the fatherland), which he derided as propaganda. 'Only cretins can take fatuousness to the point of speaking about death's dark door, and even they can do it only when they believe themselves to be a long way away from their last hour. But when Death approaches them, they hoist down their placards and run for it, like the emperor's fat court jester at Philippi, the author of the saying.' The essay was written for the Latin master, who was the friendliest of all the teachers in the school, understanding and respecting Brecht's refusal to conform. During lessons they argued like equals, and according to one ex-member of the class, Dr G. 'was one of the very few teachers for whom Brecht worked enthusiastically'. But he was furious that a would-be poet had insulted Horace, and Brecht was ordered to give back immediately the book which Dr G. had lent him. But for the intervention of a benign Benedictine priest, Romuald Sauer, who was acting as an auxiliary language teacher, the essay would probably have led to expulsion from the school. Sauer defended the cynicism as the product of 'a schoolboy brain confused by the war',[37] but the narrow escape must have made Brecht more cautious, though his proclivity to 'bad' behaviour was exacerbated by his aversion to the militaristic loyalism equated with 'good' behaviour by jingoistic teachers – many of them old men, already pensioned off, who had returned to replace colleagues who had enlisted.[38]

Brecht's poetic identity was beginning to crystallize excitingly round the realization that he was not alone in his dissidence: his songs could make him into a spokesman for the mavericks, perhaps even a leader. The first time he used the name Bertolt Brecht was to sign the published text of a poem, 'Das Lied von der Eisenbahntruppe von Fort Donald' ('The Song of the Fort Donald Railwaymen'), a narrative ballad, which he composed to sing to his friends, accompanying himself on the guitar. According to Hermann Kasack, a reader for the publisher Kiepenheuer, he made an unforgettable impact when 'with his thin, light voice he sang his songs and ballads to the guitar, on which he could scarcely play more than two or three chords, emphasizing each syllable very precisely and rhythmically, and also when he spoke, the words crackled like electric sparks'.[39] The Fort Donald song was the first of many poems and ballads which implicitly invited listeners to identify with an antisocial group – a band of pioneers or adventurers or workers in undeveloped territory, pitting their strength against nature. The implication was that manly virtues could thrive better in a less cluttered environment. The male gangs in the songs formed a flattering image of the friends who liked to go around with him, while Paula's male nickname cemented her membership of the gang.

There was also an intensely private element in the poems and songs, concerned only with the individual's relationship to the hostile nature which would eventually annihilate him. The 'Hymne an Gott' starts:

> Deep in the dark valleys the hungry are dying
> But you show them bread and let them die
> But you reign for ever invisible
> Gleaming and grim over the endless plan.

Destined to make the German ballad catch up with Nietzsche, Brecht looked balefully at the aftermath of God's death. Nature in these poems is not neutral and indifferent: it is vicious and invulnerable. Against vultures, pestilence, floods, wolves, sharks, storms at sea, famine, even the strongest of men are helpless. The adventurers who set sail on absinth seas would have done better to stay inside their mother's wombs 'where it was peaceful and you could sleep and just exist'.[40]

But what were his models? There was no vogue at this time for the narrative ballad, and though he knew a few songs by Goethe and Heine, he was not familiar with any folk-songs. As a child he heard the songs that had become popular, and sentimental ballads about robbers. In the paper factory, women workers could be heard singing these songs and improvising lines – not always without a certain irony – when they forgot the original words. One song which caught his imagination was Adolf Martel's 'Das Seemannslos ('The Seaman's Lot') which contains the line 'Stormy the night and the sea runs high' – a line that will recur in several of Brecht's plays and songs. He loved the way that popular songs tacked cursorily from one subject to another or reduced a major natural disaster to a rhythmic couplet.[41]

His enjoyment of music was not isolated from his sense of humour. Max Hohenester remembered how he performed his songs with melodies he had made up:

An irresistible force emanated from the slight, restless figure of the young Brecht, irony and mockery always curling lightly around his mouth and his owlish eyes which were like those of his beloved Wedekind occasionally looking almost melancholy, filled with a precocious wisdom.

He didn't sing well but with infectious passion, drunk on his own verse, ideas and images as other people are on wine, and intoxicating his listeners as only youth can.[42]

His voice ranged from very deep notes to surprisingly high ones, and he composed his own melodies, but they were eclectic, drawing on popular tunes and ballads. On the guitar his facility for finding acceptable chords killed any ambition to acquire expertise; his standing joke was: 'I can play the gramophone superbly.' Rudolf Prestel, who once went to the opera with him, noticed that he was following the music with outstretched fingers. He had a talent, he explained, for listening with his fingertips.[43]

Music made poetry more usable, more valuable in the power games he enjoyed. Most of his poetry-writing at this time was connected in one way or another with music. It was in 1916 that he wrote an oratorio, and a poem called 'Die Orgel' ('The Organ') was dedicated, at his father's prompting, to Klemens Haindl, owner of the paper company. Brecht's Christmas present to Ernestine Müller was a collection of

German love-songs. She never forgot a remark he made in 1917: 'I must become famous, so as to show people what they're really like.'[44]

Friends of his who called at the house would be admitted – disapprovingly if they were female – by Fräulein Roecker, most likely with the phrase: 'He's upstairs again.' The attic room, which had a double door, was divided into a large living-room and a small bedroom. On the inner door notices admonished the visitor to bring sound understanding and good ideas, leaving his prejudices at home. The floor was permanently littered with books, manuscripts and newspaper cuttings. Above the iron bedstead his guitar would be hanging; the array of pictures and drawings on the walls changed with his enthusiasms. When he had a passion for Napoleon, portraits and battle plans were in evidence. Subsequent heroes – Nietzsche, Hauptmann, Wedekind – received visual tribute, with charcoal drawings by Caspar Neher. When Brecht, after cutting his hair short, had a life-mask made, in plaster of Paris, this, too, appeared on the wall.[45]

On New Year's Eve 1917 he invited his friends to a 'Reunion of New Year Spooks' at 6 o'clock in the ice-cream shop in the Kreuzstrasse. They were instructed to bring 'Tankards. (Toboggans) Wood (in a rucksack). Mouth-organs. Humour. Cigarettes. Rubber boots. Feeling for Romance. Fun. Objective: Nervous convalescence. Tobogganing by starlight. Tea in the forest. Duelling with concierges.' When writing messages to his friends, whether in invitations like this one or in admonitions nailed to doors, he was incidentally ridiculing the solemnity of the German language. The words, the syntax and the tradition of formality all tended to exclude breeziness; breeziness was therefore all the more conspicuous when it forced its way in, and many of his remarks must have sounded even more bizarre than they seem in English translation. At midnight seven boys were sitting around a camp fire, drinking each other's health, when, almost absent-mindedly, he said: 'The fire would be even nicer if only a naked whore were jumping over it.'[46]

If fun was all the funnier with a leavening of mock-seriousness, real work, as opposed to school work, could best be done playfully. His instinct was to ricochet off other people. Most writers hate to be interrupted: what is done afterwards does not continue in a straight line from what was done before. But discontinuity appealed to Brecht more than the idea of a single form which is 'right' or 'inevitable'. Interruptions served as a reminder that there was no such thing as inevitability. The course of history could have run quite differently if events had been interrupted in different ways. Friends with literary ambitions were invited to his attic 'dungeon', or to alfresco meetings by the city moat or on the river bank. They read their poems or excerpts from their plays, listened to his criticism, ventured comments on his work and, as modifications were proposed and adopted, it became impossible to define either plagiarism or originality. Like Shakespeare, he appropriated any good material he could find, and like Villon he composed ballads for performance to music derived from popular tunes and other ballads. He also loaned drafts of work-in-progress to friends, who were encouraged to make marks or notes in the margin against anything that particularly struck them – whether good or bad.[47]

The main influences were Villon, Büchner, Rimbaud, Verlaine and Wedekind. (A classmate claims to have found evidence in an old diary that Brecht was already recommending Villon and Rimbaud in 1913–14.) When his father gave him an edition of Wedekind's work in about 1914 he found, abrasively formulated, ideas he went on appropriating. 'Morality is the best business in the world', wrote Wedekind in *Der Marquis von Keith*. Sin he explained as 'the mythological term for bad business'. One of Brecht's earliest ambitions as a playwright was to outstrip Wedekind. 'I can write,' he noted in a 1916 diary, 'I can write plays, better than Hebbel, wilder than Wedekind.'[48] And he often performed Wedekind's ballads and songs to his friends.

His deepest commitment was to having fun, and working sessions were not always distinguishable from rampages of juvenile debauchery, which involved staying up all night and singing homemade songs with Caspar Neher and his other friends, including Müllereisert and the club-footed Georg Pfanzelt, his senior by four years. Pfanzelt, whom he nicknamed Orge, had left the Realschule for a job in the municipal savings bank. A good musician who could play both piano and guitar, he was the closest of Brecht's friends. They sang together and went for long walks. At night they often accumulated a band of followers, male and female. Many of these brought a mouth-organ or guitar, and Brecht would lead his clique through the old part of the city, singing and plucking at his guitar, which would possibly be missing a string or two. Sometimes they would climb over the fences and through the barbed wire above the city wall on the Graben, Brecht playing the guitar, one friend playing the violin, others the mouth-organ, others holding a swinging lantern on a long string. Those who could not play an instrument could sing or hum. Singing to his guitar, Brecht could already interweave life and legend:

> Brown sherry in the belly
> And still entangled in our legs
> The girl who's been scrambling our eggs.
> Into the morning air –
> In between all this –
> Each of us has done a huge piss.

In the verse, as in the calculated debauchery, there is a Rimbaudesque defiance of conventionality.

Neher had been the first to volunteer, leaving in 1915, and by 1917 most of Brecht's classmates had to join up, but with his cardiac defect Brecht was exempt. Just after his nineteenth birthday, together with three classmates who had remained civilians, he sat for the *Notabitur*, the 'emergency school-leaving certificate', which set the wartime seal on his education.

In April 1917, together with the three classmates, he volunteered as an auxiliary war worker. His first job was to do clerical work in a military orderly room; his second was in a market garden, cutting down trees and transplanting saplings. Having lost most of his friends and followers to the army, he involved himself more closely with Paula, whom he wooed by singing and writing poems to her. Soon she was spending a great deal of time in his 'dungeon'. 'I've given Bittersweet a little ring. She trembled and kissed me. We haven't discussed anything.'

At the end of May, when Neher came home on leave, he found Brecht in bed. Somehow he had strained a muscle in his stomach. Neher went to sit with him, grumbling about girls, and Brecht talked about Paula, whom he had just discarded. She had taken up with a student of commerce. As soon as he could get up again there was a partial revival of the old marauding spirit – nocturnal excursions through the town with lanterns, mouth-organs and guitars.

In June he began a serious collaboration with Neher on a play, *Sommersinfonie*, with characterizations partly determined by Neher's drawings. From the middle of June Neher was living in barracks and did not have to go back to the front line until the beginning of August. Brecht went on writing to him regularly, demanding in return drawings and a diary account of what he did.

In the summer, thanks to a recommendation from Rudolf Hartmann's father, Brecht was employed as a private tutor by a *Kommerzienrat* (Councillor of Commerce), Herr Kopp, who had a villa on the Tegernsee, a lake south of Munich. 'For three hours a day I have to hammer lessons in; after that I'm lord of the manor.' Here he wrote the poem 'Romantik', which he dedicated to Ernestine, but also used on Paula and other girl-friends. His 14-year-old pupil, Conrad Kopp, especially needed help in Latin, but Brecht tutored him in several subjects during the morning, and in the afternoons took him out walking or swimming or boating. 'Herr Brecht mostly went about with his Schopenhauer under his arm. I never saw him wearing anything but knickerbockers with a cap and spectacles.'[49]

The qualities that determined Brecht's development emerged during his boyhood and adolescence. His self-confidence and his vitality were both so remarkable that he could make people feel privileged to be in his company, reacting to him with the unstinting generosity that is usually reserved for the beautiful and the famous. With his quick mind, his willingness to accept both sides of a contradiction and the pleasure he took in challenging convention, he could give a great deal of pleasure and stimulation to the admirers who surrounded him, encouraging them to acknowledge feelings – sexual feelings, and resistance to the war, to authoritarianism and conventionality – they might otherwise have suppressed. Brecht gave a great deal and took a great deal. Skilful in manipulating people, he was ruthless both with girls and with boys who were younger or weaker than he was. He felt entitled to take, not because of what he gave, but because his needs were so intense and because he knew he could get away with it. If he tried, he hardly ever failed to make other people feel more or less what his mother felt – that he needed and deserved all the help and protection they could offer him.

2 / Apprentice Swindler

It may have been partly to please his father that the 19-year-old Brecht arranged to resume his studies; he may have been camouflaging his way of pleasing himself. At the beginning of October 1917 he enrolled in the Philosophy Department of the Ludwig Maximilian University in Munich. The headmaster of the Realgymnasium wrote to warn the university authorities about their new student, and his personal appearance at this time must have reinforced the warning. Whereas Walter was usually immaculate in his appearance, his brother's fingernails were usually black, his jacket dirty. One girl in Augsburg called him the gnome.[1]

When he made the 40-mile journey to the university city, he was in no sense settling himself there, partly because home was within easy reach, and partly because he was already anchored to friendships and even working relationships such as boys seldom form before they go to university. The most important of the working relationships was with Caspar Neher. Even while he was away in the army, Neher received a stream of encouragement and advice from the authoritative 19-year-old, who was unconsciously laying the foundations for a fertile theatrical partnership, clarifying his own ideas while passing on pregnant advice, at once responding to Neher's anti-heroic inclinations and fortifying them: 'The Adam is wonderful. One understands immediately from the completely missing neck that you see him as no hero – an ingenious piece of ingratitude, dear Cas. Eyes that look piously upwards with no brow to hinder them – an ethical insight!' Comments like these influenced the way Neher saw his own work, just as he, by drawing Brecht's characters, would influence the way Brecht saw them. Even now Neher's drawings served as an anvil for Brecht to hammer out his ideas:

The walker is wonderful. He's moving inexorably, big beyond all measure, dark and whipped on by willpower as well as discipline ... it seems to me a good caricature – or what you and I agree on calling caricature: discovery and representation of what is intrinsically meaningless in a meaningful way, or the *raison d'être* which the individual imparts to meaninglessness, in that *it is* meaningless. The uncannily vivacious uselessness of this expectorated heap of

humanity which stretches out its legs in front of itself and *exits* belongs to the
same desperate comedy.

The 'Walker' was one of three works by Neher Brecht tacked to his
wall.[2]

He also confided to Neher that he was frustrated in his relationship
with Rose Maria Aman, who had another lover:

Suffering is good, you're never more aware of your *self* than when you're
suffering. So I can't kiss Rosmarie any more (she has soft, moist, full lips in the
pale, thirsty face). . . . The most you can do is take what you can take. . . . There
can be no God *because* otherwise I wouldn't be able to stand it – *not* being a
God . . ! Her eyes are fearfully empty, small, evil, sucking whirlpools, her nose
is turned up and too broad, her mouth too big, red, thick. The lines of her little
neck aren't clean-cut, her posture is cretinous, her gait slovenly and her stomach
sticks out. But I'm fond of her. (Although she isn't clever and isn't nice) I really
like her all the more. It's painfully absurd. Am *I* pretty?[3]

Later he would seem indifferent to other people's opinions of him, but
at the end of 1917 he was begging Neher to pass judgement: 'Can't you
tell me what you think of me? . . . I'm not asking simply out of vanity.
But it's so quiet in the country. I can hear only my own voice. It could
get hoarse. . . . I don't want to know what I am. Only what you think of
me.'[4]

At Munich he registered for courses on a variety of subjects, including
criticism and inorganic experimental chemistry, but this was an old
student trick for obtaining money from parents. You produced receipts
for registration fees which needed to be renewed and then decided
against renewing. But, to begin with, he did exert himself. 'It's advantageous to rush. From 8.0 to 11.0, from 12.0 to 1.0, from 3.0 to 6.30,
from 7.0 to 10.30 in laboratory, university and theatre. Every day. I gorge
myself on everything within reach and read voraciously. I'll digest it all
later in the army.' He was rushing so much that he took to 'arriving
systematically late', but he gave himself time off to go home most
weekends. 'I don't want to start up any friendships here. They're all
dreadful idiots in spite of their cultivated manners.'[5]

Brecht's restlessness in Munich can be gauged from the rate at which he
moved from one furnished room to another. His first was on the third
floor of a house in Maximilianstrasse. In November 1917 he had moved
to one in Adalbertstrasse. His father arranged for him to be provided

with coal, which was in short supply. Hans Otto Münsterer first visited him in a student hostel in Paul-Heyse-Strasse, where he had a large audience for the dicta displayed outside his door, such as 'A poor idiot is an idiot; a rich idiot is rich.'[6] By the beginning of the second term he had moved again, to Kaulbachstrasse.

He went home for the Christmas holiday. Max Hohenester and another former classmate, Fritz Schreyer, were in Augsburg: together they went skating, and ate ice-creams at the shop where they had celebrated as New Year spooks. 'But I scarcely know them any longer. Death out there has made them fat. Hohenester is like Jehovah.'[7]

At the beginning of February he wrote: 'I'm still at home and in the mornings I write songs for the guitar, which I can't sing to anyone in the afternoon. Though at lunchtime Paul Bittersüss is splendid.' But in the autumn of 1917 he had been introduced by a lecturer to Hedda Kuhn, a young student of medicine who had impressed him with her paper on Heinrich Mann's novellas. According to her, Brecht's reason for going home at weekends was that he had more to eat there. His favourite food was pancakes. She was often invited to his home, but by now his mother – nearly always drugged with morphine – was incapable of sustained conversation. His father wanted Hedda to pressure Brecht into persisting with his medical studies and to promise his mother that she would never leave him.[8] But she had never even introduced him to her father.

His decision to study medicine has been sentimentally attributed to concern for his ailing mother but, according to another student, he never seriously studied the subject. One advantage of registering for it was that it was the likeliest subject to delay call-up; another was that when he eventually enlisted he could become a medical orderly instead of being sent to the front. The only medical lectures he attended were on venereal diseases. He maintained that if you looked a girl in the eyes, she would tell you the truth, but he was still extremely nervous.[9]

At Munich he was fairly regular in attending a seminar conducted by the 40-year-old Artur Kutscher, a specialist in contemporary German literature. He also went, occasionally, to other lectures, saying he wanted to console his father by taking a PhD in Literature, but on finding he would need to sit examinations in three subjects he changed his mind. Kutscher was a friend of Wedekind – later his biographer and editor of his collected works – and at the end of January, when the university term finished, Wedekind was present at the celebration. Brecht had made good use of the collected edition of Wedekind's plays he had been given: by 1918 the copy was showing signs of wear. He had set many of

Wedekind's ballads to music, finding 'simple but very catchy tunes' for them. He did particularly well with the blind boy's song.[10]

> Was I wrong the world to cherish
> Like a cup of holy wine?
> While God leaves the good to perish
> Sinners are doing fine.

Wedekind's salty immoralizing exerted a formative influence; his verse often reiterates the point that virtue is not its own reward and that wisdom is not advantageous. The cuckoo's song ends:

> Your brain can be rich as Croesus
> And your life as poor as a beggar's.

From *Baal* to *Dreigroschenoper* the songs in Brecht's plays will pivot on a strikingly similar cynicism.

Wedekind made star appearances in his plays, and Brecht was 'regular and enthusiastic in his attendances' when his idol acted in Augsburg. He probably saw both Lulu plays, *Der Erdgeist* (*Earth Spirit*) and *Die Büchse der Pandora* (*Pandora's Box*). Wedekind played the animal tamer in *Erdgeist* and the name part in *Der Marquis von Keith*. Between 1901 and his death in March 1918 he had also been a regular performer at Munich's first cabaret, *die elf Scharfrichter* (*The Eleven Executioners*). Here was a man, at last, who could be admired and emulated:

He had only to walk into a lecture hall where hundreds of students were making a noise, or into a room, or onto a stage, with his distinctive walk, his sharply chiselled bronze skull slightly tilted and thrust forward, and silence fell immediately. Although he wasn't a particularly good actor – he even kept forgetting the limp he'd prescribed himself and didn't know the lines – as the Marquis von Keith he outshone many professional actors. He filled every inch of space with himself. There he stood, ugly, brutal, dangerous, with close-cropped red hair, hands stuck in his trouser pockets, and you felt the devil himself couldn't have shifted him. . . . He sang his songs to a guitar accompaniment in a brittle voice, slightly monotonous and quite untrained. Never has a singer made me feel so excited, so shaken. It was the enormous vitality of this man, his energy, that gave him his personal magic and enabled him, while showered with ridicule and scorn, to perform his brash hymn to humanity.

Brecht had already found that given aplomb, vitality and a guitar, you do not need a trained voice or a well-shaped face to make yourself diabolically attractive and exciting to an audience. 'He looks as though he couldn't die. He was a personality like Socrates and Tolstoy.'[11] It was not long after Wedekind's death that Brecht began to wear his own hair cut much shorter.

The day before Wedekind died Brecht and Ludwig Prestel had been singing his songs in the open air, on the banks of the Lech. After reading about his death, 'Brecht arranged a nocturnal memorial celebration in Augsburg, and he went to Munich for the funeral. The corpse was in an open coffin. 'The disdainful, studied twist of the lips, the blasé, cynical expression had vanished. At first you thought he was smiling, but then you realized he'd already grown out of the habit.'[12]

It was Brecht's verse and his guitar that led him towards the theatre: in March he told Neher: 'I want to write a play about François Villon, who was a murderer, highway robber and balladeer in the fifteenth century in Brittany.' It was easy to identify with a balladeer who became an enemy of local society, but behind the first draft of *Baal* many of the impulses were negative. Like Beckett, Ionesco and Genet, Brecht wrote his first play as a gesture of rebellion against current theatrical practice: he disliked both Schillerian romanticism and expressionism. 'I'm in favour of closing the theatres for artistic reasons.' But generally he was feeling disenchanted. His mother was ailing; Neher was still at the front; Pfanzelt was likely to die young: 'He's got heart trouble. . . . His brothers, his father died young.' 'You mustn't be tricked into forgetting that art's a swindle. *Life*'s a swindle. Art's the simpler one. More organized. More meaningful. Stronger.'[13] So to succeed in life and art you had to be a swindler.

But he refused to be swindled by the 27-year-old expressionist play-wright Hanns Johst. Kutscher considered him to be comparable with Lenz, Grabbe and Büchner, and on 30 March 1918 his third play *Der Einsame: Ein Menschenuntergang* (*The Lonely One: Downfall of a Man*) was discussed by the seminar. The hero is the nineteenth-century play-wright Christian Dietrich Grabbe, whose raptures are translated into exclamatory, over-explicit prose: 'Oh! This sensation! Not for a king-dom would I give it up! This God-Almighty feeling! Heaven and earth subject to my will! I am the world!' Brecht was particularly irked by the sixth scene, in which Grabbe insults his mother for conceiving him in 'lechery and cheap lustfulness' and making him the son of a postman and a washerwoman. He goes on to beg hard-earned money from her to buy schnapps. Brecht called the play 'idealistic' – a word he used as an insult.[14] Johst's play was merely a clumsy restatement of the assumption that artists are generically different from other people. As a poet himself,

Brecht could see that the poet must be an ordinary creature of physical appetite.

Like Brecht, Johst was influenced by Rimbaud, but unlike Johst, Brecht could absorb the influence into forceful torrents of words which convey real feeling, real experience. During the summer term, to discredit his teacher's assessment of Johst's work, Brecht read the seminar a paper attacking his 1917 novel *Der Anfang* (*The Beginning*).

He ... looked sharply, almost piercingly, through his spectacles, observing coldly. He was wearing his hair cut like a brush and, above his forehead he had shaved off a broad stripe of about 1½cm, which was clearly visible next to the fast-growing stubble and somehow it seemed to underline the hard, sharp strength of his nature. He read his paper in a harsh voice, articulating clearly, without any sign of wanting to compromise or to look his listeners in the face. Applause, laughter, fidgeting and hissing made no difference to him.

He condemned *Der Anfang* as 'smelling of midnight oil and sweat',[15] and said he was going to write an 'antithesis' to *Der Einsame*. He would trump the play with *Baal, eine dramatische Biographie*.[16]

He started by working through the printed text of Johst's play scene by scene, paralleling the action but producing scenes that were full of theatrical vitality, and materializing what had been idealistic. Within a month of seeing *Der Einsame* he already had *Baal* half finished.[17] He was intending to call the play *Baal frisst! Baal tanzt!! Baal verklärt sich!!!* (*Baal Gorges Himself! Baal Dances!! Baal Is Transfigured!!!*) Baal is the anti-type to Johst's Grabbe. In both plays the writer is seen in relationships with his mother, with a young friend, with a fiancée, with the friend's fiancée, and with a musician. Many of Brecht's names derive from Johst: Ekart from Eckardt, Johannes from Hans, Anna – in later drafts she becomes Johanna – from Anna, Grabbe's sweetheart.

When Brecht's character is addressed as Herr Baal, the name of a fertility god is ironically coupled with a title denoting bourgeois respect. Like Wedekind's Lulu, Baal represents an apotheosis of sexual appetite. He lacks any sense of justice or responsibility. Other people are there to be plundered. 'When you've slept with her,' Baal tells Johannes, who is romantically in love with a virgin, 'perhaps she'll just be a heap of flesh, faceless.'

Early on in the first draft Brecht discriminates between good verse and bad. Verse by Stramm and Novotny – the stage direction does not even specify which poems – are read out by the boss's nephew and dismissed by Baal (who is still a clerk in his host's office) as rubbish; his own verses, which are less literary, less idealistic, will emerge as better literature. Baal says he could have put up with the food and the chatter but not with the wine or the verse. Brecht, who from the beginning had thought of poetry as something useful, usable, singable, had practical reasons for rejecting the abstraction, the complexity and the literariness that had grown cancerously into so much German verse. When Johannes talks rhapsodically about his love for 'the sweetest of women', Baal answers: 'When you embrace virginal hips, warm life pulses in your hands, and in the fear and bliss of the creature, you become a god. In the dance through hell. Hupp! And whipped through paradise. Hupp! Hupp!'

Overlapping with Brecht's determination to contradict Johst was a strong impulse to justify himself, not merely as a poet but as a man. Throughout his life he gave the impression that guilt feelings had never troubled him. Even if they never held him back, they were obviously still troubling him when he wrote the first draft of *Baal*. His treatment of the mother-son relationship shows that much of the play's energy derives from the need to deal with a heavy load of guilt: Brecht did not find it as easy as Baal does to shrug off the suffering he causes by indulging his natural appetites. To some extent he was writing about the sufferings of the girls he discarded. He prided himself on freedom from sentimentality, but he was not unaware of their pain, or of the disparity between the intense pleasure they gave him and the apathy he would feel later. Even this discomfort, though, was less troublesome if he transformed it into a ballad he could perform:

> If you ask me 'What about the loving?'
> I'll tell you: 'I just can't remember . . .'
> What her face was like I don't now know.
> All I know is that I kissed it then.

This makes the same point as the line in the play about the faceless heap of flesh.

At the age of twenty Brecht was less tough than he liked to appear: he felt ambivalently envious of the men who were brutal to girls they no longer wanted. Should he encourage himself to defy his moralizing mother and grab everything he fancied? In an oratorio he started, two of the figures are the Mother and God. The Mother comes to the aid of her suffering son, but complains: 'My womb has a curse on it because of you. But you were like a child who did not know it was sinful, and ran into hell as into a playground. I beg you to come back and repent.' But

God is glad to have someone who can stand up to him. 'Didn't you notice how beautiful your voice became when you got angry and scolded me? Were you not taller when you stood up straight?'

Much of *Baal* - in its first draft - was autobiographical, and Paula was told that he had 'written into a few scenes of a play some things which will perhaps one day convince you that I love you very much'.[18] The first draft also contains more self-pity than was allowed to remain.

I was born to suffer and there's no peace for me. ... I want to give birth to something. ... Love's like a whirlpool that rips your clothes from your body and leaves you naked after you've seen heaven, immeasurably blue. ... Summer sings out of me with a soft and resonant voice. ... I hate romantic reverie, why isn't this work over? It's by divine command, cursed, holy and ravenous. Music gushes out of me. I can't stop it.

Brecht is strongly influenced by the Expressionists he claims to despise, but his formulations are exceptionally forceful. He was convinced that in dealing with life you have to get the upper hand. In the play he uses images that relate the individual to nature, combining the cosmic and seasonal with the private and subjective. Baal tells Anna that love is like trailing a naked arm in cool pond-water, weeds between your fingers. In later versions of the play this comparison will be transferred to a scene with Johannes, who will have told him of a dream in which juniper trees have been making love to his girl. Baal will describe summer clouds as swollen with love like sponges, and female limbs as resembling plants in the wind. The naïvety of the animism is disguised by the exhilarating sensual intensity.

Johst's mother-son scene provoked Brecht into writing one in which the mother grumbles rather in the manner of the mother in Brecht's poems.

> My mother tells me every day: It's awful
> When a grown man behaves like that
> And talks like that, when other people don't think about such
>   things...

She tells him that

> I'm sending her to her grave
> And the day will come, when I'll want to dig her up with my nails
> But then it'll be too late, and then I'll realize what I've lost
> In losing her, but I should have thought of that before.

In the second draft of the play Baal's mother nags at him for playing truant from the office for three days. She slaves away, she says, day after day, washing and sewing, but gets nothing from him, except anxiety. 'Your wickedness and obstinacy are sending me to my grave. Then you'll want to dig me up with your nails, if you still have any left after the way you've lived.' The sequence culminates in the news that he is sacked. When his mother weeps, he tries to comfort her: he will make money, he tells her, by selling poetry.

Brecht wants to demolish the fence of vetoes that has been erected by religion and bourgeois convention. (The Old Testament prophets had denounced nothing more violently than the orgiastic worship of the god Baal by the Phoenicians and Canaanites.) Spilling his identity beyond repressive circumscription, Brecht's Baal becomes more like an animal and more like a god. When another girl, Sophie, says she can't understand why she feels so weak, Baal explains: 'You can smell me. That's how it is with animals.' Later he asks her why a man can't make love to a plant; later still, tiring of women, he makes love to Ekart, a travelling composer.

Another semi-autobiographical scene (which was to be suppressed later) shows Baal at the point of repenting. With church bells ringing in the background, he is determined to start 'a new life . . . quiet, peaceful, contemplative'. He would 'certainly make a good Christian' because he 'can't bear to see suffering'. But he changes his mind as the Corpus Christi Day procession approaches, and interferes when boys start cutting down young birch trees for use in the ritual. This outrages the worshippers, who attack Baal, using umbrellas and prayer books as weapons. The confrontation is between true reverence for nature and narrow-minded piety.

In this draft Baal's experience prefigures that of Brecht, who had not yet worked either as a theatre critic or as a musician in cabaret. At the newspaper office Baal hands in his scurrilously disparaging review of a *Don Carlos* production and defends himself against a young poet whose work he has re-written. When it emerges that he has been in prison and has appeared in a variety show, he is sacked, but he pleads: 'Gentlemen, listen to me. I went out of my depth and lost my nerve. . . . I've turned over a new leaf. . . . I've worked like never before. . . . I'm not going to let myself be pushed backwards. I'm staying here.'

To call Baal an asocial man (as Brecht did later)[19] is to misrepresent him: 'I thrive on enmity. Everything interests me, in so far as I can eat it.' Baal is a play about appetite and the futility of either resisting or explaining. As the beggar says in Scene 13, 'You understand nothing. But you feel a lot. Understandable stories are bad stories.' Brecht was to devote much of his subsequent life to telling understandable stories.

The chaplain calls Baal an animal. His mother is more successful in inducing remorse, as was Frau Brecht, but Brecht's father, like his schoolteachers, often inflamed his anticonformism. After losing a suitcase of his father's on a train, he was defiantly unrepentant: 'First, you could have done the same thing yourself; second, I hope you never get it back; third, I hope the new owner of the things needs them more than you did, and fourth, you can easily get new things.'[20]

In his relationship with Paula, Brecht alternated between tenderness as great as the tenderness towards his mother, and hardness like the hardness towards his father. 'She's wonderfully soft and spring-like, shy and dangerous. Each day I lead myself into temptation, to deliver myself from all evils.' Far from being indifferent to religion, he found – as others had – that a little blasphemy made sex spicier. Sometimes he felt: 'Love won't survive unless we're apart from each other more.' But it was a stable relationship: 'Either Bittersüss is there. Or she isn't there. Then I wait for her.' By the beginning of July he was sure: 'I've got her totally.'[21]

A real relationship with a real girl helped to make Johst's play look ridiculous and expressionism look masturbatory and idealistic. 'Mysticism, spiritualism, consumption, inflated ecstasy are getting out of control and everything reeks of garlic.' Not that *Baal* is devoid of expressionistic self-indulgence; its confusion arises partly from attempts to catch his own moods by the tail, partly from stylistic incongruities.

Side by side with autobiographical ingredients and anti-Johst ingredients, a powerful influence was Verlaine. Hanging opposite Brecht's bed in his 'dungeon' was the painting of Baal Caspar Neher modelled on Verlaine. Rejecting Syrian features, he had painted a debauched, red-nosed Baal, and it was on this that Brecht's eyes fell every morning when he woke up. In the introduction to the 1918 Weimar edition of Verlaine's selected poems, the poet is characterized as looking, under the influence of absinth, 'more and more like Socrates or a faun'; in the 1919 draft of the play Brecht describes Baal as having 'the precise skull of Socrates and Verlaine'.[22] The 1922 edition of the script shows Baal as Neher had painted him, using photographs and drawings of Verlaine, whose relationship with Rimbaud is mirrored in Baal's with Ekart: the homosexual lovers travel euphorically together until murderous violence supervenes.

There is nothing shy in the writing of the play, but Brecht was too shy to dictate his text to the typist his father provided, so it was his friend Otto Bezold who spent most of the weekend 18-19 May 1918 in the factory, dictating from the manuscript and hurrying over the more obscene passages. On Monday evening, 20 May, after they had checked the typescript together, Brecht rewarded Bezold for his services with the gift of the manuscript.[23]

Like Brecht's other friends, Bezold found it impossible to refuse him anything. When Brecht wanted skulls, Bezold stole two from a Franconian ossuary. One of them was placed on the table in the attic workroom, which was furnished ironically: on a music-stand in the corner stood an open score of *Tristan und Isolde* and a baton.

Assuming that Brecht started work about a fortnight after seeing *Der Einsame*, it had taken him five weeks to write the play. In June the text was retyped over a weekend and eight carbon copies were made. The play now had twenty-four scenes. Brecht went on making changes and dictating scenes himself to typists. At the end of July he showed Kutscher a copy, but his comments were 'enough to make you puke'. Brecht also sent a copy to the theatre critic Alfred Kerr, who did not like it, and to Johst, who did not reply. Brecht wrote another letter to the playwright: 'I quite understand if you say *Baal* and anything else I go on to write if I feel like it are nonsense, but if you say nothing, then I must think you want me to take offence.'[24]

In July he took Paula into the mountains and to the Starnberger See. Now, for the first time, she missed a period. Frightened, he asked Neher to pray for him.

A child would destroy all my peace of mind. This would cause more of a scandal than is worth while, if only because it would go on too long, and I might have to leave for India. ... I'm afraid you'll laugh, but I'm still more afraid that *I can't* laugh. Of course I wasn't careful, not a bit, it would have ruined the fun, it wouldn't have been aesthetic and then: it didn't work. After all I'm not playing Tarot. I *can't* hold any trump cards back. ... I've made her quite brave, discussed nothing with her, concealed nothing from her and she hasn't *once* reproached me. Although she didn't want 'it', and set her mind against it hard. But it was so beautiful. Nothing about it was vulgar, and I loved her more afterwards than before. ... Her little face is like a child's when she's afraid or happy. And the little face is like this now (too) often.

Working on the chorale that now prefaces *Baal*, he incorporated the line: 'But even Baal's afraid of babies.' (In a letter to Neher he had written: 'The strongest men are frightened of little babies.')[25]

The pleasures of summer were overshadowed not only by the prospect of premature paternity, but also by the fear of being called up, and by the protracted absence of Neher, who had not been in Augsburg since the beginning of August. Missing his 'brother in art', Brecht wrote regular letters and tried, unsuccessfully, to interest newspaper editors and galleries in drawings Neher sent home from the front. 'I think these people find them too radical in their humanity. Which is exactly what gives them their value.' But since some of the editors and dealers had said the drawings and sketches were not topical enough, Brecht advised Neher to tackle more political subjects, 'Seen as a whole, of course – symbolic in the style of Goya.' Neher was encouraged to keep a diary: 'Don't forget that Lionardo [*sic*], whom I greatly love, wrote a great deal, and he never did anything without a good reason.'

Brecht also asked for a photograph: 'You also have a very beautiful face.' He also made valiant efforts to boost Neher's morale: 'Remember, when things are going badly for you, that life (elsewhere, of course) is very beautiful, wonderfully beautiful, and littered with adventures and full of colour and dizziness, and with plenty of space for the grandest of gestures. But really you can only manage to make them if you grit your teeth and don't give in.' Neher sent back drawings, pictures and passages of diary, but he refused to go absent without leave, and he grew tired of receiving detailed bulletins about his friend's amours. When Brecht enquired about which unit to apply for if he was called up, Neher suggested that he should let the little girl choose which uniform she liked best. Apologizing, Brecht urged him to come home on leave. 'It's possible. I've asked around. It must be possible. A year at the front is too much. Make a fuss. Heavens above, don't let them take advantage of you.'[26]

In September he came back. They swam in the river, climbed trees, had fun. But the pleasure Brecht took in these activities derived partly from a compulsion to steep himself intimately in Nature. You must be naked, he says in a poem, when climbing the tree.[27] You must press your back into the painful branches and, groaning, climb to the top, where you rock with the same movement that the tree has enjoyed for hundreds of years. In the water, rising bubbles show that a fish has swum through you. Lying on your back you should be as passive as if you were among the stones under the water or as if a woman were carrying you.

Delicately this merges a death-wish with a yearning to be back inside his mother's womb, and an unmistakable lust for sexual intimacy with Nature. Like Baal, who at one point wants to sleep with plants, Brecht claims in one poem (written the following year) to have 'committed buggery with the thick stones' and in another to have a love-bite on his neck, given to him by the earth. But the hunger for physical fusion with the surface of the earth is as much a matter of hatred as of love. He cannot bear living in a world which has no use for him. Later, Marxism would give him a sense of purpose, but as yet he had no way of proving to his mother that he was not a wastrel or to himself that the earth was not 'full of cold wind', that one did not arrive uninvited and leave 'covered with scurf and scabs'.[28]

3 / The Marching Corpse

If the decision to study medicine was aimed at reducing the likelihood of being sent to the front, the stratagem succeeded. When he was finally called up at the beginning of October 1918, he had about three weeks in a barracks and, inadequately trained, was posted as a medical orderly to an emergency military hospital which consisted of wooden huts erected in the fenced playground of an Augsburg primary school, the Elias-Holl-Schule. In Ward D, where he had to work, there were a few patients with cholera or dysentery, but most were suffering from venereal disease, which was a petty offence known as *Kavaliersdelikt*. The medical officer, Dr Ecker, sat at a microscope, examining specimens, and Brecht was probably given rather less to do than he later implied to Sergei Tretiakov: 'I bound up wounds and painted them with iodine, I gave enemas and blood transfusions. If a doctor told me: "Brecht, amputate this leg", I'd have answered "Right, Herr Doktor". If I'd been told: "Brecht, a trepanning", I'd have opened the man's skull and poked about in his brains.'[1]

As at school, Brecht treated the discipline as a challenge: how many rules could he break with impunity? He used his local fame and his charm to soften his superiors. He was allowed to sleep at home and, according to Münsterer, he did not always report for duty in person. One morning the kitchen-maid arrived to ask whether the medical officer had any orders for her. His school-friend Heiner Hagg was astounded at Brecht's nonchalance. 'I saw him strolling around, his hands deep in his pockets to stop his trousers from falling down. Also, he was wearing yellow sandals, and often he had no tunic on, only a pullover. He was usually bareheaded, or carrying a kind of riding whip. Of course he wore no belt. He was more of a civilian than a soldier.'[2] His temperament fitted him to be a rebel, but not a revolutionary: he felt no involvement and not even much sympathy with the rebellion in Germany that ensued on the end of the war.

Karl Marx had expected Germany to launch a proletarian revolution in Europe, and to Lenin it seemed tragic that none of the German parties could lead the workers into insurrection. The party Brecht probably joined was only half-heartedly Marxist – the Independent Social Democratic Party (USPD) which had been formed by defecting Social Democrats, contrite that the SPD had supported the war loan in 1914. The only party to favour revolutionary violence of the Soviet variety was the Spartacus Union, led by Karl Liebknecht and Rosa Luxemburg. In 1917–18 both the Spartacists and the USPD had been fomenting agitation, but most people had become politically lethargic. Even when the shooting began on 10 November 1918, according to Harry Graf Kessler, 'they did not lose their *sang froid*. . . . A great contrast to 1914, when they were all impatient to sacrifice themselves.'[3]

The new Chancellor, Prince Max von Baden, had been negotiating for an armistice, but at the end of October the naval high command ordered the fleet into action. This provoked a naval mutiny at Kiel, followed by uprisings in Wilhelmshaven, Hamburg, Hanover and Cologne. In the north the government could no longer count on its troops to obey orders, while in the south Kurt Eisner, the Bavarian USPD leader who had been in prison, rallied so much support that, with soldiers and members of the Bavarian Peasants' League among his followers, he could capture the military headquarters in Munich. On 9 November he proclaimed a Bavarian republic with himself at the head of it. Two days before the armistice was signed, the Kaiser abdicated, and a council of People's Delegates assumed power. Workmen, peasants and soldiers all had to elect spokesmen, and Brecht claimed he was one of those elected as a *Soldatenrat* (soldiers' representative), though, as Münsterer writes, 'The *Soldatenräte* were not much more than middlemen, mostly nominated by the officers themselves to make reports on the men's complaints about bad catering and suchlike everyday affairs, and they were generally used to make the men collaborate when unpopular measures had to be forced through.' Pfanzelt later said that Brecht was never a *Soldatenrat*.[4]

Prince Max von Baden resigned, announcing that the Kaiser and the Crown Prince intended to give up their rights to the throne, and that Friedrich Ebert, who was to succeed as Chancellor, would form an assembly to organize a new constitution. But without waiting for the abdication, Ebert's second-in-command, Philipp Scheidemann, proclaimed to the crowd outside the Reichstag a Social Democratic republic. Later in the day Karl Liebknecht, who had been in prison till October, addressed the crowd outside the palace, proclaiming a Socialist republic.

For weeks after the armistice leaderless bands of troops were on the rampage. Even in Berlin the government could not check the revolutionaries. Forming a joint cabinet with the USPD, Ebert had to concede that sovereign power resided in the councils, but when the Berlin councils elected an Executive Committee he was suspicious of it: was it a front for the Spartacists and the extremists? Desperate to restore order, he aligned himself prematurely with the army commanders. When a Congress of Councils met in Berlin on 16 December the majority turned out to be moderate and anti-Spartacist. Though demagogues went on trying to stir up rioting and demonstrations, officers could safely wear their cockades and epaulettes in the streets of Berlin by the middle of December. 'It is a big difference from mid-November,' wrote Harry Graf Kessler.[5]

The communist rebellion began on 5 January 1919. Workers occupied the offices of the newspaper *Vorwärts* and the Wolff Telegraph Bureau. But by now demobilized officers and soldiers, unable to settle down as civilians, were being recruited by free corps commanders such as Colonel Reinhard. Supplied with weapons and ammunition from regular army depots, the free corps used flame-throwers, machine-guns and artillery quite brutally. On 10 January, at the *Vorwärts* building, when six rebels emerged with a white flag, five of them were shot, and the survivor was sent back to say that surrender must be unconditional. The next day the free corps crushed the feeble residue of organized resistance. Karl Liebknecht and Rosa Luxemburg were both captured on 15 January. He was shot by a captain, ostensibly for trying to escape; she was shot by a lieutenant and thrown into a canal.

In Augsburg leaflets were being burnt in the streets. Together with Münsterer, Brecht, who was demobilized on 9 January, attended rallies and election meetings organized by the rival parties, though he was describing himself as an 'independent Independent'. 'Proceedings in the meeting-halls are not altogether conventional', wrote Münsterer. 'One works one's way right to the front of the seats in the balconies and galleries to aim a long-range gob of spit at the bald pates of the speakers.' The boys were 'constantly in a state of excitement for our hearts were beating on the far left, if less from political understanding than from adolescent aggressiveness'. And in a 1928 note on his position during the Spartacist uprising, Brecht was to write: 'We all suffered from a lack of political convictions and I also from my old incapacity for enthusiasm.'[6] Erwin Piscator, the pioneer of political theatre in Germany, was lacking at this time in neither. He was twenty-five in December 1918 when he joined the Communist Party, and there were many who believed that Ebert and the SPD had betrayed the workers. It would be impossible now to unite the German Left; as Kurt Tucholsky put it, the socialist government was like a radish in the garden of the republic, red on the outside but white underneath.

At meetings Brecht took copious notes,[7] and before the end of the month his adolescent aggressiveness was filtering into his new play, *Spartakus*. But the writing is two-edged. He relishes the militancy of the Spartacist, Glubb, who wants to change the world, but he also relishes the refractoriness of his anti-hero, Kragler, who refuses to do any more fighting. He has had enough. 'Everyone is top dog inside his own skin.' His girl may be pregnant by another man, but he will still be more comfortable in bed with her than on the barricades. Her father and her lover are both vulgar war profiteers, but it is more sensible to counter their materialism with egoism than with idealism. There is a strong strain of romanticism in the girl, Anna, who commits herself to Kragler when she sees him on the point of siding with the revolutionaries. But as soon as he can count on not being alone in bed, he opts for survival. Like Brecht, who had pretended to study medicine and took pleasure in defying expectation, Kragler makes weakness into a strength: he has the courage of his own cowardice. And like Baal, he is fortified by indifference to bourgeois morality. What he has learnt from the war is how to stay alive.

Spartakus is set in Berlin, and Brecht, who had never been there, had to depend on newspaper reports. 'The revolution, which had to serve as a background, was of no more interest to me than Vesuvius is to a man who wants to cook a saucepan of soup on it.' He admitted that the play was not as good as *Baal*: its main purpose was to earn money. He was taking less trouble to project ambivalence than he had in *Baal*, but this helped the new play to make an impact on young malcontents. Ernst Fischer, Brecht's junior by a year, had heard conversations in the army about the Russian Revolution, but it was not until the early 1920s that Bolshevism attracted him as an alternative to the purulent decadence of post-war Austria. Watching a performance of Brecht's play in 1922, he felt he was seeing an image of himself, distorted 'to the point of recognizability'. What Kragler seemed to be disrupting was the bourgeois twilight, 'sentimentality and business, domesticity and turpitude, high-mindedness and opportunism'.[8] While the moon is rising, red and menacing, the dead soldier stops the gramophone. 'The old song is ended and now *the other thing* begins....' The man who is returning from mass murder sees that it has all been for nothing. Brecht, who had not been at the front, could speak to those who had.

Though he was already sceptical about individuality – his characterization never depends on drawing a firm outline around personality traits – Brecht was no less sceptical about socialist ideas of collectivity. His instincts were anti-didactic and anti-political:

> The serpent in paradise was the first teacher; she wanted to 'teach' people what is good. Revolutionaries belong to the teaching profession; I mean the important revolutionaries, the ones who get rid of the Kaiser and introduce communism, while the conservatives who oppose them are also teachers. . . . But the free man has no principle as regards such unimportant matters. The total pacifist and the total militarist are both the same kind of idiot.[9]

In 'Gesang des Soldaten der roten Armee' ('Song of the Red Army Soldier') which Brecht performed when his friends threw a party for him at Gablers Taverne on 19 January 1919, he sang about freedom as a word which was often heard from mouths that could crack ice:

> And you saw men with tiger jaws
> Marching behind the red inhuman flag
> When the red moon swam over oat-fields
> They sleepily talk about times ahead
> For marching makes you sleepy
> Till you sleep as deep as the dead.

The poem was first printed in 1927 and soon afterwards he refused to have it reprinted – a ban which remained in operation for the rest of his life.[10]

Instead of going back to university for the 'wartime emergency term of 1919', he applied successfully for leave of absence and spent it gravitating between Augsburg and Munich, not so much to observe political events as to compile his first volume of poems, which was to be called *Klampfenfibel (Guitar Primer)*. The most striking poem in the collection crystallizes the image of a dead soldier, exhumed and resurrected by military doctors, blessed by the chaplain, and sent to fight once again for his Kaiser:

> Two orderlies to hold him up
> Are summoned in haste
> Else he'd flop in the mud
> And that would be a waste.

In a cartoon Georg Grosz had published in April 1919, a military doctor is examining a wormy skeleton and pronouncing it fit for war duty. According to the publisher Wieland Herzfelde, Brecht said that the cartoon gave him the idea for the poem. Both men must, in any case, have heard the saying 'They're digging up the dead', which was commonplace at the end of the war.[11]

Neher was producing glowing watercolour illustrations for *Klampfenfibel*: 'Baal playing the guitar, Orge with the rope under the tree, violet shipwrecks and the gruesome march of the dead soldier with commotion and flags in the blue spring sky.' Energetic and prolific, Brecht surprised his friends almost daily with new verses, and their reactions helped him to decide which to preserve. He was also hoping to earn a thousand marks by writing a novel: he talked about it to Neher on 27 January, when they were on the train to Munich.[12] They wanted to learn the waltz in time for the Kutscher seminar party on 3 February and, after a walk through the snow, talking mainly about Brecht's girl-friends, they went to several dance-bars. The following evening, after seeing two one-act plays by Strindberg, they got more practice in dancing.

Three days after the seminar party, Brecht attended a meeting organized by the USPD in the large Odeonsaal to protest against the deaths of Rosa Luxemburg and Karl Liebknecht. Brecht was seeing a good deal of Neher, who wrote in his diary: 'it's quite wonderfully lovely to be alone together like this. He expounds his aesthetic and I argue against it.'[13] Neher drew an illustration for Brecht's poem 'Der Himmel der Enttäuschten' ('The Heaven of the Disappointed'), and they tried to sell their combined work to *Simplicissimus*, the satirical weekly. Together they visited Müllereisert, who was ill, and then left Munich to spend three days with the pregnant Paula at her grandparents' house at Kimratshofen in the Algäu. Her parents wanted to avoid the scandal that would have built up around her pregnant presence. Returning to Munich, Brecht tried to teach Neher how to play the guitar.

They took little interest in the difficulties of Kurt Eisner, who had embarked on an extravagant programme of social welfare policies, despite the shortages of food and fuel, the price-rises and unemployment. The majority socialists, who had defeated the USPD in the January elections, were demanding a return to parliamentary government. After an ineffectual appeal to the ideal of socialist revolution, Eisner capitulated. He was on his way to the Landtag (the Bavarian representative assembly in Munich) to make his speech of resignation on 21 February when he was shot by a young nobleman. Only an hour later a member of the Workers' Revolutionary Council forced his way into the Landtag, and shot at the majority socialist leader, Erich Auer. Demonstrators stormed down the streets of Munich but the next day, according to Neher, who travelled to Augsburg with Brecht and the sister of his friend Georg Geyer,

we were in fits of laughter all the time, despite the gravity of the situation, and the hour passed very quickly. Then we arrived here. It was the same picture as in Munich, perhaps worse and more harmless-looking. During the night marauders had broken into several shops in the Bürgermeister-Fischer-Strasse and Bahnhofstrasse, and looted them. There had been shooting, but nothing more. A crowd of people contemplating revolution with downcast faces.[14]

In their home town, Brecht and his friends went out drinking and singing. They joined demonstrators marching in commemoration of Eisner. In the afternoon Neher did drawings for Brecht's poems, and in the evening, until the curfew, they went out for a walk in the town. Armed soldiers were patrolling the main street.

Four days later, back in Munich, they joined another procession to mourn Eisner. It wound its way to the cemetery. There was shooting all over the city; Neher wrote: 'It was like a pain, as if naked violence wanted to grab back everything it had lost. Unspeakably moving.'

In March Brecht showed *Spartakus* to Lion Feuchtwanger, who had not yet written *Jud Süss*, but was, at the age of thirty-five, already well known as novelist, playwright and drama critic. He was dramaturg at the Munich Kammerspiele. The young man who presented himself at Feuchtwanger's flat was 'slight, badly shaven, shabbily dressed. He kept close to the walls. . . . He has a long, narrow skull, with strongly prominent cheekbones, deep-set eyes, black hair growing down over his forehead . . . from his appearance you might take him for a Spaniard or a Jew or both.' After reading the script, Feuchtwanger was so impressed that he telephoned the young author, who 'got very worked up, so that his dialect became almost incomprehensible. Certainly he'd written this play just for money, but he had another one which was really good, and he'd bring me that.'[15] When he read *Baal*, Feuchtwanger agreed that it was the better play.

By 10 March Brecht had started on a new play about David and Absalom, but in April, after Feuchtwanger had reacted favourably to *Baal*, Brecht energetically revised it. He 'cleaned away' much of the residue deposited by Verlaine and Johst. Feeling now that the original was 'unactable', he asked Jakob Geis, the dramaturg, to retrieve it from the Munich Residenztheater, and substitute the new version.[16]

Since the beginning of the year communists had infiltrated the local soldiers' and workers' councils, which became more refractory. Unemployment had exacerbated the dissidence, and meetings in beer cellars erupted into so much belligerence that Johannes Hoffmann, the new majority socialist leader, who was intent on stabilizing the country, withdrew his government from Munich to Bamberg, leaving the stage free for radical intellectuals to put on a political performance as members of a new central revolutionary council for the prevention of counter-revolution – Gustav Landauer, who had presided at the obsequies for Rosa Luxemburg, Ernst Toller, the playwright, Erich Mühsam, who attacked the majority socialists in verse, and Franz Lipp who, as foreign minister, immediately wrote to the Pope complaining that Hoffmann had taken the lavatory key away with him.

After only six days these amateur republicans were upstaged by a more experienced revolutionary, Eugen Leviné, a Russian, who had been ordered by the Communist Executive in Berlin to take over the party in Bavaria. On 13 April, with the backing of the local councils, he proclaimed the dictatorship of the proletariat. Thirty-six years later Brecht would speak in meretriciously glowing terms of changes visible in Augsburg:

The old city was suddenly full of new men, who trooped in from the suburbs, and there was an unfamiliar liveliness in the streets of the prosperous, of officials and tradesmen. For a few days women of the working class addressed the quickly improvised councils, reproaching young workmen who were wearing army clothes, and factories obeyed orders given by workers.

No one could guess from this how Brecht was spending the time. In between shifts of intensive work on the revision of *Baal*, he and his friends were 'having fun in Gablers Taverne and Zanantoni's ice-cream parlour, where he chatted with madame, danced with the waitresses to guitar music, and showed off in front of them'.[17]

When Otto Bezold joined in a discussion at a communist meeting, it was to make the point that the well-being of the workers was ultimately dependent on the entrepreneurs, who had to take both the risk and the responsibility. His courage was admired – but not emulated – by Brecht and his friends. In private arguments Brecht defended the workers' and soldiers' councils, but called Bolshevism a disease which would eventually be rooted out, if only at the cost of destroying the people.[18]

The dictatorship of the proletariat was short-lived. Anticipating military intervention, Leviné began to recruit a people's army. Hoffmann appealed to Berlin for help. The troops that marched southwards were joined by free corps recruited in northern Bavaria by such men as Franz Ritter von Epp. One of his recruits was Otto Müllereisert, who was undeterred when Brecht threatened not to attend his funeral. Brecht's brother Walter also volunteered and served under von Epp. On 1 May a well-equipped army of 22,000 men advanced on Munich. Dozens of people were accused of revolutionary activity and summarily shot. Landauer was beaten to death, Leviné executed, Toller and Mühsam imprisoned. When a mixed gang of soldiers and students, armed with revolvers and hand-grenades, irrupted into Feuchtwanger's flat, ordering him to open his drawers and cupboards, they found a manuscript titled *Spartakus*. Fortunately for him some of the students knew his work, and he insisted that the play was not propaganda material.

In Augsburg on 2 May the distant noise of cannon fire did not stop Brecht from reading his new version of *Baal* to his friends. 'Large sections of the first part have been cut,' wrote Münsterer, 'especially the newspaper office scenes, in which Baal reaches out for an orderly life, so the overall effect is now more anarchic and anti-bourgeois.' Tirelessly rewriting, Brecht kept reading new versions of scenes to Pfanzelt, Münsterer and Bezold, working from their reactions and suggestions to make new changes. Never has the act of writing been less solitary; no one could have been less like Der Einsame as portrayed by Johst, though whenever Brecht's friends tried to secure a slightly larger audience for his readings he was too shy to turn up. But they were patient with him: as the charismatic ringleader in the anti-social games they played, he could create an atmosphere like the one he was distilling into his ballads and plays. Münsterer confirms this:

In 1919 all the early summer was permeated with Baal-like feelings towards the world. But the reverse is also true – the play, especially in this second and best version, itself contains a lot of the life we were leading.... There is Brecht's attic room in Blachstrasse, with the table overloaded with manuscripts, the hazel-tree copses on the banks of the Lech, there are the birch saplings nailed to the walls of houses for Corpus Christi Day, and the dirty pubs on the Graben.[19]

Brecht was in a routine of writing from six in the morning till midday, so he was too busy to attend lectures, but in the spring of 1919 he appeared at Kutscher's seminar to read a paper on Reinhard Goering's play *Seeschlacht* (*Battle at Sea*), which had been premièred on 28 September the previous year at the Kammerspiele. It should have been subtitled 'The Repentant Mutineer', he said. The students enjoyed his critique.

'Only Kutscher,' reports Münsterer, 'whose face darkened from one sentence to the next, irritably declared – with bestial gravity – that this lecture confirmed what he already knew: that the speaker was totally untalented.'[20]

Describing events later to Tretiakov, Brecht did not admit that he had been demobilized before the Bavarian republic was proclaimed.

The hospital was the only military installation in Augsburg. It appointed me to the Augsburg revolutionary committee. . . . We didn't have a single Red Guard. Nor did we get around to issuing a single decree or nationalizing a single bank or closing a church. Two days later a regiment from the troops of General von Epp, 'the peacemaker', stroked us with its wing. One member of the revolutionary committee hid in my flat till he could escape. Then Bavaria sank into the past.[21]

Brecht did not have a flat, but one of the revolutionary committee members did hide in the attic, and slept there for two nights. This was Georg Prem, appointed by the revolutionary committee as military commander of Augsburg. He was married to Lilly Krause, an active Spartacist who had been agitating for workers to be given guns; Brecht had met them in January at the election meetings, and become fond of 'Höllenlilli' – 'Lily of hell'. She served as a nurse during the fighting against von Epp, but Brecht took no part in it. He used his influence with the Spartacists, though, to help Rose Maria Aman; after the April disturbances she wanted to leave Augsburg, and railway journeys were allowed only with a permit.[22]

Brecht's uncle, Karl Brecht, was a member of the Augsburg Gymnastic Association and on Good Friday, 19 April, when a memorial celebration was held, the actress Vera-Maria Eberle recited a specially written poem by Brecht, comparing the resurrection of Christ with the survival of the fallen in the memories of their comrades. Privately Brecht commented that something should be done to commemorate the fall of so many of the association's female members.

His preoccupations were not political: if Neher is to be believed, he talked more at this time about the future of *Spartakus* than about the future of Germany. They often went to the theatre together, seeing plays by Wedekind, Strindberg, and Grillparzer. They walked out of Gorki's *Lower Depths* after the second act. Their nightly bouts of singing and drinking were curtailed by the 'lights-out', but art students still threw parties. On a riverside walk with Pfanzelt on 8 March they 'sang and screamed till our ears were ringing'. Brecht wanted to learn how to ride, and after being thrown from a horse on 25 April when he was riding with Müllereisert, he was in bed for several days, head and arms thickly swathed in bandages. He was often to be seen in riding breeches, walking up and down beside the canal, either clasping his hands tightly behind his back or hitting himself with a riding crop. He was also fond of quoting Nietzsche's line: 'If you're going to a woman, don't forget your whip.' Or he would prop himself for hours against the parapet, staring down into the muddy water.[23]

Between 4 and 11 May 1919 he paid at least four visits to the Plarrer, the Augsburg fair. On the 9th, Neher went in the swingboats with him and some girls: 'It's incredibly beautiful and full of bodies, warm and supple and vigorous.' He spent so much time at the fairground that he got to know some of the showmen and, with Max Knoblach, he went regularly to church fairs, including the annual Jakober-Kirchweih, held in August scarcely 500 yards from his home. All the Augsburg fairs featured ballad-singers, who sang moralizing songs, pointing with a stick to illustrations stuck up on a board, while playing a monotonous hurdy-gurdy accompaniment. One singer had a wooden leg and spat out tobacco juice at the end of each line, while his daughter went round with a hat, collecting for him. Titles of typical ballads were 'The Forester's Daughter', 'The Robber's Bride', 'Madness and Motherly Love', and 'The Crime and Condemnation of the Cruel Murderer Heinrich Thiele'.[24]

Brecht's own balladeering was sensational because it introduced a fairground atmosphere into the drawing-room. 'Then he planted himself in the middle of the room,' wrote Lion Feuchtwanger of Pröckl, the character he based on Brecht in *Erfolg* (*Success*), 'and with open effrontery in a horribly loud shrill voice began to deliver his ballads to the twanging of his guitar, pronouncing his words with an unmistakably broad accent.'[25]

Later in May Brecht left Augsburg to meet Hedda in Ulm, where they attended a lecture by Rudolf Steiner, but left before the end to go for a walk by the Danube.[26]

Though he did not help with *Spartakus*, Feuchtwanger recommended *Baal* to the Musarion-Verlag, which agreed to consider the revised version with Neher's illustrations. To deliver the pictures, Neher and Brecht travelled to Munich on 19 May with Walter Brecht who, while fighting for von Epp, had taken part in the siege of the city. At last, after seven and a half years, the collaboration with Neher seemed about to bear public fruit.

Though his poetic genius was inseparable from his genius for collaboration, Brecht did not slide easily into intimacy. It was only after knowing each other for eighteen months that he and Münsterer began to address each other in the second person singular. Like Müllereisert, Münsterer dressed dandyishly, always wearing elegant grey gloves; the scruffy Brecht enjoyed violating the dignity of his debonair friends. It was on 29 May, after Münsterer had taken his *Abitur* (school leaving certificate). They were sitting on a bench surrounded by chestnut trees:

Probably it was raining. Drops clattered down from the branches. Brecht had just made a real mess of my clothes and ridiculed my bourgeois manners; lucky it was dark, so no one could see how small and how frightful I looked. Suddenly Brecht turned to me with the question: 'By the way, wouldn't you (*Sie*) like to say *Du*?' I only know that I held his hand in mine for a long time, for it meant I was really accepted into the clique of outsiders.

They all enjoyed the high jinks, the drinking and the singing at Gablers Taverne in the long narrow room with painted peasant furniture and two stuffed eels in glass cases, the swimming, the tree-climbing and lying naked in the grass, the endless chatter, the ancient nickelodeon with changing transparent pictures.

Thanks to the method of working Brecht had evolved, using his friends, his guitar, and his untrained singing voice, life was like a non-stop party, in which parties occurred not to interrupt but to intensify what was going on. There was one in Neher's studio on 1 July. 'Bert sang at the end like mad,' wrote Neher, 'and the light was turned off, and what was done to the women was what must be done to women when the lights are turned off.'[27]

When the Musarion-Verlag rejected *Baal*, the news had little effect on the two friends. Brecht's father was still supporting him; he and Neher had the momentum to go on working together. Sometimes they quarrelled, accusing each other of egoism, and sometimes Brecht would pontificate about the dangers of letting love-affairs get in the way of work. Neher must stay in control of the situation, as Brecht did, even after Paula gave birth to his son at the end of July. Neher, Müllereisert and Georg Pfanzelt travelled with him to Kimratshofen. The baby was named Frank, after Wedekind, and the baptism was followed by a meal in a restaurant. Paula sat between Müllereisert and Neher.[28] Just over three weeks later the three friends went back again to see her and the baby. Pfanzelt played the organ, and Brecht sang two of his more recent songs, 'Luzifers Abendlied' and 'Baals Choral'.

It was in September that the soprano Marianne Zoff arrived in Augsburg to work at the Stadttheater. Brecht soon became aware of her, but Hedda Kuhn was to be given the next leading female role in his life, and sixteen months were to elapse before she was supplanted (in 1920) by the singer. The relationship with Hedda had begun in about August 1918; 'Hedda made things diabolically difficult for me, and I fought with the devil, and I often lost. . . . She had a lot of pleasure and she suffered a lot; she could have got away unscathed or she could have fought back . . . she had nails on her fingers.'[29]

Writing for the *Augsburger Neueste Nachrichten*, the schoolboy Brecht had reviewed books; the 21-year-old Brecht became a dramatic critic in October 1919 for *Der Volkswille*, the daily paper published by the USPD in Swabia and Neuburg, edited by Wendelin Thomas, whom Brecht had met in January at the election meetings. His first assignment was to review Ibsen's *Ghosts* at the Stadttheater. He signed himself B.B., though at home he was still Eugen.

He felt less at home in the Stadttheater than in the Lachkeller, listening to a small troupe of entertainers led by Karl Valentin, singer, balladeer and monologuist, who wrote his own comic sketches for performance in the local dialects. Like Wedekind in cabaret, he had to capture the audience's attention in a noisy ambience. 'One immediately had the strong feeling that this man won't make jokes. He is himself a joke.'[30] Brecht made friends with him and mimed a clarinet player in one of Valentin's films. Valentin's brand of comedy exerted a decisive influence on him, and by the end of the year he had completed five one-act plays. Valentin was not so much a metaphysical clown as a folk artist endowed with naïve wisdom. 'Demonstrated here is the inadequacy of everything, including ourselves. If this man, one of the most penetrating spiritual forces of the period, brings vividly before our eyes the *complexity* of the interconnections between imperturbability, stupidity and *joie-de-vivre*, it's enough to make horses laugh and take deep inner note.'[31]

'Valentin was for me', said Brecht, 'roughly what Schoenberg was for Eisler.'[32] (Hanns Eisler had been a pupil of Schoenberg's.) Though Brecht never plagiarized Valentin, and seldom imitated him, he was inspired to an inconsequential comic surrealism, which is unlike anything in *Baal* or *Trommeln in der Nacht* (*Drums in the Night*), the play that was formerly

Spartakus. The one-act play *Der Bettler oder Der tote Hund* (*The Beggar or The Dead Dog*) contains dialogue reminiscent of vaudeville:

BEGGAR: What Napoleon are you talking about?
EMPEROR: The one who conquered half the world and then got so proud he had to have a fall.
BEGGAR: Nobody could believe that except himself and the world. It's not true. Actually Napoleon was a man who rowed a rowing-boat and had such a thick head that all the others said: 'We can't row because we haven't got room for our elbows.' When the boat sank, because they weren't rowing, he pumped his head full of air and floated, the only survivor, and because he was in shackles, he had to row on, but from down there he couldn't see where he was going and they were all drowned. So he shook his head over the world and because it was so heavy it fell off.

It is not only in this mixture of nonsense and logic that the one-act plays look forward to the anti-theatre of Ionesco: in another, *Die Hochzeit* (later retitled *Die Kleinbürger-Hochzeit – The Petty Bourgeois Wedding*), the home-made furniture disintegrates, bit by bit, together with all pretensions to respectability. In *Der Fischzug* (*The Haul*) a drunken fisherman ambushes his wife and her lover in a fishing-net, and calls in six other fishermen, who drop the human catch into the bay. In *Lux in Tenebris* a man, ejected from a brothel because he can't pay, revenges himself by pitching a tent on the other side of the road for lectures and exhibitions concerning venereal disease. The idea must have been prompted by an exhibition held in Augsburg during September by the German Association for the Prevention of Venereal Disease.[33]

In *Er treibt einen Teufel aus* (*He's Driving Out a Devil*) a village boy uses peasant guile to outwit a girl's vigilant parents. This is the play that tells us most about the way Brecht imposed his will on both women and men. The boy's self-confidence appears to be unshakeable: he behaves as though he is so certain of getting what he wants that resistance only amuses him. He can therefore afford to move easily from friendliness to obstinacy, from teasing to self-assertion through physical strength. The whole technique of seduction is slyly based on a pose. When Brecht was making passes, he may have felt insecure and desperate for love, but the mask had already begun to grow into the skin. In the play the boy is consciously using a variety of tricks which make it hard for the girl to go on saying no. He ranges between salacity and a show of offended innocence, between nonsense and logic. He knows, too, that by getting her into trouble with her father, who hits her, he is making her more likely to think of him as an ally. He is an ordinary village boy but, like the schoolboy Brecht, he has learned how to manipulate people.

In Brechtian comedy less depends on wit than on trickery, and the principal tricksters are all male. The female role is either to be duped (like Mutter Courage, who lets a sergeant distract her while a recruiting officer enlists her son) or to play a subordinate role in an intrigue (as Widow Begbick does in *Mann ist Mann*).

All this time Brecht was reading voraciously and with exceptional speed. An assistant at the Augsburg lending library testifies that he would usually return books after a day and look for new ones. 'Often it was difficult to keep up with his wishes.' After 1917 translations of foreign fiction were proliferating in Germany, and as Brecht read Kipling, Bret Harte, Knut Hamsun, adventure stories, detective stories, cheap thrillers. His imagination gave him glimpses of an alternative society without a sophisticated legal system but with a pragmatic morality based on quasi-tribal necessities, male-oriented, with loyalty to the leader as prerequisite. The private gang in his story 'Bargan lässt es sein' ('Bargan Lets It Be') which he read to Münsterer in December 1919,[34] seems to derive partly from his own nocturnal rampages through Augsburg with a gang of followers, partly from adventure stories, partly from fantasies of freebooting superiority to the restrictiveness of provincial Germany.

> In the absinth sea, questing for years –
> By his mother already forgotten –
> Grinning and cursing but sometimes in tears,
> Seeking a land where life's not so rotten.[35]

Since the early 'Das Lied von der Eisenbahntruppe von Fort Donald', he has identified in many of his poems with male gangs of pioneers or outlaws, adventurers searching – often ruthlessly – for a better world, and in the Bargan story his narrator is one of the pirates, who reports uncritically on rape, plunder and butchery. Moral disapproval is reserved for the leader's betrayal of his followers in abandoning them for the sake of the club-footed traitor, Groze, whom he loves. In *Im Dickicht der Städte* (*In the Jungle of the Cities*), males are shown to have sexual relationships with women while their main erotic involvement is with each other, and in the typescript of the Bargan story, which must have followed either Brecht's dictation or his manuscript, the name Orge appears at one point instead of Groze. It is crossed out and corrected in Brecht's handwriting. Hedda had been told that it was Bi and the club-footed Orge that Brecht loved. But whereas he was not willing to make sacrifices for Orge, Bargan is passionately self-destructive, in a way which owes something to contemporary literary fashion:

And it was only because he needed someone to need him that he had attached himself to this outcast, abandoning everything for him, and probably was quite glad that this wasn't a good man that he loved but an evil, greedy child that swallowed him, like a raw egg, at a single gulp. For I'll be damned if he didn't enjoy ruining himself and everything that was his for the sake of that little dog he had his eye on.[36]

The 20-year-old poet who wrote the first version of *Baal* had obviously vacillated, like his hero, on the verge of repenting and conforming, but within two years Brecht had hardened. The birth of a son made no more difference to his life than the sufferings of girls he discarded, so why should he mend his ways? At the beginning of 1920 Neher noted in his diary: 'So far as his woman is concerned, there's no longer any discussion of the past in my presence.'[37]

If a play had roots that damaged its chances of being staged, the roots could be cut off. Disregarding Neher's advice, Brecht tried to eradicate from *Baal* all traces of Johst's negative influence, and he wrote to Johst saying he could 'bite off the umbilical cord completely'.[38] Despite his misgivings, Neher collaborated on the revision, producing new illustrations. Another publisher, Georg Müller, now became interested in the text, and, after the manuscript was delivered to him on 11 February, he got as far as setting up the type, but no further.

Neher was seeing Brecht almost every day, and spending evenings with him, together either with Paula, who was in Augsburg again, or with Hedda. Twice in the first half of January 1920 Brecht, Paula and Neher went together to the cinema, and on the 25th the three of them were photographed together; on the 14th, 23rd and 26th the two friends spent the evening with Hedda.[39] Brecht, who liked monosyllabic nicknames, called her 'He'; Paula was still 'Bi' or 'Bie'. Neher was 'Cas', Marianne Zoff was soon to be 'Ma' or 'Mar'.

He met Marianne by going into her dressing-room at the opera house and paying her compliments. She hoped he would go away, but he sat down. He was 'spider thin ... The ascetic skull pleased me, the narrow mouth moved constantly, the dark button-eyes could sting, the small hands, like a pianist's, pleased me.' He asked whether he might smoke. She was nervous for her throat, but she let him. At the end of the performance she found him waiting for her at the stage door. He took her for a long walk, telling her about Augsburg. What she found attractive was his brightness, his 'amazing musicality', and his lack of inhibition. When he sang his 'grating metallic voice' sent shivers down her spine.[40]

Towards the end of February Brecht made his first excursion to Berlin, where he stayed with a friend of Hedda's, Frank Warschauer. The city made Munich seem provincial. 'Berlin is a wonderful affair,' he wrote to Neher. 'Can't you steal 500 marks from anywhere and come? There's the underground railway, for example, and Wegener. [Paul Wegener, the actor.] It's all overflowing with things in the most ghastly taste, but, boy, what a display!'[41]

'Once you had Berlin', wrote Carl Zuckmayer, 'you had the world.' More than Augsburg or Munich, Berlin bore the marks of defeat. 'The streets were dirty and crowded with crippled beggars – men blinded in the war or with their legs shot off, while elegant booted pedestrians hurried past.'[42] Possibly it was the first impact of the Berlin streets that would make Brecht, eight years later, respond so strongly when he saw a translation of John Gay's *The Beggar's Opera*: he had a keen eye for contemporary relevance.

Baal could not have been written in Berlin. In the Catholic south, alongside the Corpus Christi Day procession, there were plentiful vestiges of a moral tradition to provoke youthful rebellion, but in Berlin the contempt for conventional morality was both spectacular and commonplace. According to Stefan Zweig,

Boys – and not only professionals – paraded up and down the Kurfürstendamm wearing make-up and false waistlines; every schoolboy was set to make money, while senior government officials and bankers were to be seen shamelessly flirting with drunken sailors.... Girls boasted about their perversions, and in every school in Berlin they would have been in disgrace if they were suspected of virginity at the age of sixteen.[43]

Soon after his arrival Brecht made unsuccessful overtures to the Deutsches Theater with a script of *Baal*, and went to likely parties, looking out for allies. At the beginning of March he dressed up as a monk to attend a fancy dress ball at the Kunstgewerbemuseum (Arts and Crafts Museum), where his eye was caught by what looked like a hula-hula girl, wearing a black wig, with her skin dyed dark brown. When he asked her to dance he warned her 'in a soft, rather husky voice' that he was not very good at it and, finding that this was true, the girl, Dora

Mannheim, suggested they should sit down. He kept her talking into the small hours and then offered to see her home through the Tiergarten. At this hour of the morning, he said, they would hear the birds singing there.[44]

But the relationship with 'Do' was interrupted when Brecht unheroically retreated from Berlin after the Kapp *putsch* on 13 March, a right-wing attempt to unseat Ebert's republican government. In February, when the government tried to disband two of the free corps, their commanders had appealed to General von Luttwitz, head of the Nationale Vereinigung (National Association), a political organization which had been formed to consolidate anti-republican forces. When Ebert refused to be intimidated, Luttwitz ordered Captain Hermann Erhardt, one of the free corps commanders, to march on Berlin. Uncertain whether the army would resist the mutineers, Ebert and his ministers retreated to Stuttgart, and in Berlin an East-Prussian politician, Wolfgang Kapp, was named as Chancellor. When Brecht telephoned Do, the reason he gave for leaving was that as director of an Augsburg papermill, his father might need filial support against insurgent workers. In fact Brecht went to Munich, where he spent the evening laughing at Karl Valentin.

From Stuttgart Ebert called on the working class to defend republicanism, and a general strike was quickly efficacious. The Kapp government lasted only four days. But if Brecht was feeling rebellious, it was 'from having nothing to do and anxiety and to get rid of the ideas that are tormenting me. ... No greenness is coming into the trees, the trembling birds are holding their beaks shut, and there are heaps of stories, but no amusing ones.' He kissed Do on paper 'since you can't stop me there', and asked for photographs of her. But she was unresponsive. She made him feel, he said,

like an orphan. Have you no feeling at all for my little heart, which is thirsting for love? My room gets dark, I lie about on the bed, staring up for hours on end at the charcoal drawing I've tacked up on the ceiling, which strengthens my animal impulse to go out drinking again and lose my innocence daily. The best thing would be to escape to the Allgau and write a novel there.[45]

This mimics the confessional tone of his letters to Neher, but insincerely. He went on seeing Paula every Sunday, but in the poems of this period the thought of death is recurrent, and the frailty of the body is contrasted with the power of natural forces. Not that his preoccupation with death made him responsive to Thomas Mann's *Der Zauberberg* (*The Magic Mountain*). When Mann came to read from it in the Augsburg

Börsensaal, Brecht took Walter along to listen, but concluded that the tubercular patients were waging a kind of 'guerrilla warfare, whether refined or naïve, against death'. Some were showing 'a certain *savoir mourir*', and for them death was, as compared with life, 'a kind of binge'.[46]

In April, reviewing Schiller's *Don Carlos* at the Stadttheater, he compared it unfavourably with Upton Sinclair's novel *The Jungle*. Having read about a workman who starved to death in the Chicago slaughterhouses – a man who once had a vision of freedom, but got beaten down with rubber truncheons – Brecht could no longer take Carlos's 'villainy' seriously. Generally the standard was low in the Augsburg theatre: 'Fashionable novelties are produced, and nothing of the slightest originality. The actors are mere beginners and the leading man is a mediocrity who is not bad as Valentin but intolerable as Faust.' The producer, Friedrich Merz, 'forces the acting of both beginners and old hams to a level that's more or less bearable, backed by impossible sets, obviously intended to save money, and facing a totally uneducated audience'.[47]

May began with the death of Brecht's mother.

> Now it was all over, they laid her in earth
> And flowers are growing, butterflies tumbling above it.
> She – such lightness – scarcely weighs the earth down.
> So much pain though to make her so light!

For a while he found it hard to look at other people: had she ever been as healthy as they were?

I no longer remember her face as it was when she wasn't in pain. She wearily pushed the black hair off her forehead, which was bony, I still see the moving hand. ... She died among faces that had been looking at her dying for so long that they'd hardened. She was forgiven for suffering but she was wandering among those faces until she collapsed.

Brecht found it hard to forgive himself for failing – despite his articulacy – to express his love:

Oh why don't we say what's important, it would be so easy and we damn ourselves with silence. It was easy words, close behind our teeth. They fell out when we laughed and now they stick in our throat.

Now my mother is dead. ... Fingernails are no good for digging her up.

As he put it, 'I loved her in my way, but she wanted to be loved in hers.'[48]

But if we damn ourselves with silence, her death was a milestone on his road to hell. In the immediate aftermath he spat out the guilty words from behind his teeth: 'I know I've loved too much. I've stuffed too many bodies, used up too many orange skies. I should be stamped out.'[49]

But with his Rimbaudian eloquence, his control over words, and with the self-confidence that had come from winning approval from so many audiences, he could be defiant about his self-disgust, arrogant in his self-parody. He lingered in the mood of savagery. The world was nothing but a battlefield for his fight with the God who didn't exist:

All day long he's insulted me with his pale heaven. By evening he'd gone too far. I went home. (He managed to arrange that a village brass band should play waltzes in the garden of a pub as I walked past. . . . That was a dirty trick.)[50]

Tone, style, technique and attitude are Rimbaudian, but Brecht is not merely borrowing them. As with so many of his literary borrowings, he is appropriating authoritatively.

His mother's death brought him no closer to his father. The Haindl company was respectably conservative, and Brecht, though he almost never went there, must have been a constant source of embarrassment to his father. His mother's death also severed his main emotional tie to Augsburg, increasing his restlessness. 'How bored I am with this Germany! It's a good, middling country, beautiful in its pale colours and its landscapes, but the people! A degraded peasantry with a crudity that won't engender fabulous monsters, just quiet bestialization; a middle class putting on weight and a dreary intelligentsia! The alternative: America!'[51]

He did not enjoy the servility he had to affect in trying to engineer productions of his plays. The principal dramaturg at Munich's Residenz-Theater, Gerhard Gutherz, sent for him and dismissed him without even inviting him into an office. 'He may be working under pressure, but I'm not a commercial traveller.' Nor did Carl Zeiss, director of the Bavarian State Theatres, want to produce *Baal*: it was liable to cause a scandal, he said.[52]

Brecht's temporary obsession with death was a by-product of unbridled appetite for the pleasures of living: 'I go around wanting the entire world to be handed over to me. I want every single thing to be in *my* possession, together with power over the animals, and the basis for my claim is that I can exist only once.' This is the Brecht who gave his *alter ego* the name of a god: the craving for infinite power is combined with acute awareness of mortality. Nietzsche was certainly an influence, but, like Freud, who recognized in Nietzsche a precursor who might become tyrannically influential, Brecht rationed himself to reading only a part of *Zarathustra*, and he wrote about it in the third person: 'He's very nervous that more could upset his illusion. For he also loves the uncertainties that still flourish inside him. They shouldn't be resisted or the whole thing might become banal.' He relished the salty taste of his 22-year-old self but, nervous of self-intoxication, invented commandments: 'In difficult situations, make a list of all the possibilities, and then consider them. Begin by giving each one a mark, according to how acceptable it is.'[53]

His reaction to his mother's death was not a religious one, but he saw it in a cosmic perspective. 'My mother died on 1 May. Spring stirred itself. Heaven grinned shamelessly.' Some such train of thought may have led to the idea he passed on to Neher, who used it in designing an altarpiece for a church – a miserable-looking man, wearing nothing but trousers, being escorted up to heaven by two angels. Brecht went on brooding about his mother, and going to the cemetery, as well as worrying about Paula, who was losing weight and had a persistent prickling sensation in her breast. The doctor said that something was starting at the top of the left breast, but her parents refused to have her X-rayed.[54]

Hedda had been unapproachable, 'like a whirlpool that forms where there's a hole, an empty place', and when he took her for a walk in the Englischer Garten, the main public park in Munich, he told her he did not love her. Another girl, Anni Bauer, drank schnapps with him under the lantern in his studio, and after he had played his guitar to her, let him kiss her. He started to make a pass, 'but she smelt like a poor girl, and I sent her home. I'm also afraid of go[norrhoea].'

He was not writing much, but Neher's current passion for El Greco had enthused him. He was reading a book by Maurice Barrès about El Greco, and thinking of writing either a comic sketch for Karl Valentin or a book of 'visions or heavenly farces' in the El Greco style.[55] But he always found it harder to write in the summer – he felt restless – and the work he was doing sometimes struck him as primitive and old-fashioned, sometimes as crude and tentative. 'I search for new forms and experiment with my feelings like the new writers. But then I always come back to knowing that the essence of art is simplicity, grandeur and sensitivity, and the essence of its form coolness.' He began a play called *Galgei* – later it became *Mann ist Mann* – but the going was hard: he felt that it was predominantly negative and that his own tendency was to be 'exclusively positive'.[56]

Anxiety over Paula was exacerbated by her refusal to look after herself properly, though perhaps she was aiming to make him more solicitous. When she developed a temperature – while waiting for the results of a lung X-ray – she refused to stay indoors, and after learning that her lung was infected he considered writing a play about her. And one about Jesus. But – perhaps because he was still working on *Galgei* – it was easier to think in terms of the novel about how radically he wanted his art to deviate from what had preceded it. His ambition was to grip the reader 'in such a way that the tradition, which because of (all other)novels is already there, is judicially condemned to death'.[57] Whatever style the novelist chose, it tended to induce a mood which homogenized the reader's emotional reactions. Would it be possible to shift from style to style, modulating into journalese, perhaps, for the main character's death? He did not want to pivot his narrative on a conflict between inner life and external reality. Even if the hero could be presented as unambitious, 'it would still look as though one set too much value on human beings, as though it's unfavourable circumstances, etc. that make relationships unsatisfactory'. It was people, he maintained, who created circumstances, or feebly fell victim to them. Another possibility was to 'present only the inner life, detached and isolated, hard, colourless, seditious and yet submissive'. One danger here was of idolatry towards language. The third possibility was to show that there was no such thing as inner life or major conflicts.[58] It was to this approach that he would eventually gravitate.

His chief objective was extreme narrative simplicity. Could he find a theatrical coefficient for a sentence such as 'In the year ... citizen Joseph Galgei fell into the hands of evil men who were very cruel to him, took away his name and left him lying without a skin'? He was simultaneously fascinated and horrified by the idea of having the power to strip away individual identity.

He was suffering from headaches and an almost constant pressure at the back of his head. In the bright July days his window seemed too big. He was dazzled by the quantity of light, and, seen through glass, the sky looked unreal. He was impatient to finish *Galgei* and *Sommersinfonie*, 'but then expressionism will be done for, and "expression" will be thrown overboard!' Like Rimbaud he aimed at cutting himself loose from past literature, but he intended, unlike Rimbaud, to persevere in his project. He was already alert to the mistakes of the new generation of writers, which took its boredom for pessimism, its irresponsibility for courage, its fecklessness for energy.[59] Brecht intended to learn from Van

Gogh, 'who nearly always sees the future as blacker than the present, which is already too black'. It was necessary to work 'darkly and obstinately, laying no stress on inspiration and spitting on effective ideas. ... In any case one should be wary of "wit", of grandiose notions, tasteful arrangements and smoothness.' What mattered was 'the intrepidity of the human heart, which shows things as they are and loves them like that'.[60] Though Brecht would dedicate himself to making things different, there would always be a large part of him that loved them the way they were.

With girls he oscillated between loving them as they were and criticizing them like démodé literature. Hedda irritated him when she described what had happened to her. Her narrative was:

all false and cosmeticized and unstylish, the sentences are like pimples or abscesses, swollen and unhealthy in colour. And then nothing is objective, and I don't like value judgements. Also feel hostile to intimate confessions, don't like scenes, sit there as if on hot bricks: none of it's true. But I like listening to Bi. I know what she's like, and she doesn't distort anything.

Her conversation was not unstylish. Some of her remarks he called 'wonderful'. For instance: 'Of course I can swim! But only twice. Then I'll be so tired I'll die.' He was also allergic to nervous laughter. When he went out for a walk in August with Rosa Marie Aman, he found her immature and insecure: 'her laughter's no less unsettling than a haemorrhage'.[61]

Neher never got on his nerves the way girls did. They spent an afternoon together in the middle of the month at Possenhofen: 'It's better with a friend than with a girl. We lay in the water (77°F) and in the woods and then in the boat, and swam again when it was already dark. If you lie on your back, the stars go with you, above, and the current flows right through you. At night you fall into bed like ripe fruit, with lust.' Not long after this, he was writing:

> Homeless in winter with nothing
> To occupy the mind
> They lay among other creepers
> Their bodies intertwined.
> No longer pausing to listen
> They talk through the starry nights
> United in the darkness
> And also in the light.[62]

When he met Otto Zarek, who as a student had been friendly with

Hedda and was now a dramaturg at the Kammerspiele, Brecht was better equipped to give dramaturgical advice. Zarek had got stuck with the plot of a play about David. Brecht said it could be done without plotting, and demonstrated how. 'His mouth fell wide open, and shut again, with the idea inside it. His adam's apple moved as he swallowed it. He felt like rewriting the whole thing, he thought, just once more.' By giving advice Brecht had got himself going: the next day he wrote a scene between Saul and David in which nothing depended on plotting. Saul did the talking – with plenty of internal variety – while David sat there cutting his nails.[63]

In no uncertainty about his potential, Brecht was undecided about how to exploit it. Somehow he must establish his reputation and accumulate money. 'Why aren't there any pirate films? I'll write some one day. Also theatre must be used to popularize new fashions (in clothes etc.) and get paid for this by the fashion houses. And plays (books?) could be printed on newspaper with advertisements that would pay for the whole enterprise.'[64] At work here was the commercial instinct which had once led him to sell chestnuts. Later he would repress it, but would go on making shrewd deals with his literary properties.

Not devoid of narcissism, he liked to reserve time for thinking about himself, sometimes wandering along the riverbank, sometimes lying diagonally across his bed, with a newspaper and a looking glass. Hedda usually ignored the impatience in his face when he wanted to be alone. Nor was he responsive when she lay in his bed crying. Eventually she wrote to him reproachfully: why hadn't she 'had the strength to break free then from a man who didn't love me and, what's more, was crude and inconsiderate?' He felt sorry for her, but without emotion: 'she's barking at the moon, I don't hear her remonstrations. I'm miles away in India, have no one to speak for me, she'll make herself hoarse, the moon's shining.' He had 'behaved as roughly and toughly as a bull's balls'.[65]

He was less cold with Paula, who could be useful in many different ways. She even helped him, through an acting game they played, to develop his antipathy towards individualization, and his ideas about acting. 'We lie in the copse-wood and do cinema exercises.' She acted as stylishly as she talked, but it was patently a performance – not an impersonation. 'A queen is a queen, being frightened is being frightened, and Bi is Bi.' Pointing with both hands towards the undergrowth, she would exclaim quite delightedly: 'There, look, the butterfly!'[66]

His anti-naturalistic inclinations were also nourished by visits to variety theatres. One eccentric clown shot at the lights with a small pistol and hit himself on the head, making a huge bump swell up, sawed it off and ate it.[67] (This may be the origin of the sequence in the 1922 version of *Trommeln in der Nacht* in which Kragler extinguishes the moon, which was a lantern, by throwing a drum at it. Both drum and moon fall into the waterless river.)

In 1920, Brecht was already fantasizing about having a theatre of his own. He would hire two clowns, and in the interval, pretending to be spectators, they would chat loudly about members of the audience and about the play, making bets on what was to happen in the second half. In tragedies the scene would be changed with the curtain up and with the clowns strolling across the stage, giving orders. They could also interpolate comments during the action. Seeing Baal with Ekart, they might say: 'He's in love with that filthy tramp!' 'In this way the things on stage should become real again. For God's sake, it's things that should be criticized – plot, dialogue, actions – not the performance.'

What he was later to call alienation effects may seem inimical to strong emotion, but in this period there was nothing he admired more than Rimbaudesque intensity.

To be happy, function well, take time for being lazy, to be committed, only one thing is needed: intensity ... *Amor fati*. To do everything with all one's body and soul. ... To be present at one's own misfortune, dedicating oneself to it with every ounce of flesh. The only time that's wasted ... is time when you had nothing to tell yourself about things. Didn't yell, didn't cry out, didn't laugh, didn't bare your teeth, didn't press your knuckles into your temple, didn't even swim or take a catnap.

He was no more willing, at this stage, than Kragler was to give any political cause priority over his personal needs: 'I am not one of those useful members of human society which stiffen when they want to be noticed and enjoy themselves when they cause friction. But they have no understanding. All they want is to penetrate into human society. They should be cut off.' He would have been incredulous and indignant if a friend could have given him an accurate prognosis of how his writing would develop.

Still rewriting the last act of *Trommeln in der Nacht*, Brecht made it clear that the rioters who attacked the newspaper offices were deluded, poor and drunk. Kragler is 'no longer deluded, no longer one of the low. Main point: the gesture he makes in going home, taking his tunic off, tearing off his tie, putting his hands round his own throat, saying "It's a bore" and going off to bed with the woman.' In September, when Brecht went to hear Alfons Goldschmidt, a founder of International Workers' Aid, talking in a beer-cellar about the Soviet economic situation, he walked out.[68]

He was capable of behaving very roughly at parties. One Sunday in September, after singing at Otto Müllereisert's, he threw his guitar aside and pulled Otto's girl away from him. In the ensuing fight her head got banged three times. Afterwards she let Brecht kiss her bruises, but his chances of seducing her were wrecked when Neher mimicked his behaviour, grabbing hold of the girl like an orang-outang and flinging her against the wall. Müllereisert afterwards said Brecht had behaved like an orphan boy, who seemed so gentle that flies could walk freely over his face and then, after counting up to five, shat in the soup. He later spent a day with the girl, who had 'a magnificent arse', but he decided she was 'stupid, vulgar and dull'.[69]

He was still 'very much against Bolshevism', which involved 'military training for everyone, food rationing, controls, underhand scheming and economic injustices', but he was less reactionary than his father, whose mealtime monologues eventually provoked Brecht into provoking him. It was all right if apples were stolen from the garden: the produce of trees cannot *belong* to anyone. Then his father would start shouting: it was people like Eugen who'd reduced Germany to the state she was in, with closing time fixed at 11 p.m. by the Allied Commission. What had Eugen done for the community so far? Absolutely nothing. In five years' time he still wouldn't have his first medical degree. High time he got a proper job. What did his literary achievements amount to? Nothing at all. They hadn't even been put to the test. How much money had Eugen earned? Nothing. Eugen beat a hasty retreat, and in the afternoon he went to the cinema.[70]

Frank Warschauer, who had been his host in Berlin, had invited him to Baden-Baden, and the next day he left Augsburg to spend five days there. Warschauer talked about Spengler and Zionism. 'This country is going to pieces around us – it's finished, sinking, and nothing's better than Zion.' Warschauer also introduced Brecht to the work of the classic Taoist writer Lao Tse, 'who is so deeply in agreement with me that he [Warschauer] is constantly amazed'.[71]

Brecht saw Hedda in Baden and made love to her in the woods, despite fog and rain. 'Under her veil she's pale, unhealthy, lovely. Everything takes her by surprise, everything retreats from her, her oldest friends kick her aside.'[72] He told her: 'It may be the happiest time of your life and things aren't going badly for you, but you're ungrateful. ... Blame anything you can on me. I've got a broad back.' Taking her in his arms and kissing her, he made her feel better, and in the evening they ate dinner with Warschauer before he took her to the station.

Back in Augsburg the next day he did little. 'Lethargy. I kill time with matchsticks. I look critically at the weather. I walk till I'm exhausted.' He left the next day to collect Paula from Buchloe, 25 miles to the south, and take her to Munich. They had been planning to live together, and it was less than four weeks since he had seen her – she had been in Kimratshofen[73] – but she had grown fat, and he did not conceal his disappointment.

He was feeling restless, depressed, frustrated. 'I run around like a mad dog, unable to do anything. ... I always recognize straight away what's crippling me: that I have power over nobody. That whatever I'm given is a favour. That one's entitled to refuse favours.' He believed himself to be in need of help from Pfanzelt when revising the final scene of *Baal*, and though Pfanzelt promised to collaborate, he either did not have much to say or felt reluctant to spend time on it. 'It's ridiculous,' wrote Brecht, 'it's only literature, but I've humiliated myself and I'm powerless. I'm nothing. I'm ashamed.' He knew he must pull himself out of his depressive lethargy, but 'it's a damnable strain always having to think up new ways of stretching oneself and extending oneself. ... But I'll certainly get rid of my self-assurance.'[74]

None of his qualities was less likely to be evicted, but he stoked up considerable indignation when Friedrich Merz was about to leave the Augsburg Stadttheater, having quarrelled with the board of management. No public protest was made, except by Brecht, who went against the grain of his previous strictures in an open letter to the newspapers: in a single winter, he said, Merz had 'disciplined a lovelessly recruited troupe of raw young actors so forcefully that a repertoire of an amazingly high literary standard could be staged'. Reviewing Goethe's *Tasso* in *Der Volkswille*, after Merz had left, Brecht accused the management of 'seeming to understand as much about literature as a train-driver does about geography'.[75]

What alienated Brecht most of all was the social presuppositions behind plays, productions and audience reactions. *Alt-Heidelberg* was a farce which invited laughter at an old man who had worked as a servant for student fraternities. 'Young Germans have drilled him so that he can never again walk straight or have a relaxed conversation or think for himself.' On his way out after applying for a job in a royal household, the old man, wanting to tip the valet, searches for money in the pockets of his white waistcoat and, finding none, shakes hands instead. Brecht was furious that shaking hands with a servant should be funny.[76] Why should theatre thrive on social injustice? Brecht's career as a drama critic was briefer than Bernard Shaw's, but not less decisive: disliking what they saw, both writers began to evolve ideas for an alternative theatre.

After Brecht had dismissed *Alt-Heidelberg* as 'hogwash', the paper received an open letter of protest from employees of the theatre. Brecht retorted that their 'memorandum' was 'frivolous and truculently vehement'. His reviews had been as moderate as the productions allowed. Even the public's indifference did not justify the management's laziness and stupidity. In subsequent reviews he continued his attack. Could theatre exist without art? Intelligent theatregoers were being forced to withdraw 'weeping quietly and completely broken'. Brecht's last piece in *Der Volkswille* was a review of Hebbel's *Judith*, which he called 'one of the weakest and stupidest plays in our classical German repertoire'. Vera-Maria Eberle, who played Judith, 'although cold, academic, homely and in human qualities almost painfully boring', was 'competent, by no means untalented and she worked hard', but she was lacking in 'erotic fluid, obsessiveness and "neurotic intensity"'.[77] The enraged actress sued the 23-year-old reviewer for libel.

On 13 January 1921, the day after his review appeared, the paper closed down with a final warning to its readers: 'Comrades! Wake up! Counter-revolution can break out any day!'[78]

4 / Love and Anti-Love

Still living in his father's house, without financial independence but with little restriction on his liberty, Brecht was as yet uncertain of how to use either his talent or his indubitable power over other people. Wanting to possess everything and to do anything, he often found it hard to plan ahead. Why go in this direction rather than that?

In 1921 Ash Wednesday fell on 9 February, the day before his twenty-third birthday. He celebrated 'the day one is so alert and pure and repentant' by taking a girl to a ball at an art gallery in the Schwabing district of Munich. Soon abandoning her, he danced cheek to cheek with Marianne Zoff, who was dressed as a page. She was 'the most beautiful woman there, and handled the men wonderfully – very pure and majestic and quiet and bright and unapproachable, and yet not proud'. Neher and Müllereisert were there, and so was Feuchtwanger, with his wife. Brecht danced with Frau Feuchtwanger in what Marianne called a 'sensual' way. Though Marianne was the guest of honour, she was quite willing to leave early with Brecht. 'Full of bergamot schnapps we flopped into a car and nipped home . . . I couldn't sleep. . . . At one point she felt ill, at another she wept because she's never had a baby and then she looked splendid.'[1]

She had a half-Jewish lover called Recht – she was herself descended from Spanish aristocrats and Czech Jews – and on Sunday, back in Augsburg, Brecht persuaded the man to play scenes from *Richard III*. But 'he soon ran out of villainous gestures'. Marianne talked about him in bed. When he had needed money, he had stolen, wherever he went, even breaking into a cupboard in her parents' home. He had been living with her and claiming it was for her sake that he was doing it all, but now, sick of him, though still intending to marry him in the summer, she told him to move out. This reduced him to tears. She let him stay in her bed that night, but he did not make love to her. Or so she said.[2]

The first time she spent the whole night with Brecht she seemed different, more childlike – 'small gestures and a breathless little voice'.

Once, when he could not take her, she laughed quietly and happily: 'That's exactly right, that's good, that you're not always up to it. I'm less exciting already. That's very good.'[3]

Instead of putting Paula out of his mind, he was using her as material in a screenplay he was trying to write with Neher, *Die Seeräuber* (*The Pirates*). It was about a woman who grows up on the savannahs and 'gets lugged across every possible ocean'. Neher had misgivings about collaborating so closely. Should he strike out independently? But they went on working together almost every afternoon. 'I must stop being jealous, that's the First Commandment,' Neher wrote in his diary, 'and try in every way to become a man.' Like Brecht, he was short of money; perhaps the solution was to write for the cinema. 'A film must be ready by Wednesday for Stuart Webbs. No inspiration. Bert's got an idea.' Stuart Webbs, the name of a detective in a film serial, was also the name of the production company. Brecht's diary for July 1921 says: 'For a long time I idle. Then I make a big film with Cas in three days, lots of pages, 150 shots, sweating and stinking under the table. It's to be called *Drei im Turm* (*Three in the Tower*) or something like that, and it's for Marianne.'[4]

In Brecht's fantasies wealth bulked large:

comfortable, elegantly tailored, wide grey trousers, hitched up well on the waist; soft hat squashed down, face thrust forwards, rather sharp; relaxation to the point of insolence, but respect for what's material – which is nothing but work matured into visibility; generally throwing things out, sweeping things together, making things proliferate; enterprises of all kinds for friends. But raking the gold in with one hand. Even where the ground is soggy. Washing the gold clean. Piling it up, investing it, letting it circulate, always looking away from the means (gold) towards people.[5]

None of his previous girls had been as rich as Marianne, who could take taxis whenever she liked, and was accustomed to gifts of fur coats, jewellery, dresses. 'And what am I? A small, pert mess, no face visible yet, a promise people believe in.' And how much was he getting out of it? 'Clothes, soap, sunny flat, theatre, good food, music, higher feelings, indolence, people's respect, freedom from friction, travel, beauty, youth, health, art, freedom?' Should he risk 'throwing all that into the garbage in obedience to a physiological need that vanishes as soon as it's satisfied'? No, he must not get married. 'I must have elbow-room, be able to spit wherever I want to, sleep alone, be unscrupulous.' Surely his attractiveness depended on his volatility? 'On the fact that with me people live

in the light, enjoy the drama, enjoy their food, enjoy music, feel powerful, have something to work for, command respect, have adventures
without travelling, feeling simultaneously strong, fresh, renewed, self-
confident.'[6]

Within a few days of feeling so confident about his power over his
friends, he was quarrelling with them bitterly. Marianne wanted to work
as an actress and he wanted to give her a part in the film. Müllereisert,
who had no girl-friend, although Brecht had recommended him to two
girls,[7] began to talk caustically about Marianne, with the result that
Pfanzelt, who was jealous of Brecht's success with girls and of Neher,
refused to collaborate on the screenplay.

Like Brecht, Marianne was charming and provocative, not alternately
but simultaneously. One Saturday night, at the home of Rudolf Aicher
and Annie Aicher-Simson, actors at the Stadttheater, she started picking
up Brecht's cigarette to take puffs from it and offering him pieces of ham
from her fork. They spent the night together in his attic room, which he
now called 'Kraal 3', but the next day 'we're playing catch-as-catch-can.
I put the brakes on.' Within a week she was wanting to marry him. 'But
when I withdraw into my shell (and cold air comes out) she gets upset
and gets blue hands, can't cope with me.' It was tiresome for her when
he quarrelled with her colleagues, and when they made remarks about
his unwashed ears. She tried to reform him, often overcoming resistance
to wash his ears and his neck herself.[8]

Sometimes it seemed possible for them to continue the relationship
without ever resorting to the half-measures he hated:

It's obvious what is dangerous: residue, anything interrupted in its growth,
what's undigested or left behind and out of control. Slowly we get blocked up
with uncompleted affairs, half-chewed incidents. What hasn't been used up
poisons us. Anything that's buried sleeps uneasily. The earth, which should
help us to digest it, spits it out. What the wind didn't dry or the rain wash goes
on growing and poisons the earth. Why can't the Jews be disposed of? Because
for thousands of years they've been quartered, broken on the wheel, tortured,
spat at. But the spit runs out before they do. Mendaciously we've invented the
tragic mode as a defence against sad, devastatingly bitter events. Whenever the
mind's mouth is stuffed with earth, a cry echoes out through the centuries.[9]

Despite his friendship with Feuchtwanger, Warschauer, Hedda and Marianne, there is little sympathy for the Jews; on the other hand, ruthlessness is what gives force to both his thinking and his life style.

Without wanting to marry Marianne, he was possessive – a characteristic she derided as bourgeois, becoming very angry when he sent his

friends out to spy on her. She went on taking money from Recht, who was threatening to kill her. She did her best to appease him, sometimes sleeping with him. On 8 March 1921 Brecht saw them together, standing by a train at the Munich station:

I go up to them, surprised, then get in, hear an argument: 'How dare you? Is that the way you treat me? You'll get your ears boxed. You're staying there.' She gets in. He pulls her back. She asks me for help. I help her, saying: 'Stop that! You come too!' He gets in. She feels ill. Says: 'Stay with me today!' Then he sits down next to her, smiles nastily, taps his swordstick. She smiles wearily. I smoke, eager to restore calm. Propose she goes to the Aichers. We go there, in a car. He asks me not to get in. I look at Marianne, get in. He's furious. 'So far I've controlled myself. Don't come. I can't answer for the consequences.' Silent journey. She looks as if she's been raped.[10]

The jealous rival went on threatening violence, but Brecht laughed, and nothing worse happened to him than having a door shut in his face. But after he left, Recht started to strangle Marianne. Brecht thought she should get a weapon. 'If he attacks, she must shoot him, like a mad dog.'[11]

The next day she spent three hours in his Kraal. 'In happy moments she's very lovely, young. Arguments make her age and look worn out.' He felt determined not to marry her, though she went on talking, tearfully, about how much she wanted a child. 'But I trot indifferently along, not changing my expression, hedonistic and irresponsible in bed, hypocritical perhaps, capable of rising above my circumstances, rather cold, quite unpolitical.' He could see no way of separating her from Recht without bloodshed, and then, on 11 March, when she told him she had missed her period, he felt ambivalent. 'A child now, that wouldn't be pleasant. But I'm certainly pleased about it. I'm completely idiotic.' Not yet thirty, she had already had one abortion, and obviously wanted to have a child. 'Her body's better than anyone else's, she's strong and childlike, a good mother, doesn't go to pieces easily, has held out against Recht for four years and been raped.' He was incredulous at his good luck: 'Now I'm getting a child by the dark-haired Marianne Zoff, the brown-skinned girl who sings in opera. I kneel down on the ground, weep, beat my breast, cross myself repeatedly. The spring wind runs through me as through a paper stomach. I bow. A son will be born to me. Once again.'[12]

His elation was damped when he saw how extravagant she was: 'I'm sorry I haven't got money to throw around. I'm sorry too you're throwing another man's money around. If you take it to eat, that's fine, or not so fine, but perhaps necessary. But for blouses! With my child inside? I have no money. You must get a grip on yourself. I can't do it. We're poor.'

In the evening he went to hear her sing Dorabella in *Così fan tutte*. 'Her acting's very beautiful, quiet and gracious, and she sings with a slight trill, like a lark. I go home quietly.' The next day she said that if she sacrificed her jewels, her parents could buy a farm, where she could live, if he married her. He made no promise, but she stayed the night. Neither of them knew what would happen. She threatened to have an abortion, to marry Recht. But while they were in bed, she said: 'You can't live without me,' and 'Now I've got a child by you. Now you've got me.' He thought about Frank. 'I already have a child growing up among the peasants. May it grow fat and wise and not curse me! But now the unborn are setting their sights on me.'[13]

He began to feel more confident that she would have the baby, but not that she wouldn't marry Recht. Brecht was like her, she said, a gypsy who had gone from one lover to another. Now she wanted a man who could stop her from running away. 'But I don't agree: she must learn to change. There's no hold except a face. There's no tie if it doesn't work at long range. There's no love without anti-love.' She went on threatening to marry Recht, but Brecht, who was expecting 6,000 marks for a screenplay, asked her to give him three months. 'I can do nothing except cover paper with words. For four weeks I'll do everything I can to save her, run around, beg, spend all I have.'[14]

One morning when the maid, opening the door of the attic room, saw Marianne in her chemise, Brecht threw a bed-cover over her, and the maid walked through the room. Euphoric incredulity persisted: 'I'm living luxuriously with the loveliest woman in Augsburg and writing film scripts. How long till God's patience runs out and I'm sitting on the kerb with dogs pissing on me?'

The next day Recht, finally wise to what was going on, beat her up and dragged her by the hair. She was badly bruised and dazed. Brecht helped her to pack her things, and on Sunday 27 March took her to Munich, where her brother Otto was living. They were on their way there when Recht drove up: 'Are you going to Otto's?' And he trailed after them, breathing heavily. At the house he asked for a conversation with Brecht, who asked Otto Zoff to be present. Zoff was 'a small, dry, brown man with a desiccated face like Beethoven's (authentic) death mask and a quiet, sly stare'. Recht wanted Brecht to go away for two weeks.

Would he then accept Marianne's decision, Brecht asked. 'No. Never.' And he started making threats.

Brecht interrupted. 'That's your affair. Let's forget it.'

'So, you expect me, quite frankly, to make your bed for you?'

'No. You're to make nothing and do nothing.'

'What I'm going to do to you – that's another matter.'

'We won't talk about it. Let's see what you can do.'

'I have some rights in this matter. Sit down. I've got something to say to you.'

Recht went pale.

'She's pregnant. She came to me the night after the train episode.'

Recht twitched. 'What do you make of that?' he asked Zoff, who said: 'This is very strange.'

Recht was walking restlessly around, gesticulating. 'But it's simply impossible. She had her period a week ago. She showed me the bloodstain on her nightdress. We were arguing about it.' Then he asked to speak to her. When she signalled agreement, Brecht left the room, and when he was called back, Recht had been crying. 'It wasn't granted to me to make this woman happy. You do it.' Asking Brecht to withdraw if ever Marianne left him, he held out his hand. Brecht shook it. Holding Brecht's sleeve, he said: 'In business I'm said to be a hard man, but with this woman my heart is soft.'[15]

Within three days it was clear that Recht had not given up. Brecht was still determined not to marry her, while she, evidently determined not to have a child without being married, vacillated between threatening an abortion and threatening to marry Recht, who was saying that when she came back to him, the child would be his. She accepted the thousand marks he had left with her brother, and accepted the flowers he sent. He wrote to her promising to go on loving her for ever and offering to cut off his left hand, the one which had hurt her.[16]

She spent the first weekend in April with Brecht on the Starnberger See. Frequently feeling sick, she agonized about having no home, arguing that maybe there was some way she could live with Recht, though not as his wife. On Monday, in Munich, they almost missed the train back to Augsburg 'because I took her suddenly on the sofa, and she was marvellous there: fresh, lively, loving'.[17]

Offered a salary of 10,000 marks for a season at the opera house in Wiesbaden, she reopened the question of abortion. The director, Carl Hagemann, would sack her for being pregnant. Reviewers in the newspapers were praising her Dorabella, while her parents were urging her to think of her future as a singer. She was 'squinting at her brilliant career like a cockerel on a chalk line'. Possibly Brecht's 1933 ballet *Die sieben Todsünden* (*The Seven Deadly Sins*) had roots in the rivalry between her feelings for him and the pull of her career. 'You're too young,' she told him. 'You go on the swingboats. You aren't someone to marry.' Perhaps Hagemann would fall seriously in love with her. He was interesting and a gentleman and could help her in her career. Annie Aicher-Simson was also advising her against Brecht: 'That's a lover. That's not a husband.' Smoking, cracking jokes, sitting and watching her pack for one of the journeys between Augsburg and Munich, he tried to wear her down by saying that Recht had spoilt her, that she must choose between being a wife and being a coquette, that abortion was as bad as killing a child. 'She's getting used, *lento*, to the idea of having the child on her own. That's where I want her.'[18]

On Tuesday afternoon they were together in the woods to the south of Augsburg, the Siebentischwald: 'She's wonderful in the grass. People can watch us. It's worth watching.' But afterwards she admitted that at the beginning of February Recht had had her: 'a sort of rape' she called it. Brecht went off to join his brother Walter, but at two in the morning came back to whistle under her window. Unsuccessfully.[19]

All this time he was intending to marry Paula. He proposed to her, and her reply was yes – in three or four years' time. She knew she was not right for him as she was, and she wrote to say she would like to spend six months on her own, trying to change back towards her former self. He replied that he loved her and would wait; she promised to be faithful to him in the meantime.[20]

But when Marianne told him she had decided to marry Recht, he felt 'a thin little stiletto in my chest'. Probably Brecht would never want to see her again, she said. They were sitting on a bench in the cathedral square. He got up, walked away, and, when he went back, she was not there. He went to the river – then, realizing she might be waiting in his Kraal, went straight home. She was crying. '"Hold me! I can't live without you. Why do I always make the wrong decision?" And she was trembling all over her body, so I laid her in bed, and she stayed till morning.'[21]

In Munich the next day he met Paula, who was 'nice, serious and sensible. I love her, I kiss her in the bushes. Then I travel home. (We're going to wait.)' He spent the night with Marianne, who felt sick but told him she had spoken to Recht, and everything was all right. The next day he met Recht, who said they must both give Marianne time, and when they met again the following day, Recht was tearful and hysterical. He was diabetic, he said, would soon be dead, must have four weeks with Marianne, who had promised to go away with him. He alternated between calling Brecht 'dear friend' and comparing him to Robespierre, the 'pedant of freedom'. Brecht considered him 'clever as only a Jew can be, and unscrupulous as a cattle-dealer. I'm only embarrassed, not shocked. He's so old. So worn out, greasy, miserable.' In the evening Brecht made him confront Marianne, and when she said she did not want to see him till further notice, he was submissive, which gratified her. But the next day, after Brecht had quarrelled with his father about the published details of his settlement with Vera-Maria Eberle, he found that Marianne had spoken to Recht – just a few words, she said. Brecht lost his temper: 'I'll just leave you. I've had enough. Stay with him if you can't leave him!'[22]

'I'm fed up with all this,' he wrote the next day. 'Sometimes I feel nothing at all for this woman. Bi is still closer to me.' He tried to think how to extricate himself from Marianne, but then he was sidetracked into calculating how many thousands of marks his screenplays and *Trommeln in der Nacht* were going to make. Marianne wanted to send her sister to Merano as soon as he had the money, but when he saw Paula again in Munich, he felt: 'she's worth more to me than everything else put together. When I wake up she's my wife. I'm never sure of her. She's got a stronger hold on me than anyone. I love her.' Later in the day he made love to Marianne, who was planning to marry Recht and have all her children by Brecht. But 'I'm thinking a lot about Bi; she notices it.' Smoking a cigar on the train back to Augsburg, and looking out at the rain, he felt 'well satisfied to be moving, with no desires, no complaints. I'm satisfied with rain and uncertainty, hunger and responsibility, I'll face any challenge, I'm committed to keeping on the move.'[23]

But he had to face an unexpected challenge when Marianne and Paula joined forces to confront him. Making him sit down between them, they said he must choose. Which of them did he want? Both, he answered. At which they both walked away. But when he found Paula was on the same train to Augsburg, he beckoned her out into the corridor. Would she agree to a contractual arrangement by which he married Marianne in order to make the baby legitimate, and divorced her afterwards to marry Paula, legitimizing their son too? She let herself be persuaded into accepting a written agreement which could have no legal force.[24]

On 28 April he finally went with Paula to see Frank in Kimratshofen.

I felt deeply happy. I'd been afraid he'd look like a peasant. He's slim with delicate limbs and a fine bright face, curly red hair, but not curly in front, lively with large dark-brown eyes. ... He scarcely ever talks but plays in an original way (puts my hat on a toy horse) and gives away everything he gets. He quickly accustoms himself to me, plays with me and runs to me rather than to Bi, who doesn't at first hit the right note, and then holds back, afraid of being rebuffed. I at once lend him my hat, my tie, my watch, ten pfennigs. I'll ask Papa to give him a home.[25]

Marianne still seemed to be vacillating about whether to marry Recht. Without making the counter-proposal she wanted, Brecht tried to dissuade her. 'You must be capable of rising to the top with *two* children! Why price yourself so low? At least marry a millionaire! But I can tell you: when you're in labour, my hand will mean more to you than all the applause in Wiesbaden. To get satisfaction out of art, you must be an artist with body and soul, and for that you need to keep your body and soul.' When persuasion failed, he promised himself: 'On the day she gets married, I'm going to tear her out of me with all her roots, like the old whore she's gone back to being.'[26]

After starting to behave more considerately towards Paula, he had an unpleasant surprise: she had been corresponding with a café violinist, had let him kiss her, and gone to his room, where she lay in his bed. They had not made love, she said, and, to prove it, produced the man's letters.[27]

Before the end of the week Marianne had started haemorrhaging. She was going to lose the baby but, because of Recht, she did not want Brecht to visit her. He had been spending a lot of time with Paula, 'who in the days of her distress has lost weight and become childlike and beautiful and once again something true. I love her and respect her.'[28]

Two days later he was on his way to the station when a white-faced Recht tugged at his sleeve. He had been up all night with Marianne, who had lost the baby. 'Accidentally,' said Recht, 'more or less.' She had lost blood on Saturday, and they had operated on her. Brecht

staggered home as if I'd been hit on the head. ... I could strangle her. It's the dirtiest thing I've ever experienced. ... Never have I seen the swindle of whoredom, the romanticism, so nakedly exposed. That's how a pregnant whore unloads it! And to think that I wanted to have this leaky pot, trickling with liquid efflux from various men, installed in my room!

In the evening Brecht walked by the river, smoking, trying to get himself under control. He was sleeping badly, 'as if I'd committed murder'.[29]

In Munich he visited her in the nursing home. She wept and clung to his knees. 'I show her, cruelly, the pictures of Frank.' He went on seeing a great deal of Paula. 'But she's lying to me again, goes one evening to a café with a clodhopper from Kimratshofen, and I catch her slinking hurriedly away, the stupid goat! I tell her I kissed Mar two or three times in the snow one evening in the Siebentischwald. I daren't say more because she goes quite white.'[30]

He went on trying to persuade his father that they ought to give Frank a home, but Fräulein Roecker, who was against the idea, had the decisive voice on household affairs. Brecht's alternative scheme – 'no getting away from politics!!!' he wrote – was to 'give' Frank to Marianne. When she came to see him on her first day out of bed, his intention was to 'keep her through the summer' and let her keep the boy permanently. Whereas Recht was staking everything on his relationship with her, Brecht was intending to stake nothing but the son he scarcely ever saw. In his own view he was being cynical in theory and idealistic in practice, while Recht, who was desperate, talked idealistically and behaved cynically.[31]

With Paula, Brecht went on playing acting games. They pretended they were filming Schiller's *Die Jungfrau von Orleans* in the woods near the lake. 'She plays it as naïvely as a child, but also as shrewdly as a star ... she always takes you by surprise.' She said that he looked very masculine, especially in his face, when he talked, but that from behind he looked slight and small. In bed he was boyish and cheeky. He was at his best when something was happening.[32]

Needing money, he felt betrayed by his father, who was refusing to help. 'In the Marianne business he believed a stranger and wept in front of him and betrayed me and held me back, so that the woman could be taken away from me. He never *once* asked me about my child, not *once* about its mother ... he said, apropos the child, that he believed I'd "find some way of arranging things".' Brecht was giving less as a father than he was claiming as a son. 'I'm beginning to respect him less because he has so little respect for his own blood.' 'So I dawdle about ... and fritter my energy away. It will soon be so bad that I'm thrown out of the house.'[33]

Eating cherries in front of a mirror, he struck himself as looking unco-ordinated, lascivious, full of contradictions. Talking about his face, Hedda had said: 'You've got too many,' and he could see in it disparate 'elements of brutality, repose, cunning, courage and cowardice ... and it's more inconstant and characterless than a landscape under moving clouds'.[34]

5 / Urban Jungle

In August 1921, reading Upton Sinclair's 1908 novel *The Money-changers*, Brecht was thinking about the dangers of sanctifying work, as the bourgeoisie had – treating it not as a means but an end. Then, early in September, after trying to assess 'what Kipling had achieved for the nation that "civilized" the world', he 'arrived at the epoch-making discovery that really no one has yet described the big city as a jungle. Where are its heroes, its colonizers, its victims? The unfriendliness of the big city, its malevolent stony consistency, its Babylonian linguistic confusion – in short its poetry hasn't been created yet.'[1] Baudelaire had understood how poetry could be distilled from the poisonous vapours exuded by Paris, the *'fourmillante cité'*, but Eliot had not yet published 'The Waste Land' or Joyce *Ulysses* (both appeared in 1922) when Brecht started on *Im Dickicht der Städte*. Without having read Marx he was taking a step towards Marxism; without having read Engels, he was coming to treat social pressures as no less destructive than the natural forces which destroyed the bands of adventurers in his early poems.

First he thought of calling the play *Freiheit* (*Freedom*) or *Die Feind-seligen* (*The Enemies*). It was to be 'a play about conflict, East–West, with subterranean implications. Scene: the back of beyond.' In September 1920 he had read Alfred Döblin's novel *Die drei Sprünge des Wang Lun* (*Wang Lun's Three Wells*), which pointed him towards the Orient and alerted him to Taoism. Shlink, the Malayan timber merchant in *Im Dickicht*, is Brecht's first oriental character. Other possible titles for the play were *Hinterwelt* (*Hinterworld*), *Der Wald* (*The Forest*), *Dickicht* (*Jungle*) or *Georg Garga* (the main character's name). Once the idea had been conceived, he set to work quickly, writing on small sheets of thin typing paper folded in four to fit his leather notebook. He had already found that he could think better when he was not sitting still, and he worked in the open air – on the river bank, or 'walking in the avenue; not a line of dialogue in an enclosed space'. He took no interest in food or clothes or company, walking for hours to the sound of falling chestnuts. The dialogue seemed to come of its own accord, as if he were writing from memory.

In three days he finished the first two scenes, the last, and half the third. This play must not be didactic. 'If I present a conflict, it must be between the two men, not the two systems.' 'Each of the contenders must be given every opportunity, but one shouldn't want to prove anything.'[2]

Since reading Rimbaud and since developing Baal's relationship with Ekart, Brecht had been emotionally involved, through Marianne, with Recht, and now knew what it was, *vis-à-vis* a man, to feel violent hatred, adulterated with flecks of the opposite emotion. In stumbling on the idea of a motiveless conflict, Brecht had been lucky enough to discover a stepping-stone to a situation which could absorb strong personal emotions without having any direct connection to Rimbaud's relationship with Verlaine or to his own with Recht. Nor did it depend on personality or psychology. 'Concentrate neither on people's behaviour', ran one of the commandments Brecht had formulated for himself six months earlier, 'nor on their opinions.' 'Both could be wrong. What happens to people is a long story. Stop bothering me with your mistakes. Do I have to waste time on the differences between one man and another? Strain my eyes?'[3] The animosity between Garga and Shlink was like the animosity between Brecht and Recht in having no more to do with their personalities than the hostility between two boxers – Brecht was rejecting the tradition in which conflict depends on personality. But in the play little depends on rivalry over a woman. Women will be used in the fight between Shlink and Garga, but only as pawns.

The opening blow is struck in a library when Shlink tries to buy an opinion from Garga, the librarian. He is quick to realize he is being insulted, but slow to understand that if he is ever to have a chance of making a meaningful human contact, it is with his adversary. If Brecht still believed in intensity, he must have more often been aware of its absence from his relationships and activities than of its presence; perhaps he was more passionate in feelings towards Recht than towards either Marianne or Paula, who both let themselves be used. Perhaps neither Paula's commitment nor Marianne's vacillation roused him to the same intensity – made him feel so fully alive – as rivalry with Recht. ('Real life is absent', Rimbaud had written.) Brecht was irked by the feeling that Recht was not giving him a real fight, but he also felt that Recht was staking everything on Marianne, while he was staking nothing. Real life was absent.

'Spiritual combat is as brutal as the battle between men', said Rimbaud. 'I'm not visualizing faces', Brecht wrote, 'but facing visions. This is the only expressionistic element! Not trends incorporated in individuals, but men as spiritual beings.' If either Shlink or Garga has any motive for committing himself to all-out warfare, it is to test whether he can come fully alive before dying. 'I envied the happiness of animals,' wrote Rimbaud;[4] 'I've observed animals,' says Shlink, minutes before he kills himself.

Love, the warmth of another body, is our only grace in the darkness. But it's only the coupling of organs, it doesn't break through the barrier of language. ... If you stuff a ship so full of human bodies that it bursts, they'll be so lonely, they'll all freeze to death. ... Yes, the isolation is so extreme, you can't even have a fight.

According to one of Brecht's early notes on the play, Garga should look like Rimbaud: he was 'a German translation from the French into American', while Shlink uses 'an appearance of passivity' to slash through Garga's ties to his environment, forcing him to fight 'a desperate war of liberation'.[5] But the most lethal weapon in Garga's armoury is the possibility of abandoning the fight once Shlink has become dependent on it for his only intense sensations. Brecht had found with Marianne that nothing made her more tractable than an appearance of indifference. Much of the discomfort he had suffered in the triangular relationship with her and Recht could be siphoned into the dialogue. Pointing out that Garga's girl-friend, Jane, 'has a body that's worth a few dollars', Baboon, a pimp, asks him: 'Can you afford them?' Shlink's promises to Garga's sister, Mary, parody promises made by Recht to Marianne – 'I'll treat you like my wife and serve you and if I ever do you any harm I'll hang myself without any fuss.' Garga tells her she used to dress like an opera singer. At one point Mary tells Shlink she has soiled her body, which belongs to him, even if he has scorned it; this may be either echoing or parodying something said to Brecht. Scraps of his dialogues with his mother are revived in Garga's with his, when she pleads with him not to run away from his father, and to confide his anxieties to her. 'I know I'm not allowed to speak to you the way other mothers do to their sons.' In the 1922 version of the play there is more tension between the parents than in later versions, while Brecht's personal myth about having been brought in his mother's womb from the Black Forest to the city has its counterpart in the history of the Garga family, which has come from the prairies to Chicago.

Autobiography in the play is inseparable from the struggle to put Marianne into perspective. 'Like all other artists,' Brecht noted, 'the writer can probably work from the female body. Not by representing it but reconstituting its calibration in all the proportioning of the work. The body's contours become those of his composition; just as looking at the former heightens our sense of being alive, so must the pleasure we take in the latter.'[6] But the play spotlighted what had remained obscure – a relationship between two men – and the same theme emerged in the pirate story 'Bargan lässt es sein'.

In the play he borrowed freely from a Danish novel, *Hjulet* (*The Wheel*) by J. V. Jensen: a German translation had appeared earlier in 1921. A lay preacher, Evanston, attempts the 'spiritual rape' of a young journalist, Lee, wanting to steal his views of life, alienate him from his fiancée and blame a murder on him. The borrowings from Jensen are not all integrated in a way that can make sense to an audience, while the cryptically Rimbaudesque dialogue is provocatively elliptical. In a programme note for the 1922 production Brecht frivolously justifies this by saying that the text contained only extracts from the relevant conversations. Their substance had been 'difficult and expensive to get at'.[7]

Brecht, as he matured, would become more skilful at integrating his borrowings but, like Shakespeare, he went on, throughout his career, retelling old stories in preference to inventing new ones. Sometimes he would work from plays – Elizabethan, Jacobean, Japanese, Chinese, Finnish, Irish, or Gay's ballad opera – sometimes from narrative (Jensen, Kipling, Grimmelshausen). Sometimes he would bring historical or fictional characters (St Joan, Schweyk) into contemporary history, or transpose the contemporary history of Germany into a remote time or place. Whatever he took he changed, but he did not like to draw directly on his own experience or his fantasies.

Many of his variations on unoriginal themes depended on stressing the social history which had been ignored, while ignoring the personal psychology which had been stressed. Reacting against Gerhart Hauptmann and his contemporaries, Brecht condemned the 'rather stupid precision in delineating people, the reliance on content to fend for itself, the confusion of passion with hysteria'. When he went on to sketch out a play about Pope Joan, he realized that historians had never focused on such questions as 'what the Pope ate and drank, how he loved, what his clothes and his servants were like, whether he washed and how often, and what his smoking habits were! And there's no history of fashion in dress, crafts, trading or the social position of merchants, soldiers, priests.' Providing less information about public life than was now available in newspapers, history books offered nothing but 'ideological hair-splitting and vulgar attempts to inject a meaning into the whole external calendar of public events in Europe'.[8]

Brecht was still seeing Paula, who was in Nuremberg, and still admiring her natural stylishness – her impassivity, for instance, when he complained in a café about the coffee. In the middle of October, leaving for Wiesbaden, which was occupied by the French, he panicked on the train because he was carrying a revolver. When the train stopped at Frankfurt he bought a cigar box, but could not mail the revolver to Augsburg because the post office was shut. He tried, unsuccessfully, to hide it in the lavatory, but, when the train reached the frontier, he was not searched.[9]

Marianne was less impressive as Madam Butterfly than she was in her home or her bed. After telling Recht she would accept no more money from him, she had gone with him to choose an expensive fur coat, borrowing the money for it, but in her company Brecht felt relaxed, secure. In *Rheingold* her voice stood out beautifully in a 'fearfully ramshackle' production.

But the only work of art that impressed Brecht in Wiesbaden was Chaplin's short 1914 film *The Face on the Bar-room Floor*. He had never seen Chaplin, because until 1921 Germany could not import his films. In this one a painter tells the story of a girl who left him for a bloated plutocrat. She grew fat, had children, became impoverished. Overcome by talking about her, Chaplin

puts his hat on askew and goes off into the darkness, staggering right off course as if he'd been hit on the head, off course, good God, right off course as if blown by the wind, off course, the way no one ever moves. And then, getting drunker and drunker, and needing more and more urgently to communicate, he begs for 'a chalk you use for billiards' and draws a picture of his sweetheart on the floor, but it consists only of circles. . . . Chaplin's face is always impassive, as if waxed, a single twitch of expression tears it apart, utterly simple, strong, anxious. . . . A white clownface with a thick moustache, curly hair and clowning. . . . But there's nothing more moving, it's a totally pure art.[10]

The film and Brecht's reaction to it were seminal. The fattened Yvette in *Mutter Courage*, the chalk circle that Azdak draws on the ground, the Chaplinesque Hitler in *Arturo Ui* have some of their roots in this Wiesbaden experience, while the immediate effect was to make Brecht more critical of faces and façades in what he called 'the shop-window city'.

What if well-dressed women came to realize that they might one day have to wash their own blouses, and the gentlemen to realize they might lose their money?[11] Five years before his conversion to Marxism, Brecht was already dreaming the dreams of his Pirate Jenny – wanting a revolution, but universal, not social or political.

Part Two

BERLIN

6 / Bertolt and Arnolt

During the three excited weeks he had spent in Berlin at the beginning of 1920, Brecht, despite the search for allies and the attempt to launch *Baal*, had not seriously tried to establish himself, though he had known that he would want, fairly soon, to go back. In October 1921 he received a letter from Hedda, who was living there. 'To the lover with horns from too far away.' If he wanted to visit her, should she say she was his wife when she booked a room for him? 'But I've been unfaithful for months,' she added.[1]

The invitation arrived at a propitious moment. In September his story 'Bargan lässt es sein' had appeared in *Der neue Merkur*, his first publication to reach a wide readership, and though it had been advantageous to start *Im Dickicht der Städte* in Augsburg, it would be advantageous to continue it in a city more like the one he was writing about. Besides, he had reached a point at which he would do well to meet the challenges and stimuli that bristled on the hedgehog back of Berlin at the beginning of the 1920s.

He wrote to Hedda, asking her to find a room, but at the beginning of November 1921, when he arrived after an almost sleepless night on the train, staggering out into the chilly morning, struggling with two suitcases, the city seemed grey, unwelcoming, frightening, and the room had not been prepared. Hedda was more self-assured, 'unfamiliar, remote'. She gave him the letters that were waiting for him. Paula, who had been unable to contact him in Wiesbaden, had been pregnant again for at least two months, but 'it's a good letter, unhysterical, full of love and quite uncomplaining. Reading it I love her very much and feel inordinately frightened.' Two days later another letter from her arrived: everything was all right: she had managed on her own. A letter from Müllereisert confirmed that he was doing everything necessary: 'Nothing to worry about.'[2]

The next time he saw Hedda, she was less distant, but he also met her lover, 'young and strong, with a broad skull, rather a crude face, slow, tough, middle-classy'. Brecht invited her twice to the theatre, and twice she refused. He ate a couple of meals with Frank Warschauer, and he quickly met most of the dramaturgs and many of the publishers. 'Bargan lässt es sein' had made a good impression: 'People all know the story ... and they all want to be helpful to me.' He led a busy social life, motivated mainly by the urge to make money, establish a reputation, get his plays published and produced. He could manage without much sleep. During the 1920s and 1930s he would sometimes start work at six in the morning and never, according to Elisabeth Hauptmann, later than seven.[3] A typical day was described to Paula:

I wrote a scene for a film till 10, then went to the university then to the Deutsches Theater for the rehearsals, ate somewhere quickly, standing up, before a three o'clock meeting in a café with Klabund, who's helping over the contract with Reiss, chat till six about publishing the play, drinking at three bars with a young man who'd been given an advance and paid for the drinks, then I went by underground to the Skala, where Matray and Kata Sterna were dancing, then with Warschauer, Matray and Kata Sterna to Warschauer's, stayed there two hours, having 'supper' and drinking wine. Then went with Matray to Maenz's Restaurant where Granach introduced me to a lot of theatre people, and at 2 o'clock wandered home with a cigar. And all these people push each other about, write about each other, envy, despise, ridicule each other.

Klabund was the pseudonym for a tubercular expressionist poet and novelist, eight years Brecht's senior, and Ernst Reiss was the publisher he had recommended Brecht to approach. Alexander Granach was an actor Brecht admired: one of the early notes for *Im Dickicht* describes Garga as the Granach type.[4]

Brecht was sending some money to Paula, but she sent it back. He was going a great deal to the theatre, where Granach was only one of several actors he respected, but he had only contempt for the plays. 'The compassion of the dramatists (Hauptmann, Ibsen) was the beginning of the end. The plays are all two-dimensional.... There's only one view to be taken of characters and events – the writer's. The stalls are taught to be "understanding" about everything.' He was glad that in *Baal* and *Im Dickicht* he had not imposed his own views of characters and events: 'Instinctively I hold back and take care that my theatrical effects (poetical and philosophical) stay within bounds.' He did not want to interfere with the spectators' 'splendid isolation' or invite them to identify with the hero. 'There's a higher kind of interest: in making comparisons, in recognizing what is dissimilar, incomprehensible, inexplicable.' Writers of tragedy were too nervous either to side with nature against the hero or to make fun of nature, 'to mimic the repulsive mooing of the stupid cow that has swallowed a grasshopper. That's how bourgeois the theatre is.'⁵ But he attended nearly all the rehearsals of Strindberg's *Dream Play* at the Deutsches Theater under Max Reinhardt, the paragon of German directors.

A week before Christmas, when his father came to Berlin, they sat facing each other over a table in a pub. 'He took a sort of cautious interest in me, gave me 1,000 marks, talked about his business, didn't ask how things stood with Marianne, said there'd be ham and duck for Christmas – I'd be sent some.' He was polite and undemanding, not expecting his son to see him off at the station.⁶

A great deal was still to happen before Christmas. Marianne arrived in Berlin, and on 23 December Ernst Reiss offered to put Brecht under contract for a monthly payment of 750 marks. On the same day, thanks to Otto Zarek, who took him to the Wilde Bühne, a cabaret run by the actress Trude Hesterberg, he was contracted to perform for a week, singing soldiers' ballads. This would bring in 500 marks. But Marianne, who was staying with him at the Warschauers' flat, was told that her Wiesbaden contract was unlikely to be renewed.⁷

She stayed in Berlin until the beginning of the new year, which started well for him, as he negotiated a contract worth 1,000 marks a month with Kiepenheuer Verlag, leaving himself free to sell the stage rights of his plays to the Dreimasken Verlag, the Munich publishers associated with Feuchtwanger, for a further 500 marks. He also made a new friend. At the house of Zarek's father he met the 26-year-old Arnolt Bronnen, an Austrian writer who was working at a department store, Wertheim. Bronnen noticed Brecht when he took a moist cigar out of his mouth to start singing, twanging at his guitar. He was 'thin, dry, his face sallow and stubbly, with piercing eyes under short, dark bristling hair with two curls at the front. . . . A cheap pair of steel-rimmed spectacles was hanging loosely over the remarkably fine ears and the narrow, pointed nose. The mouth was remarkably delicate and it was tuned to the same dream as the eyes.' Bronnen was overwhelmed with an inexplicable mixture of strong feelings: that he had never previously looked at a human being, that what was happening now would never stop, that 'The heart beating in the small insignificant creature over there is the heart of our age', and he prayed to Love: 'Give him to me as a friend.'⁸ All this without a word of conversation.

Bronnen was not alone in reacting strongly to Brecht. 'When he picked up his guitar', reports Zuckmayer, 'the murmur of conversation stopped, the tango dancers stopped slinking into dimly lit corners, everyone squatted on the floor around him, charmed by his spell.' As a guitarist Brecht had become more accomplished. According to Zuckmayer he

loved complicated chords that were difficult to finger: C-sharp minor or E-flat major chords. His singing was raw and abrasive, often crude like a street-singer or a music-hall minstrel, and it was pervaded with an unmistakable Augsburg intonation. Sometimes he sang with something approaching beauty; his voice floated along with emotional vibratos, and he enunciated each syllable very clearly.

Writing in the third person, Bronnen claims that he and Brecht 'understood each other from the first syllable – between them, explanations were unnecessary. Their viewpoint was the same: both rejected everything that had been thought, written, printed, up to the present moment, including their own work.' The attraction was mutual; Brecht proposed a partnership. 'We'll go to theatres and rehearsals together. We'll study directors, learn how it's done. We'll unmask playwrights.' They slipped into the second person singular at their second meeting, and began to spend about twelve hours of each day together.[9]

But before the end of January 1922 Brecht was passing blood in his urine. After he had spent two days in bed, Hedda's lover, a doctor at the Charité, the main hospital in the city centre, arranged for him to be admitted as a patient. He sent for Marianne, who broke her contract at Wiesbaden and moved into a Berlin hotel. She visited him every day until she found Paula's letters in his room. She then became ill herself and stayed in bed at the Warschauers'. A doctor said her lung was affected. Brecht, too, was afraid he might have a lung infection, but fear didn't stop him from smoking.[10] It turned out that though he was not normally a drinker, his intake of alcohol had been high in proportion to his food. Hedda's lover would not allow her to visit Brecht in hospital more than once, and she was surprised to find a 'K' – signifying Catholic – tag at the end of his bed. He explained that the priest was friendlier than the chaplain.

He stayed in hospital for over three weeks but, impatient to advance his career, left before he was discharged. Marianne wanted him to go back to Munich, but he would have felt defeated had he left Berlin now and, siding with him, Bronnen fell foul of her.

The partners were together when Moritz Seeler, director of the Junge Bühne, a new theatre group, introduced himself to Bronnen. Seeler said he would like Bronnen's play *Vatermord* (*Patricide*) to be its first production. Mistaking the astonished playwright's silence for refusal, Seeler was moving disappointedly away when the quick-witted Brecht intervened. 'It's all right to give them your play, Arnolt, but on one condition: I'll direct.'[11]

Seeler accepted the condition, but since the actors were not going to be paid, Brecht had to accept the cast he was given, including the temperamental Heinrich George, the sentimental Agnes Straub and the aristocratic Hans Heinrich von Twardowsky. Rehearsals were held in different theatres – wherever free space was available – and without knowing when or where the play would open, but according to Bronnen, Brecht 'carried certainty and determination wherever he went. This thin, pale, bespectacled figure strode over the various stages ... as if he had decades of theatrical experience behind him. At first everyone was taken in, even the forceful Heinrich George.' Brecht 'prescribed an ice-cool Brechtian tone for the Pomeranian giant and grew increasingly enthusiastic as George came less and less to resemble Bronnen's nightmarish character'.[12]

George was five years Brecht's senior and already quite well known, but Brecht was not intimidated. Though it was always expressive, George's speaking did not always have enough thought behind it; Straub's was full of false inflexions. Brecht was relentless in checking them. Drily, articulating his words with precision, he would announce that everything they had done was shit. As this happened at each rehearsal it looked unlikely that they could go on working together. But, faced with Brecht's 'sadistic whiplashes', George was tolerant, Twardowsky patient and Straub tearful. As rehearsals proceeded, though, their resistance increased, and on the day that Seeler announced to the press that the play would open at the Neues Theater am Zoo, George out-shouted Brecht, pulled the script out of his pocket, swung it round his head like a tomahawk and flung it into the fifteenth row of the stalls, while Agnes Straub collapsed in hysterics. 'The rehearsal will go on,' announced Brecht, but when the actress had been helped from the stage, only Twardowsky was left, 'his well-moulded head resting on his thin hands, staring in front of him, incapable of listening or speaking. Brecht saw his chance. He cleared his throat loudly, slammed his rehearsal script shut, switched off the rehearsal light and said "Guten Tag".' When he found Bronnen in the darkness of the stalls, he 'congratulated me with the sarcasm he always employed to conceal triumph: "It would never have been any good with them in it." '[13]

Brecht was replaced as director by Berthold Viertel, who cast Elisabeth

Bergner and Alexander Granach in the leading parts. Bronnen tried to help Brecht, 'because there was this magic surrounding him: you had to help him. Everybody felt this.' Bronnen quarrelled with Seeler, and stayed away from rehearsals, living, like Brecht, mainly on pea soup at Aschinger's, a restaurant where there was no charge for bread rolls, however many you ate with your soup.

Spring in Berlin was very cold, and 'Brecht suffered. You couldn't tell whether he was hungry or freezing: he lived to such an extent off his own inexhaustible resources that he seemed to have no needs.' He went back to working on *Im Dickicht*, in which the notions of personal and public bankruptcy are sometimes merged, sometimes confused. Many of the images and some of the theatrical ideas he was evolving derive from the need to economize. When power was in short supply, he saw a production lit with headlights intended for cars. Having fallen in love with the effect, he never used coloured lighting in his theatre.[14]

In November, within three weeks of coming back to Berlin, he had realized that the analogy between city and jungle was valid. The city had 'once again become wild, dark, mysterious. Just as *Baal* is the song of the landscape, the swansong. Here's a whiff of mythology.' Questioned on what he was trying to say in *Im Dickicht*, his answer was 'The last line.'[15] The closing speech ran: 'It was the best time. The chaos is used up. It sent me away without a blessing. Perhaps there's consolation in work. It's no doubt very late. I feel quite alone.' The tone is that of Brecht's diaries.

He did find consolation in work, especially after he and Bronnen had spent Easter with the journalist Stephen Grossmann at the fisherman's cottage he had rented in Geltow. A film producer, Richard Oswald, had organized a competition with a prize of 100,000 marks for the best scenario, and Grossmann, who was on the jury, promised his guests that they would win if they competed. On their way back to Berlin they sketched out a story about 'the downfall of three worthwhile people who have to become wild beasts, increasingly destroying each other's lives as they become increasingly competent, technically, to earn their living'. This arises out of the jungle-city equation, but the action was to be set on an island: a holocaust leaves only three survivors, who establish themselves there, founding a civilization no less destructive than the previous one. The scenario did win the first prize, but thanks to spiralling inflation, the money, by the time it reached them, was worth little; the idea, when it was recycled in *Mahagonny*, was worth a lot.

Before Easter, Kiepenheuer Verlag had signed a contract to bring out

Baal in an edition of 800 copies, but in the early summer it looked as though Bronnen would eclipse his friend. After *Vatermord* had been staged in Frankfurt and Hamburg as well as Berlin, the publisher Ernst Rowohlt offered him a contract, and Herbert Ihering, the critic who was judging plays for the Kleist Prize, chose *Vatermord*. But the magic surrounding Brecht made Bronnen ask Ihering to consider *Baal* and *Im Dickicht*. Ihering then wanted to divide the prize, but Brecht was as unwilling to share it as to share a room with his brother. Brecht was then awarded the whole prize. But when *Vatermord* was to be produced in Munich, and Bronnen asked whether he would be welcome there, Brecht, after offering to put him up in Augsburg, withdrew his offer. Marianne was still hostile to him, and Brecht, 'who in the hustle and bustle of the last few months had lost a little of his natural self-assurance',[16] submitted. He arranged for Bronnen to share the small shabby room Neher had rented in the house of a 'ghastly, smelly little woman'.

After the first night, when Bronnen was comparing the play's four productions, Brecht remarked that in Frankfurt, he had heard, director and actors had all disregarded both place and time. There was one actress, said Bronnen, who had not, but she had played a small part, and he had forgotten her name, though Brecht was curious to know it. Then Bronnen remembered: she was a Viennese girl called Helene Weigel.

Neher had been corresponding with Brecht about *Im Dickicht*, and making suggestions which were received enthusiastically. Brecht considered the play to be 'at least as strong as *Baal*, and also, more mature'. Bronnen describes Neher as 'a big, tough, blond young man who wore spectacles similar to Brecht's as a token of affiliation'.[17] He was not keen to share his room but 'one glance from Brecht was enough to make him choke back his resentment for several hours'.

In Munich Brecht's ground-floor flat consisted of only two dark rooms, but he was welcome at the house of Lion Feuchtwanger, who called him the 'family poet'. When they had been working together in the study, Feuchtwanger would come out looking abstracted. The text of his play *Kalkutta, 4 Mai* carries the prefatory note: 'I wrote this play with Bertolt Brecht.' Brecht used the Feuchtwangers' house as his headquarters. His friends were all welcome there. Inflation was having its effects on hospitality, but even large gatherings from the Kammerspiele would never be offered less than tea and biscuits. One evening there, when alcohol was on offer, Neher got so drunk that he tried to kill his unwanted room-mate, but their host was just in time to stop the champagne bottle from crashing down on Bronnen's skull.[18]

The change in Brecht's fortunes came abruptly. Following his success with *Vatermord*, Otto Falckenberg, director of the Munich Kammerspiele, let his actress wife, Sybille Binder, persuade him to open his autumn season with *Trommeln in der Nacht*, directing it himself, while, thanks mainly to the director Erich Engel, *Im Dickicht* was accepted for production in Munich at the Residenztheater, while in Berlin Seeler offered a Junge Bühne production of *Baal*.[19]

Brecht's senior by seven years, Engel had trained as an actor at Leopold Jessner's drama school in Hamburg, and had been director of the Kammerspiele there for three years before coming to Munich in 1922. Brecht threw himself into a farrago of activity, intervening energetically in casting, meeting actors and bombarding them with practical ideas, singing and playing his guitar at parties, collaborating with Feuchtwanger on several plays simultaneously, and proposing ideas for collaborative work to Bronnen.

Brecht paced about the room, puffing at his cigar, listening greedily to the arguments and counter-arguments of some dozen people, made jokes, winked and stayed infallibly in his own groove. He rode his thoughts further until they were magnificent and complete in relation to a miniature audience, but by no means in their final form. Then he'd dictate them to someone or other, and there was always someone there. His brain seemed to be an outsize organism for sucking, with polyp arms to grab at material.

During rehearsals of *Trommeln*, he rewrote a great deal of his text around the actors, and he intervened strenuously in rehearsals. According to Marta Feuchtwanger, who was there, the 24-year-old author kept interrupting the 49-year-old director and yelling at the actors. Soon Brecht had effectively made Falckenberg into his assistant, demonstrating what he wanted, while the actors did their best to copy him.[20] What he had learnt from the Augsburg teachers was not to be overawed by his seniors.

Otto Reigbert, the Kammerspiele's designer, produced a set in the familiar expressionist manner, with zigzag houses and crooked walls painted on a flat background with six-foot-high cardboard screens to represent walls for each indoor locale. Neher had supplied sketches, which Brecht submitted to Falckenberg, later claiming that his friend had originated the two-part division of the stage.[21] In fact this was a commonplace of expressionist stage design.

In the auditorium, following Brecht's suggestion, placards were hung saying 'Don't gawp so romantically.' Remembering the production over forty years later, another director recalled 'a very hard, hunted style of acting'. The bourgeois family was grouped around a gigantic gramophone. In the second act Alexander Granach spat out Kragler's long sentences with a malice that puzzled the audience, which was totally unprepared for the downbeat ending. Expressionistic plays usually end with ecstatic defiance, and it looked as though Brecht's sympathies were with the rebels: no one was expecting Kragler to lose interest in them and reach out shamelessly for the pleasures that his pregnant girl-friend could provide.[22]

The production opened on 29 September, with Brecht's father and brother, the housekeeper Marie Roecker, Paula, and Karl Valentin in the audience. Reviewing the play, Herbert Ihering wrote: 'The 24-year-old poet Bertold Brecht has changed the German literary landscape overnight.... Brecht perceives class and putrefaction physically.... The evidence of Brecht's genius is that his plays bring a new artistic totality into existence, with its own laws, its own dramaturgy.' What had been most horrifying of all, he went on, about recent public events, was that people had accepted apocalyptic developments as if they were ordinary inconveniences. 'Only when we recognize that the contemporary nightmare lies in our period's deafness to its own noises, its blindness to its own grimaces, can we understand our poets.... In his nerves and in his blood Brecht is permeated with the horrors of our period. These horrors exist as stale air and dim light surrounding people and spaces.'[23]

On the night after the première there was a late-night cabaret on the stage, *Die rote Zibebe* (*The Red Raisin*) with Brecht as both writer and performer. The show took its name from the pub in the play, and the landlord, Glubb, now appeared as compère. The performers, including Brecht, stepped out of cabins like marionettes, and in the second half Karl Valentin performed a sketch devised by Brecht involving a penny-farthing bicycle.

Ihering's review helped to generate interest in Brecht. At the Deutsches Theater in Berlin, Felix Hollaender wanted to present all three of his plays, but not directed by the author. They compromised on Otto Falckenberg. Hollaender might also stage an adaptation Brecht had been making of Grabbe's *Hannibal*.

Planning his visit to Berlin, Brecht separately asked both Neher and Bronnen to find a room he could share, but he spent only a few days there, negotiating with Hollaender, before he returned to Munich. Otto Falckenberg and Benno Bing, joint directors of the Kammerspiele there, were offering him a job as dramaturg, and impatient though he was for the success he had scented in Berlin, he accepted, not wanting to lose Marianne, who was pregnant again, or to reject the offer of a regular income. On 3 November, with Feuchtwanger and Müllereisert as witnesses, the lovers were married. Neher and Bronnen were so outraged at their friend's perfidy that jealousy edged them into an alliance: they became flat-mates again.

Less than four weeks after marrying Marianne, Brecht left for Berlin to receive the Kleist Prize and to be present, during the first three weeks of December, at Falckenberg's rehearsals of *Trommeln*, starring Alexander Granach and Heinrich George. But when it opened on 20 December the influential Alfred Kerr was no friendlier than when he had read *Baal*. Brecht had 'obvious talent', but the play was 'hardly an independent piece of work, despite its natural freshness'.[24] Brecht left for Munich on the day the notices appeared.

He was in Augsburg at the beginning of January 1923, hoping to coax the offended Neher into designing sets for the production of *Im Dickicht* at the Residenztheater. Engel, who had seen his drawings, was willing to risk an unknown designer, and when Neher failed to appear for the proposed rendezvous, Brecht tried an oblique approach. He wrote to Bronnen: 'Successes affect the ovaries. Isolated successes in big cities last for two winters.'[25] The stratagem succeeded. Neher arrived in Munich and stayed on to design the production, though it was postponed: rehearsals would not begin until March.

Also in January Brecht settled with Marianne in a two-roomed flat on the ground floor of No. 15 Akademiestrasse. He worked hard, collaborating with Feuchtwanger on revising *Im Dickicht* – Bronnen noticed that Shlink's conversational style was coming to resemble Feuchtwanger's. But Brecht felt resentful at having to stay in Munich: 'In this city you can't turn round, and the people are so stupid that you need so much humour it puts you in a bad mood. It's due to the bad water.'[26]

Bronnen had lost both Brecht and Neher, but he stayed in Berlin and quickly overcame his resentment when Leopold Jessner offered to produce his new play *Verrat* (*Betrayal*) at the Prussian Staatstheater. He tried to make two conditions: that Gerda Müller, his actress girl-friend, should play the lead, and that Brecht should direct. She was acceptable to Jessner, but Brecht was not. Bronnen did not expect to be forgiven for agreeing to have the play done without him, but his next letter from Munich was a siren song.

> Can you not come you old reprobate
> you're needed   you'll be received with honour ...

what about a little letter for your friend
bidie in this southerly isle
bidie with the slight tinge of villainy?
his kidneys are nothing special but his heart's like gold
when he and his friend caskopf smoke they dream
    of their brother in the asphalt jungle and
    their eyes water.[27]

Munich was a hotbed of Nazism. It was here that in 1919 a 30-year-old ex-corporal, employed as a secret agent by the Reichswehr, joined the German Workers' Party, which had been founded earlier in the year by a worker called Drexler. It had only six members: Adolf Hitler was the seventh. In 1920 it changed its name to National Socialist German Workers' Party (NSDAP). Discovering his talents as a demagogue, Hitler imposed his private prejudices on party policy – rabid anti-semitism, belief in 'Aryan' superiority, and resentment against the terms imposed by the Treaty of Versailles. Mass unemployment and inflation were helping the party to success, and when Walther Rathenau, the Foreign Minister, was murdered by nationalists on 24 June 1922, democratic republicanism was crippled. In 1923 uniformed Nazis were parading through the streets of Munich, chanting slogans and rallying support. Like other Jews, Feuchtwanger had stones thrown at his windows and abuse shouted after him in the street.

Preoccupied with his own anxieties, Brecht underestimated the strength of the 'sad little curs', as he called them, 'the excrement of Adolf Hitler'. Shortly before 12 March, when Marianne gave birth to a daughter, his first legitimate child, he wrote to Bronnen: 'Oh, it's boring here, you drink hog-wash (warmed up) and you shit almost odourlessly.' The baby was called Hanne. He was sometimes loving and tender towards her, but he could not concentrate when she was crying, and he 'cruised around his friends' homes, looking for places to work'. Though he found it frustrating not to make more contact, 'there's so little one can do with children, except be photographed with them, even when they're of such superior quality as my daughter.... Incidentally she has inherited two qualities from her father: she's inexhaustible and insatiable.'[28]

Brecht would often disappear from the cramped flat, ostensibly to work with Feuchtwanger. As dramaturg he wanted to introduce American plays into the Kammerspiele's repertoire, but found it hard to discover what was available for translation, though he wrote to the American Play Company and tried to make personal contact with Barrett O. Clark. By the beginning of July it was doubtful whether the marriage could survive. 'Our child is going to starve. We'll have nothing to eat. Everything takes so much time.' He often came home with friends who would stay late or stay the night, and loud male voices in the neighbouring room would keep Marianne awake. 'I must drink cognac, dissect women – in short lead a real life. When various 50-year-olds claim that they're pursuing literature because they're unsuited to life, I take this to be a cheap swindle. In any case I throw myself into "living", principally because I'm too unsuited to literature.'[29]

Nearing national bankruptcy, Germany had defaulted in coal and timber shipments due to France, which gave the French a pretext for occupying the Ruhr in January 1923. When the German government ordered a policy of passive resistance, factories, shops and banks stopped work. The population of the Ruhr patriotically starved, while in Munich the Nazi movement benefited both from desperation – the German people was being violently reminded that it had lost the war – and from the distraction of the government's energies.

In Munich there were Nazis everywhere. Two actors under contract to the Kammerspiele joined the party, actors low down in the hierarchy and greedy for advancement. Other actors, if they owned books by Marx, kept quiet about them. When Bronnen arrived from Berlin at the beginning of June he was uncomfortably aware of swastikas, uniforms, strident shouting, harshly worded placards. But the young Brecht seemed to enjoy the spectacular choreography of the large-scale fascist demonstrations, and when the two friends went to hear Hitler speak at a circus, the Zirkus Krone, Brecht said: 'He has the advantages of a man who's done all his theatregoing in the upper circle.' Like Bronnen, Marianne had the impression that Brecht did not take Hitler seriously.[30]

If his relationship with her had been better, he would have been more willing to stay in Munich; the reason he gave for wanting to leave was not marriage but 'Mahagonny' (literally 'mahogany'). The word, which was later to become almost synonymous with Berlin, first

occurred to him after seeing the masses of brownshirted petty-bourgeois, wooden figures with their falsely coloured red flag riddled with holes. The concept grew out of the word and developed alongside himself: what it meant during that summer was principally a lower-middle-class Utopia, that cynically mindless table-d'hôte state, which was brewing out of anarchy and alcohol the most dangerous mixture for the witches' kettle of Europe.[31]

In January 1919 a dollar had been worth 8.9 marks, in January 1921, 64.9, in January 1922, 191.8, in January 1923, 17,972.0 marks. Struggling not just to survive this inflation but to ignore it, living life to the full, Brecht needed a large-scale commercial success and, making his decision too hastily, started dramatizing Selma Lagerlöf's novel *Gösta Berling*. He knew that the Norwegian writer had authorized Ellyn Karin's stage version – he made use of it – but Kiepenheuer was her publisher, and he was assuming he would be able to do a deal. He asked Bronnen to negotiate for him in Berlin, but the project had to be abandoned.

When a new company formed by an agent, Jo Lhermann, gave Bronnen an opportunity of directing a play, he would have liked to do one by Brecht, who did not reward loyalty by offering him one, so he resorted to Hans Henny Jahnn's *Pastor Ephraim Magnus*, but then had doubts about its relevance to the current situation. This made Brecht angry: 'What's it got to do with you if people are starving? Can you feed them by writing plays about hunger? What we have to do is get to the top, make our way, have a theatre, get our plays produced. Then it's possible to see further ahead, to do more.' In its present form, said Brecht, *Pastor Ephraim Magnus* would have run seven hours or, with Bronnen's cuts, six. He undertook to prepare a new version. The play was condensed to two hours, and when Jahnn, 'tall, slim, blond, with demonic eyes', attended the final rehearsals, there were bitter arguments. According to Bronnen, they made Jahnn so ill that he took to his bed. At the first performance some sequences worked well; others made the audience hiss. The critics were almost unanimously hostile, and the whole enterprise collapsed when Jo Lhermann's cheques were found to bounce.[32]

When rehearsals started for *Im Dickicht*, Brecht would sit silently and unobserved at the back of the stalls, but over lunch he would make suggestions to Engel about both production and acting. Engel was encouraging Erwin Faber to give Garga many of Brecht's characteristics and mannerisms: 'the nervous flying movement of the head, which grows slantwise from the neck; the grimacing grins; the tortured animation of the whole body; the hysteria; the strange graphic mimicry'.[33]

The production opened on 9 May. It was condemned in the *Völkischer Beobachter* as 'not only unspeakably stupid but also horribly boring'. At the second or third performance the production was interrupted by tear-gas bombs, which filled the auditorium with smoke. Usherettes appeared with ozone sprays, and half an hour went by before the actors could resume.[34]

Soon afterwards the play was withdrawn from the repertoire 'on account of public resistance'.[35] But Engel was to play an important role in Brecht's career. A short man with thick spectacles, strongly sculpted features and a driving energy which compensated for his lack of charm, he recognized the power latent in Brecht's dialogue. Brecht could afford a failure because so many opportunities were now presenting themselves so rapidly. In the spring of 1923 he had another chance to work with Karl Valentin. To procure a role for his brother, an incompetent actor, a rich Munich businessman put up money for a 30-minute silent film, *Mysterien eines Frisiersalons* (*Mysteries of a Barber's Shop*). Brecht wrote the scenario; Valentin played the barber, who used a carpenter's plane, a chisel, a hammer and huge pliers for such operations as getting rid of a pimple. A duellist who comes to sharpen his sabre in the salon has his head cut off while he is being shaved. After floating about, it is planted firmly on his head again, and he seems all right until the barber's assistant, who is in love with his opponent, pulls it off again with a fishing-hook. The idea of the floating head may derive from Chinese drama. Engel directed, using Blandine Ebinger, one of the actresses who attracted Brecht, as the assistant.

Brecht's friendship with Bronnen ended as his friendship began with the 23-year-old Viennese actress who had appeared in the Frankfurt production of *Vatermord*. A Jewess and a Communist, Helene Weigel had been educated at a school run by a militant suffragette who was at pains to prove that girls could reach the same intellectual level as boys. When Jessner contracted Weigel for the Staatstheater, she rented an attic studio in the Spichernstrasse, not far from Bronnen's room in the Nürnberger Platz. From his window he could see when her light was on, and when he called on her, he was always offered a hot bath – he had no bathroom – and pastries she had made herself. Brecht often called on Bronnen, and they talked endlessly about the theatre and their own prospects. 'An actress is what one needs,' Brecht declared. A little later, the light went on in the attic studio, which prompted Bronnen to remark: 'Helene Weigel lives there.' Brecht had met her only briefly in Berlin at the première of *Trommeln in der Nacht*, but Bronnen offered to 'ring her up so that you can go over'. Another sub-tenant was using the telephone, so he was out of the room longer than he had expected to be, and when he returned, Brecht had already left.[36]

Brecht told Weigel that he did not live in Berlin, and would have to go back that evening to Munich or Augsburg. She invited him to stay the night, and made up a bed for him. Later on he knocked on her bedroom door, complaining it was cold in the room she had given him, but the stratagem failed to gain him admittance to the bedroom.[37]

He seldom wrote to Marianne, who had left soon after Hanne's birth to stay with her parents in Pichling, near Linz, but in two letters written in the autumn he complained of boredom, saying that most of his evenings were spent backstage, listening to anecdotes told by stage-hands. 'It's high time you came home with the illustrious Han-neh.... Your husband has begun to smoke a pipe.... Your bed is empty and I sleep alone in the red blanket.' 'Don't you want to have another look at your progenitor ... Hah-neh? He now spits into corners of the room and has picked up seven million habits which are revolting.... When he goes into your room, he says: Salaam, Illustrious One! What a sacrilege it is that you are absent.'[38]

Marianne was unresponsive, and before the end of the year he was suggesting to Weigel that they should spend a week together in Paris.[39]

7 / Cheese-white Faces

Towards the end of 1923 Max Reinhardt was working outside Germany so much that Erich Engel was appointed as artistic director of the Deutsches Theater, and he offered contracts to both Brecht and Zuckmayer for a year's work in the *Dramaturgie*. It was in Berlin, obviously, that the main theatrical battle had to be fought; besides, Engel was intending to do another production of *Im Dickicht*, while Jessner wanted to stage one of his plays. But Brecht was not proposing to leave Munich before he had taken advantage of his opportunity to direct. After working for fifteen months as a dramaturg, he was entitled to ask for a production.

Bernhard Reich, who had been appointed in the autumn of 1923 as senior director, would have liked him to tackle a Greek tragedy, but he did not want to.[1] According to Reich,

He spoke very quietly but assertively, formulating his assertions paradoxically. Totally categorical. He met objections not by contradicting them but simply by wiping them away. He gave his interlocutors to understand that he, Brecht, regarded all resistance to him as hopeless, amiably advising them not to squander time – just to capitulate. Was this attitude, slyness, a pose, youthful self-importance or did he have an inner right to it?[2]

Pragmatically he had as much right to it as people gave him, and as he had discovered at home, at school, in the army and in his relationship with girls, he could nearly always get away with everything he claimed. Like Brecht, Reich always wore a cap as a matter of anti-bourgeois principle, whereas workmen, who wore caps during the week, were liable to affect hats at the week-end.[3]

Feuchtwanger advised him to do a Shakespeare play. He chose *Macbeth*, and Neher was already painting the scenery when Brecht baulked. Feuchtwanger's next suggestion was Marlowe's *Edward II*, a play which shows a king losing his dignity – a spectacle then rare on the German stage – and pivoting on a relationship in which two male lovers destroy each other. It had affinities with *Baal* and *Im Dickicht*; it also provided an opportunity for throwing down a stylistic challenge to the tradition of Shakespearian production which was still dominant: 'that turgid monumental style dear to middle-class Philistines'.

Feuchtwanger, who was fluent in English, suggested that instead of using Walter Heymel's translation, they should collaborate on a new one. They consulted Heymel's version, but theirs was not so much a translation as an adaptation. There is less iambic regularity in *Edward II* than in Marlowe's earlier plays, but too much for Brecht, whose rhythms, though strong, were never smooth, while the characterization becomes more strenuously anti-heroic.

According to Zuckmayer, Brecht followed Feuchtwanger's advice on 'background, construction, sequence of scenes and the mental outline', but made his own mind up about 'shape, language, atmosphere and dialogue'. Feuchtwanger and Engel told Brecht that one sequence needed a monologue. 'In five minutes, with three people sitting around him smoking and drinking coffee, he'd written it and read it out: in twenty lines of verse he'd evoked a half-putrefied, amphibian realm of death, covered in algae, deep under the waters of the earth, where a man contemplates the ineluctability of his destiny. We thought it was excellent and right for the dramatic form, but Brecht stuffed the paper into his pocket, saying it was much too lyrical for the theatre. He'd use it for a poem and write something else.'[4]

He introduces a ballad singer to the play and approximates to a fairground view of history. Though he is not writing a counter-play to Marlowe's, as he had to Johst's, his standpoint is neither that of the hero-worshipping poet nor that of the detached chronicler but – so far as he could achieve it – that of the audience at a popular sport. As Ihering would say after the first night, 'Unconsciously he lets the energy of the masses flow into his work.'

Socially and sexually, Brecht specifies more than Marlowe, who makes Lancaster call Gaveston 'base and obscure'; Brecht's Gaveston is a butcher's son. Beyond this Brecht does not try to widen the play's social focus, but he anatomizes the relationships, giving more autonomy to the characters' bodies at the expense of their will-power. Marlowe's Edward surrenders his Gaveston and surrenders his crown; Brecht's Edward refuses to loosen his grip on either but, unlike Marlowe's king, who has no real antagonist, Brecht's is confronted in young Mortimer with a scholarly nihilist who is reluctant at first to enter the political arena, but then fights with a Baal-like contempt for current values.

Holinshed, the prime source for Marlowe's play, had described Edward's final imprisonment in 'a chamber over a foul filthy dungeon full of dead carrion'; unlike Marlowe, Brecht shows Edward daubed with excrement. But it is here that the anti-heroic drive reverses itself: in abject humiliation, Edward finds the strength of self-sufficiency:

> Upon me here, for seven hours, the dung
> Of London drips. But this filth is hardening
> My limbs. Now they are firm
> As cedar wood. The stink of filth is making
> My greatness measureless.

Faced with the man, Lightborn, who is obviously sent to kill him, Edward echoes Garga's hymn to extinction:

> Rain was good; fasting filled my belly. But best
> Of all was darkness.

Early in the rehearsal period Brecht seems to have benefited from advice to him by a well-disposed old actor: 'They know you're a beginner, and they're seeing how far they can go, like children with a new teacher. Ask for a big armchair and get in their way. Drum something into them, and show that you're not thrown off course even by the most valid objections. Don't take any notice of what they tell you until you've shown that you're in command.' Brecht was self-confident enough to take advantage of this help, and he gained enough power over the actors for his writing style to seep into production style. As Bronnen had said of *Trommeln in der Nacht*, 'Brecht had written not just words, but space – mise-en-scène';[5] now, given a free hand and months of rehearsal, he could mould both, rewriting as he rehearsed, constantly giving new lines to the surprised actors, even during the final period of rehearsal.

Thinking of the *Moritaten* (ballads) and the 'panoramas' at the Augsburg Plarrer, which froze history into moments of tableau – 'Nero Looks at Burning Rome' – he made up his mind that he wanted neither a conventionally stylized decor, with curtains and rostra, nor an evocation of royalty that depended operatically on velvet, damask and coronets. With Neher as his designer, he evolved a simple visual style, dressing the lords and even the king in sackcloth.[6]

Deviating violently from German stage practice, he insisted that actions such as eating, drinking and sword-fights must be realistic and interesting to watch. Soldiers must tie nooses for hanging a man as if they had done it dozens of times before. Brecht would sit in the stalls, confidently shouting out 'Wrong, completely wrong' to the bewildered actors when actions were untruthful in relation to character or circumstance.[7] He made the actors repeat over and over again gestures and inflections that seemed important: he wanted each piece of stage business to be expressive of the whole character, and he reacted strongly against generalization, vagueness, blurring. One of his strengths lay in his ability to stand back and look at what he was doing as if from the outside. Few professionals would have noticed 'how *weird* it is that painted people who have memorized little speeches should stand on a platform and mimic episodes from human life while many other people watch in inexplicable silence'. But in talking to the actors and technicians he formulated everything simply. 'A different light. Seven o'clock in the morning.' And he dealt summarily with noise in the auditorium: 'I'll have the stalls cleared unless there's silence.'[8]

In *Edward II* he borrowed Erwin Faber, the original Garga, now star of the company at the Residenztheater, to play Edward, while Marie Koppenhöfer, the original Marie, was cast as Queen Anne. His Gaveston, the wide-eyed Erich Riewe, did not come across as sly and elegant, but as a naïve peasant, incapable of extricating himself from his dangerous situation.[9] Already Brecht was finding his way towards the style and the method of working that were to become distinctively his. Like writing, directing could become more collaborative, and he appointed Reich's girl-friend, Asja Lacis, a Latvian Communist, as assistant director. With Bernhard Reich she had been in Russia, and she had studied in Theodore Kommissarjevski's studio and had picked up from Meyerhold the idea of making actors puppet-like. When Brecht let her rehearse the crowd scenes, she tried to de-individualize the soldiers, making them march mechanically to the sound of drums. 'I tried to choreograph the extras to a strong rhythm. Their faces should be immobile and expressionless. They knew neither why they were shooting nor where they were going.... Yet something was missing from the soldier sequences.'[10] Karl Valentin was sitting in on a rehearsal and Brecht asked him how soldiers behave before a battle. The comedian answered: 'They're scared. They're as white as cheese.' So they were given white make-up to wear, which made them indistinguishable from each other. In Brecht's version of the story, it was Valentin's remark that gave him the idea of making the soldiers' faces chalk-white. Whoever originated it – and probably it derives from Meyerhold – it was one of Brecht's first alienation effects.

Despite Asja Lacis's Latvian accent, he decided to cast her as the young Edward, who dominates the final scene. The disparity between his accent and his parents' might be unrealistic, but Brecht hated stage German, and it was realism of another kind that preoccupied him. Ihering, who was welcomed to some of the rehearsals, has described how Brecht deprived the actors of 'the relaxation that creeps in so easily.

He made them take responsibility for the characters' actions. He demanded simplicity of gesture. He insisted on clarity and coolness in diction. No emotional faking was tolerated. This led to the objective, the epic style.'[11]

Carl Zuckmayer was profoundly impressed by Brecht. 'Never have I encountered such exuberant creativity, shooting up from so many roots but at the same time critically controlled.... He detested the stereotype of the wandering poet, conscious of his mission as prophet and visionary. His attitude was realistic, governed by humour and scepticism, as was his way of expressing himself.' Perversity had launched his theatrical career when *Der Einsame* had irked him into writing a counter-play; perversity was colouring his development as a director. He was quite sure that the *status quo* was wrong and he was right. Artistically he was a revolutionary, but not politically. Of the two men, Zuckmayer was the more interested in politics. He lent books by Ernst Bloch and Georg Lukács to Brecht, who knew neither of them, and showed little interest; in return he lent Zuckmayer Kipling, saying: 'You can learn from him.'[12] He was himself quick to learn from Kipling, and slower in his response to the political books loaned by friends and to the political influence of Helene Weigel, who was pregnant before *Eduard II* opened. Public events, too, were pushing him away from political apathy. One morning in November, arriving for the ten o'clock rehearsal, Reich and Lacis saw groups of actors and technicians in the street, crowding round the ones who had newspapers. In the special edition Hitler was announcing that he had ousted the treacherous government and assumed power. Law and order would be restored as soon as possible. Meanwhile there must be no gathering of more than three people in public. Brecht dismissed the actors.[13]

Encouraged by General Ludendorff, and using a Munich beer-cellar as his headquarters, Hitler was attempting to seize control of the Bavarian state government, march on Berlin, and establish a Nazi state. But the rebellion collapsed in the Odeonsplatz, when Bavarian police fired on the procession, killing sixteen Nazis. The failure of the *putsch* enhanced the government's prestige so much that Hitler seemed innocuous. To Heinrich Mann, who left Munich the same day, it was clear that there could be no return to equilibrium, but Brecht shared the general feeling that the danger had been defused. On the afternoon of 9 November he and Marianne were at the Feuchtwangers' house with Reich and Lacis. 'It might have been thought', writes Reich, 'that we were sitting in the back row of a provincial theatre, and had just seen the procession of

Spanish guards in *Egmont*. Decidedly merrier, we said goodbye to each other quickly and went home. Brecht's eyes gleamed jovially.'[14]

In December *Baal* had its first production. At the Altes Theater, Leipzig, Alwin Kronacher directed it with Lothar Körner as Baal, but neither of them was equipped to make it into a success. At the end of one lyrical passage a voice with a Saxon accent shouted down from the gallery: 'Now explain the poem.'[15]

In rehearsals of *Eduard II* Brecht had managed to restrain Oskar Homolka, the burly, ambitious, temperamental Viennese actor who was playing Mortimer, but at the first performance, on 18 March 1924, he drank too much in the interval and during the second half of the play used too much voice, gesticulating too much, not only with his hands but with his head. At the party afterwards Brecht threatened to make it impossible for him to go on working as an actor.[16] But the production was successful.

After a short trip to Berlin before the end of the month, Brecht took Marianne to Italy in the early summer, but he could no longer enjoy either her company or her physical presence. After visiting Rome, where they met Bernhard Reich, they went on to Naples and Capri. Neher was in Positano, and when Reich arrived in July, Brecht and Marianne had been there for a few weeks. Unlike Neher, who was also seeing the Mediterranean for the first time, Brecht was indifferent to the scenery. He preferred Naples, with its cinemas, sailors' bars and fairgrounds, and in Rome he had no desire to look at ruins. He grew eager to rejoin Helene Weigel. In a letter to her probably written in the middle of June from a Capri *pensione*, he said that he was expecting to be there for another week, and in another letter, written soon afterwards in verse, that he expected to be back in Germany within a week or two.[17] In July he resumed work on *Galgei* in Augsburg, and by the end of August he had drafted four acts.

8 / Berlin Attic

At the beginning of September 1924, taking up his appointment as dramaturg at the Deutsches Theater, Brecht settled in Berlin – to stay there until 1933. He moved into Helene Weigel's attic studio in Spichernstrasse and, adjusting tactfully and submissively, as she always would, to his needs, she moved out, renting a studio flat in Babelsberger Strasse. To reach the Spichernstrasse attic you had to climb five flights of stairs, cross a catwalk, open a massive iron door and go down a corridor; once inside you could look through the overhead windows at the roofs of Berlin. There was a huge cast-iron stove, but no carpets and no curtains: it looked less like a home than a place he was temporarily staying in. On a long, heavy table by the window stood a typewriter and files of newspaper cuttings, mostly from American papers. The arrival of a visitor was treated less as an interruption than as an opportunity for testing out a tricky passage and, in the light of reactions to it, typing out a new version.[1]   In October Brecht had to divide himself between Erich Engel's rehearsals for *Im Dickicht* and Jürgen Fehling's for *Eduard II*. Engel was using Neher as designer and a cast headed by Fritz Kortner, who had turned down a part in Reinhardt's production of Shaw's *St Joan* in order to play Shlink. Instead of repeating his Munich production, Engel was making the play less poetic. Brecht approved. The première was on 29 October, five days before Helene Weigel gave birth to his son, whom they named Stefan.

The working relationship with Fehling was less harmonious: cordially disliking the ideas basic to his production, Brecht could not bully him into making fundamental changes. Erwin Faber again played the king; the production opened at the beginning of December.

Brecht was still at work on *Galgei*, which he now retitled *Mann ist Mann (Man is Man)*. Conceived in about 1918, at roughly the same time as the one-act farces, the original idea had been for a play about a dim-witted Augsburger who got tricked into believing he was a missing butter merchant – a man called Pick. But having continued to read Kipling, Brecht discarded the Augsburg setting in favour of British India. Elisabeth Hauptmann's influence may have been more than catalytic here:

she had studied English and helped him to understand Kipling. The Augsburger Josef Galgei was replaced by Galy Gay, an Irishman working in India as a fish-porter, but it was no harder for Brecht to identify with him: under the new mask there was even less danger of being recognized.

Elisabeth Hauptmann, whom he had met in November, was a friend of Dora Mannheim. Blonde, brown-eyed, chubby-cheeked and Saxon, Hauptmann was to become mistress, assistant, and collaborator. He persuaded Kiepenheuer to pay her a salary for helping him with the three books he was contracted to deliver. Working at the play on his own in the summer, he had felt that not having a collaborator was like having to take responsibility single-handed 'for the whole of Versailles'. In effect she replaced Feuchtwanger. The two men seldom met now, but with her help Brecht arrived at a concept which was new to his work on the play, though it derives, like so many elements in his early theatre, from Rimbaud, who had said: *'Je est un autre'* and had insisted that the process of thinking was passive: 'It's misleading to say: "I think". One should say: "I am thought".' Brecht began to see his central character, Galgei, as a man who is more lived than living, a passive 'hunk of flesh, who proliferates inordinately, who, only because he has no centre, survives each transformation, just as water flows into any shape'

> Here is the donkey who feels inclined to survive as a pig.
> The question is: is he living?
> He is lived.[2]

Later, in his Marxist reinterpretation of his early work, Brecht would condemn Galy Gay's (Galgei's) volatility, and new lines would be interpolated to drive the point home:

> Unless we're careful not to let him out of sight
> He could become a killer overnight.

Though Brecht cannot have been unaware of the play's relevance to Nazism – a man's identity changed when he put on a brown shirt and jackboots – Brecht cynically refused to adopt a disapproving stance. Like Kragler, Galy Gay wants to survive, even at the cost of becoming someone else, and instead of being punished by the action of the play, he ends up in a stronger position. In the 'Ballade vom armen B.B.' ('Ballad of Poor B.B.') Brecht wrote

> In the earthquakes that are coming, I hope bitterness
> Won't make me let my cigar go out.

The attitude behind the play is much the same, though complicated by the mechanistic psychology of behaviourism, which was fashionable. The machine analogy struck Brecht as being valid for individual consciousness:

> We'll take a man to pieces like a machine.
> And how much will he lose? Not a bean.[3]

That men were machines which could be dismantled and reassembled was an idea that had been latent in the work of Fernand Léger and Marcel Duchamp, who had both been using the analogy to make brutal statements about the human body and its functions, while Paul Klee's technique of 'taking a line for a walk' – to use his own words – directly influenced Neher, and indirectly Brecht. Neher's drawings, like Klee's and like Georg Grosz's, perform a geometrical surgery on bodies, postures, gestures and movements. The machine analogy was also implicit in constructivism, with its premiss that the artist could best serve the whole of society by entering into direct rapport with machine construction.

From the outset Dada in Berlin had been more political than in Switzerland or France, and in his first German Dada manifesto (April 1918) Richard Huelsenbeck proclaimed: 'The highest art will be that which represents the multiple problems of the epoch.' Georg Grosz, Wieland Herzfelde and John Heartfield collaborated in 1919 on a series of seditious little reviews, which were each banned on the appearance of the first issue. Grosz's cartoons drew on the *Simplicissimus* tradition, but introduced montage, a technique which was developed by Kurt Schwitters, whose review, *Merz*, began to appear in January 1923, influenced by *De Stijl*, the magazine edited by the Dutch painter Theo van Doesburg. In his abstract *Merz* pictures Schwitters used odd scraps of material, nails, torn tickets, bits of newspaper, to play off shapes, colours and textures against each other.

For Brecht it was exciting to think that the components of human personality could be rearranged no less cavalierly. When *Mann ist Mann* was later performed on radio, the point he stressed was that no harm was done to Galy Gay; it might seem 'regrettable a man should be duped like this and forced to give up his precious ego – all he possesses (so to speak); but it's not. It's quite a cheerful affair. For this Galy Gay emerges unscathed; he comes out on top, as a man who takes this attitude is bound to come out on top.'[4] While other writers of a populist slant – Mark Twain and Theodore Dreiser in the United States, Shaw and Butler in England – had been apprehensive about the new technology, and pessimistic about determinist attitudes, Brecht was defiantly optimistic. As science increased our chances of mastering the environment, it must become easier for us to assert ourselves and enjoy ourselves, if only we could overcome antiquated moral scruples. Brecht was making no protest against the way Hitler was liberating his supporters from outmoded restraints on aggression.

Mann ist Mann may be less autobiographical than *Baal* or *Trommeln* or *Im Dickicht*, but, as in the schoolboy stories, Brecht was giving himself advice. No one could have been more eager to come out on top, or to proliferate inordinately. If he had a centre, it was subjective, and rejecting subjectivity he was hungry for transformation, willing to flow into any shape. This he had in common with those who became Nazis, but he was able to dramatize the process. *Mann ist Mann* is covertly autobiographical in being about the transition that it marks, the movement towards the drama in which the writer appears to have given up his precious ego in favour of identification with a group.

Apart from Elisabeth Hauptmann, his collaborators on the play were Neher, Bernhard Reich and Emil Burri, whose career straddled boxing and literature. Formerly a medical student at Munich and a protégé of Feuchtwanger, he worked as sparring partner with the light-heavyweight champion, Paul Samson-Körner, and he wrote two plays: *Amerikanische Jugend* (*American Youth*) and *Das mangelhafte Mahl* (*The Deficient Meal*) which Brecht considered progressive. Brecht was also working on *La dame aux camélias* with Reich, who was preparing to direct it in Ferdinand Bruckner's translation and wanted to make it more socially realistic. The star, Elisabeth Bergner, Reich and Brecht agreed that nothing should be said to Bruckner about the textual surgery, and Brecht's name was not to be mentioned in the programme. He interfered energetically with the text, introducing two realistic prostitutes into the fourth act, and reducing the pathos of the fifth by making Armand less noble, less loving and less sympathetic to Marguerite's sufferings. He also wrote in a small part for Asja Lacis – Esther, a friend of Marguerite's. Elisabeth Bergner knew that the desentimentalized ending would disappoint the audiences, and the critics (including Ihering) were disapproving, while Bruckner sued the theatre, demanding compensation for loss of royalties from provincial theatres which might have staged his version had it been successful in Berlin.[5] Brecht had not improved his chances of being allowed to direct *Baal* at the Deutsches Theater; he had not even earned any money.

*   *   *

On 27 February 1925 Erich Engel's production of *Coriolanus* opened with Fritz Kortner in the lead. Brecht, who had discussed it with Engel in detail, called it 'a model of the director's art, decisively important in the emergence of Epic Theatre. He presented the history of Coriolanus so that each scene stood independently, and only its upshot contributed to the whole. In contrast to dramatic theatre, where everything rushes towards a catastrophe.' This is to take the same view as Meyerhold, who rejected the Aristotelian idea that episodic actions were inferior because the sequence of events lacked both probability and necessity.[6]

Though Brecht made more use of collaborators in *Mann ist Mann* than in *Baal* or *Trommeln in der Nacht* or *Im Dickicht*, the new play was more original, combining the farcical comedy of the one-act plays with the wide-ranging ontological suggestiveness of the full-length plays, while using a ballad-like simplicity and preserving an admirable lightness of touch. Confusion of identity had been recurrent in comedies since the fourth century BC, but none had been written from the premiss that differences between one personality and another are negligible. Nor had Brecht previously realized how much could be achieved by developing farcical material into a larger and more ambitious pattern.

After reading some scenes to Bernhard Reich, who was pessimistic about audience reactions, Brecht tried to compromise with current taste. 'But it turned out that instead of being softened in the new version, the elements likely to alienate the audience had been emphasized.'[7] Chaplin had helped Valentin to teach Brecht that both poetry and resonance can be achieved through farce; the comic formality in the dialogue of *Mann ist Mann* looks forward to *Waiting for Godot* and backwards to the titles in silent screen comedy: 'Dear wife, I have decided today, in accordance with our income, to buy a fish. This would not be beyond the resources of a packer, who does not drink, smokes fairly seldom and has almost no passions. Do you think I should buy a big fish, or do you need a small one?' The mock solemnity of this literary style immediately cancels any implicit claim that a mirror is being held up to human nature, but neither the stylization nor the comic exaggeration undermines the points about identity and behaviour.

Brecht could claim, as he did in his prefatory talk for the radio production, that his play was relevant to the 'new human type' which was evolving. Faced with Galy Gay, the audience should not think it was listening 'to an old acquaintance talking' but to a 'new sort of type', mendacious, optimistic, flexible. 'Actually it is only seldom that he can afford an opinion of his own.'⁸ Millions of Germans were adapting to circumstances and suppressing their own opinions by joining the Nazi Party; neither the play nor Brecht's statements condemn the new mendacity, the new adaptability, while any basic ambivalence towards it is fanned into comedy. The absurd trial scene is the first of Brecht's many trial scenes in which justice is not done and is seen not to be done. With only facts and logic on his side, Galy Gay can defend himself only feebly against the nonsensical accusations of Uriah, who is ominously combining the roles of judge, jury and prosecuting counsel, after instigating the incident used to tempt Galy Gay into apparent crime – the auction of what the three soldiers make out to be an elephant. Actually it is only an elephant head and a map spread over a pole. The scene is surrealistically theatrical, but once he has testified that he was not present when Galy Gay auctioned the elephant, Galy Gay has to deny that he is Galy Gay, and to have his moustache shaved off in the hope of escaping identification.

It is not only the barbering that makes the trial scene reminiscent of Brecht's film with Valentin: in style both look backwards to vaudeville and Chaplin, while pointing forwards to Ionesco, Genet and Pinter. But the substance of the trial scene – and of the farcical jurisdiction in Brecht's subsequent trial scenes – derives partly from the absurdity of current events. In March 1924, four months after the *putsch*, Adolf Hitler had been on trial, together with nine others. Instead of defending himself he boasted that he was 'the best of Germans who wanted the best for the German people'. Though he was Austrian and was convicted of treason, the court ignored the law that treasonable aliens should be deported. He was sentenced to five years' imprisonment, but was released after less than nine months. Sentences equally grotesque for their leniency were commonly passed on hooligans involved in right-wing movements: the judges were more reactionary than the *Reichstag*,⁹ and Brecht could never feel that justice was being enforced by the courts.

Not that he was yet concerned about social injustice. His premiss was that since life is so very short, one must live it to the full, ignoring the suffering caused, and not wasting time on resisting changes in the political environment.

What moved Brecht much more than social or racial injustice was individual frailty: a sonnet written when he was in Augsburg during June describes how the man, having noticed a grey hair on the head of the girl he was about to leave, decides to spend one more day with her:

> ... And let's not waste too much time talking
> For we were both forgetting that you're ageing.
> But then my voice was silenced by desire.[10]

While he was in Augsburg he bought a second-hand car and had no end of trouble with it. He wrote a few other sonnets and read, as usual, prodigiously: 'nothing left for me in the lending libraries'. In July 1925 he went to visit Marianne and Hanne, who was now two and a quarter, and while he was in Baden, sitting with a cocktail he had mixed himself and puffing at one of his strong, black cigars, he tried to analyse his dissatisfaction. Surely this was the best time of his life. He was twenty-seven, and able to get almost anything he wanted.

So far you've been able to carry out any kind of blackguardly action, so long as it wasn't too exhausting for you. . . . What's too cold for you was your summer; if your daylight was too dark for you, it'll soon be night. . . . I've got what I want and see nothing better. There's nothing I want more than something different. . . . The old pastures – even the ones I haven't seen – are too old for me. Life is too short and it passes too slowly.[11]

His short story 'Brief über eine Dogge' ('Letter about a Mastiff'), published in August 1925, throws some light on the feeling of having everything he wanted and wanting nothing more than something different. The narrator describes how, from their first encounter, the dog is scared of him. Like Jerry in Edward Albee's 1959 play *The Zoo Story*, the narrator tries to make friends with the animal. He feeds it, eventually owns it, but even during the San Francisco earthquake, when the dog is trapped by debris, it refuses to let him release it. Looking back on the incident after two years, he still cannot understand how he antagonized the dog. The expression in his eyes has brought him success with some people. Did it repel 'this more sensitive animal'? Or was it a matter of deformity or malformation on some deeper level? Perhaps it is his mind that 'can no longer apprehend the repulsive as repulsive'. Later, as now, Brecht would be prone to moments when self-hatred was indistinguishable from the feeling that other people hated him. In preferring to deal with the collective, both in plays and in relationships, he was, like T.S. Eliot, acting partly out of revulsion against the embarrassments of individual relationships. For many communist intellectuals, such as

Ernst Fischer, the *raison d'être* of any revolutionary movement was concern for the individual personality;[12] Brecht would be attracted to Marxism more negatively.

Professionally he wanted all the power he could arrogate, but in his sexual and social relationships there were disadvantages in finding it so easy to spellbind other people: the excitement of conflict was missing, and only a limited satisfaction was to be had from devotion. He disliked going out to other people's flats, but was consistent in welcoming them to his. His social evenings followed a routine pattern. Theatre talk was followed by improvisations, in which Homolka would try to outclass Kortner. Weigel and Homolka would tell Viennese stories, and eventually Brecht would be asked to sing ballads. Taking the guitar down from the wall, he would perform his infallible magic, driving the rhythms relentlessly forward and 'cutting the words as with a guillotine.... With the word *Heldentod* (hero's death) he held the "o" up high for several seconds, so that the impudent "o" could be inspected from all sides.' Reich was not alone in finding that Brecht the ballad-singer made even more impact than Brecht the poet. Instead of appearing to bare his soul, he seemed to be letting the eccentricities and beauties of the ballads speak for themselves, but 'the performance precluded a decent, quiet response to the poetry by putting unexpected stress on insignificant passages and surprisingly little stress on highly dramatic passages'.[13]

Hostile to expressionism, he felt attracted by the new cult of objectivity, realism, usefulness, functionalism. When G.F. Hartlaub originated the phrase *die neue Sachlichkeit* in 1924, he applied it to 'the new realism with a socialist flavour', but as the phrase became fashionable, it was associated with several disparate developments including Bauhaus art, Georg Grosz's caricatures, the abolition of upper-case letters in typography, Hindemith's music and Max Beckmann's painting. According to a 1925 pamphlet published by Grosz and Wieland Herzfelde, the time was coming when the artist would 'no longer be the Bohemian, sponge-like enemy of society as before, but a healthy, clear-thinking worker in the collectivist society'. Now, as later, this was close to what Brecht wanted: to contribute constructively. 'I feel no need for a thought of mine to achieve immortality. I'd prefer everything to be consumed, rearranged, used up.' He forced himself to come to terms with the ugly, the streamlined, the functional, the interchangeable: 'After enjoying black coffee I can look more tolerantly at concrete buildings.... I believe: surface has a great future.... I'm glad that in cabarets dancing girls are being manufactured to resemble each other more. It's pleasant that there are so many of them and that they're interchangeable.'[14]

This is in line with *Mann ist Mann*, but in steering himself towards this aesthetic position, he had to overcome his ambivalence towards everything he associated with city life.

> Skyscrapers on Manhattan Island! Some notion!
> Expect them to be durable?
> It may amuse the Atlantic Ocean
> That our optimism's incurable.
> Nothing from all these cities can last
> Save the wind that has no clear intention
> And when we ourselves are sunk in the past
> We'll be followed by nothing worthy of mention.[15]

Not that he was at odds with intellectual fashion in wanting to see traditional culture displaced by thrillers, sport, spectacle and light entertainment. In the Soviet Union revolutionary artists and intellectuals had, like Mayakovsky, tried to turn their back on *belles-lettres* and the art which could appeal only to a minority. 'Think of the packed crowds at football, volley-ball and ice-hockey matches,' wrote Meyerhold. 'We shall soon be using the same stadia for dramatizing sporting events. Modern audiences demand the kind of suspense that can be generated only by a crowd of thousands.' Following the Russian lead, German intellectuals were turning towards sport and popular entertainment: bicycle races feature in Georg Kaiser's play *Von morgens bis mitternachts* (*From Morning to Midnight*, 1916) and in Joachim Ringelnatz's *Turngedichte* (*Gymnastic Verses*, 1923). Detective stories gave the impression of recording what happened, objectively and dispassionately, while the boxer Brecht most admired, Samson-Körner, struck him as boxing 'objectively' ('*sachlich*').[16]

His interest in sport had developed since he settled in Berlin. Together with Burri he watched most of the major events in the Sportpalast, constantly comparing both the public and the spectacle with those to be found in the theatres. The sporting public knew exactly what to expect:

that trained people display their particular skills in the way most suited to them, with the finest sense of responsibility but in such a way as to give the impression that they're doing it for their own enjoyment. *On the other hand traditional theatre is currently quite characterless.... A theatre without contact with a public is nonsensical....* Our theatre has no connection with the public because it doesn't know what's required of it.[17]

There was no 'sport' in the theatre; no one was getting fun out of it. 'And no one can expect other people to get fun out of what he's doing if he isn't having fun himself.' He came increasingly to think of 'new' theatre as categorically different from 'old', and of new theatre as being unstageable in old buildings. 'In the old theatres we're simply out of place with our plays, just as Jack Dempsey cannot prove himself in a bar-room fight: someone just hits him over the head with a chair and he's K.O.'[18]

Before the year 1925 ended Brecht signed a surprisingly advantageous contract for his poetry with the publisher Ullstein. Over Christmas he was working abortively on a play about Charles the Bold, and at the beginning of 1926 planning a comedy about post-war youth. It was to be called *Inflation*. Precocious suburban schoolboys trade in motorbikes and copper collected from old military telephones.[19] Working with Burri, Brecht was also drafting a play about Dan Drew, the railway pioneer. The second act was finished by 4 January.

Through Burri he met Samson-Körner, became friendly with him, and began to write the boxer's biography, which was serialized in *Scherls Magazin* and in *Die Arena*. 'Samson-Körner is a splendid and significant type,' Brecht told an interviewer. 'I wanted to familiarize myself with him.... I ask him to talk about his past, and I set great store by his opinions. People's opinions interest me more than their feelings.' A few of Samson-Körner's opinions are quoted in the twenty-three pages of the biography. For instance, 'it's important in a fight to be as angry as possible'. Brecht was still inclined to give himself advice when writing stories. The narrative is written in the first person, as if Brecht were ghosting it, and though it is not a direct transcript of Samson-Körner's words, Brecht takes trouble to reproduce his narrative style. He had been involved – before his boxing career began – in a protracted battle with another man, a black cook who took elaborate revenge for a practical joke. Another reason for Brecht's interest was that a professional boxer struck him as a man who did his utmost to turn himself into a 'human fighting-machine'. This idea was to give the biography its title – *Die menschliche Kampfmaschine*. In *Mann ist Mann* soldiers are represented as fighting machines, and the sergeant is known as a 'human typhoon'. Samson-Körner's account of the man who taught him how to box, another black called Kongo, looks forward to the divided personality of Herr Puntila: 'he maintained that when he'd been drinking he was a much better man, a man who couldn't even be compared with the sober, ordinary everyday Kongo'.[20]

Samson-Körner's reminiscences also led to the short story 'Der Kinn-haken' ('The Uppercut') which was published in the January 1926 issue of *Scherls Magazin*. One boxer describes how another drinks before a fight and gets himself knocked out, not because he drank but because he had come to dislike himself: 'A man should always do what he wants to do. In my opinion. You know, caution is the mother of the K.O.'[21]

When Moritz Seeler offered a Junge Bühne production of *Baal*, Brecht felt remote from the 20-year-old who had written it. Wanting to bring his adolescent subjectivism into line with his new *Sachlichkeit*, he poured his metal back into the melting pot, even giving the play a new title, *Lebenslauf des Mannes Baal* (*Career of the Man Baal*). Instead of iden-tifying with Baal or treating him as a hero, he tried to think of him as an abnormal case. How would the story have been reported in a newspaper? In stepping away from the autobiographical, he was stepping towards the style of his later plays. Elisabeth Hauptmann's diary records how a 'model' for *Baal* was faked. An Augsburg mechanic was invented and (perhaps ironically) named Josef K. Written in the style of a newspaper report, the account of his life made him the illegitimate son of a wash-erwoman, a man who talked impressively and lived irresponsibly. 'When A[ugsburg] became too hot for him, he left to go on prolonged wander-ings with a disreputable student of medicine, returning to A. in about 1911.'[22]

Brecht now began to work in the same way on *Im Dickicht*, looking at the events from a different angle by writing them up as a journalist might.[23] He was instinctively doing what he would later ask actors to do in rehearsal. Stanislavsky had encouraged them to think of their charac-ter in the first person; Brecht forced them to stand back from the character by interpolating 'he said' or 'she said' when rehearsing dia-logue. Besides encouraging detachment, this pitches the action away from the present tense of drama towards the past tense of narrative.

Brecht directed *Baal* himself, with scenery by Neher. Alarmed by the hectic rewriting, Seeler tried to argue in the rehearsal room. Some of the quarrels were violent, but Brecht had learnt how to keep actors on his side. Oskar Homolka was co-directing as well as playing Baal, with Paul Bildt, Helene Weigel and Sybille Binder in the cast.

On 7 February Elisabeth Hauptmann watched Brecht trying 'to bring some life into the "dead" table on the right' during the café scene. In the death scene the woodcutters were told not to 'handle Baal like a raw egg'. 'When Brecht gets no fun out of things he's done, he at once sets about making changes.'[24] He cut the play down to eleven scenes, which were set in the first decade of the century, emphasizing the industrialization of the environment, while stripping Baal of both his lyricism and his quasi-divine stature. Each scene was given a title. The production had only one performance – a matinée at the Deutsches Theater on 14 February.

According to Hans Henny Jahnn, who had come from Hamburg specially, the auditorium was overfilled. 'The performance began very late. The atmosphere was charged with tension and impatience, already poisoned. It was hot. It was abnormal.' The explosion was triggered by one of the ballads.

Baal had disappeared, the cabaret singer was alone on the stage. People in the auditorium whistled, shouted, yelled, applauded. The actress hoisted herself on top of the piano, stamped on the keyboard and sang *Allons enfants de la patrie*. The noise was atrocious. I thought panic would break out.... But there was nothing more than this earsplitting noise which went on until its originators were exhausted. Suddenly there was complete silence, and in it, from one of the galleries the words floated down: 'You're not really shocked. You're just acting. ...' The sound of an audible slap followed.[25]

Baal might not have been expected to please Hugo von Hofmannsthal, who was now in his early fifties, but he wrote a prologue for the Viennese première, which followed five weeks later, again with Homolka as Baal. The actors, appearing as themselves, discussed the new drama, in which 'repressed spiritual forces break free, creating a new form of living space, which they themselves fill'. Hofmannsthal understood that Brecht was battling against the old idea of individuality:

Our age is groaning under the weight of this sixteenth-century child fattened by the nineteenth to outsize dimensions.... We are nameless forces. Spiritual potentialities. Individuality is an arabesque we have discarded.... All the sinister events we have witnessed in the last twelve years are nothing but an uncomfortable and protracted burial of the European concept of individuality in the grave it has dug for itself.[26]

In March Brecht was invited, together with Bronnen and Alfred Döblin, to give a poetry reading in Dresden, where Verdi's *La Forza del Destino* was to be premièred in Franz Werfel's translation. Humiliatingly, though, the three guests of honour were allocated inferior seats in the opera house, and were not invited to the gala reception for Werfel. Infuriated, they returned their tickets, and it was only after a publisher, Leo Franck, had stepped in as mediator that they agreed to go ahead with the reading. Brecht included a freshly written allegory about three gods who visit Alibi where no one pays homage to them because the people are all celebrating the great Alea. One citizen of Alibi, Sibillus, persuades the gods to go with him 'to the table of the fat Alea . . . to pick up the crumbs that fall from his rich table'.[27] Though Werfel was quite plump, the audience would have missed the point if the impulsive Bronnen had not denounced Werfel and the management, describing the previous day's events. A scandal ensued, and years later, when he wrote *Der gute Mensch von Sezuan*, Brecht went back to the idea of three visiting gods who are given a poor reception.

Though he was not yet writing so schematically, he was already pinning his faith in schema and formula, as he tried to prescribe a cure for the theatre's unsporting traditionalism. On 23 March 1926 Elisabeth Hauptmann noted: 'Brecht finds the formula for "epic theatre" – play from memory (quoting gesture and posture) – and orients his writing entirely to this. He performs the sequences himself, this is how the "demonstration scenes" (as B. calls them) emerge.' The idea is in line with using the newspaper report as a model for dialogue and dramatic action. Instead of pretending that something was happening in the present tense, the actor would visibly be reproducing something from the past.

But nearly two years earlier in Berlin, at the Volksbühne in Bülowplatz, Erwin Piscator had directed an 'epic drama' about Chicago anarchists in 1886-7 – *Fahnen* (*Flags*) by Alfons Paquet. Short sequences of action were strung episodically together and, reviewing the production in the *Leipziger Tageblatt*, Brecht's friend Döblin called the play 'a stepping-stone between narrative and drama', adding that this form provided refuge when 'the coldness of a writer's feelings stops him from identifying with the characters' fates or the story's development'. If Brecht read this, the phrasing would have caught his attention: in his diary (20 May 1921) he had quoted Julius Meier-Graefe's characterization of Delacroix – 'a warm heart beating in a cold man'.[28]

With Paquet's *Fahnen* Piscator claimed to have 'crossed the threshold from the theatre of art to the theatre of the age', arguing that Paquet had tried 'to lay bare the roots of the case in the epic elaboration of the material'. This was drama which documented its period: 'it is not the inner arc of the dramatic event that is essential, but the epic course of the epoch from its roots until its last effects are represented as precisely and comprehensively as possible.'

Writing in 1929, Piscator still regarded *Fahnen* as 'the first consciously epic drama', though by then he had put the epic principle more successfully into practice in *Schweyk* (1928) and in the first act of *Boom*. Paquet and Piscator were ahead of Brecht in their formulations, but Gerhart Hauptmann had already refurbished the Aristotelian distinction between 'epic' and 'dramatic'. Like Zola (and like Chekhov) Hauptmann believed that the creative writer should apply scientific methods. 'The modern dramatist,' he wrote in August 1912, 'being a biologist, may sometimes work towards a drama which like a house, an architectural creation, never moves from the position where it has been situated. Or he may have reason to apprehend life horizontally, having already grasped it vertically. He may prefer life's *epic flow* to its *dramatic stasis*.' The biological orientation probably derives from Zola's 1880 essay 'Le Roman expérimental', which had been written under the dual influence of the physiologist Claude Bernard, who advocated observation and experiment, and of Hippolyte Taine, whose history of English literature explained style in relation to racial inheritance, the driving force of the age, and environment – physical, social and political.

In Gerhart Hauptmann's first play, *Vor Sonnenaufgang* (*Before Sunrise*, 1889), a socialist agitator tries to help a group of oppressed Silesian coalminers. *Die Weber* (*The Weavers*, published 1892; produced 1893) is innovative in giving a strong proletarian twist to bourgeois domestic tragedy, and in wrenching the action away from personal relationships and private predicaments. There is no hero or central character, and the play's focus is on a movement of rebellion. But unlike Brecht, Hauptmann lacked the technical skill and the doggedness to bring his artistic programme to fruition: this was the objective Brecht set himself. 'Actually,' he said in a speech, 'I am the heir of Gerhart Hauptmann.' This was tantamount to claiming the foremost place in current German drama, as he did when he boasted: 'After me, Piscator is the greatest living German dramatist.'[29] Piscator wrote no scripts, but he created drama in the way that a film director created cinema.

Meyerhold's criticism of Piscator was that he had 'made a new theatre, but used old actors to perform in it'. Brecht was, in the long term, to have more influence on acting style than either Piscator or Meyerhold. But he owed a great deal to both. 'We need tendentious drama,' insisted Meyerhold, 'with one object only – to serve the revolution.' And in 1925 Meyerhold had already been speaking of 'the actor-tribunal', which must 'work for a specifically propagandist purpose, revealing what is concealed behind the situation'.

In Germany Brecht was outstanding for the clarity of his realization that a new theatrical style was needed for old plays no less urgently than for new. In insisting on this, he was dissociating himself not only from the establishment but from the avant-garde, as represented by the *Junge Bühne*. After *Baal* he persuaded Seeler to put on a play by his 25-year-old protégée – formerly she had been Feuchtwanger's – Marieluise Fleisser. Before studying at the university in Munich, she had been at a convent school and her play *Die Fusswaschung* – Brecht retitled it *Fegefeuer in Ingolstadt* (*Purgatory in Ingolstadt*) – is about adolescence in a small Catholic town. Nominally the director was Paul Bildt, but it was Brecht who controlled not only the staging but the revision of the text, ruthlessly encouraging her to trust the less sophisticated side of her talent, to write like a child, to risk mistakes. Seeler again disliked the results of Brecht's textual surgery, and again failed to win the arguments in the rehearsal room. Though the production was a critical success, Brecht and Seeler never worked together again.

Not content with printed plaudits or applause in the auditorium, Brecht needed constant encouragement from collaborators. Going back yet again to revise *Mann ist Mann*, which was finally to be premièred in September 1926 (simultaneously in Darmstadt and Düsseldorf), he asked Elisabeth Hauptmann for her opinion of the opening. Wasn't it of classical stature? She agreed that it was: she almost knew it by heart. He then called the play a classic comedy.[30]

In his workroom he concerned himself less with theatrical than with social problems, but he was refining his ideas about epic theatre. His earliest formulation about it was made during an interview given in July 1926, a couple of months before the première of *Mann ist Mann*. His plays, he claimed, reflected the mood of the whole world, presenting an objective view of things. Without mentioning detective fiction, he ranked himself with the writers who simply set down what happened. 'I give the ungarnished events, so that the audience is left to think for itself.' The production should bring out the material of the action 'quite soberly and objectively. Today the meaning of a play is usually blurred because the actor aims straight at the audience's hearts. The characters ... ought to be put across quite coldly, objectively and classically.'[31] Readers of detective fiction knew exactly what they wanted. 'You want to see quick thinking (the hero's, the author's, your own), you want to understand a particular part of the plot up to a certain page and to be ignorant of the rest.' To satisfy these demands the author must have gone through a certain 'spiritual training', so that, like a variety artist, he can remain good-humoured and smiling throughout his performance. It should be possible to construct a play with mathematical precision: *ausmathematisieren* was a word he used. By the end of his work on *Mann ist Mann* he had dismantled and reassembled it eleven times, with still more reworking for certain scenes.[32]

For the Darmstadt production of *Mann ist Mann* the theatre's artistic director, Ernst Legal, decided to play Galy Gay himself, engaging Neher as designer, and Jakob Geis as director. Geis had been influenced by both Brecht and *die neue Sachlichkeit*. Writing in *Die Szene* about his objectives, he promised 'no innuendoes, secrets, ambiguities, twilight; but facts, clear illumination of every recess, impartiality, no combination of comedy and pathos'. For the first time the half-height curtain – a characteristic feature in Brecht's later productions – was used, and Begbick was given three daughters, who played jazz. In Neher's designs white and khaki predominated, and the effect, as attested by the critics (including Ihering and Kerr from Berlin) was generally brilliant, but the production did not lead to any revivals of the play.

Intending to write new plays for the new public, Brecht was aiming to deal objectively with the new collective life that was emerging: he was planning to follow *Im Dickicht* with two other plays about 'humanity's entrance into the great cities': *Der Untergang des Egoisten Johann Fatzer* (*The Downfall of the Egotist Johann Fatzer*) and *Joe Fleischhacker*. At first he made little headway with *Der Untergang*, but worked hard at collecting material for *Joe Fleischhacker*, which was to be set, like *Im Dickicht*, in Chicago – this time against the background of the corn exchange. He read Gustavus Myers's *History of the Great American Fortunes*, and studied the careers of Vanderbilt and Dan Drew, while Elisabeth Hauptmann, who was regularly clipping newspapers for him, was briefed to collect information about the exhanges in Vienna and Breslau. After consulting an economist, Dr Singer, an expert on the Chicago exchange, Brecht formed the impression that these processes were simply unintelligible.[1]

Determined to make sense of them, he embarked on a systematic study of economics. 'He had to find out about theories of money. . . . He knew that the form of traditional (high) drama was unsuitable for representing such modern processes as the distribution of the world's wheat supply, as for the life-story of contemporary man, and generally for all actions with consequence.'[2]

The sexual relationship with Helene Weigel may have involved more ideological rapport than emotional symbiosis, but it is hard to gauge her fanaticism or the part she played in converting him to Marxism, though after the première of *Mann ist Mann* he got hold of books about socialism, asking friends to list the order he should read them in. When he left Berlin for a holiday, he took books with him. 'I'm now eight feet deep in *Das Kapital*,' he wrote to Elisabeth Hauptmann. 'Now I must get to know exactly. . . .' But in the informed opinion of Hanns Eisler, Brecht never read – never needed to read – more than the first volume of *Das Kapital*.[3]

Marxism satisfied him as Christianity never had; it was useful to be freed from the belief that humanity was pitted hopelessly against the superior forces of nature. According to Engels, the 'most essential and most immediate basis of human thought' was *'the changing of nature by men'*.[4] In mastering their social organization they win mastery over their natural environment: it was not only possible but necessary to speak, as Brecht soon would, of 'changing the world'. The idea of class conflict was taking its grip on an imagination already addicted to the image of the fight. Of all the Brechtian productions in which a boxing-ring has been the dominant visual image, the first was staged in December 1926, when *Die Hochzeit* was premièred in Frankfurt, directed by Melchior Vischer, who let Brecht persuade him into modelling the set on a boxing-ring.

Marxist literature helped to focus the strong antipathy he already felt towards the bourgeoisie and its art. He never read Proust, and looked at *Ulysses* only out of interest in its technique. As Eisler put it, 'Brecht had the admirable virtue of reading only what he could use.' After advising him to read Hegel's *Aesthetik*, Eisler would later find that Brecht could almost immediately light on the passages – just as he could usually find the people – he would find most helpful. He had no interest in modernism as such, or even in literature as such. His commitment was to looking at life from underneath. If no man is a hero to his valet, heroic drama and heroic poetry must have depended on leaving the valet's viewpoint to be represented only by comic or contemptible characters. Brecht intended to balance things out.

Ever since his poems had been useful for entertaining friends and seducing girls, he had been predisposed to make usefulness his criterion. When he was invited to judge a poetry competition organized in February 1927 by *Die literarische Welt*, he found that the 500 odd entries by 400 odd poets were flawed with 'sentimentality, inauthenticity and lack of contact with reality.... Once again we find those quiet, refined, dreamy men, the sensitive side of a worn-out bourgeoisie I want nothing to do with.'[5] Since none of the entries had any practical value, he provocatively awarded the prize to a piece of doggerel which had not been entered for the competition. It had the English title 'He! He! The Iron Man!' and it was a celebration of a popular racing cyclist, Reggie MacNamara. Brecht had found it in a cycling magazine.

His own collection of poems, *Hauspostille (Domestic Breviary)* was published in 1927 by Ullstein in the format of a Prayer Book, bound in black leather and printed in double columns on Bible paper. There is a complex mixture of banter, effrontery, irony, parody and self-parody in his 'Direction for the Employment of the Individual Lessons': at any performance of the Chronicles smoking is to be recommended; a stringed instrument may be employed to provide harmonious support for the voice. 'Chapter Six is to be read principally in the white nights of June. But it is permissible for the second part of the ballad, in so far as it concerns the shipwreck, to be sung as late as October.... Chapter 8 is intended for periods of unprecedented persecution. (In periods of unprecedented persecution, the devotion of a good woman will become evident.)' To mock at religion and its calendar, the poet is producing a piquant mixture of solemnity and mockery, offering his verse, and implicitly himself, as a substitute. At the same time he is using – and will continue to use – forms, rhythms, and syntactical patterns that had been impressed in his mind by the Bible.

On 18 March 1927 Radio Berlin broadcast *Mann ist Mann*, with Ernst Legal again playing Galy Gay. The broadcast was heralded by an article in *Der deutsche Rundfunk* by a young composer, Kurt Weill, who afterwards reviewed the production of what he called 'the most powerful and original stage play of our time'. He praised the bridging passages Brecht had introduced for the broadcast: 'short sentences predicting how the plot will develop, and reminiscent of the fairground barker's style or of titles in old films'.

Brecht may have met Weill in Berlin during the early 1920s with Essenin and Isadora Duncan, but only briefly and unmemorably;[6] he was now curious to meet the author of the review. Weill, who had been taught by Busoni and had been collaborating on operas with Georg Kaiser and Yvan Goll, an expressionist who had joined the Dadaists, was due to compose a chamber opera for the summer festival at Baden-Baden, and he was looking for a text.

Brecht and Weill met at Schlichter's, a restaurant in Lutherstrasse, known for its cold buffet and salads. From that point on,' says Lotte Lenya, Weill's wife, 'Kurt and Brecht visited each other quite often and started discussing what they could do together.'[7] Brecht's *Hauspostille* contains three 'Mahagonny Songs', and the first of them punningly equates civilization with syphilis. The adventurers set out in the belief that city life is diseased. In Mahagonny

> Our ci-ci-ci-ci-civilis
> Will get cured.

The first idea was that Weill should set these three songs, together with two written in English by Elisabeth Hauptmann, 'Benares Song' and 'Alabama Song', and with an unpublished poem by Brecht, 'Gedicht über einen Toten' ('Poem on a Dead Man'). But the possibility of collaborating attracted Brecht, who was always willing to rework old material, and together they created a *Songspiel* – their own term, a variant on *Singspiel* (light opera). Though Weill was temperamentally less revolutionary, their ideas were complementary.

Brecht had seen Chaplin's *The Gold Rush* in the spring of 1926, and the Mahagonny of the poems relates not only to inflationary Berlin but also to the American boomtowns created by speculators. (Jack London may have been another influence.) Life in Mahagonny is ruled by greed for money, whisky, sex and food; the only crime is to run out of money. Brecht had already composed melodies – however eclectic – for his poems, and Weill used these in the Alabama Song and (less extensively) in the song about God's arrival in Mahagonny, while Brecht provided new verse and a minimal scenario. The end product was a provocative miniature cantata. Like Schoenberg, who had written cabaret-songs, Weill had tried his hand at them[8] but he was courageous not only in being simple but in being ironically vulgar, with the risk that the audience would miss the irony and uncritically enjoy the vulgarity. An unsigned programme note (presumably by Brecht) described the piece as 'a small epic play which draws the logical conclusions from the inevitability of the collapse of our existing class structure'. It claimed that Weill had 'begun to address himself to an audience which goes to the theatre naïvely and for fun'.

Work on the *Songspiel*, which was to be called *Mahogonny*, helped to crystallize Brecht's realization that he wanted to campaign for a new aesthetic and a breach with tradition. The sociologist Fritz Sternberg, who helped him to understand Marx's ideas, helped him to clarify his own. Sternberg explained the decline of Western drama as a historical necessity, consequent on the eclipse of the individual by collective entities. He was a friend of the painter Rudolf Schlichter, and he saw Brecht eating in the restaurant which belonged to the painter's elder brother. 'He made an impression on me. The way he sat there, the way he moved his hands. Something remarkable, unforgettable, was emanating from his face and his body.' Invited to Sternberg's table, Brecht pronounced vehement judgement on things he did not seem to understand fully. And when Sternberg compared *Baal* unfavourably to Wedekind's early work, Brecht turned to Schlichter: 'Tell me, didn't you say Herr Sternberg had taken a doctorate in economics? ... Then ask him if he'll help me when

I buy a suit. Perhaps he could help me do it more economically.' Later in the evening, when Brecht said that since writing *Trommeln in der Nacht* he no longer found a relationship between a man and a woman was enough to carry a play, Sternberg called it the first of his remarks that was not only interesting but progressive. The world war had ended the comparatively short cultural period which had begun with *Romeo and Juliet*, said Sternberg, the period in which sexual love could be central to a work of art. Before they parted, Brecht had asked whether he could send Sternberg his unpublished manuscripts; from then on they met at least once a week, and Brecht attended Sternberg's lectures. Once Sternberg told him: 'You don't think in straight lines, you think in knight's gambits. You think in associations scarcely anyone else would arrive at.'[9]

Herbert Ihering, always on the look-out for publishable controversy, filtered into the *Börsen-Courier* an exchange of views between the sociologist and the dramatist. According to Sternberg, Shakespeare's plays reflected the emergence of the individual from feudal anonymity, and conflicts between individuals were characteristic of the new age. But, as it developed, bourgeois drama had become more monotone, eventually confining itself to the man–woman relationship, and now that capitalism was declining, collective forces were ousting the individual.

Brecht, whose aversion to the idea of individuality had ripened without any help from Marxist theory, now recognized that 'this Marx was the only audience I'd ever found for my plays.... They provided him with illustrative material.' In the *Börsen-Courier* Brecht argued that Shakespeare's plays had been followed by '300 years during which the individual evolved into a capitalist' and the old drama had been defeated 'not by the consequences of capitalism but by capitalism itself'. To function as an activating force, theatre must become truer, more real, more closely intertwined with journalism and daily events.[10]

Sternberg encouraged Brecht to think of traditional literature as a superstructure created to protect the interests of the oppressors. After attending the sociologist's lectures, Brecht arranged to have private meetings with him. It was like taking instruction from a priest. Euphorically convinced that he was learning something crucial, Brecht came to believe in theatre as an instrument for teaching, for relaying the enlightenment that had made his own thinking so much more truthful. In November he wrote that the '*radical transformation of the theatre*' must correspond to the 'radical transformation of our period's mentality':

together with art and literature, theatre must form the *ideological super-structure* 'for a solid, practical reorganization of our way of living'.

Brecht was working all this time with Weill on their new art form, the 'Songspiel'. Having sung, effectively, himself, since he was a schoolboy, Brecht knew the potential of the untrained voice; Lotte Lenya had trained as a dancer and turned to straight acting, but could not read music, though she had sung on stage. Weill had been scoring the cantata for operatic voices – four male and two female – but the Alabama Song, which was to be performed by two women, called for a popular singing technique. Why not use an untrained voice? Why not use Lenya?

The Weills were living on the third floor of a house in the Luisenplatz. When Brecht arrived to audition her their landlord, Papa Hassforth, took one look at the small, badly shaven, cigar-smoking man in a leather jacket and leather cap and said. 'We don't want to give anything', as he slammed the door. Weill, who had been listening out for Brecht, hurried out to rescue him, and then Lotte Lenya sang the Alabama Song. Since it was in English – Brecht's theory was that the first world language would be a kind of pidgin English – she had learned the words phoneti-cally from another Viennese actress, Greta Keller. 'He listened,' she writes, 'with that deep courtesy and patience that I was to learn never failed him with women and actors. "Not quite so Egyptian", he said, turning my palm upward and extending my arm outward in direct appeal to the moon of Alabama. "Now let's really work...".'[11]

Subsequently when they visited him in his attic, Weill and Lenya usually found him surrounded by young people of both sexes. Bernhard Reich suspected that he was not, at heart, gregarious but needed stimu-lation from other people. Thin and fragile-looking, Brecht

paced to and fro, surrounded by blue clouds from his almost incessant Virginia cigars. Now he would throw out a lightning question to one of his seated disciples, now throw out a quick casual answer to another.... His narrow, white hands gesticulated incessantly, translating each phrase instantly into theatre language. Often he shook with silent laughter. Then he subsided into an armchair, clapped his hands on both knees, bent double until the laughter was over, rubbed his eyes with the backs of both hands and said: 'Yes, that's life.'

For serious sessions of work on the cantata, the disciples would leave the two men alone with Hauptmann and Lenya. Sometimes Brecht would play a few chords on his guitar to convey a suggestion, which Weill would always register with a serious smile, never saying no, always promising to incorporate Brecht's idea if he could.[12] The two men invariably listened to each other with respect, but never became close friends.

The première was scheduled for 18 July. Brecht wanted the performance to begin with the entrance of the two women singers in the nude, but the idea was quashed by the municipal authorities. As in the Frankfurt production of *Die Hochzeit*, eight months earlier, the set consisted of a boxing-ring – a surprise for the audience that had just listened respectfully to dissonant miniature operas by Milhaud, Ernst Toch and Hindemith. Climbing through the ropes came four men in bowler hats and two girls in straw hats. Lotte Lenya remembers how

a giant Caspar Neher projection flashed on the screen hung behind the ring, and *Mahagonny* began – with a real, an unmistakable *tune!* The demonstration started as we were singing the last song, and waving placards – mine said 'FOR WEILL', with the whole audience on its feet, cheering and booing and whistling. Brecht had thoughtfully provided us with whistles of our own, little *Trillerpfeifen*, so we stood there whistling defiantly back. Later, I walked into the lobby of the fashionable hotel where most of the audience went for drinks after the performance.... Suddenly I felt a slap on the back, accompanied by a booming laugh: 'Is here no telephone?' (This is one of the pidgin English lines from the Benares Song.) It was Otto Klemperer. With that, the whole room was singing the Benares Song, and I knew that the battle was won.[13]

By the end of July Brecht was in Augsburg again: in Berlin there were too many distractions from work but in Augsburg there were only two cinemas. He wrote asking Helene Weigel to send him all the Marxist literature she could, including the new serialized history of the revolution. Now that he was politically so committed, it was inevitable that he would be attracted into the orbit of Erwin Piscator, who was now thirty-three and had been working at the Volksbühne since 1924, and had, after quarrelling with the board of directors, opened his own theatre, the Piscator-Bühne, in Berlin's Nollendorfplatz. His 'dramaturgical collective' was headed by Felix Gasbarra, a German-Italian communist who had worked with him on earlier political productions. Piscator involved himself in the collective, together with Leo Lania, Brecht, Kurt Tucholsky, Ernst Toller, Erich Mühsam, Franz Jung, Walter Mehring, Johannes Becher, Alfred Döblin and Alfred Wolfenstein. In a press release about the arrangements, Lania described himself as 'chief'. His intention may have been to claim only administrative leadership, but it infuriated the other members of the collective, especially Brecht who, according to Piscator, strutted up and down the stage, shouting: 'My name is my trademark, and anyone who uses it must pay for it.' And in another burst of indignation he wrote to Piscator suggesting that the theatre should become overtly political and be called The Red Club Theatre. Grosz, Sternberg, Ihering and the dramaturgs could be enlisted, and membership later be thrown open to the audience. But Brecht added: 'I am not prepared to work under Gasbarra's literary direction, though I may accept his political leadership. I am perhaps your comrade but certainly not your dramaturg.' This was one of the earliest attempts to plan an artistic policy collectively, and a villa was hired on the Wannsee so that meetings could be interspersed with healthy lakeside walks.[14]

The original intention was to open the theatre with a political revue. Rehearsals were to start at the beginning of August, and the company had also acquired the rights to stage *The Adventures of the Good Soldier Schweyk*, which had not reached Germany until three years after Jaroslav Hašek's death in 1923. The theatre opened in September with a production of Toller's *Hoppla! Wir leben*, and when the adaptation of *Schweyk* by Max Brod and Hans Reimann proved inadequate, the collective was set to work on the script. Brod had given the play a conventional plot which climaxed when Schweyk blew up a jam factory. Brod had a strong copyright hold on the novel but, defying his wishes and the law, Piscator, Lania and Brecht turned the script into a satire on Austria-Hungary during the First World War. Much of the dialogue was taken verbatim from Grete Reiner's 1926 translation of the novel, and the text was oriented to a production style that would imitate the laconic narrative in which scenery and dramatis personae are summarily re-arranged. Brecht learnt a great deal from the correlation between textual revision and Piscator's ideas for the production, which was cinematic in its fluidity, with costumed characters, furniture and props set on two conveyor belts. Solid figures or objects could be swept across the stage; Schweyk could march strenuously while the conveyor belt, moving against him, kept him static, and Georg Grosz's animated drawings were projected, enormously magnified, on the screen behind him. Piscator had known Grosz since 1918, when they had been active in the Berlin Dada movement.

Yvan Goll had already introduced photography into stage action in *Der Chaplinade* (1920) and *Der Unsterbliche* (*The Immortal*, 1921). Goll used film and the projection of placards, newspaper cuttings and photographs, as well as grotesque masks exaggerating physical characteristics. Piscator and Grosz used masks in *Schweyk*, and marionettes which could be moved on a conveyor belt, so that the human characters were confronted with apparently dehumanized adversaries and oppressors who were slightly larger than life-size.

During his year as a member of the collective, Brecht had plentiful opportunities to study Piscator's methods of shifting the focus away from the individual. Ever since fighting in the trenches, Piscator had blamed the war on capitalism, and been relentlessly hostile to bourgeois art. His prime concern was to find a new language of images for communicating with a new, unsophisticated audience. To disseminate information, to spread enlightenment, and to inculcate the desire for social change, he studied the Soviet example and developed more sophisticated techniques for presenting contemporary history panoramically. Rejecting painted backgrounds, he used theatre space architecturally. Instead of encouraging the public to forget it was in a theatre, he drew attention to the fact. To interpolate objective documentation he used the detached commentator and filmic projections. Sometimes he introduced a complex theatrical counterpoint to expose the disparity between subjective impressions and objective actualities or between private ambitions and historical events. In *Rasputin, the Romanovs, the War*, while an obsequious minister reassured the Tsarina that everything would turn out all right, a list of lost battles was projected on to a screen higher than the acting space and, above the list, a film sequence showing her being shot. Brecht collaborated on adapting the script, and his unfinished play *Joe Fleischhacker* was announced for the 1927–8 season under the title *Weizen (Grain)*.

Piscator wanted a functional theatre that could speak not just through the actor's mouth but through each of its component parts. His elaborate technology, his lifts, his conveyor belts, his complex lighting plots, his projections of the human face blown up gigantically all derive from a determination to translate history into visual imagery, while making imagery inseparable from action. 'The dramatic alternated with the epic', wrote Bernard Diebold.'[15]

Piscator was a writer in the same sense as the *caméra-stilo* film directors who try to use the camera like a fountain pen, so that they can transfer their thoughts directly onto celluloid. A Calvinist who had lost his God in the trenches, a modernist who reverted to the medieval concept of *theatrum mundi*, a sculptor-engineer who moulded space and light, he was more politically committed than Brecht and, being less oriented to words, he could be more consistently hostile to traditional theatre and theatrical tradition. The main weakness of Piscator's theatre was in the texts he used, but it is not surprising that Brecht learnt so much from his display of technical and technological virtuosity. But he did not learn how to make theatre more political, less dependent on individual lives and individual details. This was later to be Piscator's main criticism of Brecht's achievement: even as a Marxist, Brecht remained primarily a poet, and even as a director, primarily dependent on words spoken by individuals. Piscator's tendency was towards bringing every element in the acting area to life; Brecht went on bringing individual characters to life. What was bound to emerge, even when shown in relation to enveloping political and economic circumstances, was their concern with themselves and with each other.

Brecht's practical involvement in Piscator's theatre might not have ended so early in 1928 if he had not decided to shelve *Joe Fleischhacker* in favour of another collaboration with Weill. They were planning to write a full-scale opera together: either a new subject would present itself or they would follow the suggestion of Hans Curjel, dramaturg at the Kroll-Opera, that they should develop the *Songspiel* into an opera.

It was Elisabeth Hauptmann who told Brecht about *The Beggar's Opera*. Prototype of the modern musical, the 1728 ballad opera by John Gay had been revived in 1920 by Sir Nigel Playfair at the Lyric Theatre, Hammersmith, where it had run for 1,462 performances. Sensing that it could also be a success in Germany, she translated it for Brecht. As Goldsmith observed, Gay had a happy strain of ballad *thinking*; this, together with his relish for low life, gave him an affinity with Brecht. But Brecht was too absorbed with *Joe Fleischhacker* to pay much attention to her work until one day in March or April, when he was lunching alone at Schlichter's, and was introduced to Ernst Josef Aufricht, a 27-year-old actor with a rich father. To set himself up as a theatrical manager, Aufricht had taken a lease on the Theater am Schiffbauer-damm, an ornate nineteenth-century building in the centre of Berlin, not far from Max Reinhardt's Grosses Schauspielhaus, and had employed Erich Engel as director and Heinrich Fischer, a protégé of Karl Kraus, as dramaturg. When Aufricht said he was looking for a new play, Brecht tried to interest him in *Joe Fleischhacker*; it was only after Aufricht had signalled for the bill that Brecht mentioned the ballad opera.[1]

The next morning Fischer collected a manuscript from Spichern-strasse, while Aufricht waited in his parents-in-law's Meinekestrasse flat. Though Fischer failed to protect the manuscript from the rain, one reading was enough to convince him and Aufricht that they had found what they were looking for. What they read was Elisabeth Hauptmann's translation with perhaps a few alterations by Brecht, but when they telephoned he said the music was to be by Weill, and he now began to adapt the text, interpolating material from Villon and Kipling. Aufricht was so unenthusiastic about Weill that Theo Mackeben, the dance band conductor, who was hired as musical director, was instructed to make a new arrangement of the original score and keep it in reserve.

Brecht and Weill had to work rapidly: rehearsals were to start at the beginning of August for an opening to coincide with Aufricht's twenty-eighth birthday at the end of the month. Borrowing the Piscator idea of using a pleasantly situated house for the dramaturgical collective, Brecht rented a villa near the beach in Le Lavandou from the beginning of June. Helene Weigel and their son Stefan stayed with him, while the Weills stayed at a nearby *pension*. Elisabeth Hauptmann and Erich Engel were also in attendance for some of the time. It was probably here that Brecht and Weill moved decisively away from the idea of operatic music. Opera is occasionally parodied in Weill's score but, as in *Mahagonny*, simple ballad-like tunes dominate. Between bouts of work Weill refreshed himself by swimming, and Lenya remembers watching 'Brecht wading out, pants rolled up, cap on head, stogy in mouth'. But never seeing him swim, she assumed he was perhaps 'slightly water-shy'.[2]

Gay had been more intent on ridiculing Italian opera than on reforming social or political abuses, but he had aimed an amusing fusillade against the Prime Minister, Walpole, who was suspected of taking bribes and of dividing himself between a wife and a mistress; both Peachum's transactions in stolen property and Macheath's with his girls allude to Walpole. Gay's opening lyric makes the point that

> The Priest calls the Lawyer a cheat
> The Lawyer be-knaves the 'Divine',
> And the Statesman because he's so great
> Thinks his trade as honest as mine.

But he did not expect to be taken seriously. It is questionable whether Brecht did, but he thought he did, and he set out to prove that the middle classes were no less criminal than the criminals. Gay's Captain Macheath was a highwayman; Brecht moves the action to the Victorian period, making Mack a burglar and stick-up man, while Peachum organizes a gang of beggars, equipping them to masquerade as disabled, like the war-victims Brecht had seen in the streets of Berlin. Brecht's Mr and Mrs Peachum aspire to bourgeois respectability. Unlike Gay's Peachum, Brecht's can claim that his activities are not illegal, and he complains when the chief of police, Tiger Brown, fails to give him protection.

After not quite a month in Le Lavandou, Brecht left to go on working at the text in Utting on the Ammersee, a small resort thirty miles from Munich, while Weill went home to compose the music. By the end of

July Brecht was back in Berlin, and soon after rehearsals began on 1 August, the Weills appeared in Aufricht's office. 'Tomorrow, I'll play you my music,' Weill said, 'and I have one other request. I'd like my wife to play Jenny, one of the whores.' This annoyed Aufricht, but, as he put it, 'she looked talented, moved well and I liked the look of her. "Weill will compose a song for me too," she said in the doorway. She's rather cheeky, I thought. Also: little Weill really doesn't deserve such an attractive wife.' Aufricht agreed to try her out for three days of rehearsal. The next day a piano was rolled onto the empty stage of the theatre and, as Aufricht put it, 'the gentle little man with the glasses started to play and sing in a soft, metallic voice that expressed his intentions precisely'. Aufricht was delighted with the music and with the Polly Peachum he had agreed to try out – Carola Neher, the extraordinarily pretty actress Feuchtwanger had introduced to Brecht in Munich. (She was not related to Caspar Neher.) Since November Brecht had been divorced from Marianne; Carola was now married to Klabund. Aufricht liked her mobile, expressive, 'flat, regular-featured face with its cat's nose', and called her 'a marsh flower under the Soho moon'.[3]

After three or four days of rehearsals she left for Davos, where her tubercular husband was seriously ill. Telegrams to her went unanswered, and when Aufricht finally telephoned, she spoke in a low voice. Klabund was in agony, she said, but the part must not be given to anyone else.

On 14 August he died, and when she came back to rehearsals, she found many of Polly's lines had been cut. She made no protest until the evening of the first run-through, a week before the opening night. After a series of altercations about script changes and changes to moves, she said she would not play such a small part. The weary actors had to wait in the auditorium while Brecht sat down with her at a small table on stage and began to write. At five o'clock in the morning the actors were still waiting, and exhausted: either they must rehearse the final scene or go to bed. Aufricht went on stage, where she was obstinately rejecting every new line Brecht proffered. When Aufricht suggested they should work in his office to let the rehearsal continue on stage, she threw the script at his feet and walked out.

Though he was unwilling to lose her, Brecht did not want to pursue her himself. 'Take a bouquet of roses, Polly's wedding dress and Erich Engel, and see if you can make her change her mind. You know what you're losing if you can't get her back.' The two men followed her to a modestly furnished flat, handed the roses to the maid, and waited for an hour, only to be told: 'Madam is receiving no one today.'[4]

Brecht and Aufricht had a week to find and rehearse a new leading lady. They also lost Engel, who told Aufricht that he had never worked on a Brecht show which had not been a disaster. For the final week Brecht directed himself, and Engel warned Aufricht he should have something ready to put on when *Dreigroschenoper* flopped.[5]

The indications were that it would. Helene Weigel went down with appendicitis, and during a lunch break the brothel scene was rewritten in the Hotel Bristol so that her character, the brothel madam, no longer needed to appear.[6] At one rehearsal the cabaret singer, Rosa Valetti, who was playing Mrs Peachum, stopped in the middle of the 'Ballade von der sexuellen Hörigkeit' ('Ballad of Sexual Dependency'), refusing to 'sing such filthy words'. The song had to be cut.

A blonde music-hall actress, Roma Bahn, was engaged to replace Carola Neher. She had only four days to learn music and words, and a new problem developed when the musical comedy star, Harald Paulsen, enlisted the services of a fashionable tailor and appeared as Macheath carrying a sword-cane and wearing a double-breasted jacket, tight trousers, white spats, patent-leather shoes, a bright blue silk bow tie, and a bowler hat. In the ensuing argument he threatened to give up the part rather than the bow tie, while Brecht, anxious not to lose him, used his intuitive understanding of theatrical dialectics. Incongruities can be made into counterpoint, disadvantages turned to advantage. Remembering the *Moritaten* at the Augsburg Plarrer, and perhaps remembering Piscator's production of *Schweyk*, which had opened with a Czech folk-song, accompanied by a hurdy-gurdy, Brecht hit on a solution which looked like a compromise. He cashed in on Paulsen's vanity by opening the show with a *Moritat* about the evil deeds of the man in the blue bow tie. The lyric for 'Mäckie Messer' ('Mack the Knife') was written in one night, and so was the music. 'Anyone who knew Brecht's intonation,' says Zuckmayer, 'anyone familiar with his melodic diction (as it emerges, for example, in the broadsheet-seller's song in *Eduard II*, which he composed himself) must realize that the famous organ-grinder bars of "Mack the Knife" derive from his inspiration and suggestions.'[7] Paulsen wanted to sing the new ballad himself, but Kurt Gerron, who was playing Tiger Brown, was made to double as the ballad-singer who enters with a Bacigalupo barrel organ to open the show.

The title *Dreigroschenoper* was contributed by Feuchtwanger. Brecht and Weill, who had discarded their original title *Gesindel* (*Riff-Raff*), had been thinking of *Ludenoper* (*Ragamuffins' Opera*), – while Karl Kraus contributed a second stanza to the Jealousy Duet between Polly and Lucy. Fritz Kortner's contribution was the suggestion that the Bach-like final chorale should be cut; it was saved when Caspar Neher rallied to the support of Kurt Weill. But it was agreed after the dress rehearsal, which lasted until six in the morning, that 45 minutes had to be cut from the running time, and one of the songs to be dropped was the Solomon Song, which Lenya was to have sung. So much of Peachum's main scene was cut, too, that the actor Erich Ponto turned up at the theatre in the morning with his bags packed. But he relented.

Because Brecht had admitted friends to rehearsals, news of the disasters leaked all over Berlin. Some said the show should never open; rumours reached the actors that Aufricht was searching frantically for a surefire success to salvage his career as a producer.

On the opening night the audience responded uncertainly to the fugal overture and when Gerron, about to sing the line about the shark's teeth, turned the handle of his barrel organ, no sound came out. He sang the first stanza unaccompanied, and the orchestra improvised support for him in the second. In the next scene the audience was unresponsive when Peachum explained his trade, and neither the comedy in the wedding scene nor Polly's Pirate Jenny ballad aroused any enthusiasm. But the duet Macheath sang with the police chief, Tiger Brown, about their army days in India, the Cannon Song, ended in a furore of applause, stamping, and shouted demands for an encore. The actors had been instructed not to repeat any of the songs, and they tried to go on with the dialogue, but their words were drowned by persistent shouting from the audience until Aufricht nodded his permission for an encore. After that almost each song had to be repeated at least once.

But in the interval, when he went jubilantly backstage, he found the placid Weill shouting that the place was a pigsty. He was not going to let Lenya continue, he said. Her name had been omitted from the programme. When she told him that nothing would stop her from going on, he recovered his self-control. Carola Neher was in the audience. At the end of the show she asked: 'How long is the other girl contracted for?'[8]

Alfred Kerr and Ihering, the two most influential critics, had been irked to find they were sitting next to each other, but in the morning they were equally encomiastic. According to Kerr, it was a magnificent evening and a pioneering work. Ihering welcomed the production as 'heralding a new world in which the barrier between tragedy and comedy is removed. This is a triumph of the open form.'[9] When the production transferred to a bigger theatre, Carola Neher took over from Roma Bahn: with actors he admired or desired, Brecht was seldom unforgiving.

The success was repeated by productions in Munich, Leipzig, Prague and Riga: for the first time in his life he had a very large income. He was thirty-two.

To at least one observer, Harry Graf Kessler, who enjoyed the production on 27 September, it was 'Piscatorially primitive and proletarian in its approach (apache style).' But a triumph of his own deviant eclecticism helped to steer Brecht away from Piscator. Success derived mainly from a combination of elements that were nearly all deeply rooted in Brecht's theatrical thinking. Replying in October to a question from the magazine *Die Dame* about the reading that had exerted most influence he wrote: 'You'll laugh – the Bible.'

While Weill was providing a highly commercial coefficient to what Hindemith called *Gebrauchsmusik* (music for consumption), Brecht was coining a form of *Gebrauchsreligion*; at the same time as exposing the hypocrisy of a shady businessman like Peachum, who traded mercilessly on psychological principles picked up from morality, Brecht was making money out of the exposure. One of his premises for the play was Proudhon's maxim 'Property is theft' – itself a justification for literary eclecticism – but there is nothing in either the text or the music of *Die Dreigroschenoper* to stop a property-owning bourgeois audience from enjoying itself: no attempts to reform contemporary abuses, no allusions to contemporary politics, and no irony, even, that is not double-edged. It was not wholly insulting to the bourgeoisie to expatiate on what it had in common with ruthless criminals; the arson and the throat-cutting are mentioned only casually and melodically, while the well-dressed entrepreneurs in the stalls could feel comfortably superior to the robber gang that aped the social pretensions of the *nouveaux-riches*.

Brecht could profit from Paulsen's vanity because it chimed with an irony he was already planning to exploit in the contradiction between the gentlemanly appearance of the criminals and the violence of their behaviour. In the wedding scene, for instance, the gangsters wear dinner-jackets, but their deportment is at odds with their clothes, which makes a point about the covert violence of those who are habitually well dressed, but it would not matter if this failed to emerge. Not that Brecht was intending to be ingratiating or 'culinary' (to use his word for theatre that is merely entertaining). Working hurriedly, he had slipped into a style that came naturally, introducing many of his predilections into the dialogue. Those who allow themselves to be moved too easily are ridiculed in Peachum's sequence with Filch. Disliking empathic acting,

Brecht incorporates scenes in which characters perform: this makes the actors act, as it were, inside inverted commas. Disliking linear narrative and loving ballads, he writes digressively, extravagantly taking space for songs which are relevant only thematically. 'Pirate Jenny' is sung by Polly in the wedding-party scene, partly to snatch the scene away from the mood of celebration (as in *Die Hochzeit* and in so many of his subsequent wedding scenes which go sour), and partly to accommodate a sadistic vengefulness which is at odds with the more culinary components of the theatrical experience, visual and musical. As in Polly's next song – an explanation of why she gave herself to the first man who took her without asking – the anarchic spirit of *Baal* is still alive. If society stands in the way of a man's or a girl's natural appetite for happiness, it deserves all that's coming to it.

In 'Pirate Jenny' the rancour is counterbalanced both by Weill's catchy music and by the song's irrelevance to the on-stage situation: the pretty bride is entertaining her guests by impersonating a maid in a cheap hotel and singing about the maid's fantasy of revenge against the people who take her for a non-entity. Because of her, the hotel will be spared when the pirate ships fire on the town, but when the pirates ask her which of the townspeople are to be killed, she will say 'All of them'. In the end she will sail away on the pirate ship. The lyric looks back to Brecht's early poems about bands of adventurers, but it also looks forward to his Marxist maturity. The revolutionary does not emphasize his relish for bloodshed, but it is indispensable to the revolution he is wanting. In Brecht there was always a strong nihilistic thrust, but in the consciously positive work it is carefully controlled.

To compensate for lavishing time on digressions, he has to economize over crucial bits of dramatic narrative. Given songs instead of show-downs, the audience feels that its intelligence is not being underestimated. But while many of the ironies are subtle, Brecht never gets to grips with the fundamental contradiction underlying the text. The sentimental optimism – man is good but society makes him evil – assorts oddly with the suggestion that violence is as natural to us as it is to the shark. The difficulty Brecht had with the artificially happy ending is one sign of a conflict that remained unresolved.

Nevertheless the production was not only cheaper than any of Piscator's, it was incomparably more successful. 'It's the fashionable show, always sold out. . . . "One simply has to have seen it"', wrote Harry Graf Kessler.[10]

By the autumn of 1928 Brecht felt fully committed to communism. He wrote to Bernard von Brentano, Berlin correspondent of the *Frankfurter Zeitung*, about 'our dialectical activity', asking him to spare time for compiling an anthology of quotations from Hegel, Marx, Engels etc., setting out 'the basic principles of dialectical materialism'. Brecht also involved Sternberg, who had been giving him essays by Marx and Engels, in an abortive collaboration on a 'sociological' version of Shakespeare's *Julius Caesar*[1] and in discussions with Piscator about a new production of *Trommeln in der Nacht*.

In the newspapers Brecht was arguing that Piscator's revolutionary activity was relevant only to the theatre, not to politics, and not even to the drama. Though Brecht was as avid to sit in on his rehearsals as he had previously been to sit in on Reinhardt's, Piscator now felt unrelaxed in his presence: 'Brecht, you'll have to leave. I can't go on rehearsing when I know you're there.'

As his name became more famous, Brecht was besieged by visitors – aspiring playwrights, directors and actors, admirers in search of philosophical enlightenment, idealistic Nazi students. In discussion with groups of four to ten people, he enjoyed himself and argued skilfully but, as he told Sternberg, he felt no more obliged to express his own opinions than he did when writing dialogue in a play. What he said was devised to provoke, to stimulate, to generate dramatic tension.[2]

With the Piscator-Bühne out of action until September, the Theater am Schiffbauerdamm emerged as the leading left-wing theatre. After *Dreigroschenoper* transferred, Aufricht staged Peter Martin Lampel's *Giftgas über Berlin* (*Poison Gas over Berlin*), a polemical play about the army, and when the chief of police threatened to close the theatre, Brecht supported Aufricht's resistance to censorship. Permission was granted for one private performance, but thanks to some young communists who caused an uproar in the auditorium, the play was then banned as a danger to public safety.

Together with Neher, Brecht and Weill had been working intermittently at their *Mahagonny* opera. Confirmed by the success of

Dreigroschenoper in his proclivity for lyrical digression from the dramatic line, Brecht incorporated some of his early Augsburg poems, including 'Tahiti', and a few of the 'city' poems he had written after settling in Berlin. Leokadia Begbick is borrowed from *Mann ist Mann*, while the hurricane derives from the report in the *Chicago Daily News* (22 September 1926) which was in Brecht's file of American newspaper cuttings. The point is to compare the destructiveness of nature with human destructiveness.

Marieluise Fleisser had written *Die Pioniere von Ingolstadt* (*The Pioneers of Ingolstadt*) as a sequel to her *Fegefeuer in Ingolstadt* and, with Lotte Lenya (whose part in *Dreigroschenoper* was recast), this went into rehearsal at the beginning of March 1929 under the direction of Jakob Geis; but Brecht usurped control of both actors and script, which he radically revised in rehearsal, overriding the authoress's resistance. Expecting her to be no less submissive than before, and assuming that the collective will coincided with his, Brecht decreed that in this theatre other playwrights should be no more rigid or proprietorial about their texts than he was. Marielouise had given herself to him in bed, and he treated her play, like her body, as something he could use. Wanting a secluded setting for a lovers' meeting, she had set it 'by the churchyard'; Brecht placed the action directly in front of some tombstones.

One day Aufricht found a small actor waiting patiently for an interview. He told the man that he looked like a tadpole, but he could go down to the stage and ask Brecht to cast him as the village idiot. He was given the part, and Brecht soon afterwards advised Aufricht to offer him a three-year contract. His name was Peter Lorre.[3]

The evolution of Brecht's ideas about drama and acting did not proceed in a straight line, but he was gravitating still further away from the psychological approach to personality and motivation. In *Im Dickicht*, he said, he had deliberately disregarded motivation, looking at actions as pure phenomena; perhaps the next step would be 'to show characters without any features at all'. The activities reported in contemporary newspapers could not be dramatized through forms like Ibsen's: 'Petroleum cannot be manipulated into five acts ... fate's no longer an integral power but more like fields of force to be observed as they send out currents in opposite directions'. He saw himself as a theatrical Galileo whose task was to bring drama into line with Einstein.

The acting he admired tended to hold back from both characterization and emotionality. As the maid (or second messenger) who announced Jocasta's death in Jessner's *Oedipus*, Weigel had, according to Brecht,

called out her 'Dead, dead' in a totally emotionless, penetrating voice, and her 'Jocasta is dead' without any grief, but so firmly and irresistibly that at this moment the naked fact of her death had more effect than any private pain could have evoked. Her voice was not given over to horror, but perhaps her face was, for she used white make-up to indicate the effect death has on all who are present at it.

It is improbable that Brecht had never told her about the clown-white faces of the soldiers in *Eduard II*; it is equally improbable that they had never discussed how she should make up for *Oedipus*. When he cited this exemplary performance in a newspaper interview, he did not mention the actress's name. But in performance understatement was habitual with her, and it was not misleading to contrast her with the actors who 'put themselves and the audience into a trance'. Instead of inviting the public to take a cool look at the bizarrerie of Richard III's behaviour, they encouraged it to identify with Richard III. Brecht hated theatrical magic –

> The mysterious transformation
> That supposedly goes on in your theatres
> Between dressing-room and stage: an actor
> Leaves the dressing-room; a King
> Appears on stage.

Actors should study 'the theatre which is played on the street'. The woman from next door mimicks the landlord; men show giggling girls how, ostensibly resisting, they draw attention to their breasts. With a crowd of passers-by as tribunal, a man describes a street accident, imitating now the old man who was run over, now the driver. Without implying that the accident was unavoidable, and without pretending to be either of them, he demonstrates what they did. Nor does he mind being interrupted: he can answer questions and then resume his performance.

> But you must not say: The man
> Is no artist. To erect such a barrier
> Between you and the world, only excludes you
> From the world. If you deny that he
> Is an artist, he could deny that you
> Are human, and that would be
> More shaming. Say rather:
> He is an artist because he is human.

The professional actor may be more skilful, but acting is

> As rudimentary to man as eating and breathing.[4]

Another writer might have chosen a market as a better example of the 'theatre which is played on the street', but Brecht had come to hate trading.

On 10 April 1929, less than two weeks after the opening of *Die Pioniere*, and the same month that text and score of the completed *Mahagonny* opera were sent to the publishers, he chagrined all the other members of his sexual collective by marrying Weigel. 'It couldn't be avoided,' he told Carola Neher, meeting her with flowers on her arrival in Berlin at the station, 'but it doesn't mean anything.' She then used the flowers as a weapon.[5] Elisabeth Hauptmann's reaction was the most extreme: she tried to kill herself, while Marieluise Fleisser announced her engagement to another writer, Helmut Drews-Tyehsen.

Brecht's decision to marry Weigel was a decision to form a new partnership, comparable to the one he once had with Bronnen, but still more one-sided. 'An actress is what one needs,' he had said. His instinct told him that, unlike Marianne Zoff, Weigel was unhysterical and stable, with an enormous capacity for devotion. She would willingly subordin-ate her own career to his. Forty years later she would say that during the fifteen years in which she did not act, 'the thought did not even occur to me the whole time, because there was really something to be done that was sensible, practical and important: to make it possible for Brecht to work and the children to grow up'. She was less feminine than Marianne Zoff or Paula Banholzer, but her masculine qualities must have appealed sexually to the side of Brecht that made him want to call Paula Paul, while Weigel's political faith may have been a factor in the feeling of security she gave him. To some extent he used her as a political conscience; later he would do this to two of the other women most important in his life, Margarete Steffin and Ruth Berlau. Max Frisch noticed that Brecht would behave quite differently, in political conver-sations, when Weigel was in the room. She always gave glib party-line explanations of anomalies, while he became visibly less open-minded.

She was, in both senses, a totally committed ally. Ernest Bornemann remembered enraging Brecht by comparing a passage in one of his plays with a passage in a Hemingway story. Brecht shouted: 'Get out, get out, get out. No, show me your identification first. Show me your passport so I know where you belong first. Then take your exit permit and go.' The shouting brought Weigel 'out of the kitchen, a frying pan in her hand; and without having the vaguest desire to know what the argument was all about, she joined her husband in shouting loyally: "Yes, go, go, go", swinging her frying pan like a sword'.[6] Whereas most writers diffuse energy on quarrelling with their wives, Weigel assiduously protected Brecht from people likely to waste his time. Her relationship with him was not primarily sexual, but she came closer than any of his other women to replacing his mother. Probably his ability to write such good parts for women roots back to these two. But, though it was not true that the marriage 'doesn't mean anything', it did not mean that he and Weigel would be sharing a flat and a double bed. In Berlin they lived separately; but after going into exile together they would live together – in the same house or flat but not in the same bedroom.

In the spring, when Kiepenheuer Verlag published the *Dreigroschenoper* lyrics, Brecht's old detractor Alfred Kerr denounced him for plagiarizing K. L. Ammer's German translation of Villon. On May Day Brecht was with Fritz Sternberg when they saw police shooting workers who were defying the ban on demonstrations. Brecht would go on talking about this, years later, when he was in exile, but in May he was preoccupied with defending himself in the *Börsen-Courier* against Kerr's accusation: 'I must declare truthfully that I unfortunately forgot to mention Ammer's name. This in turn can be attributed to my fundamental laxity in questions of intellectual property.'[7]

Aufricht naturally wanted to follow *Dreigroschenoper* with another Brecht-Weill musical, and Brecht promised something similar. Inspired by Shaw's use of the Salvation Army in *Major Barbara*, and – to judge from marks in the margin of Brecht's copy – by Lenin's remarks on the Army in his book on Feuerbach, Brecht sketched out a synopsis for *Happy End*, a comedy about gangsters and salvationists in Chicago. In the middle of May 1929, a few weeks after completing the *Mahagonny* opera,[8] he and Weill had set out in their new cars for the south of France, where they had worked so successfully on *Dreigroschenoper*. On the way Brecht crashed his Steyr but he had not lost his commercial flair: he arranged for it to be replaced with a new one in return for his participation in an advertising gimmick. An illustrated account of his 'instructive motoring accident' appeared in the magazine *Uhu*. He went back to work with Weill in Berlin, where Aufricht, who wanted to celebrate his twenty-ninth birthday with the opening of *Happy End*, had gathered the same team – Engel, Neher, Mackeben, with Carola Neher as the Salvation Army lieutenant, Heinrich George as a gangster and Peter Lorre as an oriental.

Finally rich enough to occupy more living space, Brecht moved close to the Kurfürstendamm, choosing an elegant five-roomed top-floor flat in Hardenbergstrasse. He and Weigel furnished it sparsely with low tables surrounded by low stools, and a rocking-chair in the corner.[9]

During 1929 and 1930 he was reading Marx, Engels, Lenin and (less thoroughly) Hegel: there are underlinings and annotations in his copies to prove it. He also read articles in Marxist periodicals summarizing the major classics of Marxism-Leninism. *Unter dem Banner des Marxismus* (October 1929) contains an essay by W. Adoratski – 'Lenin über die Hegelsche Logik und Dialektik'. In an indented quotation from Hegel, Brecht underlined the phrase: 'recognition of internal contradiction as driving forces for development', and the phrase: 'that contradictions dissolve themselves not into absolute nothingness but essentially only in the negation of their particular content'.

An article by Wilhelm Reich on 'Dialectical Materialism and Psycho-Analysis' in the same magazine is heavily annotated. Reich was defining the ego as 'a result of the impact of external reality on the willpower', and was looking for examples of the ways that opposites could unite in a phenomenon which would then be transformed into its opposite. Brecht put a mark against the assertion that 'whether an activity is rational or irrational is determined by its social function'.[10]

His Marxist convictions were hardening at this time, as Eisler says, into Leninism,[11] which sharpened his ambivalence towards commercial success. He began to divide his time between working on the story about gangsters and on *Lehrstücke* – didactic plays to expound communist doctrine. Plenty of plays had already been written to promulgate communist ideas, but Brecht found a new way of using dialectical materialism as a structural principle. The first *Lehrstück*, written for performance at the Baden-Baden Festival, was published in April 1929 by *Uhu*. Titled *Der Lindberghflug* (*The Lindbergh Flight*), it was a cross between a radio play and a cantata. Hindemith and Weill composed the music for alternate scenes and collaborated with Brecht on the script. The work was to be performed on the radio before being staged.

Flying was an experience that had been unavailable to Shakespeare and to Brecht's grandparents; the first solo flight across the Atlantic could be celebrated as exemplifying a human triumph over the hostile forces of nature. But it must be represented as a collaborative triumph, not a piece of heroism. The first draft lays great stress on Lindbergh's identity;[12] subsequently the airman presents himself in the most impersonal way Brecht could contrive, announcing his name, age, family background and nationality before cataloguing his equipment and summarizing the preparations that had to be made for the flight.

The forces of nature – fog, snow, rain – are personified, as is sleep, when the pilot sings a duet with its seductive contralto voice. In other sequences the writing aims at a newspaperish factuality. The fifteen scenes have titles like 'Throughout the flight all the American newspapers speak constantly of Lindbergh's luck.'

The first performance at the festival was on 25 July, and three days later it was followed by a sequel, *Das Badener Lehrstück vom Einverständnis* (*The Badener Didactic Play about Acquiescence*) which was set entirely by Hindemith, though he maintained that Brecht's socialist leanings had nothing to do with music.[13] Four airmen have crashed and need help. The question 'Whether Mankind helps Man' was projected on a screen. Human inhumanity is demonstrated in a series of episodes. Brecht and Hindemith stayed on stage throughout the performance. During the projection of a film prepared by Engel, showing stills of dead bodies, the audience became restive, Brecht ordered the speaker to announce: 'Repeat showing of the badly received portrayal of death'. The sequence was then repeated.

In another sequence a clown on stilts with long hands and a huge head kept complaining of pains. Two other clowns advised him to cut off the limbs that were hurting. (Brecht may have been thinking of the Biblical injunction about plucking out the offending eye, or he may have been remembering the clown he had seen hitting himself on the head, causing a huge bump, which he sawed off and ate. In Brecht's hands the business of sawing limbs off one by one becomes a vaudeville variant on the theme of dismantling the individual personality.)

The clown was played by Theo Lingen, who was now married to Marianne Zoff. He had been given a bladder of blood which he had to squirt.

For the audience that was really too much. And as they sawed my head off . . . it started the biggest riot I've ever seen in a theatre. Everything that wasn't nailed to the walls flew to the stage. My fellow-actors fled, and as I peered through my gauze shirt at the raging and yelling audience, I could see opposite me in the front row a dignified, white-haired gentleman sitting there perfectly calmly.

This was Gerhart Hauptmann, who had come at Brecht's invitation.[14]

The message of the play is that until the world is changed, real help is not to be expected. The pilot, who wants to be famous, is sent off the platform; the three mechanics, who willingly embrace anonymity, are praised for their acquiescence in the natural 'flow of things'. 'Who are you?' the chorus asks. 'We are nobody.'

Language and rhythms are biblical; the dismissal of the pilot from the stage – a symbolical annihilation – is like an excommunication. Communism is beginning to provide Brecht not just with an alternative morality but with a religion that promises a kind of redemption. Because they discard personal identity, the three mechanics are absolved by the chorus from death. They must march 'with us'. By battling against oppression they can help to change the world. They can survive, but not personally.

When Hindemith asked for a statement to be published in the score that the clown scene was optional, Brecht not only refused but introduced revisions that would have entailed alterations to the music. When he remained adamant, Hindemith withdrew his music, so Weill had to write new music for a new version, while the Badener piece received no further performances.

In his notes on *Lindbergh* Brecht stressed that it had 'no value if you don't learn from it. It has no artistic value to justify a production which is not meant for teaching.' The object was not to serve radio, but to change it. The performer should not identify with the character but remain detached. He should pause at the end of each line. Performance was exercise, a step towards the discipline which was necessary to freedom.[15]

Much of Brecht's success, both as a writer and as a man, was to develop out of his failure to complete his play about the egoist Johann Fatzer. As in the Fleischhacker play, he was trying to explain the economic collapse of 1917–19 and the failure of the revolution in the West. In the summer of 1927 he had made little headway; in the autumn of 1928 he was still complaining about the difficulty;[16] he had not abandoned it by the beginning of 1930, but the experiment represents his last attempt at a semi-autobiographical play. As in *Mann ist Mann*, a group of four soldiers is in danger of severe punishment. Listed as dead during the third year of the war, the crew of a tank stays in hiding. The men may be shot as deserters unless there is a revolution against the war. Fatzer, the strongest personality, seems dependent for his survival on the others, but he is pushed forward by their weakness, and eventually he can survive only by leaving them behind. At first Brecht identified with the wily Fatzer; the emphasis on his egoism came later, when Brecht introduced a chorus and an anti-chorus to judge him. The reversal parallels the swing against Baal.

One of the other soldiers, Koch (re-named Keuner), is given authority to liquidate the individualist: a theme Brecht will use in *Die Massnahme* (*The Remedial Measure*). The change of attitude and the change of dramatic style are inseparable: Brecht is experimenting in the play at eliminating the self in favour of the collective. Fatzer's guilt had centred on 'the fallacy that they could stop the war as individuals. So when they abandon the masses for the sake of survival, they have already lost their lives; they never find their way back to the masses.'[17] If Brecht was finding his way to the masses, it was by changing his dramatic style.

Undoubtedly his commitment was sincere, but he had been sincere in his partiality to simultaneous girl-friends. Could he lead a double life as a playwright? Rehearsals of *Happy End* were due to start at the beginning of August 1929, but Brecht was still at Utting, with the script unfinished, when Weill devised a stratagem: after sending Brecht a telegram to say that the production was cancelled, Aufricht left Berlin, taking both his wife and Lenya with him. Within two days Brecht was at the theatre. Aufricht and Lenya drove back from Warnemünde, taking turns at the wheel. Though the third act was still unfinished, Brecht was sufficiently reassuring for rehearsals to start, but he was introducing a new character, a female gangster boss known as the Fly – a part to be played by Weigel. So many of his lines were reallocated to her that Heinrich George walked out of the production, and he was replaced by Oskar Homolka. When run-throughs started, there was still no final act, and at one rehearsal Kurt Gerron had a shouting-match with Brecht. 'Without your fat belly you couldn't earn a living.' 'You were supposed to write a play, not come here and shit on the stage.'[18] Brecht then threatened to walk out unless the actor was disciplined. The rehearsal went on until four in the morning, but Brecht never completed the final act, and he rejected the detailed proposals Engel made for clarifying the plot.[19] When Engel walked out in protest, he took over as director. Engel returned before the opening and helped to construct a makeshift ending.

Brecht was trying to compromise between Marxist didacticism and showbiz. He involved Bernhard Reich and Asja Lacis in rehearsals, together with Slatan Dudow, a Bulgarian cinéaste he had consulted at Baden-Baden over the film sequences. All three criticized both script and production, which unsettled the actors. Having promised to write the third act in rehearsals, Brecht modulated into polemics, with Ford, Morgan and Rockefeller ironically pictured as saints. He refused to let his name appear on the programme as author, but when Weill insisted, agreed to take responsibility for the lyrics. Authorship was attributed to

Elisabeth Hauptmann, who was credited for adapting a story which was said to have appeared in the *J and L Weekly*, St Louis: 'Under the Mistletoe' by Dorothy Lane. It was not obvious at the time that this was a hoax – like the claim that Baal had been modelled on a mechanic – but after Brecht's death, Hauptmann admitted that she had not written the script.[20]

On the opening night the first two acts went extremely well. Two of the best Brecht-Weill songs were premièred – 'Bill's Ballhaus' and 'Surabaya-Johnny', and it looked as though the show would be another big success. But in the third act the Fly, discovering that one of the Salvation Army officers is her long-lost husband, proposes a merger between her gang and his organization: the world was too corrupt for any distinction to be made between thieves and those who beg for money. The audience became increasingly restless until Weigel's departure from script – presumably prearranged with Brecht – forced it into hostility. She shouted Marxist slogans and even read from a pamphlet.[21] It was only the final piece of audience provocation that had been rehearsed: what came down was not the curtain but two stained-glass church windows as hymnal music struck up – 'Hosanna Rockefeller'. But the number broke into raucous jazz. The audience reaction was tumultuous, but Brecht and Weigel had turned a potential success into a flop, which cost Aufricht 130,000 marks.[22]

In March 1929 the *Mahagonny* opera had appeared on Piscator's list of possible future productions, but almost a year elapsed between its completion in April 1929 and the Leipzig première in March 1930. There were several reasons for the delay. One was that after the collapse of *Happy End*, Aufricht was no longer eager to work with Brecht, while Brecht, who had little contact with Weill, was less concerned about *Mahagonny* than about the work he was doing with a more politically committed and more radical composer. Hanns Eisler, who knew him much better, saw himself as a messenger who was giving Brecht practical information about the working-class movement. At the same time the deteriorating political climate, though it made *Mahagonny* more relevant, made it harder to produce. Gustav Stresemann, the moderate who had steered Germany into the League of Nations, with a seat on the Council, died at the beginning of October 1929, and at the end of the month the Wall Street crash precipitated an international crisis. Brecht's urge to make a clean break with the past was no isolated phenomenon: millions of Germans were joining the Nazi party because Hitler was promising to make things vastly different when it seemed impossible to make things worse. The Nazis were hostile to much that was fashionable, including 'decadent' modernist art, which they associated with the Jews and with Negro jazz. When Weill was curious enough to attend a brownshirt rally in Augsburg, he was astonished to hear himself denounced, together with Albert Einstein and Thomas Mann, as a danger to the country. Unrecognized, he slipped away.[1]

Had Brecht and Weill refused to make compromises, the opera would have remained unperformed. When Dr Emil Hertzka, the Viennese music publisher, told them that no opera house would produce the brothel scene as it stood, a love poem about cranes and a cloud was interpolated. Finally a contract was signed with Gustav Brecher, director of the Leipzig Opera House, but Brecht's involvement with Eisler exacerbated his disagreements with Weill during rehearsals. Brecht wanted placards to be brandished during the finale, while Mahagonny burns, to satirize the bourgeois attitude to social problems; Weill's view was that the evils exposed in the opera were not peculiar to capitalism or to the bourgeoisie. Neher, who had not followed Brecht into Marxism, probably exercised a moderating influence. He was now based in Essen as production manager of the municipal theatres. The resultant slogans included 'For the Natural Disorder of Things', 'For Higher Prices' and 'For the War of All against All'. Not wanting the names and the references to be so American, Weill proposed German alternatives (Jakob Schmidt, Johann Ackermann) for Jack O'Brien and Jimmy Mahoney. The published score provides alternative names.

Before the show opened, Nazis were demonstrating in front of the opera house. Lenya, who was sitting with Weill's parents in the auditorium, noticed 'something strange and ugly' in the atmosphere: there was an 'electric tension around us'. One middle-aged man was seen later on simultaneously applauding and booing. Suddenly 'war cries were heard in the auditorium. Hissing, applause that sounded sinisterly like face-slapping.' One man produced a shrill whistling sound by blowing through a key, while his wife whistled through two fingers.[2] Women fainted, people shouted for the curtain to be lowered. By the beginning of the final scene, 'fist fights had broken out in the aisles, the theatre was a screaming mass of people; soon the riot had spread to the stage, panicky spectators were trying to claw their way out, and only the arrival of a large police force cleared the theatre'. At the following evening's performance, policemen lined the walls of the auditorium, and the houselights were left on.[3]

Two days later, when another production of the opera opened in Kassel, there seemed to be nothing communistic about the on-stage demonstration in the final scene: 'Mahagonny', as Weill put it, 'like Sodom and Gomorrah, falls on account of the crimes, the licentiousness and the general confusion of its inhabitants.'[4]

It was apropos *Mahagonny* that Brecht made a detailed and explicit formulation about epic theatre. Marx and Sternberg had convinced him that works of art were not only being conditioned by the network of publishers, newspapers, opera houses and theatres that mediated between the artist and the public, but being judged according to their value as material for the network. The intention in *Mahagonny*, he said, was that 'some irrationality, unreality and frivolity should be introduced in the right places to assert a double meaning'.[5]

Copying a lay-out device of Lenin's, Brecht contrasted epic theatre with dramatic theatre by listing the qualities of each in parallel columns. Instead of offering sensations and squandering the spectator's capacity for action, epic theatre demanded decisions from him and tried to stimulate his capacity for action. The premiss for dramatic theatre was that human nature could not be changed; epic theatre assumed not only that it could but that it was already changing.[6]

While Brecht's thinking became more rigidly Marxist, more austerely orthodox, *Dreigroschenoper* was scoring commercial success all over Europe. After the Paris production opened in October 1930, the 25-year-old Jean-Paul Sartre was one of many who got to know the songs by heart and often quoted the phrase 'Erst kommt das Essen und dann die Moral' ('First comes your stomach, and your conscience follows'). Throughout Germany the show was so fashionable that it set fashions: girls wanted their boy-friends to be more like Macheath, more gangster-ish.

Brecht and Weill had no difficulty in selling the film rights for 40,000 marks. Signed on May 1930, the contract guaranteed them full artistic control over the material, with extra payment for their involvement in adapting it. G. W. Pabst, who had directed *Die Büchse der Pandora* (*Pandora's Box*) – two of Wedekind's Lulu plays sandwiched into a film starring Louise Brooks – was engaged for the *Dreigroschenoper* film, with Leo Lania and Ladislaus Vajda (the scriptwriter for *Die Büchse der Pandora*) to write the screenplay.

In July 1930 Pabst and Lania went down to Le Lavandou, where Brecht was trying with Elisabeth Hauptmann to combine Salvation Army material with Chicago stockmarket material in a new play, *Die heilige Johanna der Schlachthöfe* (*St Joan of the Slaughterhouses*). It soon became evident that his new ideas for *Die Dreigroschenoper* were oriented to his new ideology and not to box office success. He produced a new title, *Die Beule* (*The Bruise*) and, collaborating with Slatan Dudow and Neher, a new story in which Peachum's organization is scaled up to a trust and Macheath's to a gang of 120. The guests at his wedding to Polly include dukes and a general, and the Queen's coronation is invaded by Peachum's beggars. A car chase culminates in Macheath's arrest, but he is bailed out by a bank which has been taken over by Polly and the gang. As in *Happy End*, Brecht was eager to blacken the banks.

If the film company had accepted the new story-line, much of Weill's music would have had to be scrapped, but the producer, Seymour Nebenzahl, offered Brecht full payment for his treatment, on condition that he withdrew from the film. His reaction was to sue the company for breach of contract, while Weill, angry that music by another composer was to be interpolated, joined forces with Brecht.[7]

They also collaborated on the next *Lehrstück. Der Jasager* (literally 'the yes-sayer') was based on the fifteenth-century Noh play *Taniko* (literally 'the hurling into the valley') by Zenchiku. Elisabeth Hauptmann had translated some of Arthur Waley's English versions into German. Her translation of *Taniko* follows Waley's, which alters the play's meaning and omits several sequences, including the last.[8] The senior pupils of a temple school are to go on a dangerous pilgrimage across the mountains, led by a Yamabushi monk, who is changed by Waley into a teacher. A junior pupil, whose father is dead, wants to go on the pilgrimage so that he can pray for his sick mother. He too becomes ill on the journey, and the pilgrims throw him into the valley, but the monk turns out to be a reincarnation of the Yamabushi sect's founder, and the boy is restored to life. This resurrection, which expresses Buddhist belief in reincarnation, is omitted by Waley, who makes the teacher submit reluctantly when his senior pupils insist on observing the ancient religious custom that anyone who fails on the journey must be hurled to his death. The boy acquiesces.

About three quarters of Brecht's script consists of Elisabeth Hauptmann's 1929 German translation of Waley's English,[9] but Brecht took the secularization even further. The school is no longer a temple school. The pilgrimage becomes a scientific expedition, and the boy is anxious to fetch medicine for his mother from physicians in the city beyond the mountains. (The idea may have derived from the illness of Brecht's mother, but little emotionality is involved.) In this altered context the ancient custom seems incongruous, but, at pains to demonstrate the necessity for self-sacrifice, Brecht makes the chorus speak in praise of acquiescence, and when the boy is asked, he agrees to die. Affectionately, the others execute him. ('Lean your head on our arms, just relax.')

After fumbling in successive attempts to shape his *Fatzer* material, Brecht had almost accidentally found a model he could use. The stylized story-telling of Noh drama offers a means of alternating between action and choric comment without any loss of clarity or intensity, while preserving unity without observing the Aristotelian unities. In most Noh dramas, action and emotion are not dramatized directly, but presented through a mixture of narrative and re-enactment. Noh drama deals with past events and the need for fatalistic acquiescence; Brecht's early didactic plays deal with the need for submissiveness toward the superior wisdom of the Party. Unlike the Japanese dramatists, Brecht never uses ghosts as narrators, though in his best didactic play, *Die Massnahme*, the central character is dead, and in all the didactic plays after *Der*

Jasager, he preserves the Japanese form and indirectness in language that is stylized but not mannered.

According to Elisabeth Hauptmann, he saw the troupe of Japanese actors which visited Berlin in October 1930 and again in January 1931 with a programme that included scenes from Kabuki plays. Ihering's review pointed out that unlike French or German actors, they could communicate the gist of their performance to an audience ignorant of the language. From action, gesture, facial expression, stage business, it was easy to understand a servant's lust for vengeance or a widow's gratitude to the avenger of her husband's murder. In his theatregoing, as in his reading, Brecht was interested primarily in what he could adapt. He made a fragmentary note on 'the Japanese technique of acting', saying it can be 'transported away and applied to conditions which are essentially different'.[10]

It was significant for him because he learnt that understanding of theatrical action should not depend on understanding of the spoken word: twenty years later, when he had his own company, he would maintain that acting should be intelligible to the deaf.

The first production of *Der Jasager* was premièred in Berlin at a school, the Zentralinstitut für Erziehung, on 23 June 1930. In May, during one of their normal choir practices, the boys of the school were told by the music teacher, Professor Martens, that they were going to perform an opera. When the text was read to them, the older boys were astonished, while the young ones did not understand why the boy had to die. The teacher was played by one of the boys, Otto Hopf, who found that 'these short, sharp, simple sentences aroused, first, a certain scepticism, but scepticism is always the first step towards conviction'. In rehearsal, despite the hot summer, the boys were excited by both music and text. Reviewing the performance, Brecht's old friend Frank Warschauer complained that 'these yes-sayers are strikingly reminiscent of the yes-men during the war. .... This school opera artfully insinuates a view of life containing all the evil ingredients ... of reactionary thinking founded on mindless authority.'[11]

Der Jasager was afterwards performed at a school in Berlin-Neukölln, a working-class district, where Brecht asked the teachers to report on the boys' reactions. He also arranged meetings to question schoolboys. Did they agree with the message? Did it coincide with their experience? Was the play suitable for performance in school? Their comments were so negative that he rewrote the play, multiplying the illness into an epidemic. The boy's death becomes a sacrifice of one for the sake of many – a point reminiscent of *Die Bibel*. He also wrote a companion-piece, *Der Neinsager*, about a boy who refuses to be sacrificed. In this play there is no epidemic and no reason for throwing him to his death except the ancient custom of sacrificing anyone who falls ill on the expedition. But this boy is no traditionalist: he says that from now on it should be customary to scrap old customs which are evil.

The most substantial of these *Lehrstücke* is the most austere, and a main factor in the evolution of *Die Massnahme* was Brecht's rapidly growing friendship with Hanns Eisler, whose brother, Gerhard, had been working for the Comintern in China. For six months Eisler was in Brecht's flat every morning from nine o'clock till one, scrutinizing the text, commenting, collaborating.[12]

Brecht never used the courtroom situation more imaginatively than in *Die Massnahme*. Instead of featuring a corrupt judge (as in so many other plays) or a judge like Azdak in *Der kaukasische Kreidekreis*, who incarnates folk wisdom, Brecht puts the chorus in the judicial role, making it representative – as he did in the Lindbergh play – of the Party's wisdom. As in the first version of *Der Jasager*, an important mission is endangered by one person: unless he dies, the others cannot go on. Four agitators have had to kill a comrade who was working with them in China. In re-enacting the events that led up to their decision, they take it in turns to play their victim – an ingenious dramatic device which deprives him of individual character, while implying that each of them sympathizes with him. De-individualization also features in the initiation sequence. Before setting out, they renounce their personal identity:

You are no longer yourselves – you no longer Karl Schmitt from Berlin, you no longer Anna Kjersk from Kasau and you no longer Peter Savich from Moscow, but all of you are nameless and motherless, blank leaves for the Revolution to write its orders on.

Unlike Lindbergh, and like his three mechanics, they are content to become anonymous. As a member of Piscator's dramaturgical collective, Brecht had insisted on the commercial value of his name, and in most of his plays much depends on identity, but in this text the rhythm of his prose registers strong approval for anonymity, lending glamour to something intrinsically unglamorous. He must have wanted to inspire in the audience a religious sense of duty, though he may have been unconscious of this intention. Certainly he was under the influence of biblical rhythms and reiterations:

Whoever fights for communism must be able to fight and not to fight, to tell the truth and not to tell the truth, to serve and refuse to serve, keep promises and not keep promises, take risks and avoid risks, be recognizable and unrecognizable. Whoever fights for communism has of all virtues only one: that he fights for communism.

The liturgically balanced phrases point to an affinity with T. S. Eliot, while the acquiescence to martyrdom parallels that of Becket in *Murder in the Cathedral*, which was written a few years later. In reaching for a discipline, Brecht has swung – both in form and in attitude – to the opposite extreme from *Baal*, though this, too, was influenced by the Bible.

The line 'Lean your head on our arms' is again used (as in *Jasager*) before the agitators shoot their comrade. He has proved incapable of subduing emotion to reason as determined by Party policy. Watching coolies whipped for slipping in the mud, he tried to help them instead of waiting for them to rebel. Instead of letting an innocent man be arrested for distributing subversive pamphlets, he drew attention to himself and his comrades by attacking a policeman. He refused to make friends with a capitalist who could have been useful in the fight against imperialism. (Obliquely Brecht wanted to justify the alliance formed by the Chinese communists with the Kuomintang.) And instead of preserving his anonymity, the young comrade continuously acted impulsively. In the earliest printed version of the play, he fell sick, like the boy in *Jasager*. His final and unforgivable error was to take his mask off. Communism appealed to Brecht – as Anglo-Catholicism did to Eliot – partly because it offered an alternative to egoistic preoccupations. Like Eliot, Brecht tried to remove all traces of autobiography from his work, and he was reticent in talking about his past. When Eisler was in Augsburg with him during 1929 or 1930, Brecht invited him to the house in Bleichstrasse, where he met Brecht's father and brother, but Brecht said nothing about his mother.[13]

To make the climax of *Die Massnahme* less brutal, Brecht added a sequence in which the young comrade consents to be killed. His features have changed since he put the mask on – devotion to the cause has altered his personality – but Brecht could not forgive him for taking off the mask that had relieved him of his identity, merging him into the collective. His sin is the same as the pilot's.

The main intention was to instruct through performance. Brecht wanted the play to be performed in schools, with children taking turns at each of the roles, and identifying successively with the conflicting viewpoints. In 1956 he told me that I was not entitled to criticize the play's moral values until I had acted as one of the four agitators *and* as a member of the Control Chorus. 'Then you have seen it from every angle, and only then may you judge.'[14] Judgement is always of the essence in Brecht's plays, which is one reason for the recurrence of courtroom scenes: drawn into taking sides, the spectator is being drawn into making a political judgement of his own.

The next didactic play Brecht started was *Die Regel und die Ausnahme* (*The Rule and the Exception*), in which, as in *Die Massnahme*, a communist court condones a murder. But it would have been bad propaganda to go on glorifying acts of violence – and, abandoning it, he started *Die Ausnahme und die Regel*, which deals with the injustice of a bourgeois law-court. The merchant is another bourgeois character denied any redeeming features, while the coolie is another proletarian character denied any flaws. Again the action involves a perilous journey – this time in Mongolia. The merchant dismisses his guide, suspicious that he has been too friendly towards the coolie. Carrying all his master's baggage, and unable to find his way without a guide, the exhausted coolie has good reason to feel resentful, but instead he offers to share his water with his master, who actually has more water than he admits. Guiltily apprehensive when the coolie approaches with a raised water bottle, the merchant shoots him dead.

In the courtroom scene Brecht returns to the device he had used in his schoolboy parable about the Balkan Wars, but this time the audience is roused to a higher pitch of indignation at the legal injustice: the verdict goes against the coolie's penurious widow. In spite of plentiful provocation, the man failed to attack his oppressor: how could the merchant have known that this man was exceptional?

Having rejected bourgeois ethics during his youth, and the ethic of theatrical professionalism in his work on *Happy End*, Brecht needed to feel that communism offered an alternative ethic, and when Hindemith, together with the other directors of the summer music festival in Berlin, refused to première *Die Massnahme*, Brecht turned to the alternative channel. He and Eisler sent a joint letter to the committee, withdrawing 'this important production' and making it over to workers' choral societies, amateur theatrical companies, school choirs and school orchestras. It was intended 'for those who neither pay for art nor are paid for it but want to create art'.

At the general elections, on 14 September 1930, the Nazis, who had previously held only twelve seats, won 107: 6,500,000 people had voted for them, making their party the largest in opposition to the SPD, which won 143 seats. Unemployment was to reach six million by 1932: economic hardship was working against moderation and liberalism. The Communists, who previously had 54 seats, now won 77, while on the streets clashes between Nazis and Communists became more frequent. On 13 October, the day a new Reichstag opened, Harry Graf Kessler wrote:

In the afternoon, on the Leipziger Strasse, the windows of Wertheim, Grünfeld and other department stores were smashed. In the evening on Potsdamer Platz demonstrators were chanting: 'Deutschland erwache', 'Jude verrecke' and 'Heil, heil', and were continually dispersed by police patrolling in vans and on horseback. ... The street scenes reminded me of the days just before the revolution, the same crowds, the same Catiline-like figures lounging about and demonstrating.[15]

At the *Dreigroschenoper* trial on Friday 17 October (when filming had already begun) the Nazis among the large and fashionable crowd in the public gallery could support neither the Marxist playwright nor the Jewish film producer.[16] Brecht's argument was that the audience expected the author's intentions to be accurately expressed. The counsel for the film company impugned his attitude to literary property by citing his plagiarism from Ammer's Verlaine translations. Enraged, Brecht tried to interrupt, and then stormed out of the court. After the judge had ruled that his case should be heard separately from Weill's, Weill won and he lost. But he received 16,000 marks compensation, and won a moral victory when the film ended up with a plot surprisingly close to the one he had proposed.

When he was invited to direct *Mann ist Mann* at the Staatstheater he introduced a song about the 'flow of things' to be sung by Helene Weigel as Widow Begbick; looking at the river, you are never looking at the same water – so long as your foot stays in the water, the waves that break over it will always be new ones.

The revision, as well as the production, brought the play closer to the *Lehrstücke*, and it ended with the words '*Quod erat demonstrandum*', spoken by Begbick. The presentation of the soldiers was partly derived from Kabuki and partly in line with the clown sequence in *Das Badener Lehrstück*. Theo Lingen (who had played the clown) was one of the three soldiers. Using masks, padding and stilts, Brecht made them into mutant specimens of humanity. Two were monstrously tall with overgrown fingers hidden by gloves, the other had exorbitantly wide shoulders, which made his arms look short. Galy Gay (Peter Lorre) was small and, at the outset, unequivocally human, but he was progressively dehumanized. As Ihering reported, 'he went from personality to mask, from an identifying acting technique to reporting, from the dynamic to the static'.[17] As in Kabuki, change was externalized by means of 'masks' formed with greasepaint and powder; Galy Gay had four successive masks in this production – a refinement of the idea used on the soldiers in *Eduard II*. The design was by Neher, whose drawings had so often helped Brecht when he was evolving characterization.

Talented though he was as a synthesizer, Brecht had not yet integrated the committed seriousness of the austere chamber-plays into a play on the same scale as *Dreigroschenoper*. *Die heilige Johanna der Schlachthöfe* results from an ambitious attempt to combine the two modes, bending dramatic tradition towards Marxist assumptions.

The use of blank verse to dramatize negotiations about the price of meat represents an ironic attempt at adapting a classical form to deal with the contemporary market-place.

> Do you remember, Cridle, how some days ago –
> We wandered through the slaughterhouse, it was evening –
> We stood before our new packing machine?
> Remember, Cridle, think of that great bull
> Who blond and big and dull looked up to heaven
> As he was killed: to me it was as though
> I died with him. Oh, Cridle, oh, our business
> Is a bloody one.

The stylistic inflation warns both actor and audience against being taken in: how much genuine emotion is there, if any, behind the show of compassion? 'The heroes are businessmen. They fall out over prosaic issues – profits – and take prosaic actions.... I am going to let these "heroes" speak in Shakespearian verse. This verse form rightfully belongs to them, for the enterprises of the dealers and brokers are no less consequential – a matter of life or death for tens of thousands – than the battles of generals in Shakespearian wars.'[1] The mixture of two kinds of language implies a contrast between two kinds of civilization: would it have been possible for heroic values to survive in an industrialized society? But Brecht's motivation, as in *Baal*, was partly parodistic: Schiller's St Joan play *Die Jungfrau von Orleans* (1800-1) is written in sub-Shakespearian blank verse.

In 1927, answering a questionnaire for the magazine *Filmkurier*, Brecht had been asked to say when in his life he had laughed loudest. His answer was: 'When I heard that Shaw is a socialist.' But in *Die heilige Johanna* he draws – for the second time – on Shaw's *Major*

Barbara, and also on *St Joan*, which was premièred in 1924. Shaw had taken the orthodox radical view of the Salvation Army as a tool used by capitalists to protect the survival of their system, but Brecht went back to Engels, who accuses Louis Bonaparte of importing from America salvationism, 'which fights capitalism in its religious way and so breeds an element of the primitive Christian class struggle, which can one day be quite fatal for the prosperous people who are today financing it'.[2]

To convince Johanna that working-class people are evil, the meat tycoon Pierpont Mauler arranges for her to be shown over the slaughterhouses, but the only dishonesty she encounters is the result of penury and desperation. The play Brecht started in 1929, *Der Brotladen* (*The Bread Shop*), assumed that all evil-doing had its source in oppression and poverty. As he wrote in a note, 'Our re-working of what is, classically speaking, tragic, must always refer back to the bread shop. Depriving a mother of her children – near the bread shop, a terrible blow. Idem, away from it – liberation. Freedom: a permanent necessity when one has bread in one's pocket, but no use when one is hungry.'[3]

After the Wall Street crash, the US had suspended its loans to Europe, which exacerbated the unemployment crisis in Berlin, intensifying Brecht's determination to find the roots of this suffering. His heroine in *Die heilige Johanna*, a lieutenant in the Black Straw Hats (Salvation Army), is no less resolute: 'I'm going to find out who's to blame for all this.' Brecht was collaborating closely with Elisabeth Hauptmann and Emil Burri, who both came to work in his studio every morning to discuss the new play, taking turns to type out dialogue and notes. Sometimes they brought with them sequences they had drafted; sometimes Brecht gave them ideas to develop before the next working session.[4] Most of the material stayed in his possession, and often he would work on it without them, revising and versifying what they had written. The other collaborator subsequently given a credit was a teacher, Hans Borchardt; Brecht also involved Bernhard Reich and the critic Walter Benjamin in detailed discussion of the work in progress. As soon as *Happy End* flopped, Brecht began talking to Reich about an alternative treatment of the Salvation Army material, and in the summer of 1930 Benjamin spent a good deal of time with Brecht and Burri in the south of France, preparing the play.

Six years Brecht's senior, Benjamin had gone to Russia when his academic career had been aborted by the rejection of his thesis on the origins of German tragedy. Together with Herbert Ihering and Bernard von Brentano, Benjamin and Brecht had been planning since about

January 1930 to launch a new periodical, *Krisis und Kritik*, to be published by Rowohlt. Georg Lukács came to one meeting, but Brentano lost his temper with him,[5] and in February 1931 Benjamin withdrew, having come to believe that a new periodical oriented to dialectical materialism would only be exploited by the bourgeois intelligentsia for its own purposes.

In Berlin Brecht was working simultaneously on *Die heilige Johanna* and collaborating with Slatan Dudow on a film, *Kuhle Wampe*: together with the thinking he had done about the screening of *Dreigroschenoper*, this helps to account for the film-like freedom of movement from one locale to another in *Die heilige Johanna*.

Apart from Shaw, his principal sources were Marx and Upton Sinclair. Brecht's copy of Marx's *Lohnarbeit und Kapital* (*Wage Labour and Capital*, ed. Kautsky, 1922) has markings in the margin against the paragraph which rejects the view that the cost of goods is determined by the cost of their production: it is the turbulent upward and downward movements of prices that determine production costs, and this is dangerous for bourgeois society. As in *Im Dickicht*, Brecht focused on the Chicago of Sinclair's *The Jungle*, taking over his reminder that it was possible for a worker in the slaughterhouses to fall into a boiling vat and be made into lard. In *The Moneychangers* Sinclair pointed to the central role of the stock exchanges in industrial activity and, appropriating this point without quite understanding it, Brecht made Mauler, in manipulating the Chicago meat market, depend on information received in a series of telegrams from New York. Brecht's assumptions about the economics of employment in the meat industry seem to derive mainly from Marx's explanation of the way that the demand for labour was determined by 'expansion and contraction of capital'. At the same time Brecht was trying to dramatize collective pressures through the actions of individuals. Whereas Piscator had depersonalized his drama, and Toller's had gravitated towards anonymity, Brecht makes one temperamental man – Mauler – dominate a huge area of commercial activity, while the failure of a general strike is represented as resulting from the action of one woman – Johanna – who fails to deliver a letter. A local Salvation Army leader then takes it upon himself to promise that his organization will, in future, encourage workers to be submissive.

Yet the play represents an important step forward. As the *Lehrstücke* had shown, Brecht was not quite in control of his religious inclinations, and unaware of why martyrdom appealed to him. But the case he makes out for violence is more cogent than in *Die Massnahme*. Johanna cannot go on condemning the violence advocated by the Communists,

> Only force can help, where force prevails, and
> Only human beings help, where human beings are.

Brecht's blank verse, which is flexible and muscular, adds resonance to his pronouncements, but though the lessons in market economy are put into the right mouths, he makes capitalists talk as though they accepted the premisses behind Marxist analysis and, as in *Dreigroschenoper*, he is writing directly and simplistically about human goodness and human evil. Mauler starts off by preaching about the poor:

> They're evil people. I have no feeling for them
> They are not innocent but are themselves butchers.

As in the *Lehrstücke*, the message is that man must change before the world can change.

Nevertheless, the play is powerful and moving, especially in its treatment of Johanna, the generous-spirited girl who – like the young agitator in *Die Massnahme* – causes only trouble by attempting to relieve suffering. In the final scene her declaration of her new-found faith in violence is outshouted by the capitalists and salvationists, who can now afford to canonize her because she has helped to preserve the *status quo*.

Early in 1931 the Soviet writer Sergei Tretiakov paid a long visit to Berlin. Brecht had met him the previous spring, when Meyerhold's production of his play *Scream, China* had arrived in Germany. Brecht had responded enthusiastically. The play struck him as 'finding totally new means of expression',[6] and in 1931, together with Walter Benjamin, he became interested in Tretiakov's 'factographic' technique, which had affinities with Piscator's production style. Tretiakov used facts, documents and interviews not just to provide information about social reality but to induce the desire to change it .

In the middle of May Brecht left Berlin, with Elisabeth Hauptmann and Emil Burri, going through Augsburg, Lausanne and Marseilles to Le Lavandou, where Kurt Weill, Lotte Lenya and Bernard von Brentano were holidaying. At the end of May Benjamin arrived, bringing a collection of Kafka's stories, *Beim Bau der Chinesischen Mauer*. Though Brecht was later to become impatient with Kafka's 'defeatism', his first reaction was positive.[7] In the middle of June Brecht travelled to Unterschondorf on the Ammersee, where Helene Weigel was staying with Stefan and the baby daughter born in October 1930 – Barbara.

Preparing the film *Kuhle Wampe* with Slatan Dudow, the novelist Ernst Ottwalt and the composer Hanns Eisler, Brecht was determined not to lose control of the material. Sacrificing their right to an advance, they formed a company establishing Brecht and Ottwalt as co-authors, Dudow as director, Eisler as musical director, and Robert Scharfenberg as producer. The film deals with the problems of worklessness. Kuhle Wampe is a huge camp, a city of tents for refugees from the depression. The fate of one family, the Bönikes, encapsulates the revolutionary message Brecht had been prevented from importing into the *Dreigroschenoper* film. The demoralized son kills himself, but the daughter's boyfriend makes his mind up to discover the causes of the misery. Thanks to proletarian cultural and sporting organizations – the same organizations financed the film – he works his way towards class-consciousness. The leading actors were Hertha Thiele and Ernst Busch. Busch had worked for Piscator in 1927, played a policeman, Smith, in *Dreigroschenoper*, and one of the agitators in *Die Massnahme*. The film was completed in the spring of 1932 – only to be banned by the censor.

Brecht again worked with Dudow and Eisler in his adaptation of Gorki's 1907 novel *Mother*. A dramatization of it had been commissioned by the Berlin Volksbühne and completed by the playwright Günter Weisenborn and the Volksbühne's dramaturg, Günther Stark; but when Weisenborn, an admirer of Brecht, submitted their version to him, he was told that they had not realized the novel's full theatrical potential. As so often, Brecht's inclination was not to revise or rewrite but to reconstruct. The Volksbühne withdrew from the project and so did Stark, but Weisenborn joined forces with Brecht, Dudow and Eisler. In the new version, titled *Die Mutter* (*The Mother*), the focus, as in *Die heilige Johanna*, is on the emergence of a revolutionary: the audience is expected to learn what Johanna and Pelagea Vlassova learn – that the only alternative to injustice and oppression is revolution.

Much of the dialogue is evangelistic, while, drawing on Gorki, Brecht skilfully uses action to reinforce passages of argument. Pelagea's conversion results partly from listening to Pavel, her revolutionary son, and his activist friends, who expound elementary economic principles to her, and partly from being subjected to the brutality of the Tsarist police, who vandalize her home while searching for a printing press. When she undertakes, soon afterwards, to distribute leaflets in a factory, she sees for herself how workers are treated. Brecht considered the adaptation as 'a sociological experiment in revolutionizing the mother'.[8] His play places less emphasis than Gorki's novel on the way her thinking has been conditioned by religion, but, as in *Die heilige Johanna*, a major climax centres on the rejection of God in favour of a new faith in revolutionary violence. After Pavel has been killed – the martyrdom theme persists – neighbours offer the bereaved mother their condolence, but she rejects the Bible they want to leave her, and the book gets torn during an argument between the landlady and the poor tenant she is about to evict, disregarding the biblical injunction to love your neighbour. Gorki's Pelagea is finally arrested; Brecht's is shot, carrying a red flag, during a demonstration.

But the syntax, the hard-edged simplicity and the forceful paradoxes in Luther's translation of the Bible are still exerting a strong influence on Brecht's style, especially in such secular hymns as 'Lob des Kommunismus' ('In Praise of Communism'):

> The stupid call him stupid, and the dirty call him dirty.
> He is against dirt and against stupidity.
> The exploiters call him a crime
> But we know:
> He puts an end to crime.
> He is no folly, but
> The end of folly.
> He is no riddle
> But the solution.
> He is the simple
> That is hard to achieve.

The straightforwardness and symmetry sweeten the paradoxes, while much depends on the offer of a faith as panacea. Communism's yoke is easy, its burden is light.

As a piece of theatre *Die Mutter* is more assured and less realistic than *Die heilige Johanna*. In 1930, contrasting epic with dramatic theatre, Brecht proposed 'narrative' as an alterative to 'direct action'. It was advantageous to be working, so soon afterwards, on adapting a prose narrative, and instead of translating it all into stage action, he let Pelagea tell some of the story in monologues. Other characters – the schoolmaster for instance – are given soliloquies, so the dialogue moves between two levels, while the interpolated songs introduce a third.

In November 1931 Brecht was approached by a director, Ludwig Berger: a new adaptation of Shakespeare's *Measure for Measure* was to be staged in January by the 'Gruppe Junger Schauspieler' (Group of Young

Actors). The group had been formed in November 1930 in protest against the programme planning and in order to stage revolutionary drama for proletarian audiences.[9] After working with Berger, Brecht deviated into constructing a new plot. Instead of abandoning the project when the group withdrew, he went on working. Shakespeare's plot was cut back into serving as a base for *Die Rundköpfe und die Spitzköpfe (Roundheads and Sharpheads)*. He was writing about the rise of Hitler as he once had about the Balkan War – by building an allegorical superstructure on a parable.

Shakespeare's Duke becomes a Viceroy whose political behaviour is conditioned (as Hindenburg's might have seemed to be) by his private interests as a landowner. Shakespeare's Angelo is replaced by a Hitler figure who is brought in to avert the crisis threatened by '*Die Sichel*' (The Sickle), a Communist organization which is inciting the tenant farmers to rebel against extortionate rents. Racism will work as a diversionary strategy. In the country of Yahoo there are two physical types, the Tschuchen, who have round heads, and the Tschichen, whose heads are pointed. Angelas at first wins a great deal of popular support by blaming all the country's difficulties on the Tschichen – he intervenes during a lawcourt sequence in favour of a round-headed tenant farmer, whose sharp-headed landlord is condemned to death. But the landlord, de Guzman, has a beautiful sister, Isabella, who, like Shakespeare's Isabella, is about to go into a convent, and Brecht retains from *Measure for Measure* both the deputy's offer to spare the brother's life in return for the sister's favours, and the bed-trick in which the virgin's chastity is reprieved by substituting, under cover of darkness, the body of another woman who had previously been the deputy's mistress. In his sexual greediness Angelas is more like Goering than Hitler, whom he does resemble, though, in his demagoguery and his fanatically racist interpretation of materialism.

Brecht satirizes the roundhead tenant farmers who – seduced by the prospect of paying no more rent to sharp-headed landlords – forget the need for solidarity with sharp-headed tenants. While working on the play Brecht was writing to ask the political theorist Karl Korsch what methods and constructions of Marxism-Leninism had taken on an ideological character. And what experience had the working class had of exploiting its industrial power politically? The implication is that racism diverts vital energy from the essential conflict between rich and poor. Brecht had faith in the Communist dogma that international capitalism was fomenting anti-Semitism in order to deflect energy from the class struggle, while Hitler is presented as no more than a puppet manipulated by industrial tycoons.[10] The seventeen million people who were to vote for Hitler in March 1933 were not primarily industrialists. In 1930, 28.1 per cent of Nazi Party members were manual workers, and a further 25.6 per cent were salaried employees.[11] Nor could Hitler be removed, as Angelas could, once the danger from the left had receded.

Two of the scenes are set in lawcourts, an appropriate setting for the kind of public discussion Brecht wanted to write. One of his ideas was that a new theatre should be built in Berlin, constructed like a lawcourt, and each evening two famous trials would be recreated: 'For instance the trial of Socrates. A witch trial. The trial of Georg Grosz, who was prosecuted for blasphemy because of his cartoon "Christ in a Gasmask".'[12]

Since *Happy End*, Ernst Josef Aufricht had been forced to sell the Theater am Schiffbauerdamm, but the cabaret star Trude Hesterberg wanted to play Begbick in *Mahagonny*, and a rich banker was sufficiently enamoured of her to finance the project, with Aufricht as producer. They took the Theater am Kurfürstendamm. Neher was not only designing but co-directing with Brecht; Lenya was to play Jenny and Harald Paulsen to play Jimmy Mahoney. Weill agreed to make substantial cuts in the score, but with Alexander von Zemlinsky, Schoenberg's brother-in-law, as musical director, there was no danger of musical vulgarization.

Rehearsals widened the rift between Brecht, who refused to be a mere librettist, and Weill, who refused to subordinate his music to the dialogue. They both brought their lawyers to the theatre. Once, after being photographed with Weill, Brecht knocked the camera out of the newspaperman's hands. As Weill walked away, Brecht called him a 'phoney Richard Strauss' and threatened to throw him down the stairs. Knowing that Brecht must somehow be kept away from rehearsals, the Machiavellian Aufricht offered 3,000 marks towards a production of *Die Mutter* by the Gruppe Junger Schauspieler with Weigel in the lead. 'My gamble paid off. Brecht gave priority to the cellar-theatre and left us in peace upstairs with *Mahagonny*.'[13]

Rehearsals for *Die Mutter* started in December with Ernst Busch and Theo Lingen in the cast. Nominally the director was Emil Burri, but as usual Brecht usurped – and Neher designed, using photographic projections.

> A few indications
> Set the stage. Some tables and chairs.

> The indispensable sufficed. But photographs
> Of the great adversaries were projected on screens
> behind and quotations from socialist classics
> Painted on cloth or projected ...

With his hostility to mystique, Brecht believed that amateurs and professionals should work together, and one of the amateurs he used in *Die Mutter* was Margarete Steffin, a slight girl of twenty-three with the liveliness that was often a concomitant of tuberculosis. She played the servant girl in the scene about the collection of metal for the war effort. Brecht had been drawing on memories of attempts to organize school-boys at the Augsburger Realgymnasium and, endowing Pelagea with something of his own guile in manipulating other people, he makes her succeed in discouraging other women from contributing to the collection. A working-class girl who had joined the communist youth organization while still at school, Margarete Steffin could be used as a touchstone for the validity of emendations to the script. He gave her a monosyllabic nickname, 'Muck': *mucken* is to grumble or sulk, and the allusion was to her characteristic reaction if he put his hand under her skirt during rehearsal.

> Angry, remote, you sit facing me.
> 'How dare he, a complete stranger?'
> And my astonishment is not yet over
> When your growing pleasure gets quite visible.
> Still remote you copy down new dialogue
> And suddenly reach out to take my hand.

She was living on the edge of Berlin, in Zehlendorf, and she could not risk letting him stay for long in her room.

> Quickly despatched, he seemed unwelcome
> To have him there seemed really unpleasant.
> So the urge to be there slowly left him.
> All desires now seemed to him quite crude
> And his urgency now felt indecent.[14]

After opening at the Wallner theatre on 12 January 1932, the company went on to give private performances for works councils and delegates of various radical and proletarian organizations.

In Berlin freedom was visibly being eroded by the Nazis, and in *Die Mutter* – especially in the illegal printing scene and the sequences in which Pelagea Vassova outwits the guard at the factory and the warder in the prison – hints were being thrown out to the audience about how to defy a totalitarian regime. Questionnaires were distributed at each performance, and changes made to the text according to points that arose. The economic crisis had emptied many theatres, putting actors out of work. To make the production as mobile as possible, Neher had designed a simple set consisting of canvas or sacking stretched on a metal framework, and a big screen for photographs, slogans and subtitles to be projected. Decor and props could be packed into one car. But the only way Brecht could devise to signal for the slide to be changed was to make the scenery-painter sit in the front row of the audience with a washing-line in his hand. When he pulled it, a bell sounded backstage. The intention had been to tour working-class districts, but in February 1932 the police banned the production as 'not in keeping with fire regulations'. The actors tried to defy the ban, but performances were constantly interrupted.[15] After one, Weigel was invited to meet a group of women, who were disappointed that she was so young, but asked her whether in the current situation she recommended direct propaganda such as Vlassova used in the copper collection sequence.

In the first scene Weigel stood in the centre of the stage and, making no attempt to characterize, spoke Vlassova's lines as if she were telling the story in the third person. And when she tried to discourage the revolutionaries, she 'allowed her own exuberance to shine through the character's anxiety'. She made good use of the elongated vowel sound in 'Jaa' at the end of Scene 12 when talking to workers who refuse to accept leaflets from her. 'Her posture bowed (an old woman) the actress raised her chin high and smiled, using head-voice to pronounce the long drawn out word quietly, as if she understood the temptation to let things drift. ...' 'She was more playfully relaxed than ever,' wrote Ihering in his review. 'It was not only masterly, it showed that certain acting talents are released only in this style.' Alfred Polgar wrote: 'Remarkable how Mutter Weigel, the further the play advances and the more she ages, the younger she becomes. (Ideological rejuvenation?) She almost verges on playfulness.'[16]

Though Brecht took enormous pleasure and possessive pride in her artistry, she had to realize that it could not bring her closer to him emotionally. She was already expert at repressing jealousy, but found it hard to tolerate the intimacy with Margarete Steffin, who inspired fiercer passion than Elisabeth Hauptmann ever had, while collaborating with him no less closely on his writing. Affectionate but tough, positive but stringent, Steffin functioned like a proletarian conscience grafted on to a middle-class writer.

Although Weigel had borne him two children, Brecht found he could keep his distance and could explain himself to her in writing: 'Out of small psychic disturbances, which could have many sources and are mostly inexplicable, arising partly from misunderstandings, partly from exhaustion or irritability, caused by work, and so coming from outside, an incurably bad mood begins. I then can't avoid an unhappy and certainly unpleasing tone of voice, and you make unfriendly or tragic faces.' Urging her not to allow the physical to be determined by the psychic, he claimed that he felt better disposed to her than he seemed, even during quarrels. Giving so much of his energy to his work, he dreaded exhausting rows. Other people might need to say hello on arriving, say goodbye on leaving, articulate personal feelings, celebrate birthdays and make statements about how happy or how miserable they were. But 'it would be much pleasanter to avoid all this. What do you think?' (These were the norms of his behaviour with Eisler: they never shook hands or greeted each other or said goodbye.) In another letter, probably written soon afterwards, he protests against her refusal to let Steffin live with them. 'For one thing, her illness wasn't infectious.' Weigel should not make too much of the affair: 'I love you, and no less than I always have.'[17]

Max Frisch noticed how it was impossible to display warmth in Brecht's presence. He used the same vocabulary to express toleration or respect or affection, as if he were clamping down on a sentimental streak in his temperament. He hated demonstrations of familiarity and, unlike most men, behaved in exactly the same way when women were present.[18]

He had learnt how advantageous it was to give no sign of feeling even an occasional twinge of guilt, and it must have been useful, in the long relationship with Weigel, to have the clouded political horizon as a distraction from the domestic front. His verse reflects unfeigned outrage at the failure of the German Socialist Party (SPD) to stop workers from drifting into the Nazi Party. That white terror should not be countered by red terror was a liberal idea that induced acquiescence to the rise of Nazism. The workers might have been willing to fight, if only a united front could have been formed.[19]

Brecht had been frustrated in his efforts to launch *Die heilige Johanna* on the stage, but in April a radio production starred Carola Neher – Brecht had from the outset had her in mind for Johanna – and Fritz Kortner.

Nor had Brecht succeeded in having *Kuhle Wampe* screened. After it had been banned in March by the Berlin censor, the radical press agitated for it to be released, and on 11 April Ernst Toller and Herbert Ihering were among the speakers at a protest meeting. Another was organized by the 'Neue Filmgruppe' of the Junge Volksbühne and the 'Liga für unabhängigen Film' (League for Independent Cinema). This time Brecht, Eisler, Dudow and Ottwalt were among the speakers. On 21 April, when the censor reconsidered the film in a revised version, permission was granted for it to be shown, provided that further cuts were made. The film was premièred in Moscow during May, and Brecht went there, together with Dudow. They were greeted at the station by Tretiakov, Piscator, the Reichs and a bevy of photographers. Reich was now Vice-Chancellor at the University of Theatrical Arts, but he was living, with Asja and their child, in a single room divided into two parts. Brecht spent the evening there. 'Eggs, bread, butter, tea, caviar.'[20]

Piscator had arrived in 1932 to make a film which was not to be finished until 1936 – *The Revolt of the Fishermen of Santa Barbara*. He struck Brecht as 'feeling very persecuted, but he is well looked after. Complains about the lack of organization – rightly, but he intervenes too little, relies on other people and gets left alone, instead of proving himself to be reliable.' Brecht went to see the thousandth performance of *Turandot* at the Vakhtangov Theatre in a production that was thirteen years old. Tretiakov, who showed him around Moscow, seemed pro-prietorially proud of everything. 'They're his soldiers, his lorries. But, unfortunately, not mine.'[21] Brecht went with Asja Lacis to see Alexander Tairov's production of *Dreigroschenoper*, which left him unimpressed. At the end of the month *Kuhle Wampe* was given its first public performance in Berlin.

In the summer, as usual, Brecht left Berlin, going back with Weigel and the family to Unterschondorf on the Ammersee, and to Utting, which he liked so much that he bought a house there. 'Roughly in the middle of the garden stand wonderful pine trees, almost black. It is like stepping into a small forest. They surround a rather dark carp pond.'[22]

Having consulted Karl Korsch while writing *Die Rundköpfe*, Brecht made his acquaintance on returning to Berlin in the autumn. A political theorist who had been expelled from the Party, Korsch was hostile to Lenin's insistence on materialism, and the ensuing Soviet rejection of the subjective dimension in the dialectics of change. He hated the system in which centralized bureaucracy counted for everything, individual conscious-ness for nothing. He was trying to evolve a new scientific method, and in November he started a course of eight lectures on Marxism at the Karl-Marx-Schule in Neukölln. Together with Alfred Döblin, Brecht attended not only the lectures but discussions in an Alexanderplatz café and in Korsch's Tempelhof flat.

Brecht wanted to form an association ('Gesellschaft für Dialektik') with the object of arriving at a new dialectical formula. A study group began to meet in Brecht's studio, involving, besides Elisabeth Hauptmann, Slatan Dudow and Bernard von Brentano, Korsch himself and several of his associates – Hanna Kosterlitz, Paul Partos and Hans Langerhans. Brecht was critical of Korsch for wanting 'to cut the umbilical cord of Leninist ideology and for placing too much faith in the proletariat', but agreed with him that the German Communist Party had been too submissive in its relationship with Moscow. Brecht was to remain dependent on Korsch for explanations of Marxist aesthetics: 'You will go on being my teacher for life.'

Earlier in 1932 Hindenburg had won 19.4 million votes against the Nazis' 13.4 million, but after attempting to illegalize Hitler's SS and SA, Brüning's government resigned at the end of May. Franz von Papen became Chancellor, with a cabinet of reactionary aristocrats and bureaucrats. The SS and SA were allowed to kill people in broad daylight: von Papen's only reprisal was to depose the Socialist Prussian premier on 20 July for being incapable of maintaining order. Hitler's position was further strengthened by the elections at the end of July, when the Nazis, who had had only 107 seats in the Reichstag, won 230, becoming the largest Party, though without commanding a majority. Brecht and Eisler were among the artists who protested in a political revue called *Wir sind ja sooo zufrieden (Oh Yes We're Sooo Satisfied)*.[23]

Before von Papen's regime was overturned at the end of 1932, reparations were abandoned, and Germany was allowed parity in armaments. It was the army that finally took control when General Schleicher replaced von Papen. Determined to keep Hitler from power, Schleicher tried to establish an alliance with the left, but von Papen, aiming to effect a comeback, stage-managed an alliance between the Junkers, the industrialists and the Nazis.

Though Arnolt Bronnen had veered rightwards, Brecht remained on good terms with him, as he did with many reactionary artists and intellectuals, including Rudolf Schlichter and Ernst von Salomon. At Brecht's New Year's Eve party, these three were among those who drank to a bloodless Fascist putsch. By January 1933 it was obvious that Hitler would soon be in power, and when the former Soviet commissar for education, Anatoly Lunacharsky, came to Berlin for an eye operation, Brecht mentioned that he might soon have to emigrate. It had been in the Party's interest, as well as his own, that he had worked for it as a non-member, but he had probably been on the Nazis' blacklist ever since his poem about the marching corpse. Even in exile, said Lunacharsky, he could go on writing plays.[24]

Observers outside Germany still expected the army to check Hitler's rise to power, but the officer corps was tired of intervention in parliamentary politics. Hindenburg would have preferred to have von Papen as Chancellor, but he would have been powerless without the support of the Nazis, which could be won only by making their leader chancellor. On 30 January Hindenburg gave his consent.

Hitler insisted on the immediate dissolution of the Reichstag, with new elections to follow in March. During February, Goering, as Prussian Minister of the Interior, unceremoniously made the police subordinate to the SS and SA. And on 27 February 1933 the Reichstag building was burnt. The communists were blamed, but the fire was probably organized by the SA and the SS in order to give the Nazis a pretext for the arrests which followed.[25] During the night of the 27th, 4,000 communist officials and Party members were rounded up, together with writers and intellectuals who had resisted Nazism. Brecht was clever enough not to be at home. He was in the private clinic of a friendly doctor – possibly for an operation or possibly because it was a safe place. Without returning to his studio he went to the flat of Peter Suhrkamp, the publisher, who helped him to escape with Weigel and Stefan to Prague – a journey they could make without visas.[26] Their two-year-old daughter Barbara was in Augsburg with Brecht's father.

Austria was still independent, and they went to Vienna, where Weigel's family was living. There they met Eisler, who had just arranged for a Viennese production of *Die Massnahme*, while Peter Suhrkamp and Fritz Sternberg put Brecht in touch with Viennese publishers. It was obvious that none of them could go back to Berlin in the near future; it was not obvious that Brecht would stay in exile until he was fifty.

Part Three

SCANDINAVIAN EXILE

Exile was going to make Brecht react to the passage of time in a new way. In Berlin, as in Munich and latterly in Augsburg, he had been alone only when he wanted to be, and no writer had done more of his work collaboratively. He liked to work alone in the mornings and with collaborators after lunch.[1] In Berlin, even before *Die Dreigroschenoper*, he had been writing scripts with a view to immediate production, just as initially he had written verse he could perform immediately to friends. Now he would have to live in countries where few people spoke the same language.

In Vienna and Zürich language would not be a problem, but of the people he observed in Viennese coffee-houses he would later write: 'Most of them did not give the impression of doing much, but it seemed certain that whatever they did was done principally in order to collect opinions about it.... The opinions were collected so that they could be exchanged.' He never needed chit-chat, but he always needed company.

In March 1933, hearing that Feuchtwanger and Döblin were both thinking of settling in Zürich, he left Weigel in Vienna to explore the possibility of joining them. In Zürich he was talking on the telephone in his hotel bedroom to Alfred Döblin when a voice shouted through the wall: 'Is that Brecht?' He shouted back: 'It's possible.'[2] In the room next door was Kurt Kläber, editor of *Linkskurve* and a Party member – Brecht had met him through Bernard von Brentano. The novelist Anna Seghers had also come to Zürich, and they all needed somewhere to live. After a few days in a hotel at Lugano, where he met Feuchtwanger, Brecht accepted an invitation from Kläber and his crippled wife, who wrote fairy-tales, to stay at their house in Carona, an isolatèd village on Lake Lugano. He searched unsuccessfully for a house in the Ticino, where the Kläbers had for several years had a holiday home, but he soon summoned Weigel to take over the job of house-hunting and to arrange for their furniture and possessions to be sent on from Berlin.

He enjoyed mornings spent in the Kläbers' garden, reading the papers and discussing the news. 'One digests things better with other people, and things are now pretty indigestible.' But he did not want to live in

Carona without a car. He would have preferred to settle in Zürich, but it was too expensive, and so, according to Brentano, was Basle. Meanwhile Brecht longed for the presence of Anna Seghers and her economist husband, Johann Lorenz Schmidt-Radvanyi: 'Schmidt is no Marx, but all the same. ...'[3]

It should not have been hard to guess the Nazis might try to use the two-year-old Barbara as a means of luring him back to Berlin. Thanks to an Englishwoman called Anderson, who was doing welfare work in Vienna, her parents learned she was in danger. Miss Anderson offered to smuggle the child out of Germany, and on 1 April Barbara was picked up outside Augsburg and put on a train that carried her safely to Switzerland.[4]

The problem of where to live was still unsolved when Brecht received an invitation to Paris where Kurt Weill had been commissioned to create a ballet for the Viennese dancer Tilly Losch. An illegitimate grandson, it is said, of King Edward VII, her English husband, Edward James, had made a financial arrangement with George Balanchine, who had formed a dance company, Les Ballets 1933, and agreed to tailor one of his new ballets for her. Like Weill, Brecht had left most of his possessions in Berlin; the books that he constantly kept with him were Hašek's *Schweyk*, a German anthology of Arthur Waley's translations from the Chinese, *Lebensweisheit des Confucius im alten China*, Voltaire, Virgil, Terence, and Ovid's *Metamorphoses*.[5]

He settled into a small left-bank hotel and, when Aufricht appeared, tried to interest him in the idea of a theatre modelled on a lawcourt. Why not set up a Theatre of Judgement to stage trials of prominent public malefactors, classical and contemporary? Nero could be arraigned for burning Rome and Goering for burning the Reichstag.

Refusing to write a mere scenario, Brecht insisted that a ballet could have songs in it, and *Die sieben Todsünden der Kleinbürger* (*The Seven Deadly Sins of the Petty Bourgeois*) pivoted on the notion of having a singer and a dancer as sisters. Anna 1 tells the story, while Anna 2 dances it. Brecht drew on material he had collected for *Joe Fleischhacker* and *Dan Drew*, while, as in his *Hauspostille*, he subverted conventional values: the seven sins are shown to be bourgeois inventions. There is nothing evil about a girl's appetites, but the healthy spontaneity of the dancing Anna is subjugated by the calculating Anna who is obedient to the moralizing of the petty bourgeois family, which cares for nothing except success and security. To buy a house for her parents, Anna takes only rich lovers and lucrative jobs. Once again the setting is a mythical

America, and once again the pattern is of rustic innocence – Anna comes from Louisiana – corroded by life in the big city. The premiss is that industrial civilization drives the two sides of the self into disharmony. Brecht will return to this idea in *Der gute Mensch von Sezuan* (*The Good Woman of Setzuan*), making the good woman pose as her uncle to protect herself from the consequences of her own generosity. Effectively, like Anna, she is splitting herself, and, as in the early work, Brecht is suggesting that there is no coherence or consistency in personality.

Weill used four male voices for the mother, father and two sons who moralize spuriously – the mother is sung by a bass. The ballet was premièred on 7 June 1933 at the Théâtre des Champs-Elysées, with Losch and Lenya as the two Annas. Audiences were unenthusiastic; Serge Lifar's comment was 'C'est de la pourriture de ballet' ('This is ballet gone rotten'). Undeterred, Edward James translated the libretto into English; *Anna-Anna*, the new title, would be less offensive to the middle-class London public. When it opened at the Savoy, Weill was able to report (with some exaggeration) that it was 'the great success of the season and furthermore Lenya is a great hit'.[6]

Brecht's first visit to Paris did not induce the euphoria that Berlin had thirteen years earlier, but he played with the idea of settling in Paris, and he enjoyed himself still more in May, when Margarete Steffin arrived. He tried to get work in the film industry, and he discussed with Aufricht a production of *Die Rundköpfe und die Spitzköpfe* – its relevance to the situation was now obvious – but none of these prospects was to materialize.

Weigel stayed in Vienna with the children until an invitation arrived from a kindly, 61-year-old Danish novelist she had known for fourteen years. Karin Michaëlis lived on Tuno, a small island south-east of Aarchus, north of Fyn, the second largest island. In the third week of June 1933, Brecht travelled out to join them there. Ernst Ottwalt and his wife had also arrived as refugees, and since Whitsun, Karin Michaëlis had had another house guest – Hans Henny Jahnn, author of the play Brecht had decimated for Bronnen to direct. The two men did not have much to say to each other.

Brecht soon decided to settle in Denmark. 'Switzerland is too expensive, has no cities, and is a theatrical set (but without performers).' Karin Michaëlis helped him to find a house in Skovbostrand, a village near Svendborg, on Fyn. His father and Weigel's both contributed. The contract was signed at the beginning of August.

Resigned (more or less) to living in exile, Brecht did not abdicate from political activity, although Weigel had signed a declaration that in Denmark he would. In June he had written to Johannes Becher, Secretary of the Bund proletarisch-revolutionärer Schriftsteller (League of Proletarian and Revolutionary Writers). Though not a member, he suggested that a conference should be held 'to establish definitively the aims and methods of our future work'. Left-wing bourgeois writers should be made aware 'of lacking a stand and of their defencelessness', and they should be educated politically.[7]

Dreigroschenoper was not the only work of Brecht's to have been produced in Denmark. *Trommeln in der Nacht* had been staged in Copenhagen, *Der Jasager* had been published, and *Mahagonny* was due to open at the end of the year, but his name was not familiar to the public. The playwright Svend Borberg took responsibility for introducing him in a series of newspaper articles, and translated *Die heilige Johanna* in the hope of having it produced. One of the leading actresses at Copenhagen's Theatre Royal, Bodil Ipsen, wanted to play Johanna.

On the west side of the house in Skovbostrand was a stable that could be enlarged to make a study. Weigel enlisted the help of a young architect, Mogens Voltelen, and one day he arrived with a strikingly attractive 27-year-old actress, Ruth Berlau. Until the house was ready, the Brechts were living in a cottage near Karin Michaëlis's house, and, always willing to cook for guests, Weigel invited Voltelen and Berlau to eat. Berlau had played Anna when *Trommeln* had been produced at the Theatre Royal, but she had since been more involved in amateur agitprop productions. By forming a radical company of her own she had caused something of a stir, partly because her husband, Dr Robert Lund, was an eminent doctor whose books were translated into several languages. She was twenty years his junior. She had also made a bicycle trip through the Soviet Union and published a rapturous description.

She was surprised when Brecht got up from the meal, compote in hand, to withdraw from the room without a word of explanation, but when he emerged from his siesta, she told him about her Workers' Theatre. His advice was that she should buy a cinema projector for it. From the beginning they spoke to each other in the second person singular, but she did not yet know how rarely he used this form.[8] She was thinking of translating *Die Mutter* into Danish and directing an amateur production. He said he had no spare copies, but showed her his working copy. It was not until she had left that he discovered she had taken it with her.

*　　*　　*

During the second week in September he went back to Paris, where he had left Margarete Steffin, who was helping to compile a selection of his poems. He now sold it to a new publishing house founded by Willi Münzenberg.

Many of the people Brecht wanted to meet in Paris had not yet returned from their summer holidays, so he went to see Feuchtwanger, who had settled in Sanary-sur-mer, as had several other literary refugees from Nazism, including Franz Werfel. In 1930 Feuchtwanger had published *Erfolg* (*Success*), a *roman-à-clef* in which Hitler appears as Rupert Kutzner, Brecht as Kaspar Pröckl, and Ludendorff as General Vesemann. The 1932 novel *Der jüdische Krieg* (*The Jewish War*) was ostensibly about Josephus and the Jews in Roman times, but actually about the present situation. Feuchtwanger had obtained extremely good terms for his new novel *Die Geschwister Oppenheim* (*The Oppenheims*) which was to be published in Amsterdam. It was about the current Nazi persecution of the Jews. He now had a car, a secretary and a married couple to look after his house and garden, so it was easy to convince Brecht that for German writers in exile the novel was a useful medium.

One of the partners in Querido, Feuchtwanger's German-language publishing house in Amsterdam, was Fritz Landshoff, formerly a co-proprietor of Kiepenheuer Verlag, which had published Brecht's series of *Versuche* (*Explorations*). Another Dutch publisher, Allert de Lange, had a German section, and two other former employees of Kiepenheuer were working for it, Hermann Kesten and Walter Landauer. Landshoff, Kesten and Landauer came regularly to Paris, looking for émigré German writers and offering a monthly retainer. Besides signing a contract, Brecht offered Kesten a 'pact of literary friendship' such as he had concluded with Feuchtwanger and Döblin. To Kesten he explained that he was not so much a writer as a 'teacher of behaviour', and that, as a Marxist, hostile to bourgeois civilization, he was prepared to undermine the whole economic and literary existence of his opponents, but he was also extremely helpful to friends – Caspar Neher, for instance. Kesten indignantly rejected the proposal.[9]

By writing a novel Brecht would be able to develop the narrative he had proposed for the film of *Dreigroschenoper*, and to clarify his feelings about material conceived before his conversion to Marxism. After the success of the show, a *Dreigroschenroman* would appeal to publishers and, aiming at the highest possible advance, he whetted the interest of both Münzenberg and Allert de Lange, so as to play one off against the other.

His attempts to penetrate into the French film world were unsuccessful, although Slatan Dudow, who had formed an alliance with Jacques Prévert, was directing a political feature film, *Seifenblasen* (*Soap Bubbles*). Brecht met Jean Renoir, who was friendly, and gave him dinner in Meudon, but did not offer any work. Generally Brecht disliked the Parisian atmosphere: 'showy groups, or rather cliques, with no perspective'.[10]

He was staying at a hotel in the rue du Four, almost next door to Walter Benjamin, and they saw a great deal of each other. Brecht urged him to settle in Denmark, where he would be able to live more cheaply, and when Brecht left in December, Benjamin wrote: 'the town is now quite desolate for me'. He had to settle Brecht's hotel bill, and wait a long time for the money to be sent from Denmark. On the way back there Brecht met his father in Strasbourg, but he now felt so alienated that his letter to Weigel, written on the train, refers to 'Walter's father'.[11]

Back in Skovbostrand Brecht renewed the invitation to Benjamin: 'It is pleasant here. Not at all cold, much warmer than in Paris. In Helli's [Helene's] opinion you could live on 100 krone a month (60 Reichsmarks, 360 francs). Besides, the Svendborg library can get *any* book for you. We have wireless, newspapers, playing cards, and soon we'll have your books, fires, small cafés, an extraordinarily easy language, and the world is disintegrating *more quietly* here.'[12] The other friend Brecht wanted as a neighbour was Karl Korsch, who was offered access to Brecht's books, which had arrived from Berlin in chests, and to Walter Benjamin's library.

A friend he missed even more was Elisabeth Hauptmann. In Paris, she had helped on the selection of poems for the volume that was to be titled *Lieder Gedichte Chöre* (*Songs, Poems, Choruses*), but she was not to be dissuaded from the intention of going to the United States.

Settling down again in Skovbostrand, Brecht was settling down into the relationship with Weigel. With her diligent housekeeping, she eased his way into a working routine more arduous – because more lonely – than the one that had been interrupted when he escaped from Berlin. The workroom was heated to be warm enough for him to start writing regularly at 8 every morning. He was sensitive to cold and always nervous of catching colds.[13]

Undoubtedly he was a genius, but the quality of his achievement would not have been so great if his output had been smaller. No writer has ever organized his life more ruthlessly to squeeze every last drop from the sponge of his talent, and no writer has depended more on collaborative stimulus from other people or on a routine buttressed by an efficient and protective wife. Exile would make him depend less on collaborators and more on Weigel, who would have liked to collaborate but was never allowed to.

The relationship with Berlau developed slowly: she claimed that two years passed before he kissed her. As with Margarete Steffin, intimacy grew through collaborative work, while it was easier for Weigel to tolerate his infidelities when they seemed inextricable from his need to work collaboratively. When she saw that Brecht was singing to Berlau, she glared suspiciously, but when they read scenes from *Die heilige Johanna*, Weigel played Frau Luckerniddle to Berlau's Johanna. And Brecht played chess with Dr Lund. 'He really was a snob in relationships with scientists,' Berlau said.[14] He collaborated with her on her novel *Jedes Tier kann es* (*Every Animal Can Do It*): 'I brought the raw material; Brecht did the formulating.'[15]

When Margarete Steffin arrived in Denmark, Brecht arranged for her to stay with Berlau and Robert Lund, who became her doctor. On Christmas Day she confessed to Berlau that she was in love with Brecht, but she went on staying in their house for three months: it took Brecht all this time, according to Berlau, to muster enough courage to tell Weigel that Steffin had arrived in Denmark. Jealous of the women who helped her husband with his work, Weigel had been learning how to type, but even as a secretary she could not compete with Steffin, who was not only quick and accurate as a typist, but good at understanding how he wanted scripts to be laid out on the page. Adamant that the tubercular Steffin could not be accommodated in the same house as the children, Weigel helped to furnish a room for her in Skovbostrand, and provided food, which Brecht delivered in the second-hand car Berlau had found for him. The double journey took only four minutes.[16]

Though comfortably situated in a well-run household, able to work and not frustrated sexually, Brecht had no outlets for intellectual conversation or political activity. 'The existence of the Party is currently doing more to hinder than to encourage the formation of a united front among the émigrés. We're waiting for directives, lines, settlement of accounts, regroupings etc. etc. It's all centralized, and the centre doesn't answer.'[17]

After consulting with the Bund, Brecht sent an open letter to Heinrich George, asking him not to ignore the arrest of another actor, Hans Otto, who had been beaten up by the SA and taken to a hospital. 'We understand that you are not suspected of having anything against the present regime. .... You yourself and your colleagues have been turned into puppets overnight. You will be wretched theatre-functionaries tuned to ruthlessness, directed by torturers, doing your work, which will consist of being loyal to traitors, and you won't even have enough influence for that to be regarded as an atrocity.'[18]

Skovbostrand was a pleasant place. 'The island of Fyn is called the garden of Denmark. Everything is green, so far as one can see, and, more important, the people have good trading relationships with England. The fruit trees have to be propped up with wooden supports, and the fishermen stab their lances into the floodwater and in a few hours collect dozens of eels.' Copenhagen was only five hours away, but Brecht seldom went there, and when visitors arrived – Müllereisert, for instance – Berlau would meet them and act as chauffeuse on the long journey. But Brecht was restless, frustrated at being denied the fame that *Dreigroschenoper* had seemed to promise. 'I'm bored.' 'One day I'm going to be successful.' 'I'm a modern classic.'[19]

Even if Danish was 'extraordinarily easy', he seldom attempted to speak it, preferring to depend on Berlau and Steffin to interpret. But he frequented pubs around the harbour, and studied the techniques used by whores to cajole sailors into giving away their savings; and in his pidgin-Danish he had long conversations with the local cigar merchant. He also learned to read Danish, but liked only books by J. V. Jensen and J. P. Jacobsen.[20]

Talking about his work in the theatre, he resigned himself to using the past tense, and he now bracketed himself with Piscator. 'We wrote texts ourselves – plays, too, in my case – or we cut those of other people in pieces and stuck them together so differently they were unrecognizable. We interpolated music and film, everywhere putting the lowest things at the top: what had been tragic we made comic, and vice versa. We let our characters sing whenever it was least motivated.'

He maintained that 'theatre in its traditional form has become completely meaningless'. Ibsen's and Strindberg's plays were unmoving and uninstructive, except as evidence about 'the way human relationships – especially between men and women – were regarded in earlier cultural periods'. 'In modern society what goes on inside the soul of an individual is totally uninteresting. Only in feudal times did the sufferings of an individual – a king or a leader – have any influence.' Today even Hitler's private sufferings were irrelevant.[21] But in *Die heilige Johanna* Brecht had made market activity largely contingent on whims and decisions precipitated by one eccentric individual's inner life.

If he was now overstating his case, it was partly because his intention was to promote his plays as representative of the new culture. There was nothing he wanted more urgently than Danish productions of them, and Berlau introduced him to Per Knutzon, who had directed *Trommeln* and now showed interest in *Die Rundköpfe und die Spitzköpfe*. In March 1934 when Hanns Eisler arrived in Skovbostrand, Brecht worked with him and Margarete Steffin on reorienting the play to current events in Germany, stressing the relationship between Fascism and bourgeois materialism. The play was now subtitled *Reich und Reich gesellt sich gern (The Reich and the Rich Flock Together)*.

The only play Brecht started during 1934 was a short *Lehrstück* called *Die Horatier und die Kuriatier (The Horatians and the Curiatians)*. The initiative came from Eisler, who spoke of a Red Army commission and of the propaganda value the play could have if performed in American, English, French and Scandinavian schools. To begin with Eisler collaborated on the text, and when the Party ordered him to attend an international music congress in Prague, Brecht felt abandoned. Margarete Steffin took over as collaborator. Written almost entirely in blank verse, and using a Chinese convention by which a single actor stands in for an army, the play deals with a war motivated by the need to unite the Curiatians against an enemy in order to stop internal dissension provoked by social inequality. The Curiatians are better equipped than the enemy they attack, but the Horatians outwit them and defeat them. The first battle is won by the Curiatian bowmen, and the second by the Curiatian lancers, but in the third, although the Horatian swordsmen run away, the more heavily armed enemy is slow in pursuing. Separated from each other, the pursuers are defeated: 'The retreat was an advance.' The purpose of the play is to offer comfort and advice to all those – himself included – who had retreated from the Nazis.

Most of Brecht's creative energy was now channelled into his *Dreigroschenroman*. The original intention had been to transfer the action to Berlin: in February he said he was working on 'the story of three old men in Berlin'.[22] He had never been in London, but he did not finally let this deter him from setting his action there: nothing depends on topography, and little depends on evoking a sense of place, though narrative and characterization are often reminiscent of Dickens. He was determined to eliminate all the romantic elements from the story he had told in the *Dreigroschenoper*. Macheath is now middle-aged, bald, double-chinned and glamourless, a businessman who runs a chain of shops as an outlet for stolen goods. Polly, now nicknamed the Peach, is still sexually attractive, but there is no love between her and Macheath: she marries him because she cannot afford an abortion to terminate a pregnancy started by another lover. Nevertheless, Brecht wanted the book's front cover to be illustrated with a photograph he had of Carola Neher as Polly. Twelve months later his idea for the dust-jacket would be a drawing of Peachum, arms extended, offering a yacht and his daughter for sale. There would be a price-tag on each: £15,000 on the boat, £7,000 on the girl.[23]

Insistently, the novel defines the businessman as the criminal who is never brought to justice. Although the pleasures of buying and selling are almost as rudimentarily human as the pleasure of eating, drinking and making love, Brecht had arrived at the dogma that all business deals are tainted with criminality. The final episode, a lawcourt scene, is a dream. George Fewkoombey is an archetypal victim – having lost a leg as a soldier in Africa, he is hanged for a murder committed by Macheath. But in the dream epilogue he is judge at the trial of a man accused of criminally inventing a parable that has been used in pulpits for two thousand years to induce acquiescence.

As in *Die heilige Johanna*, Brecht was at pains to demonstrate the workings of economic processes, and the novel gave him space for a stage-by-stage exposé of how business is done. He shows how a dishonest middleman involves Peachum in the business of selling the Admiralty unseaworthy ships for use as troop-carriers in the Boer War, and eventually he has to choose between total ruin and arranging for the middleman to be murdered. In the world of the story, the criminal is capitalism, and the premiss is that human innocence, which existed once in an Eden-like society, will one day be revived by an egalitarianism which will somehow exempt citizens from the need to own property or do business.

Undeniably Brecht can be accused of crude thinking, but an apologia is built into the argument: 'Nothing is more important than learning to think crudely. Crude thinking is the thinking of great men.' On a beam supporting the ceiling of Brecht's study in letters cut out of black cardboard and stuck up with thin nails were the words: 'Truth is concrete.' On a window-sill was a small wooden donkey which could nod its head. 'Even I must understand it', said the sign he had hung around its neck. Walter Benjamin, who was by no means crude in his thinking, defended Brecht's position:

'Crude thoughts belong to the household of dialectical thinking precisely because they represent nothing other than the application of theory to practice. ... Action can, of course, be as subtle as thought. But a thought must be crude if it is to come into its own in action.'[24]

For the enemy of Fascism in the 1930s the greatest evil was inaction, and subtlety could look like its ally:

> There are uncritical people who never doubt
> And there are scrupulous people who never take action ...
> With the murderer's axe raised above their heads
> They ask themselves whether he isn't human too ...
> You can make mistakes
> By acting with too little thought,
> But the mistake in time of danger
> Is to go on thinking too long.[25]

Deciding to join Brecht in Skovbostrand, Benjamin had his books sent on from Berlin and he arrived at the end of June. Brecht, who had been suffering from a kidney disease, was in hospital, where he had to stay for over four weeks, but when Benjamin visited him there on 3 July they talked about Benjamin's paper 'Der Autor als Produzent' ('The Author as Producer'), which he had delivered in Paris on 27 April at the Institute for the Study of Fascism. It praised Brecht for formulating the demand that intellectuals should not supply material for the media without trying to transform them. And they talked about Rimbaud's *Le Bateau ivre*. Had Marx and Engels read it, Brecht said, they would have recognized the work of a man unable to tolerate the repressiveness of the class infecting even the Crimea and Mexico with its mercantile interests.[26]

When Benjamin called again the next day, Brecht said that he often pictured himself being interrogated by a tribunal: was he really in earnest? He would have to admit that no, he wasn't. He thought about art too much to be serious. Did this mean that his work would have no effect? 'I sometimes wonder whether writers like Hauptmann aren't, ultimately, the only ones who really get somewhere. You know, writers of real solidity.' Perhaps he identified both with the three agitators in *Die Massnahme* who have to justify themselves, and with the young comrade who was not a serious revolutionary. Perhaps the play's secret subject is his attempt to annihilate the more personal part of his personality, to make his features permanently indistinguishable from those of his Marxist mask. Unlike his parents, who had neither the wisdom nor the power to control him, the Control Chorus is omniscient and irresistible while the play endorses its assumption that dogma is good, emotion anarchic and therefore evil. 'A poet', said W. B. Yeats, 'is never the bundle of accident and incoherence that sits down to breakfast; he has been reborn as an idea, something intended, complete.'[27] Brecht had always been a poet, and always disliked the notion of individuality, but the commanding idea of impersonality had not been born until he read Marx and Lenin. As an idea it worked powerfully on his *Lehrstücke*, but had less effect on his other plays, which continued to revolve around characters brought vividly to individual life.

Brecht's children saw more of their father than they had in Berlin. They called him 'Biddi' and Weigel 'Helli'. When they were ill, he read to them – sometimes from the Bible, sometimes his own stories. Then he would go back into his room and walk up and down for hours in creaking shoes. Barbara was allowed to go around naked during the summer, and Stefan, together with his school-friend, Markussen, was welcome to join the adults and take part in conversation.

Nothing mattered more to Brecht than the sense of participating in the fight against Hitler. 'I'm constantly planning blows against the robbers who are based in the south.' But after nine months in Skovbo-strand, he found it hard to make any plans. He was more privileged than most of the other refugees, but he could no longer function as a play-wright, and there was little point in developing his theories about theatre when they could exert no influence. Though he counted himself lucky to have a publisher in Amsterdam, he was not enthusiastic about writing books. By the last week in September he had two ideas. One was for a short satire on Hitler in the style of a Renaissance biography. This was to be called *Ui*,[28] while *Tui* was to be a long novel set partly in China. It would be an encyclopaedic survey of intellectual follies.

Intellectually he could convince himself that like the Horatian swords-men who had won by retreating, he had been right to leave Germany, but as a refugee, isolated in provincial Denmark, he found few outlets for his aggressive impulses. He was lucky to have Benjamin as a neigh-bour and, besides Müllereisert, his visitors included his old Augsburg friends Georg Pfanzelt and Rudolf Hartmann. He also received a visit from his 65-year-old father, who urged him not to go on attacking the regime. Brecht, who refused to be muzzled, heard later that his father intended to disinherit him.[29]

At the age of thirty-six he could not accuse himself of having wasted his life, but he argued with himself about whether he had exploited his potential to the full: 'I've lived not for myself but very publicly, for since the 21st year of my life I've become well known for my literary works and many other enterprises associated with them. I also already have pupils and have often advised or guided other people.'[30] The false antithesis is revealing: he needed to feel that living publicly was unselfish.

In the autumn, until Brecht left for London on 3 October, Benjamin noticed that he was lapsing into vindictiveness. Visiting Benjamin, who was unwell and reading *Crime and Punishment*, Brecht attributed the malaise to Dostoevsky, trying to substantiate the diagnosis with a story about a childhood illness of his own, which he blamed on a friend who had played Chopin when he was too feeble to object. Chopin and Dostoevsky were both particularly injurious to health, he said. He was himself reading *The Good Soldier Schweyk*. 'It became evident that Dostoevsky simply could not measure up to Hašek, and Brecht included him without further ado among the *Würstchen* (little sausages).'[31] Another word Brecht had taken to using for work he considered useless or uninstructive was *Klump* (lump or clot).

In the autumn of 1934 Brecht spent almost three months in London, staying at a boarding-house in Calthorpe Street, where Karl Korsch was lodging. In Paris he had arrived with work to do and a theatrical production in view; he arrived in London uninvited but not unhopeful. Surely he could arrange for one of his plays to be staged, or get himself commissioned to write a film, or at least interest a publisher in translations of his work. But despite the recent production of *Anna-Anna*, it was hard to see how any of his plays could have been mounted in the London theatre, which struck him as 'antediluvian',[1] and although Hanns Eisler, who was in London, put him in touch with Berthold Viertel, who had been making films in England since the previous year, he was less helpful than Leo Lania. Brecht wrote two poems for the new version of Lania's play *Das Ölfeld* (*The Oilfield*), and they collaborated on a scenario about a Viennese doctor, Semmelweis, who had specialized in puerperal fever. Lania then tried, unsuccessfully, to interest Alexander Korda in the project. Many refugees from Germany had settled in London. Most prominent were the actors. Elisabeth Bergner had starred for C. B. Cochran in *Escape Me Never*; Adolf Wohlbrück became much more famous as Anton Walbrook. Conrad Veidt and Oskar Homolka both worked in British films before moving on to Hollywood; W. H. Auden married Thomas Mann's daughter Erika to give her British citizenship. But the famous were vastly outnumbered by the obscure:

> In a grey city, full of market cries,
> We met those who had lost their face.
> Whoever we met looked away.
> Whoever we followed walked faster.

Lonely, Brecht sent love poems to Margarete Steffin, and wrote to Weigel, who had left for Vienna and Zürich: 'Perhaps you can recruit a few people on your travels for Svendborg.' He also asked her to investigate the possibility of acquiring Czech citizenship: he had heard in London that this was possible.[2]

Trying to raise funds for the fight against Fascism, he approached

Princess Elisabeth Bibesco, who had previously contributed. When she invited him to dinner at the Savoy, Eisler persuaded him to accept, but turning up in his everyday clothes, he was so intimidated by the hall porters that he did not even mention the Princess's name. 'I tried to penetrate into this Babylonian tower by another entrance. But there I met such a tide of superior, richly dressed and obviously remorseless people that I gave up all hope.' He reported that London was 'an evil and tough little city. The natives are among the most malicious in Europe.'³

After going home, late in December 1934, he did not have time to settle down. Piscator had been elected as President of the International Association of Revolutionaries of the Theatre (MORT) with Johannes Becher as Secretary of the German section, and in January Brecht was invited to a conference of directors in Moscow. Piscator wanted to 'collect a few good people for a constructive discussion'.⁴ This was to take place in April, and it was at Piscator's suggestion that a Brecht evening was arranged for 12 May at the headquarters of the Deutsches Theater Kolonne Links, a left-wing German language theatre. While Brecht was naturally eager to revisit the city which ought to be the hub of resistance to Nazism, Piscator wanted him to co-operate in expanding MORT into a cultural organization that would produce its own films, promote plays and publish a newspaper, besides serving as an international cultural centre for anti-fascists. Ernst Ottwalt and Bernhard Reich were among the German exiles now in Moscow, as was Carola Neher, who had remarried. At the Brecht evening in May she performed some of his songs.

A German-language theatre would have commanded support, but Piscator's plans were ominously at odds with those of Gustav von Wangenheim, founder and director of the Gruppe 1931. Wanting to stage both *Die Dreigroschenoper* and *Die Rundköpfe und die Spitzköpfe*, he started negotiating with Brecht about a part for Weigel in the film *Kämpfer* (*Warriors*), which he was to direct. With Piscator Brecht discussed the creation of a film studio, and of a German theatre in the Ukraine, but none of these projects materialized. At the beginning of May a German-language theatre was founded at Dnepropetrovsk, but when one of its directors approached Weigel about joining the company, Brecht advised her against committing herself for more than two months. Travelling by lorry, the company was performing in Ukraine villages and holding discussions in market-places. 'It certainly won't be first-class, and I doubt whether it's even third-class.'⁵

Tretiakov, who had translated *Die Massnahme*, *Die Mutter* and *Die heilige Johanna*, was in no position to help – he was already out of favour and was shortly to disappear. Dedicated to a narrow interpretation of social realism, the Moscow theatre was to prove inhospitable, but at first Brecht felt optimistic. In an interview he said that in both Paris and London the theatre had struck him as belonging to the year 1880: 'Only one theatrical city now exists in the world: that's Moscow. And it's only in the Soviet Union that great developments in theatrical art are still occurring.'[6]

He was glad to see the Reichs, Ernst Ottwalt, Carola Neher, who had grown rather fat and nervy, and Alexander Granach, who at the Brecht evening directed German-speaking amateurs in two scenes from *Die Rundköpfe und die Spitzköpfe*. Apart from a mild friendship with Wilhelm Pieck, Brecht made no close contacts with the German communist politicians; but the Hungarian leader, Bela Kun, who was present at the Brecht evening, responded enthusiastically, afterwards inviting Brecht, Piscator, the Tretiakovs and the Reichs to his home. When Kun asked Brecht to sing, he demurred: he was out of practice, had no guitar with him, had forgotten how to sing. Kun was so insistent that a guitar was fetched. Still Brecht hesitated, but when Piscator and the Reichs joined in the persuasion, he sang the 'Legende vom toten Soldaten', but with none of the old spellbinding magic. The applause was only polite.[7]

The most important event of his visit occurred in May, when he saw a troupe of Chinese actors. The leading actor, Mei Lan Fan, made almost as strong an impression on him as the Balinese dancers had made on Antonin Artaud four years earlier, just before he formulated his ideas for a Theatre of Cruelty. Mei Lan Fan performed without make-up, or lighting, never hiding his awareness that an audience was watching and, like the man in Brecht's 1930 poem about the street accident, he gave the impression he would not mind if he were interrupted in mid performance. 'He confines himself from the outset to simply quoting the character he's playing.'[8] Making no attempt to describe the production or the physical appearance of the actors, Brecht writes about Mei Lan Fan in the singular, as if he had been doing a one-man show. Brecht's art depended on using almost everything he could observe and observing little he could not use. As in his encounter with Noh plays four years earlier, he isolated the qualities that could contribute to the theatrical style he was evolving. In some early handwritten notes on Mei Lan Fan's troupe, he criticized Chinese acting technique as unrealistic, ceremonial, stiffly symbolical and psychological. 'It is the person, not the action, that is alienated.' But in the draft for his published essay, he attacked Chinese theatre for encouraging the audience to focus its attention on the star performer. Unlike Artaud, he did not want to watch actors conveying information about the character's internal state – or about their own. He concluded that the art of Chinese theatre had 'become rigid. But its eminent technique of the alienation effect could help us if put at the disposal of our quite dissimilar tasks.'[9] He may have been intuitively aware that he could put the model of Chinese drama to better use than Japanese. Whereas Noh drama, which was feudal in its provenance, invited acceptance of the *status quo*, Chinese plots more often revolved around the need for social justice in a corrupt society.

Mei Lan Fan reminded Brecht both of the crude acting at the Augsburg fairs, and of what he had done in his own productions to discourage the audience from empathy.[10] His use of the word *Verfremdung* (alienation) dates from this performance in Moscow: previously he had used *Entfremdung* (distancing) for the defamiliarization necessary to stop an event from seeming natural, readily acceptable: in his native dialect, Swabian, *entfremden* and *verfremden* are synonymous.

The function of this defamiliarization was criticism; nothing should be exempt from the question: is this necessary? The performance should help the spectator to develop that detached stance 'with which the great Galileo observed a swinging chandelier. He puzzled about this swinging as if he had not expected it and failed to understand it. In this way he arrived at the laws that were operative.' As a poet Brecht was perhaps hoping for the same kind of didactic dialogue with the audience as he had carried on, since his schooldays, with his band of disciples. Aware that his talent was founded on perversity, on seeing things differently from other people, he tried to win converts for the alternative viewpoint. Theatre should pluck commonplace occurrences out of their normal perspective and show unfamiliar backgrounds littered with commonplace occurrences. In the Augsburg fairgrounds he had been struck by the portrayal of such events as Charles the Bold's flight after the Battle of Murten: 'Deliberately the fleeing commander, his horse, his retinue and the landscape are all painted to convey the impression of an extraordinary event, an unexpected catastrophe.'[11] Mei Lan Fan could 'suggest passion without pretending to lose his self-control. He can, for instance, chew at a lock of his own hair. To exhibit the symptoms of emotion (raised voice, tightened neck muscles, heavy breathing) is to risk infecting oneself with emotion; better to signal it mechanically – for instance by abruptly showing a white face, after concealing white make-up in one's hands and clasping them to one's face.'[12] Once again Brecht was thinking of the soldiers in *Eduard II*.

Not that *Verfremdung* depends on stylization. Nor does it obviate the need – Brecht agrees with Stanislavsky on this point – for truthfulness. Does an angry man really speak like that? Is this how an offended man sits down? Brecht wanted both dialogue and gestures to be submitted to the public for a verdict.

Vsevolod Vishnevsky's 1932 play *Optimistic Tragedy* had been banned in the Soviet Union because in advocating collaboration with the Social Democrats in Germany, it deviated from Comintern policy. During Brecht's two-month stay in the Soviet Union there was a shift of policy towards support for a Popular Front, and he twice read his poem 'An die Gleichgeschalteten' ('To Those Who Have Come into Line') on Moscow radio. He also took part in planning a periodical, *Das Wort,* which was to begin publication the following year with himself, Feucht-wanger and Heinrich Mann on the editorial board.

Brecht did not learn until he returned to Denmark that he had been stripped of his German citizenship with effect from 8 June 1935. Together with his children, Stefan and Barbara, he was named in a list published by the Nazis on 11 June.[13]

One of the letters waiting for him in Skovbostrand was from Paula, who
was now Paula Gross. Frank, now nearly sixteen, was living with her
again, having been with her mother. Paula wanted him to study dentistry
and wanted Brecht to help financially, but his reply was that he neither
liked the idea nor could afford it. The most he could send, he said, was
fifty marks a month for the next year, 'and even that isn't certain, though
I'll do my best'.[1]

In the middle of June he was working with Eisler on a new operetta
about female pirates. He may have wanted to develop the 'Pirate Jenny'
idea from the song in *Dreigroschenoper*. His stay in Skovbostrand was
even briefer than the previous one. Before leaving on 15 June with Karin
Michaëlis for an international conference in Paris, he asked Walter Benjamin to book rooms for them, 'not too dear but without bugs', either in
his hotel or in Slatan Dudow's. Delegates came from all over the world.
One woman travelled fourth class from Greece, her fare paid by a group
of workers, but then had no opportunity to make a speech.[2]

Brecht's speech was not calculated to please either liberals or Party
members who were committed to a United Front. The atrocities of the
Fascists were not unnecessary, he said. They were not lying when they
claimed these to be essential for the preservation of bourgeois society.
'Those of our friends who are just as incensed as we are over the cruelties
of Fascism, but want to preserve the *status quo* in property relationships
or profess their indifference to whether it is preserved, cannot fight
strongly or persistently enough against the barbarism which is gaining
ground so rapidly.' As in *Der Dreigroschenroman*, he insisted that
brutality had its root in 'the business transactions which can no longer
be conducted without it'. For Walter Benjamin Brecht's presence at the
congress was 'the most enjoyable – almost the only enjoyable – element in
the whole proceedings'. But his speech was ignored by both the Party press
and the socialist newspapers. The only consolation was that the delegates' behaviour provided material for his satirical *Tui* novel: 'Again and

again one is sadly forced to the recognition of how little penetrates inside people's minds.' It took four days to decide that culture must not be destroyed: 'If necessary we will sacrifice 10–20 million human beings for it.'[3]

Having failed in both Paris and London to get any of his plays staged, he was heartened by the news that in New York the Theatre Union, a group backed by the American Communist Party, wanted to stage *Die Mutter*. But when Paul Peters, who had translated and adapted the script, forwarded a copy of his text, pleasure gave way to anger: 'You don't believe that the American worker can do without a naturalistic form. No doubt you will be upset that I am nevertheless not agreeable to a naturalistic production.'[4] Through V. J. Jerome, cultural organizer of the American Communist Party's agitprop division, Brecht offered to help in the production if his fare was paid to New York. Jerome, who knew Eisler, arranged for a representative of the theatre, Manuel Gomez, to visit Brecht in Skovbostrand, where a contract was signed, guaranteeing him control over the text.

He was expecting more from the New York production than from Ruth Berlau's amateur production, but this caused him less chagrin. Like George Orwell, he had unshakable faith in the native wisdom of the working class. 'Just get on with the practical work', he advised her. 'You'll see – your workers will make changes themselves.' Pelagea was played by a charwoman, Dagmar Andreasen, who scrubbed steps at the railway stations, while many of the amateur actors were unemployed. Some of them came to rehearsals mainly because of the coffee and sandwiches Berlau provided, but her enthusiasm had its effect on them. There were more communists among them at the end of rehearsals than at the beginning.[5]

She persuaded Brecht to make the long journey to Copenhagen for one of the rehearsals, which was held in a cellar. He laughed out loud several times before whispering to her: 'It's funny when workers want to play at being actors. And tragic when actors can't play workers.' But he helped them by speaking lines for them. They understood the tone he wanted, and began to laugh apologetically when they got it wrong. 'Good,' he shouted. 'Because anyone who can laugh at himself is already half a god. God laughs at himself all day long.'[6]

Afterwards he addressed a long poem to them:

> Your first school
> Should be where you work, your home, your part of town.
> Should be streets, underground railways, and shops.

> Everyone there
> You should observe. Strangers as if they were friends, but
> Friends as if they were strangers.

Assuming that members of the Theatre Union in New York were workers, he wrote them a long verse letter, complaining in detail about the naturalism in Peters' translation:

> The great stage space
> You fill with furniture. The smell of coal
> Comes from the hearth.

Why should workers be scared of new forms?

> For the exploited, constantly deceived,
> Life too is a constant experiment.

What he could not know was that the company had little interest in him or his work. At a board meeting in April, Gomez had proposed 'Gorki's *Mother* in the Eisler operetta', and five weeks later the board commissioned Peters to translate the 'libretto'. Eisler, who arrived in New York early in 1935, created a favourable impression; Brecht left on 7 October, sailing on the S.S. Aquitania, and, as if to tutor himself in arrogance, wrote a poem on board, comparing himself to Columbus. He was met at the jetty on 15 October by Peters and the director, Victor Wolfson who, disappointingly, was twenty-three. He had staged a festival of plays written by coal-miners on strike in West Virginia. He immediately disliked Brecht, finding him 'without human charm. . . . He has no soul, no heart, no prick.'[7]

Albert Maltz and George Sklar, members of the Theatre Union's production committee, corroborate each other's accounts of Brecht's behaviour in rehearsal and of the smell that emanated from underneath the unvarying clothes – grey silk shirt and leather jacket. 'The stench of his unwashed body', says Maltz, 'made it an ordeal to sit beside him.' In rehearsal, says Sklar, 'Brecht would sit in the audience, mutter to himself, then take off like a Beechcroft plane, hop up on the stage and start screaming in German.' 'He had a voice', says Maltz, 'that would have humiliated the fight announcer at Madison Square Gardens; . . . I can still hear after thirty years his Prussian drillmaster's call *Sitzung*, i.e. meeting. We often had several a day.'[8]

With Eisler's help he forced Wolfson to recast the leading part and to reinstate the original third act. By the beginning of November the whole of the original text was being used, 'thanks to a nice little piece of dictatorship'. But rehearsal conflict came to a head after a shouting match with the 18-year-old musical director, Jerome Maross. Told that his music was shit, he replied 'that he was trying to make music out of shit'. On 9 November Brecht was thrown out of rehearsal after the pianist threatened to 'break every bone in his body'.[9] Eisler left with him.

Believing the Theatre Union to be under Party control, Brecht appealed to the General Secretary, who could do nothing. It was agreed that V. J. Jerome should act as arbitrator, but within two days Brecht was ignoring his rulings: 'Ah, but I am not a Party member. I need not keep the agreement. But you are Party members and are under discipline.' They explained that they were not Party members.[10]

Cuts and textual changes were made in his absence, and there was a row about the song 'Get up! The Party is in Danger'. Wolfson insisted on having it sung not to the audience but to the ailing Pelagea. When Brecht jumped up on the stage to argue, Wolfson had him thrown out of the theatre. The designer, Mordecai Gorelik, found him and Eisler outside the stage door. 'They asked me rather piteously if I could fetch them their caps which they had left inside in their haste to escape from the theatre. They were apparently afraid to go in again.' Gorelik was the only one to be in sympathy with Brecht's ideas, which reminded him of Japanese precision. 'Yes, yes, Japanese,' Brecht agreed. 'Let it all be elegant, thin and fine, like Japanese banners, flimsy like Japanese kites and lanterns, let's be aware of the natural features of wood and metal.'[11]

The play was due to open on Tuesday 19 November. Over the weekend of the 16th–17th Brecht again contacted Jerome, threatening to inform the critics, 'those of the bourgeois press too', that his text was being mutilated. He also threatened to picket outside the theatre. At a run-through for several hundred people who had mostly contributed to the costs of the production, he stood up and shouted in German: 'This is shit! This is crap! I won't have it!' And he walked out, followed by Eisler.[12] The critic Brooks Atkinson called the play a technically interesting but emotionally weak exercise in the art of theatre; in his opinion the production was more interesting than the play. Other reviewers were almost equally unfavourable, which would not have mattered so much if audiences had responded well. Brecht and Eisler still hoped to put the play 'into the political and artistic shape it deserves', and when they were refused extra rehearsals, they complained that the Theatre Union was no better than a Broadway management. '*Die Mutter* has been totally spoiled for us here (stupid textual mangling, political ignorance, backwardness of every kind, etc.).' Writing for the *New Masses*, Brecht complained that it had been absurd to cut straight from the twelfth scene which showed how in 1914 the bulk of the proletariat rejected the Bolshevik programme, to the fourteenth which showed the Revolution of 1917. Picture-book Russianized costumes had been introduced at the last minute without consulting Gorelik, and most of the dialogue had been wrongly pitched. Only in a few passages had the actors 'spoken with the same sense of responsibility as a statement made for the record in a court of law'.[13]

Brecht stayed in New York until 29 December, but he achieved little. He negotiated for an American edition of his novel, which was to be translated by Desmond Vesey under the title *A Penny for the Poor*, with the verse translated by Christopher Isherwood. Brecht was impressed by Clifford Odets's *Waiting for Lefty*, which he saw at Madison Square Gardens, but Odets's next play, *Paradise Lost*, expressed no more sympathy for exploited workers than for those 'who will soon be unable to afford a cab'. This was characteristic of a vague 'something is wrong' feeling, similar to the alarmism which, in Germany, had won votes for Hitler. Brecht urged Jerome to write a regular newspaper column to enlighten the cultural leftists.[14] But the Party was aiming to consolidate an alliance with the middle classes against fascism, war and censorship. The Workers' Laboratory Theatre had been renamed Theatre of Action, and some of Wolfson's interference with Brecht's script had been prompted by Party guidelines. The Bible-tearing scene was omitted, as were the Bolshevik slogans in the final scene, while the song 'Praise of Communism' became 'Praise of Socialism'.

In New York, Brecht saw something of Georg Grosz, and a little of Kurt Weill, but it was with Eisler that Brecht spent most of his time. They went to the cinema together almost every day, seeing mainly gangster movies – preferably James Cagney's – and they played chess. 'It is only with great difficulty that one can work here,' Brecht wrote, 'and it's more boring than in Skovbostrand. Christmas was frightful. Eisler and I were with people who had no children, and someone went on interminably singing Scottish ballads.'[15]

In December he met Marc Blitzstein, who played his song 'The Nickel under Your Foot'. Brecht urged him to write a musical about prostitution in all its forms, and this led to *The Cradle Will Rock*. Even with artists he met only once, Brecht had a galvanizing effect. But he did not make a good impression on Americans he met casually. Gomez describes him as 'enormously vain – as well as enormously energetic, enormously stubborn, enormously sarcastic and enormously difficult'. A Theatre of

Action worker said: 'he would look at you strangely, not straight on. . . . He seemed to regard you as a kind of mechanism to be studied.'[16]

Before leaving New York he wrote to Gorki with details of the takings, which had totalled $16,031. At 5 per cent the royalties came to $801.56. The American translator and Eisler each had 30 per cent of this, leaving $320.62 to be divided between Gorki and Brecht. 'Please let me know how much I should send you.' Although his travelling expenses had been paid, he added, he had paid for his own accommodation during the rehearsal period.[17]

It was less boring in Skovbostrand after Karl Korsch arrived in January 1936. He had been living in London until his residence permit was withdrawn. He was suspected of being a Nazi informer. Settling with his family in Skovbostrand, he worked at a book on Marx. 'We don't know when he'll leave,' Brecht wrote. 'His suitcases are always packed. He discovers all one's weaknesses, and he'll make immediate proposals. . . . Listening to him is strenuous. His sentences are very long. In this way he teaches me to be patient.'

Once again Brecht used his house more as a base than as a home. In April he left again, this time for London, where Hanns Eisler had arranged for him to be employed as one of the scriptwriters on *A Clown Must Laugh*, a film of *I Pagliacci* to star Richard Tauber. Fritz Kortner was principal scriptwriter; Eisler, who was musical adviser and conductor, was living in Abbey Road, where Brecht found a room on the other side of the street. He was offered £500 but when he persisted in making unwanted suggestions he was paid off. Outraged, he asked Eisler and Kortner to walk out with him, but neither of them wanted to.

In London Brecht read Stanislavsky's *My Life in Art*, 'feeling envious and troubled. The man has brought a system into existence, and the result is that in Paris and New York they become students of Stanislavsky. Need that be so? Really we're living in an ivory tower.'[18] Brecht grew determined to bring a system into existence.

Through Eisler he met the 56-year-old Stefan Zweig, a rich and elegant man. Brecht talked about *Die Rundköpfe*, mischievously asking Eisler to play the song about 'the enlivening effect of money'. Zweig swallowed the insult in silence. Eisler went on to sing two other songs. Eventually Zweig said: 'Interesting'. Apologizing for the first song, Brecht called it a trifle, written 'to help the cause a bit'. 'Don't call it a trifle, Herr Brecht', said Zweig. 'It is perhaps your best work.'[19] He then took Brecht out to lunch, choosing a particularly cheap restaurant.

When Berlau arrived in London they began to draft *Freuden und*

Leiden der kleineren Seeräuber (*The Smaller Pirates' Pleasures and Sufferings*). He also resumed work with her on *Jedes Tier kann es.*

In May, Margarete Steffin, who had been in Moscow and Leningrad, arrived in London. In July Brecht – without leaving London – attended another international congress of writers. As at the one in Paris, proposals were made for the defence of culture against barbarism. André Malraux and H. G. Wells were the two writers Brecht expressly attacked in his satirical poem 'Inselbriefe 1' ('Island Letter No. 1').[20]

In July the first issue of *Das Wort* was published. Living so far from Moscow, Brecht could do no more than make suggestions (which could easily be ignored) about contributors and contributions. Before leaving London he did a deal with an agent, arranging for W. H. Auden to be offered an advance of £25 if he would translate any of Brecht's plays. Returning to Skovbostrand at the end of July, shortly before Walter Benjamin did, he tried to secure for *Das Wort* the rights of Benjamin's essay 'Das Kunstwerk im Zeitalter seiner technischen Reproduzierbarkeit' ('The Work of Art in the Age of Its Technical Reproducibility').

The delay over the Copenhagen production of *Die Rundköpfe* was due to Per Knutzon's success with another production, a satirical musical which ran for over a year. With the actress Lulu Ziegler as his codirector, he had formed an experimental company, which presented the musical as its first production. It was only in the autumn, when the long run was drawing to its close, that they could concentrate on preparing *Die Rundköpfe*. Knutzon was running his company as a collective, but Brecht urged him to cash in on Lulu Ziegler's popularity by giving her star billing.

Knutzon baulked at Brecht's demand that each line of dialogue should be studied in relation to the social gesture immanent in it. Unable to direct the Danish actors himself, and unable to manipulate Knutzon, Brecht became highly irritable and dogmatic: 'A rich man can't ever be friendly,' he told the actors.[21] To stay in Copenhagen would have been to risk an explosion: he withdrew to Skovbostrand, leaving Weigel to represent his interests at the Riddersalen Theatre, where she arranged for him to be involved in the final rehearsals. The gulf between his ideas and Knutzon's was not too wide for the production to be more Brechtian than any since his own 1931 staging of *Mann ist Mann*.

Die Rundköpfe opened on 4 November 1936, just over three weeks before the ballet *Die sieben Todsünden* opened at the Theatre Royal. The heads of the Sharpheads were about 20 cm in height. The masks had distorted noses, ears, hair and chins. The Huas (like the soldiers in *Mann ist Mann*) had gigantic hands. The decor incorporated many ideas deriving from Brecht's work with Neher. The set consisted only of four large movable screens, slightly curved. The spotlights were visible, and scene changes were only partly concealed by a low curtain. Iberin was not made up to resemble Hitler, but some of his gestures were Hitlerish, and so was his relationship with the microphone, which became almost a sexual object.[22] During a speech about peace, the huge barrel of a cannon was lowered from the flies, pointing at the audience. On his way to prison, the tenant farmer walked through the auditorium and, to Brecht's intense satisfaction, the public was allowed to eat, drink and smoke during the performance.

But rumours about rehearsal rows reached the most influential critic, Frederick Schyberg, who sided with the director against the play, which he dismissed as undramatic, unpoetic and inhumane, condemning Brecht as a 'pale sectarian with scant talent'. Other local critics were almost equally disparaging. One wrote: 'Brecht champions himself in the programme as creator of the epic drama. We would have preferred it if he had created dramatic dramas.'[23] Offended by the characterization of the opportunistic prioress and by Iberin's trick of camouflaging his safe with a picture of the Madonna, local Catholics joined forces with local Nazis to have the play banned. They took it to be the work of a Jewish communist. The public outcry was helpful. It brought crowds to the Riddersalen, where the production ran for 21 performances.

But *Die sieben Todsünden* did not fare so well. At the first night the King said: 'No, that's not what the famous Royal Ballet is there for.' And when the Nazi government complained to the Danish ambassador in Berlin, the ballet was taken off after its second performance, dashing all the hopes Brecht had been nourishing for three years of using the Danish theatre as a base for launching his international reputation.

He felt relieved when he was not refused permission to renew his residence permit, but 'enough of my friends are saying that I must opt either for reactionary substance or a reactionary form. Both together would be too much of a good thing. And a prominent communist is saying: "If that's communism, then I'm not a communist." Perhaps he's right.'[24] The ambiguity is characteristically Brechtian, but underneath the joke there was a serious doubt. Exile and short runs both eat acidly into a playwright's confidence.

At the international conferences in Paris and London he had felt no rapport with non-communist writers, but after his two Copenhagen productions he concentrated on plannning a society for an exchange of views between artists 'seriously concerned with the correct presentation of the world and of the conditions necessary for human existence'. The idea had evolved from conversations with Mordecai Gorelik, and Brecht wanted to name the society after Diderot. In the period of the Encyclopaedists, some such idea might have been feasible, but in 1937 it was as naïve to speak of 'the correct presentation of the world' as to expect Thomas Mann, Auden, Isherwood, Eisenstein, Archibald MacLeish, Georg Grosz, Piscator and Tretiakov to join a collective and to write reports on their technical problems for other members. To Jean Renoir, Brecht wrote: 'It will take some time, but what will emerge will be the picture of a new art, anti-metaphysical and social.' The society's object would be 'to collect the experiences of its members systematically, to create a terminology, to analyse scientifically the theatrical forms of human togetherness'. Benjamin and Korsch would not have qualified for membership, not being creative artists; Feuchtwanger was not invited. Among those who had worked with Brecht in the theatre, Eisler was on the list, but not Weill or Hindemith; Gorelik but not Neher; Piscator, Dudow and Knutzon, but not Engel.[25]

The Spanish Civil War began in the middle of July 1936 with an army revolt; at the beginning of October the insurgents appointed Franco as head of state. The danger to the Spanish republic was as alarming to non-communists as to communists. Acting on Slatan Dudow's advice, Brecht collected material from newspapers and started work on a piece calling for armed intervention. *Die Rundköpfe* had evolved out of his work on *Measure for Measure; Generäle über Bilbao (Generals over Bilbao)*, which derived from J. M. Synge's one-act play *Riders to the Sea*, was Brecht's first play which had a current political crisis as its starting-point. It was drafted by the end of March 1937, and one of the final drafts was dated June 1937.

In Synge's play the mother, having failed to stop the last of her sons from becoming a fisherman, resigns herself to his death: 'No man at all can be living for ever, and we must be satisfied.' Brecht's play, which was revised as *Die Gewehre der Frau Carrar (Señora Carrar's Rifles)* prefigures one of his themes in *Mutter Courage*: in both plays a mother tries to stop her two sons from risking their lives in the fighting. Following the pattern of *Die heilige Johanna* and *Die Mutter*, he builds his action around the conversion of the central female figure to militancy. After the death of the older boy she not only encourages the younger to fight, she decides to fight herself. Stylistically, though, the play is less progressive than Brecht's earlier work. Taking his own joke seriously, he put progressive content into a reactionary form. It is the only one of his plays which he described as 'Aristotelian (empathy) drama'.[1]

The insistence on the inevitability of violence is Leninist, and with Johanna, Vlassova and Carrar, Brecht is contradicting what he said in *Mann ist Mann*. Instead of praising the 'new human type' that acquiesces in external pressures, he is glorifying the nonconformist. But far from renouncing the play he had directed so successfully in 1931, he saw how its message could be inverted by transferring the action to Nazi Germany, satirizing the transformation of the inoffensive fish porter into a 'fighting machine', and substituting a stolen car belonging to an SA man for the elephant Billy Humph.[2]

*　　*　　*

In the summer of 1937, accompanied by Ruth Berlau and Karin Michaëlis, Brecht attended another writers' congress in Paris. The declared object was to discuss the attitude of the world's intellectuals towards the Spanish war. But the topic delegates discussed most urgently in private – and even sometimes in public – was André Gide's defection from the Party. In 1932 he had written that he would gladly sacrifice his life for the success of the Soviet Union. But he went on declaring himself to be an individualist. In June 1936, four days after arriving in the Soviet Union, he made a speech at Gorki's funeral. 'The great international and revolutionary forces', he said, 'have the responsibility to protect culture and make it illustrious.'[3] But before leaving he had seen that Soviet culture was monolithically dedicated to the glorification of the state. Ostensibly, 'self-criticism' was encouraged, but with the Party line as the only norm. At the model collective he visited, the houses were identical, each containing the same ugly furniture and the same portrait of Stalin. Along with the uniformity of style went uniformity of opinion. At first he could find no mention in the papers of the Spanish Civil War, and people he met were nervous of venturing an opinion until, a few days later, *Pravda* sided with the republicans.

Far from having been emancipated, the workers were being exploited, and so deviously that they could not see who was to blame. The fattest wage packets were going to Party members, conformists and informers. The model town of Bolchevo was populated entirely by ex-convicts, but the privilege of living there was reserved for those who had informed on fellow-prisoners. Generally workers did not have freedom of movement; if a man wanted to leave his factory job, he would lose the living-quarters to which it entitled him, and possibly be unable to find an alternative job. Thousands of people had been deported, while art that was nonconformist or obscure was denounced as 'formalist'. In Leningrad Gide was invited to address a society of students and writers, but he was not allowed to say that the majority of people can never respond to what is new and difficult in a work of art.[4]

Gide's pamphlet *Retour de l'URSS* caused consternation. Gide had been celebrated in the communist press as the greatest living French writer; now he was denounced as a fascist monster. The Russian delegates coupled his name with Trotsky's, and Michael Kolzov, the *Pravda* correspondent, improvised parodies of his book.[5]

It was Kolzov (Ernest Hemingway's model for Kharkov in *For Whom the Bell Tolls*) and André Malraux who proposed that the congress should be adjourned and resumed in Madrid, as a gesture of solidarity with the republic. Malraux, Arthur Koestler and George Orwell had been in Spain the previous year; Hemingway, Stephen Spender and many other writers had gone early in 1937. But Brecht had no desire to go. While the crew in *Das Badener Lehrstück* care little for individual survival, he cared a great deal for it and, apart from *Die Gewehre der Frau Carrar*, his only contribution to the republican cause was a speech he sent to be read in Madrid: 'Though long – all too long – defended only with intellectual weapons, but attacked with physical weapons, culture, which is itself not only an intellectual phenomenon but also, more particularly, physical, must be defended with physical weapons.'[6]

Braver, and more impetuous, than her lover, Ruth Berlau decided that she would fly to Madrid with Kolzov. Brecht tried to dissuade her and, failing, returned to Denmark, where he found that some of the actors from her production of *Die Mutter* had left to fight in Spain. In *Frau Carrar* he had roundly asserted that to stay aloof from the fight was tantamount to supporting the generals; for him, though, there was no question of fighting with any weapon but the pen.

In Spain Berlau made friends with Kolzov's wife, Maria Osten, and she went to the front with Egon Erwin Kisch and the Norwegian playwright Nordahl Grieg. Ernst Busch was there, and 'his voice gave courage to many fighters'. She received letters from Brecht in verse and prose, begging her not to take risks, and instructing her to reread morning and evening the lines:

> He whom I love
> Has told me
> That he needs me
> So
> I take great care
> Watch my step
> Fearing that each raindrop
> Could kill me.

When she finally wrote to him, announcing her return, he drove to meet her at the harbour, but on the ship she had met a Swede who had been fighting in Spain, and she stayed on board with him, disembarking at the next port to take him with her to Vallensback. Brecht drove disconsolately home:

> And all through the hours of his journey
> He felt ashamed.[7]

Once again he stayed only briefly in Skovbostrand, but long enough to complete *Der Spitzel* (*The Informer*), a sketch about the fears of a teacher and his wife that their schoolboy son will denounce them for anti-Nazi remarks. Brecht wanted to characterize Nazi Germany in a few short plays which could perhaps be staged in Paris.[8] In September he went back there. Aufricht was preparing a new production of *Dreigroschenoper* in French at the Théâtre de l'Etoile, with Raymond Rouleau as Macheath and Yvette Guilbert as Mrs Peachum.

At the same time a Paris production of *Die Gewehre der Frau Carrar* in German was being rehearsed by Slatan Dudow at the Salle Adyar with Helene Weigel in the name part. After paying another visit to Feuchtwanger in Sanary-sur-Mer at the beginning of October, Brecht went back to sit in on Dudow's rehearsals.

Weigel did not play Señora Carrar's neutrality as if there were no alternative to it, or even as if it were the natural attitude to adopt. She made the woman's feelings appear to be mixed, while an aggressiveness became visible, even when neutrality was what she was fighting for, so this helped to make the conversion plausible. The performance produced something of a rapprochement between husband and wife. Writing to Karl Korsch, Brecht said: 'Helli was better than ever. She has lost nothing during the long gap. . . . Her acting was the best and purest that could so far have been seen anywhere as part of Epic Theatre.' And the performance inspired several poems, almost as though he felt he had wronged her by centring so many on Margarete Steffin and Ruth Berlau. He admired Weigel unstintingly – as an actress. She showed everything

> That was needed for understanding
> A fisherwoman, but did not transform herself fully
> Into this fisherwoman and she played
> As if partly absorbed with thinking
> At the same time, always asking herself:
> What was it really like?[9]

The play was premièred on 16 October 1937. The poster announcing the two performances proclaimed: 'Brecht's new work is dedicated to the Spanish people's heroic battle for freedom.'

Soon after the middle of October he returned to Skovbostrand – to a house with no housewife in it. After some additional performances of *Carrar* in Paris, she went on to play the part in Prague. 'Above all,' he advised, 'give pride of place to tempo. When you need pauses, it's easy to forget that. You must have tempo between the pauses. Without increasing your volume.' But later in the month he sent her a summons in Party jargon: 'The marital and filial council had decided to recall you without delay to carry out your duties and resume your activities here. You are to report as soon as possible to the undersigned.'[10]

Before leaving Prague she had talks with E. F. Burian about a Czech edition of the play, and she visited her relations, while Brecht negotiated with the publisher Wieland Herzfelde, who was bringing out a collected edition of his work.

In Paris, during September, he had been discussing with Piscator the possibility of a play about Julius Caesar, and towards the end of October he wrote asking Weigel to find a copy of Theodor Mommsen's *Römische Geschichte* (*Roman History*) for 'the Caesar play' if she went to Vienna. He started writing the play in blank verse. One fragment that survives is the advice of a dying Roman father to his son:

> look after the slaves!
> For they are human too, which means they are mortal.
> It is a shame to let them die, when they have cost
> you so much.[11]

Brecht used the same kind of irony in the self-contained scenes he went on writing for the play about conditions inside Germany. He also aimed several volleys of satirical poems at the same target:

Not one piece of coal would come out of the earth
If the Minister weren't so wise. Without the Minister of Propaganda
No woman would let herself be made pregnant. Without the Minister of War
There would never be a war.

This comes from one of the 'Deutsche Satiren' ('German Satires') which he wrote in 1937–8 to be broadcast in German from Moscow. He achieved a more crisply epigrammatic style in his *Kriegsfibel* (*War Primer*):

> CHALKED ON THE WALL:
> They want war.
> The writer
> Is already dead
>
> WHEN THEY HAVE TO MARCH, MANY DON'T KNOW
> That their enemy is marching in front of them[12]

In another poem he described the refugees, restlessly settling close to the frontier and eagerly questioning each new arrival for news of developments at home. Worst of all, for him, was the impossibility of settling down:

Leave the sapling unwatered
Why plant another tree?
Before it's as high as a doorstep
You'll be glad to leave.[13]

18 / Caesar and Galileo: Businessman and Rebel

Regarding Julius Caesar as 'the prototype of all dictators', Brecht had begun by February 1938 to rework the Caesar material into a novel, which he titled *Die Geschäfte des Herrn Julius Caesar* (*The Business Deals of Mr Julius Caesar*). He wanted to show that a society based on slavery would come, eventually, to enslave all its citizens. But, as he conceded in a letter to Karl Korsch, 'In spite of everything, Caesar represents progress and ... it's hard to make it clear that this progress ceases to exist for the new dictators.'[1]

Brecht was trying to copy Feuchtwanger's method of dressing modern fascism in Roman guise, but instead of concerning himself with a collective subject, Brecht, though he believed himself to be an anti-individualist, was once again focusing on an individual, and the novel is an early attempt at the sort of iconoclastic deconstruction that has since become commonplace. Brecht puts Caesar into an unflattering perspective by showing him through the eyes of his private secretary, the slave Rarus, and his banker, who is called Mummlius Spicer. As in *Die heilige Johanna*, Brecht suggests that the individual who appears to be dominant is manipulated by invisible economic forces – this Caesar is desperately in debt. The real power is in the hands of the moneylenders. All his military and political initiatives are diversionary gambits; the overriding objective is to evade his creditors. As in *Dreigroschenroman*, Brecht was intent on proving that business transactions led inevitably to violence; as in the speech he made at the 1935 Paris congress, he extended his argument from the private world of business to the public world of politics, but the plausibility of the narrative is damaged by introducing modern financial and political concepts.

In the middle of February, at the Borup High School in Copenhagen, using the set of an amateur production of *Frau Carrar* by Ruth Berlau, Brecht co-directed with her a single German-language performance of the play with Weigel in the part. This was mainly for their Danish friends, including the 69-year-old Danish poet Martin Andersen Nexö, but critics attended too, and Schyberg pronounced Weigel 'ultimately too intellectual to become entirely a fisherman's wife'. Brecht maintained that 'the play was written for her, and in such a way that it did not work without her'.[2] In any case she was happy to be acting again: she gained ten pounds in weight. The evening also included a recital in Danish by Bodil Ipsen of Spanish poems and, finally, of Brecht's poem about Weigel.

Using newspaper reports and stories told by émigrés, Brecht was achieving great verisimilitude in his scenes about the reign of terror in Germany and its human consequences. Later they would constitute the play *Furcht und Elend des Dritten Reiches* (*Fear and Suffering in the Third Reich*). He had at first intended to write five scenes, but by the beginning of April he had completed twenty-seven, many of them very brief. In one a Jewish wife, deciding to save her non-Jewish husband's career by leaving him, says goodbye over the telephone to her friends, choosing her words carefully. In another a perplexed judge has to deal with a robbery in a Jewish shop. Another treatment of lawful injustice is set in a prison yard, where two bakers are in conversation. One was arrested for mixing bran into his bread, the other arrested a year later for failing to incorporate bran as the new law required. Most of the scenes are about dilemmas created for middle-class intellectuals. A doctor takes refuge in the term 'professional malady' when he has to describe injuries inflicted in a concentration camp; a physicist can no longer consult Einstein. As Brecht said, the series constituted 'a catalogue of attitudes, the attitudes of keeping silent, looking over one's shoulder, feeling frightened etc. – behaviour in a dictatorship'.[3]

For Brecht, what lay ahead was likely to be even bleaker than the five years of exile that lay behind. Since 1936 it had been obvious to him that war was inevitable. In November 1936 Mussolini had proclaimed a 'Rome–Berlin axis', and within three weeks both fascist governments had recognized Franco's regime in Spain. Openly defying the Treaty of Versailles, Hitler had remilitarized the Rhineland, and Japan, about to invade China, made an anti-Comintern pact with the Germans. On 11 March 1938 Nazi troops entered Austria, which became part of the Third Reich.

> IN THE CALENDAR THE DAY IS NOT MARKED.
> Every month, every day
> Lies open. One of the days
> Will be marked with a cross.[4]

Foreboding tarnished all the pleasures of living with a devoted wife and two children in a comfortable house on a beautiful island and with two mistresses not far away. A poem written after an unexpected snowstorm uses the contrast between white snow and greening hedges to crystallize some of the other contradictions. His thirteen-year-old son draws him away from the prediction of war he is writing to inspect a small apricot tree. The tree can be protected from the cold with a sack; the child cannot be protected from the war. Rainclouds hang above the Danish Sound, while the sun brightens the garden. The pear trees have leaves but no blossom yet, the cherry tree blossom but no leaves. The twittering of starlings mingles with the distant gunfire – Nazi naval exercise.

In March or April he sent Piscator nineteen of the disconnected scenes he now thought of making into a play. 'It could be extraordinarily suitable for production in America. ... The so-called democracies are very interested in the effects of swastika dictatorship on the various (social) levels. ... You could interpolate documentary material. I think of the style as being like Goya's in his sketches of the civil war.' He maintained that the overall effect was unlikely to be depressing: he compared the play with a Brueghel painting or a cycle of drawings by Daumier.

In May Brecht went to Paris, where, with Slatan Dudow, he co-directed a cast of émigré German actors. Eight scenes were staged in the Salle d'Iéna under the title 99%; Helene Weigel played the Jewish wife and one other part. The music was written (under a pseudonym) by Paul Dessau. The first-night audience laughed a good deal and applauded enthusiastically at the end of each scene,[5] but unfortunately the performance did not lead to a French-language production.

In the *Neue Weltbühne* Walter Benjamin reported: 'At last, after five years in exile, the special political experiences that this audience has in common found expression on a stage.' *Das Schwarze Korps*, the journal of the SS, attributed the audience's laughter to amusement at Brecht's failure to understand what was happening in Germany: he was presenting an absurd subversion of all moral and legal norms.[6]

When one scene, *Der Spitzel* (*The Informer*), was published in *Das Wort*, it won praise, as no previous work of Brecht's had done, from Georg Lukács, who had established himself in Russia as the leading theoretician of socialist realism. He welcomed the new realism in Brecht's work, acknowledging a 'vivid, many-hued and graduated way' of 'representing human destiny'.[7]

After returning to Skovbostrand in June, Brecht went on to develop his theatrical theory, stimulated by his wife's quintessentially epic performances in *Frau Carrar* and in *Furcht und Elend*, and by anxiety at having written both plays in a naturalistic and old-fashioned mould. In the eight-page essay 'Die Strassenszene' ('The Street Scene') he reverted to the anti-illusionist argument he had advanced in the blank verse poem of 1930 – that acting on stage should be modelled on the street-corner acting of a man demonstrating what happened in an accident. The actor should be like the man in wanting neither to reproduce nor to induce emotion for its own sake. The demonstration must have a social purpose: it must help either to expose attitudes that tend to cause accidents or to establish who was responsible.[8]

Later in June Walter Benjamin came back. With a big garden at his disposal and a writing-table by a window overlooking the Sound, he would have nothing but chess to distract him from writing his book on Baudelaire. 'Next door is Brecht's house, where there are two children I like, the radio, supper, the friendliest reception, and, after we've eaten, one or two prolonged games of chess with Brecht. The newspapers arrive here so very late that it is an effort to open them.'[9]

Both men enjoyed their conversations, though Brecht was uncertain how critical he could afford to be about Stalin. Tretiakov had been arrested as a Japanese spy and had probably been liquidated. Carola Neher had also been arrested: 'If she has been condemned, there must have been substantial evidence against her, but one does not have the feeling that one pound of crime is met with one pound of punishment.' Soviet poets were in great difficulty: 'If Stalin's name is not mentioned in a poem, it is taken as a sign of ill will.' Brecht came closer to complaining about Soviet deviation from Marxist communism when he said: 'Marxism lends itself all too readily to "interpretation". Today it's a hundred years old and what do we find?' He had been talking about his deep-rooted hatred of priests, and implying that Marx's theoretical doctrines were being appropriated and exploited by what was virtually a priestly sect. Or, as he formulated it a few weeks later, 'The struggle against ideology has become a new ideology.' Always a man who enjoyed standing up in the middle of a conversation to act out a point, he leaned over the seated Benjamin to personify the state. Assuming 'a sly, furtive expression ... and with a cunning sidelong glance at an imaginary interlocutor, he said: "I know that I *ought* to wither away." '[10]

What he wrote was liable to be less sophisticated and less critical than what he said. On the Moscow Trials his only written comment was:

With total clarity the trials have proved the existence of active conspiracies against the regime and proved that these nests of conspirators were responsible for both domestic sabotage and certain negotiations with Fascist diplomats about the attitudes their governments might take towards a possible change of regime in the Union. ... All the scum at home and abroad, all the parasites, professional criminals, informers joined them. All this rabble had the same objectives as they (the conspirators) did. I am convinced that this is the truth.[11]

Working on the Caesar novel in July 1938, Brecht tried to regard nothing as inevitable. Historians were too fatalistic. Even slavery could have been overthrown – the slaves formed two thirds of the Italian population. 'I have to show how the effort to preserve slavery forced the whole people into slavery. Not a single senator or banker in the Caesarian period had as much personal security, opportunity for political initiative or freedom of movement as almost everyone had in the age of Cicero.'[12]

His conversations with Benjamin constantly reverted to the Soviet Union. It was clear to Brecht that after the dissolution of the First International, neither Marx not Engels had kept actively in touch with the working-class movement. Nor could a socialist economy exist in one country. 'Inevitably rearmament has sent the Russian proletariat back to phases of historical development which have long ago been passed – among others, the monarchic phase. Russia is currently subject to personal rule. Only idiots can deny this.'[13]

He shocked Benjamin on 24 July by going over to read him a poem:

> Harvesting your fodder, we stood, crouching ...
> For your stall, thou protector of the family,
> We groaned under heavy beams. We
> Sleep in the wet, you in the dry. Yesterday
> You coughed, beloved pacemaker.
> We were beside ourselves.[14]

Could Brecht possibly be writing about Stalin? 'I did not dare entertain the idea.' But then Brecht called it a poem in honour of Stalin, who had, he said, immense merit. The writings of Trotsky showed that suspicions could be harboured, and if, one day, they proved to be justified, it would become necessary to fight the regime, and publicly. But – 'unfortunately or, if you prefer, thank God' – the suspicion was not yet a certainty.[15]

Observing his friend at such close quarters, Benjamin noticed 'the destructive element in Brecht's character which jeopardizes everything almost before it has been achieved'. Habitually he tried to avoid risks – in not going to Spain, for instance, or in consulting Benjamin about whether to publish in *Das Wort* an attack on Lukács – but he had compulsions that made him quarrel with directors and collaborators and embark on courses of action which could only be self-defeating. He was aware of this tendency but saw it as belonging to the period: 'If the history of our time is handed down to the future, the possibility of understanding my manic qualities will be handed down with it. The times we live in will form a backdrop for my mania. But I'd really prefer people to describe me as a *moderate* manic.'[16]

Thinking he had discovered in himself a capacity for moderation, he wanted to cultivate it, but, believing that Hitler was going to win the war, he felt uncertain whether moderation was a luxury or an indispensable necessity. Life would go on: in spite of Hitler there would always be children. But Brecht was also capable of an impassioned vehemence which made an impact on Benjamin 'equal in strength to the power of fascism'. Because Brecht's writing was his only weapon, he brandished it with disproportionate ferocity. Considering whether to include his verses for children in the volume of *Gedichte im Exil* (*Poems in Exile*), he said: 'In fighting against that lot nothing must be neglected. What they're planning – make no mistake – is nothing trivial. They're planning for thirty years into the future. Colossal things. Colossal crimes. They're totally unscrupulous. They're out to destroy everything. Under their blows every living cell recoils.'[17] This was to lavish demagoguery on an audience of one, but Brecht had to convince himself that his verse could help to avert the cataclysm.

Writing in his *Arbeitsjournal* (*Work Journal*) on 16 August, he catalogued the tasks that lay ahead. The Tui novel was less urgent than the Caesar novel, which must be finished before he could settle down to writing on *Die Haltungen Lenins* (*Lenin's Attitudes*) or to rewriting *Baal* as *Die Abenteuer des bösen Baal, des Asozialen* (*The Adventures of the Evil Baal, the Asocial Man*). 'Thirty years are not too much for what remains to be done.' He also saw a need for 'a small realistic novel with heroes for the proletarian youth'.[18]

But it was hard to believe in Moscow as a centre for artists who knew what needed to be done. Stalin's attempt to impose unity on the arts paralleled the attempt being made in Nazi Germany. Together with the French decadents, the German expressionists, the surrealists and the cubists, Brecht was denounced by Lukács as formalistic. In conversation with Benjamin, Brecht dismissed Lukács as an enemy of creativity, an *apparatchik* interested only in exercising control over other people. Drafting two articles for *Das Wort* – where he never published them –

Brecht aimed more respectful blows at Lukács's position, arguing that realism should not be ascribed merely to a particular historical form of the novel – Balzac's or Tolstoy's, for instance. Shelley was more of a realist than Balzac, and as rival exemplars, Brecht cited Cervantes, Swift, Grimmelshausen, Dickens, Voltaire and Hašek. Realism was not a matter of form, Brecht insisted. 'Our concept of realism needs to be broad and political', and he proposed five principles. Realist art should expose the network of causes operating on society. It should show the dominant viewpoint to be the viewpoint of the dominators. It should be created from the viewpoint of the class which has proposed the broadest solutions for the most urgent social problems. It should focus on 'the dynamics of growth'. It should be concrete, but should encourage abstraction. Realist writing was not to be identified with the sensuous writing in which everything could be tasted, visualized, smelt, felt. Realism must be gauged by measuring the work of art not against other reputedly realistic works of art but against contemporary reality.[19]

One of his complaints about Lukács was that in concerning himself primarily with consciousness, he transposed everything from objective into subjective terms. Brecht's concern was with the external world. This was why he preferred Hašek to Joyce or Gide. *Ulysses* was a catalogue of descriptive methods; *Les Faux-Monnayeurs* was a novel about the difficulties of writing a novel. *Schweyk* was 'the only great popular narrative of our time'.[20]

Between his work and the world Brecht aimed to keep the traffic of influence running in both directions. In September 1938, when England and France acquiesced in Germany's plans for the annexation of Sudetenland, he wanted to reflect developments in his Caesar novel: 'the breach of contract which wipes Czechoslovakia off the map and finishes off France's claim to be a great power. They conduct only predatory wars. They defend the plundering only when it's their plunder to keep. They constantly sacrifice political power for the sake of commercial advantage, whenever this astonishing choice has to be made.' Together with Fritz Sternberg, who was staying in Skovbostrand on his way back from a Scandinavian tour, Brecht sat by the radio till three in the morning, listening to news bulletins in various languages. As he saw it, England was reluctant to fight a war which would be won by her Russian ally, Russia reluctant to fight for it to be won by the generals, and France reluctant for it to be won by the popular front.[21]

Brecht was glad to be distracted from the bad news when the American filmwriter Ferdinand Reyher arrived in Denmark on 28 October to stay for a week. They met several times, and played chess. Brecht revealed his hopes of living in America and, discussing past and future plays, mentioned that he had been researching the life of Galileo. Reyher encouraged him to believe that Galileo could help him to gain an entrée to the United States. They agreed that he would produce an outline for a film story, which Reyher would then try to sell in Hollywood. Only afterwards would Brecht write the play.[22]

Within three days of Reyher's departure Brecht had settled down to work, but, following his instinct, he wrote the story as a play. Ten days later (17 November) he had finished nine of the fourteen scenes; the whole play was finished by the 23rd. Its original title was *Die Erde bewegt sich* (*The Earth is Moving*), and he later thought of calling it *Die Schlauheit des Überlebens* (*The Cunning of Survival*). On 2 December he wrote to tell Reyher that the play now existed. 'It has a monumental part, and if one could get it into the hands of an important, influential actor, it might lead to a production.' Were American productions dependent on actors? Could Reyher 'suggest an approach for having it produced'?[23]

But for Reyher's visit to Denmark, the play would not have been written so quickly, but probably it would have been written. Margarete Steffin told Walter Benjamin that the idea had been 'haunting him for some time', and he had thought at one stage of rewriting it as a *Lehrstück* for the amateur actors who had performed *Frau Carrar*. His research had been extensive. He had studied Erich Wohlwill's long book on Galileo, together with astronomical work by A. S. Eddington, J. H. Jeans, Henri Mineur, Galileo himself, Francis Bacon and Montaigne. Brecht also consulted the Copenhagen physicist Christian Möller, and he owned a copy of Leonardo Olschki's 1927 book *Galileo und seine Zeit* (*Galileo and His Time*) which praises him as an exemplar of 'the moral courage which overcomes the fear of profound mysteries and recognizes the discovered truth as the object of adoration and the goal of infinite striving'.[24]

Leben des Galilei (*Life of Galileo*), as it was renamed, is Brecht's only play to centre on a famous historical figure, but this was an easy step to take from the Caesar novel. Like Caesar, Galileo does not interest Brecht as an individual – little of his private life comes into focus – but as a meeting-point of historical forces, a man driven into taking responsibility for the future. Brecht could hardly have believed his own decisions to be equally vital for humanity, but his awareness of extreme crisis and his need to adopt a committed attitude towards the future helped him to project himself into Galileo's situation. 'Dark times' is one of the key phrases in Brecht's poems of 1938. One section of his Svendborg collection is prefixed with the motto:

> In the dark times
> Will they also sing?
> They will also sing.
> About the dark times.

Was he, when writing about the seventeenth century, escaping into the brighter past? 'Aren't there plenty of indications that night is coming and none that a new age is beginning? Shouldn't we therefore maintain an appropriate attitude for people heading into the night?'[25] Brecht usually had less reason than most of his contemporaries to blame himself on this score. When he looked into the past, he was searching for clues about the future.

The 1938 version of the play is less pessimistic than subsequent versions, and less critical of Galileo, who is made to declare: 'I insist that this is a new age. If it looks like a bloodstained old hag, then that's what a new age looks like.' Twenty-eight years later, when Dürrenmatt asked him whether the world could still be represented theatrically, Brecht replied yes, it could, but only if it were conceived as alterable.[26] Brecht's Galileo is a man who could alter the world by giving humanity a different view of its importance. To discredit the Ptolemaic cosmology, which put the earth at the centre of the universe, would, in Brecht's opinion, have been to subvert the Church's authority over scientific questions at the same time as upsetting the old view of the relationship between earth and heaven, and with it the assumption that the hierarchical ordering of society reflected a hierarchical universe: 'And the earth rolls gaily round the sun, and the fishwives, merchants, princes, cardinals and even the Pope roll round with it. The universe lost its centre overnight.' Brecht makes Galileo think and talk in a modern way about the macrocosm and the social order, but his principle was: 'Learn from history, but at the right moment throw it away. Don't be bothered by historical accuracy.' The real subject of the play is the difficulties and dangers of asking for the truth to be recognized when the truth is subversive. A senile cardinal (who may derive from the senile Grand Inquisitor in Schiller's Don Carlos) is made to insist: 'I am walking on a fixed earth.' But when, like Brecht and like Kragler, Galileo has to choose between dying as a martyr and surviving as a coward, he chooses to live.

The 1938 draft of *Galileo* contains an anecdote subsequently incorporated in Brecht's *Keunergeschichten* (*Stories of Herr Keuner*). Galileo tells the story of a Cretan philosopher who works seven years for the agent of a repressive regime without answering the question 'Will you work for me?' When the agent dies, the philosopher gets rid of the body, fumigates the house, and answers 'No'.[27] As the exemplary survivor who apparently submits to pressure but succeeds in smuggling his *Discorsi* out of the country, Galileo was intended as a model for the intellectuals who stayed inside Germany. Later Brecht would apparently submit to pressure in East Germany but would succeed in creating the Berliner Ensemble.

'It accords with historical truth', he wrote, 'that the Galileo of the play never turned directly against the Church.'[28] But the confrontation between Galileo and the Church is falsified by making him speak like a precursor of dialectical materialism and by implying that he pioneered a purely materialistic rebellion. Static sequences of rhetoric are incorporated to represent Galileo as a passionate believer in mankind's reasonableness:

My hope lies in the old woman who with her hardened hand feeds an extra bundle of hay to her mule on the night before the journey, with the sailor who has foresight enough to buy provisions for the days that will be lost when there's no wind or too much, with the child who stuffs a cap on his head when he's made to see it may rain. They all submit to evidence. Yes, I believe in the gentle power of reason over humanity.

Much of the play's action turns on his outrage and Galileo's discomfited incredulity at the Church's refusal to be convinced by irrefutable evidence.

At the same time Galileo is viewed in relation to the rise of natural science, which Engels connected with the ascendancy of the bourgeoisie: for both the manufacture and the distribution of their goods merchants needed the knowledge and the terminology that science could provide. Engels's notes on the history of science, which mention Galileo, argue that 'science owes infinitely more to production' than production owes to science. This point emerges in the discussion between Galileo and the Curator, who tells him off for disliking commerce, arguing that physics is in great debt to the demand for looms.[29]

Equally Marxist is Brecht's treatment of Ludovico, the rich landowner who wants to marry Galileo's daughter. Ludovico's vested interests are in the preservation of the *status quo*, which Galileo threatens, and Virginia's personal happiness falls prey to the conflict of interest between the two men. Embittered, alienated and dehumanized, she turns to religion for comfort, and in the final scene behaves more like her father's gaoler than his daughter. The antipathy between Galileo and Ludovico is as impersonal as the battle between Shlink and Garga, but the father-daughter antagonism belongs to the realm of personal relationships.

The historical Galileo, who maintained that scientific research and theological dogma dealt with two different kinds of truth,[30] felt more ambivalent than Brecht's Galileo about the Church's authority, and the Inquisition had difficulty in collecting evidence against him. According to Wohlwill's book, the injunction against Galileo was a forgery, contrived by the same cardinal, Roberto Bellarmino, who in 1600 had engineered the execution of Giordano Bruno. But Brecht was not interested in making a case against the cardinal. His concern is to demonstrate that the Church is both an oppressive force and an instrument used by the dominant class to preserve the *status quo*.

During Galileo's lifetime it would have been impossible to organize the Italian peasants into rebellion, but Brecht makes him veer towards a revolutionary attitude. 'I see their divine patience,' he says of the Campagna peasants, 'but where is their divine anger?'

Although Galileo derives enormous enjoyment from food and drink, Brecht projected a great deal of himself into the character. 'He's more of a pleasure-fancier than any other man I've met,' says Barberini, one of the cardinals. 'His thinking proceeds out of sensuality.' This corresponds to the most empathic of Brecht's working notes on Galileo: 'As a confirmed materialist, he insists on physical pleasures. He wouldn't actually drink while working, but what matters is that he *works* in a sensual way.' Describing his character in a letter to a Swedish painter, Brecht spoke of a

tough physicist with embonpoint and a face like Socrates – a noisy, full-blooded man of humour, the new type of physicist, earthy, a great teacher. Favourite posture: belly stuck out, hands on the two cheeks of his arse, always gesticulating with a fleshy hand, but economically. Costume not ostentatious, except at official functions, comfortable trousers for working in, shirtsleeves, or especially towards the end, a long, yellowish-white soutane with wide sleeves, tied with a cord over the belly.[31]

The early years of working collaboratively with Neher had habituated Brecht to picturing clothes and postures in graphic detail. But it was not until much later that he emphasized Galileo's self-indulgence in order to associate him censoriously with the development, three centuries afterwards, of thermonuclear physics. The first version of the play was only just finished when, in December 1938, it was announced that Otto Hahn and Fritz Strassmann had split the uranium atom. This did not stop Brecht from claiming in a newspaper article published on 6 January 1939 that the play was about 'Galileo's heroic struggle for his modern scientific conviction'.[32] It was when revising the play six years later that Brecht expressed doubts about whether it was right to pursue scientific knowledge if the pursuit led into areas that might be dangerous for humanity.

Like Brecht, Galileo surrounds himself with disciples, working pleasurably in their company, instructing them by Socratic questioning, and testing his own ideas against theirs. The build-up of the group around Galileo prepares for the recantation scene, which achieves an effective climax. If Galileo recants, the bells will be rung. His disciples wait, hoping for the silence to continue, but belatedly the bells start booming. Galileo enters, visibly transformed by the trial – one of the rare offstage trials in Brecht's work – just in time to hear Andrea del Sarto say: 'Unhappy the land that has no heroes.' Instead of greeting Galileo, his disciples shrink away, and Andrea abuses him. His answer to what he has overheard is: 'Unhappy the land where heroes are needed.' This Galileo is neither heroic nor prone to guilt feelings. Fear of physical pain is enough to make him recant, but, as in so many Brecht plays, guile, when offered as an alternative to heroism, turns out to be satisfying fare. There is no catharsis, but when Galileo gives Andrea the copy of his *Discorsi* which has been hidden inside his globe, the strong sense of danger is spiced by the topical allusion: 'Be careful when you go through Germany if you're smuggling the truth under your cloak.' Like the Cretan philosopher in the anecdote, Galileo is rewarded for years of patience by a final triumph over the agent of the oppressive power.

Brecht also wanted his play to be staged in Copenhagen, where the actor Poul Reumert, who would make an excellent Galileo, was influential enough to get the play on. While he was working on the play, Brecht was so often visualizing Reumert that he sometimes told Ruth Berlau 'Then you see Reumert come on stage', when he meant Galileo. Unfortunately, five years earlier, he had said in an interview: 'We must move right away from old-fashioned naturalistic acting, from the emotionally heightened dramatic acting of Emil Jannings, Poul Reumert and in fact the great majority.' It was too late to back-pedal, although Brecht considered *Galileo* to be a naturalistic play: '*Leben des Galilei* is tech-

nically a big step backwards, like *Frau Carrars Gewehre* all too opportunistic. The play would have to be completely rewritten to capture this
"breeze that blows from undiscovered coasts", this rosy dawn of science.
Everything more direct, without the interiors, the "atmosphere", the
empathy.'[33]

It was in January 1939 that he heard Michael Kolzov had been arrested
in Moscow. 'My last Russian contact over there. Nobody knows anything about Tretiakov. . . . Or anything about Neher, who's supposed to
have transacted Trotskyite deals in Prague on behalf of her husband.'
Stalin and his new GPU chief Yezhov were drastically purging the
intelligentsia as well as the Party, the government, the army, the func-
tionaries in collectives and the engineers. Bernhard Reich and Asja Lacis
had stopped writing to Brecht; Margarete Steffin, writing to friends in
the Caucasus and in Leningrad, had been getting no answer. Bela Kun
had been arrested. Meyerhold had lost his theatre and was allowed to
work only in opera. 'Literature and art seem to be covered with shit, and
political theory to be down and out. What prevails is a thin, bloodless
proletarian humanism, bureaucratically propagated.' Brecht's 1939
poem on the execution of Tretiakov is titled: 'Ist das Volk unfehlbar?'
('Is the People Infallible?')

> The innocent often have no proof.
> So is it best to keep silent?[34]

Brecht's diary for 12 February 1939 records that Galileo's Dialogues had
given him the idea for presenting theory by means of dialogue in a work
to be called *Der Messingkauf* (*The Purchase of Brass*). The object was to
analyse theatre's substance, ignoring form, just as a man might buy a
trumpet not to play it but for the sake of the brass. He intended to write
a four-sided conversation about new ways of making theatre,[35] but there
are six speakers in the sketches he completed: a philosopher (Marxist),
an actor and actress, a dramaturg, and a stage-hand or electrician to
represent the worker's viewpoint. Brecht incorporated several poems,
essays, scenes and rehearsal exercises for actors. The philosopher's views
on the function of theatre echo views Brecht had already pronounced.

Der Messingkauf was to remain unfinished, but Brecht wrote for it a
great many fragments, varying in length between a few lines and a few
pages. Though he still vetoed empathy, he conceded that no restraint
should be put on the actor's use of emotions or on his presentation of
them. Brecht stressed the importance of comedy more than he had before

– 'A theatre where you can't laugh is a theatre you can laugh at' – and also the agitprop value of theatre; his actors had not been 'high priests of art'. Their function as political human beings was to use art or anything else for their social objective.[36]

During the first half of March 1939 he resumed work on a play he had started in about 1930 in Berlin. Its first title had been *Fanny Kress oder der Huren einziger Freund* (*Fanny Kress or the Whore's Only Friend*); the second title was *Die Ware Liebe*, which means *Love is a Commodity* but sounds like 'die wahre Liebe' (true love). To be a prostitute is to be the goods and the retailer; realizing this, a young girl starts to keep the functions separate, running a tobacconist's shop dressed as a man, while wearing more feminine clothes to remove in her other career. In Berlin Brecht had written five scenes, four of which were still usable. The part was designed for Weigel: with her deep voice she could have switched effectively into the male impersonation. Though the disguise element reminded him of charades, he could develop ideas he was formulating in *Der Messingkauf*, and since there was no prospect of a production, he would compromise less than he had in *Frau Carrar* and *Furcht und Elend*. The play would have to be stored with his other unproduced scripts, and 'You don't make concessions for your drawer.'[37]

Condemned, like the Flying Dutchman, to staying on the move, Brecht could not settle down to work on *Der gute Mensch von Sezuan* (*The Good Woman of Setzuan*) – his new title for the prostitute play. On 13 March 1939 German troops marched into Bohemia and Moravia, which became a 'protectorate' under the command of Constantin von Neurath. 'The Reich is growing larger,' wrote Brecht. 'The housepainter is sitting in the Hradschin.' The next day Slovakia was placed under German 'protection'. Brecht had not only lost the collected edition of his work, which Wieland Herzfelde had been publishing in Prague; it was clear he could not go on 'sitting on one of these little islands when the butchery seems about to start. This year each new week without a world war is simply an unbelievable stroke of luck for mankind.'[1]

Thanks to Georg Branting, the Swede who had sailed back from Spain with Ruth Berlau, Brecht escaped to Stockholm on 23 April 1939. Together with the writer Henry Peter Matthis, Branting, a prominent Social Democrat, arranged for Brecht to be invited by the National Association of Amateur Theatres to give a lecture. 'I have put my little house on the market. The formalities are naturally time-taking. Then there's the packing of books and furniture, and the children's identity papers have to be put in order.'[2]

He pretended that he was going to give a five-month lecture tour in Sweden, and, during March, applied to the Danish police for Weigel and the children, who had no passports, to be given exit visas. The police made no difficulties, but before Margarete Steffin could cross the border, she had to become a Danish citizen. She did this by a marriage of convenience, and after Brecht had been in Sweden a week, she, Weigel, and the children followed him. Once again they settled on an island; once again a house was put at their disposal. It belonged to the sculptress Ninan Santesson, a friend of the actress Naima Wifstrand, who had translated *Die Gewehre der Frau Carrar* into Swedish, and played the name part in March 1938. The island was Lidingö, near Stockholm, and the house was in the middle of a small fir-wood. 'My workroom, previously a sculptor's studio, is 7m. in length and 5m. in width. I also have several tables.'³ His books and his furniture were sent on afterwards from Skovbostrand.

He lectured at the students' theatre in Stockholm on 4 May 1939. For at least two generations, he argued, theatrical experiment had been conducted along two lines which had seldom come together. Vakhtangov, Meyerhold, Reinhardt, Okhlopkov, Stanislavsky and Jessner had tended to improve theatre's capacity to entertain; the experiments of Ibsen, Tolstoy, Strindberg, Gorki, Chekhov, Hauptmann, Shaw, Kaiser and O'Neill had been aimed to heighten drama's educational value, as had his *Dreigroschenoper*, he said. The only director he grouped with these playwrights was Piscator. In Berlin, because of his rival claim to the paternity of epic theatre, it had been expedient to attack him; here it was expedient to claim him as an ally, praising him for submitting facts to an audience which had been required to arrive at political decisions. Traditional empathic acting had tended to unite the audience and nullify the educational value of the production; Piscator and Brecht had tended to divide the audience into two mutually hostile groups.

Georg Branting was present at the lecture, together with representatives of Social Democratic trade unions, who agreed to sponsor a new amateur theatre company. Brecht had already written the play *Dansen* for the Copenhagen workers' theatre; he turned out a similar play which was produced in August 1939 by the Amatorteater Riksforbund in a Stockholm adult education institute. It was called *Was kostet das Eisen?* (*What Price Iron?*) and Brecht, who was again debarred from political activities, used the pseudonym John Kent. Both *Dansen* and *Was kostet das Eisen?* are agitprop plays aimed against neutrality and non-aggression pacts. The comedy is farcical and the effects unrealistic. 'The iron merchant must wear a wig with hairs that can stand on end; the shoes must be very big.'

In the summer of 1939 Brecht's brother Walter, who was still lecturing on the manufacture of paper at the Technische Hochschule in Darmstadt, came to speak in Stockholm. Visiting Brecht in Lidingö, he brought the news that their father had died in Augsburg during May. Theo Lingen, who had adopted Brecht's daughter Hanne, now a girl of sixteen, was resisting Nazi pressure to divorce her half-Jewish mother.

In Sweden Brecht's social life was more actively interwoven with his work than it had been in Denmark. He saw a great deal of Matthis, and of two other Swedish writers, Arnold Ljungdal and Johannes Edfeld. The four men collaborated on a scenario for a children's film, *Wir wollen fliegen* (*We Want to Fly*).⁴

The émigré German actors Hermann Greid and Curt Trepte, who were helping to organize amateur theatricals for the Social Democratic unions, often came to Brecht's house. The painter Hans Tombrock, an ex-miner, became a close friend. He produced a series of drawings – as Neher once had – to illustrate Brecht's poems and plays, while Brecht encouraged him to use 'the principle of the social group as a category of pictorial composition'. Alternating texts and pictures, Tombrock produced a number of large panels for community houses. Brecht persuaded him to paint the workers larger than life-size, looking both ill at ease and dangerous. 'One must have the feeling: there sits the true builder of seven-gated Thebes, the conqueror of Asia, who is darkly pondering the lies about his conquests and his buildings.'[5]

Brecht was also friendly with Naima Wifstrand, who in the summer of 1939 may have helped to start the mental processes that led to the writing of *Mutter Courage*. The part was probably written with her in mind, though Berlau maintains he had conceived it much earlier. Wifstrand read to him from Johan Ludvig Runeberg's early nineteenth-century ballads about the Russian-Swedish war. His canteen woman, Lotte Svard, was one of the models for Brecht's canteen woman, though Svard offered herself among the goods that were for sale. In Bernard Shaw's translation of Runeberg,

> And the dear young soldiers' heroic mood
> She loved in its full display.

Naima Wifstrand also made specific suggestions for the play, and it is probable that Brecht from the beginning thought of using it to pave his way into Sweden.

At this early stage the theme of love as commodity was probably common to both the plays he was writing. In May, struggling with *Der gute Mensch*, he had the idea of making the prostitute's lover an out-of-work airman. He wanted to avoid charm and chinoiserie. 'The girl must be big and strong, the town big, dusty and uninhabitable. ... I'm thinking of a Chinese suburb with cement factories etc. There are still gods there, but already aeroplanes.' Still working on the play in the middle of July, he was badly behind the schedule he had set himself.[6]

Later he would boast that even in exile he had never let a day pass without working, but his routine was interrupted by the outbreak of war. When the non-aggression pact between Russia and Germany was ratified on the last day in August, Brecht's reaction was: 'The Union is saving itself at the cost of leaving the world's proletariat without watch-words, hope or help.' In the evening he heard an English infantry officer on the radio, addressing German front-line soldiers: 'Otherwise we'll teach the rulers of Germany to deal decently and honourably with neighbouring nations. Good night.' At 8.45 the following morning Germany warned all neutrals not to fly over Polish territory, and then Hitler spoke to the Wehrmacht. 'Hitler's radio speech was strikingly insecure: "I am determined to be determined." Strongest applause when he said "Traitors have nothing to expect except death".' On the German radio Brecht heard 'the military marches that create a mood for dying', and on the English radio arrangements for evacuating three million people from London.[7]

With Matthis, Ljungdal and Edfelt he attended a lunch at the town hall in honour of Thomas Mann, who was appalled at the non-aggression pact, while his daughter Erika found it understandable and logical, if scarcely conducive to peace. On 3 September, when England and France declared war on Germany, Brecht's analysis was: 'The German government wants war, the German people doesn't. The French and English governments don't want war, the French and English people do – to stop Hitler.' The next day he noted: 'I was fairly sure the English would pull back at the last minute. But Churchill seems to have brought it off.'[8]

It was obvious that the RAF would not halt the Wehrmacht's advance by dropping leaflets on Germany. According to the Swedish papers, news of victories were being greeted in Berlin restaurants with shouts of 'Heil Hitler!' By 10 September German armies had overrun Pomerania, Silesia and western Poland. Brecht tried to go on writing *Der gute Mensch*, but found much of his dialogue too casuistical, and he could not combine the parts into a whole.[9]

On 17 September Russia invaded Poland from the east, after an article in *Pravda* had heralded the military action by blaming Poland's military collapse on the suppression of minorities. Brecht saw that Russia might enter the war on Germany's side, and, in any event, the principle 'the USSR doesn't need a foot of foreign soil' had been abandoned. It was a pity that 'it seems to Stalin impossible to declare war in a revolutionary way, as a people's war, as a proletarian action'. Instead, the Russians had embarked on a 'singularly Napoleonic' invasion of foreign territory, usurping 'all the Fascist cant about "blood brotherhood"'.[10]

The war gave a new edge to his ambivalence at having to live in exile:

One night recently
I had uncomfortable dreams and dreamed
  I was in a city
Where the street signs were in German. I woke up
Drenched in sweat, saw the pine tree
Black as night below my window, and was relieved to know:
I was in a foreign land.

Putting the prostitute play aside, he worked on *Mutter Courage*, which looks forwards by looking backwards. Before 1914 Europe had never come closer to a world war than during the Thirty Years War (1618–48) which, constantly renewing itself, had devastated huge tracts of central Europe. Though even Brecht could not have believed that the impact of his play would be strong enough to stop Hitler, he claims to have 'imagined that the playwright's admonitory voice would be audible in the theatres of various great cities, warning that if you sup with the devil, you need a long spoon'. But judging from Margarete Steffin's diary, he did not start work on the play until 27, 28 or 29 September. It was finished by the beginning of November.[11]

As in *Frau Carrar*, the action revolves around a mother's efforts to keep her children alive, but Mother Courage is financially dependent on the war, selling drink and goods to the soldiers. Brecht could not have written the play without his early experiences of composing verse to perform with guitar accompaniment and his later experience of reworking John Gay's ballad opera. The characters in *Mutter Courage*, like characters in a ballad, are painted in primary colours – the brave son, the honest son, the dumb but big-hearted daughter, the opportunistic priest, and so on. We are told what the cook's name is – Peter Lamb – but to us, as to Mother Courage, he remains 'the cook', while characterization rests partly on touches of the kind Brecht had already used in his ballad 'Surabaya Johnny' in *Happy End*. Like Johnny, the cook keeps his pipe in his mouth when making love. These are less individuals than types, while many of the main statements are made through ballad-like songs. But the earthy vitality of the prose and the verse fuels the action as it ranges over twelve years of the Thirty Years War, robustly reconstituting the guile of recruiting sergeants, the conflicts and power games of officers and underdogs, the manœuvrings of a primitive business-woman, practised in the art of survival but unsuccessful in teaching it to her children.

Brecht owes something to Schiller's blank verse trilogy *Wallenstein* (1797–9), a sub-Shakespearian history play, which spreads its focus from the central heroic figure to take in the soldiers – their courage, their appetites and their greed for plunder. Superficially Brecht's soldiers look more realistic, but he makes them philosophize rather like the characters in *Dreigroschenoper*, articulating assumptions he wants to discredit, as when the recruiting sergeant condemns the anarchy of peace, praising war for the order it brings, or when the chaplain rationalizes procrastination by saying that the Lord will provide.

According to Brecht's notes, the Thirty Years War was one of the first large-scale wars to be caused by capitalism. As in the *Dreigroschenroman*, he is at pains to show that trading is always criminal and often murderous. In one scene Mother Courage could save the life of her honest son by paying a bribe of 200 florins, but by haggling she loses him. More important, the association between trading and killing is implicit in the play's central image, the wagon which is both a shop and a mobile home: to earn a living for herself and her family she pursues fighting wherever it breaks out. War was 'the continuation of business by other means'.[12] As she says, 'If you listen to the big shots, the war's being fought just from fear of God and for everything that's good and beautiful. But look closer and you see they're not so stupid as all that. They're in it for what they can get. Otherwise the small fry like me wouldn't go along with it.'

Writing for Sweden, Brecht opened his action there, not in 1618 but in 1624, a year of relative calm after six years of violence, but also the year Wallenstein's army marched into Bohemia. The play reveals parallels between seventeenth-century events and contemporary events, but his history of the years 1624–36 is quite unlike that of the history books. After the death of Marshall Tilly, Mother Courage apprehensively asks the chaplain whether the fighting will stop. The retort is scornful: 'Because the field marshal's dead? Don't be childish. There are dozens like that. You can always find heroes.' But none are to be found in this play. Wallenstein is not even mentioned; Tilly and Gustavus Adolphus are kept offstage. The focus is on the Courage family, customers, a camp-follower, and hangers-on. For Brecht, as for Brueghel, history is the history of the small fry, who always constitute the majority. When the chaplain, hearing the salvo of cannon-fire at Tilly's funeral, exclaims: 'This is a historic moment', Courage is angrily sorting out merchandise brought in by her dumb daughter, who has been assaulted on the way back to the wagon. 'The historic moment for me is the knock on the head my daughter's had.'

Brecht owned Gustav Glück's *Brueghels Gemälde* (*Brueghel's Paint-*

ings) and *Das grosse Brueghel-Buch*, which Weigel had given him in about 1934 in Denmark. He particularly liked *Dulle Griet*, which depicts a fury as the originator of war, but gives her the features of a servant, helpless and handicapped. In his notes about alienation effects in Brueghel's narrative pictures,[13] Brecht stresses the contrasts in the landscapes – an Alpine peak in a Flemish landscape. Each element, by 'alienating' the others, forces them into clearer focus. The landscapes are mostly populated, and the people are often more absorbed in their own work (ploughing, fishing, sweeping) than in watching a catastrophic event such as the fall of Icarus. Similarly Brecht will give space in the foreground to activities such as plucking a chicken, and when he shows how a disaster can impinge on an idyll, he will use each to heighten the impact of the other. In rejecting literary traditions, he was all the more open to visual influences, especially when he found images of brawling and bustle that could be translated into theatrical terms. His plays are no more realistic than Brueghel's paintings, but both convey a strong sense – almost a strong smell – of life being lived.

The story of *Mutter Courage* goes back to *Frau Carrar* (and to Synge's *Riders to the Sea*), but instead of trying to keep her children out of the war, Courage tries in vain to keep them alive without breaking her habit of living by the sword. The fortune-telling she fakes in the first sequence, drawing death cards for each of the three children, is intended as a warning to them and as a reminder to us, not of tragic fatality but of probability. The sequence also performs a negative function in reminding us that she is not *fated* to go trying to earn a livelihood from war. One of Hitler's favourite quotations was 'War is the father of all things', and he attributed it not to Heracles but to Clausewitz. *Mutter Courage* is Brecht's attempt to demonstrate that those who live off war will perish by it.

The play also continues the argument started in *Galileo* about the unhappiness of the land that needs heroes. Courage tells the cook that it is only a bad general who needs heroism. 'Whenever you find such great virtues lying around it always means there's something rotten. ... If a captain or king is really stupid and leads his men into the shit, then they've got to be brave as hell, which is another virtue. Or if he's too mean and doesn't hire enough soldiers, then they've all got to be just like Hercules. ... In a decent country virtues aren't needed. Everybody can be perfectly ordinary, run of the mill, and, for all I care, cowards.' The style of arguing is close to that of Schweyk, while the inversion of conventional morality is in line with the attitude implicit in Brecht's earlier works, especially *Dreigroschenoper* and *Die sieben Todsünden*. What is new in *Mutter Courage* is the clarity of focus on the discrepancy between the values that prevail in war and the values that prevail in peace. In the second scene, Eilif, the brave son, is rewarded by his captain for stealing cattle and butchering the peasants who tried to stop him; in the eighth scene he is condemned to death for behaving in exactly the same way during peacetime. Criminality depends not on the action but on the perspective.

Brecht's pen may also have been guided by thoughts of Hitler during the chaplain's attempt to woo Courage. Boasting about his powers as a preacher, he claims: 'With one sermon I can put a whole regiment into such a mood that it looks at the enemy as if it was a flock of sheep. With their mind fixed on ultimate victory they care no more about their lives than about a smelly old footcloth that they don't mind throwing away. God has given me the gift of eloquence. When I preach you can no longer hear for yourself or see for yourself.' If he was not thinking of Hitler – or even if he was – Brecht may have been remembering the jingoistic journalism he had been writing in 1914. In any case he had compounded the idea with a surefire form of theatrical irony: the chaplain, trying to make himself more attractive to the woman, is doing himself no good.

Courage is realistically portrayed as a tough woman, mean enough to be proprietorial about shirts when there are wounded men who desperately need bandaging, but generous enough to offer schnapps when an old peasant woman collapses; cold enough to go on haggling when her son's life is in danger, but humane enough to reject the possibility of a quiet life with the cook when she realizes that she is being offered a home on condition that she abandons her daughter. It would not be good for trade at the inn he has inherited if visitors had to confront a dumb girl with a scarred forehead. Unhesitatingly the mother sacrifices the lover for the sake of the daughter.

Playwrights in the Ibsen tradition had tended to ignore or to minimize contradictions and anomalies in the behaviour of their characters; Brecht welcomed them, making theatrical use of what he had learned from Marxist theory about contradiction. Besides, the more self-frustrating Courage appeared, the easier it should be for the audience to see that her line of action was self-defeating. Fortunately Brecht's line of action was also self-defeating: the result of admitting so many contradictions is that her individuality emerges more strongly. By trying to discredit her, he makes her unforgettable. Except that her three children had different fathers, we learn little about her past, but we come to know her in the present tense, while another reason for her vividness is that Brecht was reaching through her to two of his most neurotically sensitive areas: his hatred of trading and his knowledge (rooted in affectionate memories) of maternal love. Several of the play's key sequences pivot on a conflict between Courage's maternal instincts and her more masculine lust for profit. In the first scene she loses Eilif because she is tricked into leaving him alone with the recruiter when the sergeant feigns interest in buying a belt buckle. (In the 1939 draft of the play she momentarily forgot Eilif to offer the sergeant a drink; in later drafts Brecht tried to harden her.) The haggling that costs her second son his life is protracted less because she cannot afford the price demanded than because she cannot bear to be worsted in a deal, and because Brecht wants to demonstrate that trading is, in effect, murderous. When the dead body is brought in, she pretends not to recognize it – a denial reminiscent of events preceding the crucifixion – and, with a good actress in the role, the audience recognizes the effort it costs her. If Weigel was to give the definitive performance in the role, it was partly because she had to some extent served as model for it. She was brave enough to make artistic use of Brecht's ambivalence towards her, which was inseparable from ambivalence towards characteristics he regarded as typically Jewish.[14] She had the makings of a good businesswoman. If she could sell the Danish house they had lived in for more than she had originally paid, he was the chief beneficiary, and his appreciation of this was tinged with admiration, but also with contempt. His success with Courage depended partly on enriching the characterization with tensions and contradictions that derived from his ambivalence towards Weigel and the Jews.

Courage's only surviving child, Kattrin, is assaulted and left with a scar because Courage takes the risk of sending her out on a business errand, while the later incident, in which Kattrin gets herself killed, could not have occurred unless Courage had left her alone in order to buy goods in town. It is mainly because she is so convincing as a mother that Brecht makes the audience feel more for her than he intended it to. When she displays affection for her children, it is often in a tough or apparently grudging way. Eilif is slapped on the face in the presence of his captain because he took an unnecessary risk with his life; to console Kattrin after the offstage assault, Courage produces from a sack the red high-heeled boots which had belonged to the prostitute Yvette. 'Put them on quick before I change my mind.' And after deciding against the cook's offer and stopping Kattrin from running away, Courage feeds her, like a baby, with a spoon. But the tough dialogue counterpoints the tenderness of the action. 'Don't imagine I sent him packing because of you.'

Because we identify with Courage more than Brecht intended, her cumulative sufferings come closer to tragedy than intended. The structure is more epic than tragic, the episodes being almost self-contained, but the deterioration in her situation is continuous, despite fluctuations in profits. Set in the seventeenth year of the war, the ninth scene of the play shows her outside a half-dilapidated parsonage during a particularly harsh winter. 'In Saxony a man in rags wanted to give me a bundle of old books for two eggs, and in Württemberg they offered me a plough for a little bag of salt. Why go on ploughing? Nothing grows any more, only thorns. In Pomerania the villagers are supposed to be eating young children, and nuns have been caught carrying out highway robbery.' Like Brueghel, Brecht can introduce nightmarish imagery without becoming unrealistic.

Mutter Courage is a history play of a new kind, but the history, as in this speech, is neatly subordinated to the personal suffering of the character, which can be focused through voice, stance and clothes indicative of penury and extreme cold. In the Solomon Song (written for the *Dreigroschenoper* but cut) Courage and the cook sing as beggars outside the parsonage, using Solomon, Caesar, Socrates and St Martin as examples to prove that wisdom, courage, honesty and altruism are virtues that bring no rewards. Although the setting could scarcely be further removed from the Augsburg Plarrer, the cook's commentary, spoken between the verses, seems to derive from the showmen at the fair, while the very inappropriateness of the attempt at panache makes its theatrical point, and the begging prepares quite movingly for the moment when, rejecting the cook's offer, Courage lets her maternal instinct dominate.

Brecht's main object in making Kattrin dumb was to provide Weigel with a part she could play in Sweden without speaking the language. At the beginning of November 1939, Ninan Santesson's sister started work on the translation, but the production did not materialize.

Brecht did not fare any better with the radio script *Das Verhör des Lukullus* (*The Trial of Lucullus*), which was almost ready by 11 November. After being approached by the composer Hilding Rosenberg, he was commissioned to write a text for broadcasting. In Denmark, as a by-product of his work on the Caesar novel, he had written 'Die Trophäen des Lukullus ('Lucullus's Trophies'), a short story in which the poet Lucretius refuses to give a flattering answer when the Roman general asks what his fame will rest on. Perhaps, says Lucretius, he will be remembered for bringing the cherry tree to Europe.

In the radio play Brecht is preoccupied, as in *Mutter Courage*, with the quantity of human life expended in warfare, and while blaming the leaders, who do not have to put their own lives at risk, he advances along the line of Nietzschean argument he had used in *Die sieben Todsünden* – that ideas of good and evil are evolved by the dominant class as an expedient endorsement of its own interests. Setting his radio play in a heavenly lawcourt, Brecht shows the Roman general behaving with an arrogance proportionate to his earthly reputation, but here he has to face a tribunal consisting of a peasant, a slave, a fishwife, a baker and a prostitute, whose values are neither those of aristocratic Roman society nor those of the twentieth-century church. The general tries to disqualify the fishwife by arguing that people who cannot understand war cannot judge it, but, as a mother who has lost her son in battle, she satisfies the court as understanding war's consequences, and, repeating the verdict of the story, the tribunal finds that Lucullus's only creditable achievement is his introduction of the cherry tree. On the debit side of the balance are the 80,000 deaths he has caused.

With Margarete Steffin as his collaborator, Brecht completed the play within a few days, but the only performance it had was given by a workers' theatre group in a hall belonging to the Stockholm Jewish community, where Hermann Greid directed it as a shadow play. It was wiser to preserve the anonymity of the actors in case they were accused of revolutionary activity.[15]

After writing these two plays so quickly, Brecht went back to his Caesar novel. Working at it in the perspective of current events – Russia had attacked Finland at the end of November – he was acutely aware that historians were liable to confuse motive with end product. In making a pact with Stalin, Hitler might have been preparing either for a war with the western powers, or for making peace with them. Much would depend on how long the Finnish war lasted, but retrospectively everything would look quite different.[16]

By the beginning of 1940 it was becoming dangerous to stay in Sweden: before long the German army would be marching into Scandinavia. Brecht was still hoping for an entry permit to the United States, and during 1939 he had been trying, through the novelist Halldór Laxness, to base himself temporarily in Iceland, in order to cross the ocean from there. But Ferdinand Reyher had not, apparently, succeeded in engaging the help of the Committee for Refugee Writers at the League of American

Writers. Brecht had been hoping a visa would be issued to him by the middle of 1939, and when the silence persisted, he turned to Hanns Eisler, who was in Mexico. Anxious to help, he enlisted the novelist H. R. Hays, who had good contacts, but Fritz Kortner was exerting himself more effectively on Brecht's behalf. In Hollywood Fritz Lang was persuaded to start a fund for Brecht and his family. Lion Feucht-wanger offered to pay Brecht's fare to the Soviet Union, while Kortner recruited Dorothy Thompson, a well-connected journalist, to put pressure on the State Department for the issue of entry visas to the Brecht family, to Steffin and to Berlau.

In January 1940, when Weigel was invited to teach at the drama school Naima Wifstrand ran in Stockholm, Brecht helped by devising exercises for the students. They should work through simple actions like folding linen and putting it away, and through variations like eating with abnormally small or abnormally large pieces of cutlery. Passages from the Bible could be dramatized, and games could be made to turn serious: women light-heartedly faking a quarrel for the benefit of their husbands in the adjoining room come to blows as genuine jealousy is engendered. Dialogue could be practised with one side of it spoken from a gramophone record.[17]

When he looked at the rather 'dilettantish' book Hermann Greid had written on Marxist ethics, Brecht again felt prompted to set exercises. The sentences containing the words 'should' or 'ought' irritated him as stemming from a morality that was restrictive and outdated. He advised Greid, for the sake of the forthcoming class conflict, to censure only on grounds of stupidity, not of morality: he should replace 'you pig' sentences with 'you fool' sentences. For instance, 'you should not sleep with your mother' was once a 'you fool' injunction, for in primitive societies it signified great confusion in ownership and production relationships. But since it could no longer be rendered in a 'you fool' sentence, it would have to be cut.

The fifth scene of *Mutter Courage* contains the germ that was to grow into *Der kaukasische Kreidekreis* (*The Caucasian Chalk Circle*). Rocking a baby she has rescued from a house that was about to collapse, Kattrin ignores Courage, who tells her to give it back to its mother. The next scene makes no reference to the baby or to Kattrin's maternal instincts, but the story 'Der Augsburger Kreidekreis' ('The Augsburg Chalk Circle'), which Brecht wrote in January 1940, is evidence of a connection between Kattrin and Grusche in *Der kaukasische Kreidekreis*. In the story, which is set in Augsburg during the Thirty Years War, a maid, Anna, rescues a baby which has been abandoned. Years later, when its mother claims it, the case is heard by a judge who is 'famous throughout Swabia for his crudity and his wisdom'. A chalk circle is drawn on the ground, the child put inside it, and the two women are ordered to pull it out. Anna, who cannot bear to hurt the child, lets the mother yank it out of the circle, but the judge decides in Anna's favour.[18] The idea derives partly from a judgment of King Solomon, who is said to have decided a similar case by offering to cut the disputed child in half, and awarding it to the woman who withdrew her claim. Another source was Klabund's free adaptation of Li Hsing Tao's thirteenth-century play *Chalk Circle*, which introduces the test of the circle, though the judge, who is the father of the child, already knows who the real mother is. In both these sources the child is restored to its mother; in both Brecht's variations, the mother deserves to lose her child, which is awarded to a woman who will care for it better. As so often, he is demonstrating that justice has little to do with the law.

A 1908 photograph of Walter Brecht, Eugen Berthold Brecht and their mother. In 1908 Eugen – as he was called – started at the Royal Bavarian Realgymnasium. See p. 8.

The schoolboy Brecht with his friends Otto Müller (left), who adopted the name Müllereisert which Brecht invented for him, and Georg Pfanzelt (centre), whom Brecht called Orge.

Brecht with Paula Banholzer in 1918. 'She's wonderfully soft and spring-like, shy and dangerous. Each day I lead myself into temptation. . . .' See p. 33.

The opera singer Marianne Zoff, Brecht's first wife, with their daughter Hanne in Munich, 1923. 'There's so little one can do with children, except be photographed with them.' See p. 93.

Brecht's first play, *Baal*, produced at the Deutsches Theater, Berlin, on 14 February 1926 with Oskar Homolka (centre) as Baal, Sybille Binder (seated) as Emilie and Paul Bildt (left) as Ekart. The performance caused pandemonium in the overcrowded auditorium. See p. 115.

Brecht in 1927 with Elisabeth Hauptmann in his Berlin attic studio, Spichernstrasse 16. 'It looked less like a home than a place he was temporarily staying in.' See p. 104.

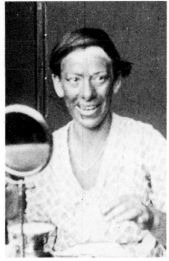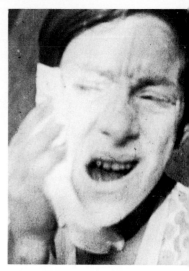

Three stills from a film Brecht made about 1929 of Helene Weigel at her make-up mirror. Marvelling at the expressiveness of her face, he showed the stills to friends, asking them what the expressions meant, and passing their answers on to her – anger, happiness, envy, compassion, and so on.

Brecht with his son Stefan in 1931.

Brecht during his second visit to London. He stayed in Abbey Road from April to July 1936. See p. 196.

Brecht with Helene Weigel in Lidingö, Sweden, where they lived from May 1939 until April 1940. 'In Sweden Brecht's social life was more actively interwoven with his work than it had been in Denmark.' See p. 221.

Brecht with Margarete Steffin in 1941, shortly before her death at the age of 33. For four days after she died, Brecht did not smile. 'It's like losing one's leader at the very moment of going into the desert.' See pp. 251 and 255.

Ruth Berlau in 1945 or 1947. Her pregnancy coincided with his work on *Der kaukasische Kreidekreis*. 'A message can be bottled in a play: maternity must be presented favourably.' Their son, who was to be called Michael, after the child in the play, lived for only a few days. See pp. 284 and 288.

Brecht with Caspar Neher in 1948. From *Baal* onwards, Neher's sketches helped Brecht to crystallize his characterizations and to plan key postures for actors. After *Mutter Courage* opened in Berlin, he wrote: 'The designs for *Courage* weren't good. We waited for you till the last minute, and then had to improvise.' See p. 329.

Helene Weigel in the Berlin production of *Mutter Courage*. She enters singing her song and striding beside the wagon, which is pulled along by her two sons. At the end of the play, childless, she pulls it herself.

Brecht at the country house in Buckow he bought in 1952, considering it to be 'peaceful and boring enough for work'. See p. 361.

20 / Near the Finland Station

In January 1940 Winston Churchill had urged the neutral countries to side with Britain before Hitler attacked them; after less than a year in Sweden, Brecht realized that he would soon have to make yet another move northwards, and in April he appealed to the Finnish writer, Hella Wuolijoki, for an invitation to Finland. With this in his possession, he could probably obtain an entry visa, but if she was willing to help, she must act quickly. Once again he had a narrow escape: on 9 April Germany invaded Norway and Denmark; eight days later Brecht, together with his family and Margarete Steffin, boarded a steamer bound for Helsinki. He left his books and his furniture with Swedish friends. For the first week in Helsinki, the Brechts stayed in a hotel near the central railway station, and they rented a small unfurnished flat in Tölö, a working-class district, moving in on 26 April 1940. 'Helli drove around in a van and within two hours collected the furniture we needed, borrowing from five people we didn't know yesterday.' 'It is a splendid thing that even (or especially) in these dark times, so much spiritual solidarity prevails in the different countries.' The most helpful Finnish allies were Hella Wuolijoki and the poet Elmer Diktonius, Brecht's senior by two years. The Finnish President, Ryti, had made a pact with Nazi Germany, but he had enjoyed *Dreigroschenoper*, and Wuolijoki used her influence to procure entry visas and residence permits for the family.[1]

During the first week in May, Brecht was feeling sufficiently settled to resume work on *Der gute Mensch von Sezuan*. It looked as though Finland would remain neutral, but he was intending to move on in the summer to the United States. On the day he left Stockholm, a telegram had arrived from Piscator, offering him a job as 'lecturer in literature' at his New York drama school. Confident that this would procure the necessary visas, Brecht booked tickets for a transatlantic steamer leaving on 5 August. Eating his midday meals at the station, and knowing that his future depended on a visa, he was in the same predicament as thousands of other refugees from Nazism. His *Flüchtlingsgespräche* (*Refugee Conversations*), which he started in Finland – modelling them on

Goethe's *Unterhaltungen Deutscher Ausgewanderter* (*Conversations of German Exiles*) – begin with a conversation between two strangers at a Helsinki station restaurant. They instinctively look over their shoulders when they talk politics. Ziffel is tall and fat with white hands and a sense of humour rather like Hašek's; Kalle is small with the hands of a metal-worker.

KALLE: The passport is the noblest part of a man. And it doesn't come into existence so easily as a man does. A man can come into existence anywhere in the most frivolous way and for no logical reason, but a passport never...
ZIFFEL: You could say that a man is only the mechanical holder of a passport.

They are also in agreement about the importance of indiscipline. In war, says Kalle, a soldier can save his life by disobeying orders. 'In my opinion', says Ziffel, 'mankind is not yet ready for a virtue like the love of order.'[2] Brecht laughed uproariously when he was writing the conversations.

Hermann Greid had travelled to Helsinki on the same boat as the Brechts, and Arnold Ljungdal had followed soon afterwards. Most evenings they all met, together with Diktonius, at Wuolijoki's house.

On 10 May, the day Neville Chamberlain resigned, Germany invaded Holland, Luxembourg and Belgium. Within four days the Dutch army had surrendered; within three weeks Belgium had. At the end of the month British troops were being evacuated from Dunkirk. The artist, Brecht wrote to Hans Tombrock, must invest personal activity with historical significance: 'I mean if the newspapers, on a certain day, report that the Chinese have invaded Setzuan, you must then ask yourself what did Tombrock do on that day.'[3] Brecht chose his subject-matter knowing he would regularly ask himself the same question.

On 10 June Italy declared war on England and France; Brecht, together with Margarete Steffin, was for the tenth time revising *Der gute Mensch*. 'Jealously I protect my mornings, recently, since the news has become so bad, I consider whether I should switch off the early morning radio. The little box is next to the bed, my last action at night is to switch it off, my first in the morning to switch it on.'[4]

On 14 June, the day the Germans marched into Paris, Brecht wrote that the war was 'the solution of a problem, in fact it is the consequence of Germany's arrival too late in the imperial distribution of the world market (in turn the result of the tardiness of the bourgeois revolution and its creation of national unity)'. A few days later he cut out from an English newspaper German newsreel photographs of Hitler performing a victorious jig on 17 June when he heard that France was ready to surrender. But Brecht doggedly went on applying himself to the play he had started in Germany and continued in Denmark and Sweden. By 20 June it was 'generally speaking, finished'.[5]

The opening obliquely reflects his belief that the postwar climate would be lethal to human goodness. Fascism, he believed, could be defeated only by another form of fascism or by democracy, but he had no faith in England as a champion of democracy. In Setzuan catastrophe seems to be imminent: 'Many people think that only the gods can save the situation.' The three gods who visit the half-westernized city are investigating whether goodness can survive in a world of poverty and hardship. For Brecht the war was inseparable from the alienation which had been forced on the labourer. The play is an allegorical recipe for the way goodness must disguise itself to survive the dark ages. The gods have been briefed that 'the world can stay as it is if enough good people are found, who can live in a way fit for humanity'. Atheists, complains one of the gods, are saying that the world must be changed because no one can *be* good and *remain* good.[6] The formulations are reminiscent of the dying plea made by Brecht's saint of the Chicago slaughterhouses:

> Make sure that when you leave the world
> You have not just been good but are leaving
> A good world.

Until about August 1940 Brecht had called the good-hearted prostitute Li Gung and her cousin Lao Go, but he then changed the names to Shen Te (which means divine virtue) and Shui Ta (flood tide).[7] The central dramatic device of splitting Shen Te into two halves harks back to earlier de-individualizing devices Brecht had used. In his 1931 production of *Mann ist Mann* he had, by using masks, refined on his original idea of how the fish porter would be transformed into a soldier. Shen Te's transformation into her tough male cousin Shui Ta is – on the surface at least – more a matter of choice, but the strength of Brecht's theatrical parable depends partly on his skill in suggesting that she has no real alternative. Having bought a tobacco shop with money given to her by the gods, she cannot protect herself against spongers and parasites except by resorting to a drastic change of identity: a disguise. Brecht is dealing in a new way with the question he made Mr Peachum raise:

> We'd all prefer to be good.
> But circumstances don't allow it.

Human nature is fundamentally good, but society is stopping us from behaving as generously and benevolently as our instincts tell us to. 'Being evil is like being clumsy,' Shen Te tells Yang Sun, the unemployed pilot. 'When we sing a song or construct a machine or plant rice, we're being generous.' She finds it easy to behave altruistically and difficult not to:

> To trample on fellow creatures
> Isn't it a strain? The vein in the forehead
> Swells with the effort of being greedy.

Brecht made the same point in a poem about the lacquered Japanese demon mask on the wall of his study:

> Pityingly I see
> The forehead's swollen veins, showing
> The strain of being evil.

He centres his play on the theme he had treated in his schoolboy parable on the Balkan War – justice versus necessity. Goodness prompts Shen Te to deal justly with her neighbours, to return the 200 silver dollars she has borrowed, to help the water-seller by pretending she was a witness when the barber injured his hand with a hot curling-iron. But, infatuated with the unscrupulous pilot, who needs 500 silver dollars to bribe the employer who could create a vacancy by sacking another pilot, Shen Te vacillates, nearly losing both her lover and the shop she has sold to raise money for him.

Certainly there is a strong theatricality in the coexistence of two morally different persons inside a shared body. Mark Twain, who had parallel reasons for wanting to show that goodness had nothing to do with nobility of birth, produced a comparable image of moral duality in his story 'Those Extraordinary Twins' – one of the Siamese twins is good, one evil. Later, in *Herr Puntila*, Brecht will produce a comic variant on the Jekyll–Hyde idea – a man who is good when drunk and evil when sober. The point lies in the ambiguity of moral identity.

In the concluding scene of *Der gute Mensch* – a lawcourt, with the three gods as judges – Shen Te tries to explain why she disguised herself as her cousin Shui Ta:

> To help both others and myself was too hard.
> Oh, your world is difficult. So much trouble and despair.
> The hand you hold out to the needy
> Gets bitten off. Those who help the lost
> Get lost themselves. So who can
> Refuse to become bad, when you can't live
> Without eating?

The implication is that the atheists are right: the world needs to be changed.

On 22 June 1940 France signed an armistice with Germany; a week later Brecht wrote: 'One world power has collapsed and another is being shaken to its very foundations since I started the last version of *Der gute Mensch von Sezuan*.' It had given him more trouble than any of his previous plays, and the finishing touches could have been added only if it had been staged. 'Only performance can decide between possible variations.'[8] Like *Galileo* and *Mutter Courage*, it had to remain untested.

It was difficult in 1940 to believe that the world could be changed for the better, and impossible to believe that current changes were merely superficial. 'The world is now changing every hour,' Brecht wrote at the beginning of July. 'I can remember how, gradually, more and more disappeared.' German newspapers had been published in Austria, Czechoslovakia, Switzerland and the Saarland. 'One by one they collapsed. The radio remained, but one day Vienna went silent, another day Prague.' Then, successively, the radio stations in Warsaw, Copenhagen and Oslo had been silenced. Then Paris. 'Now, of the western democracies, only London remains. For how long?'[9]

21 / Puntila and the Sawdust Princess

By the beginning of July 1940, it was obvious that Brecht could not expect to have an entry visa to the United States in time to sail on 5 August, though in April, thanks to Piscator, he had received another invitation – to lecture on literature at the New School for Social Research from May until January 1941. But his life-style changed when Hella Wuolijoki gave him the use of a small house on her estate at Marlebäk in Kausala.

She is giving us a villa between lovely pine trees. We talk about the silence out here but it is not silent; it is only that the sounds are more natural, the wind in the trees, the rustling of the grass, the birdsong and the sound of the water. The estate house, white, with two rows of big windows, eight in each, is over a hundred years old, built in the Empire style. The rooms are worthy of a museum....

We are very sleepy; probably because of the unfamiliar air. The smell of the pines alone is intoxicating, and also the smell of the wood. Beneath the pine trees are plentiful wild strawberries; gathering them makes the children tired. I'm afraid the cooking will be hard for Helli. The oven has to be heated, and there's no water in the house.

But he got on extremely well with his plump hostess. Estonian by birth, she had come to Helsinki in 1904 to study philology, and she now spoke six languages. She had been married to Sulo Wuolijoki, a lawyer and Social Democrat politician, and she had managed several timber firms. She had an inexhaustible repertoire of stories about her estate.

Constantly shaking with laughter, she tells stories about the guile of simple people and the stupidity of their superiors, shifting her half-closed eyes slyly from side to side and accompanying the speeches of the characters with epic, fluent movements of her thick, beautiful hands, as if beating time to a music audible only to her.... Over her island and her moorland she carries her great weight with flabbergasting energy, and her embonpoint has something Chinese about it. She seems to run the estate with a very light touch: she's never dictatorial.[1]

Margarete Steffin, who was seriously ill, was for the first time allowed to live as a member of the family. Weigel was no longer nervous that she would infect the children with tuberculosis.

Ruth Berlau had gone back to Copenhagen, but Brecht asked Hella Wuolijoki to invite her: 'Once the Nazi apparatus gets to work it will be impossible for all her collaboration with me to be kept secret. . . . In my opinion she can't go back until the war is over.' She had intended to stay in Denmark, fighting for the resistance, and in Lidingö she had been visiting him only during holidays, but in a letter from Finland he now urged her to come, insisting that he needed her for his work, and promising that she would in future be included in all his travel plans. But when she arrived, Weigel was not prepared to extend the same tolerance to her as to Margarete Steffin. Told there was no room for her in the house, the imperturbable Berlau got hold of a tent and pitched it in the garden. Brecht gave no sign of thinking her behaviour abnormal, and he often went to work with her in the tent, where she had a typewriter. But Hella Wuolijoki sided with Weigel, and banned the intruder from the house, though Brecht pretended that in Copenhagen he and Weigel had stayed with Berlau, and in Skovbostrand she with them.² There were violent quarrels about whether she was to travel with the family to America, and Berlau, who began to drink heavily, insisted that she was not going to be sent home. Brecht tried to reassure her: 'You are not to worry, I am thinking of you and will not leave without you.'³

The crucial work on *Der gute Mensch* had been done remarkably soon after settling into the flat in Tölö, but Brecht made little headway with either of the new plays he tried to sketch out: one about a French girl who, during the German occupation, dreams she is Joan of Arc; one about a blind beggar outside the ministries when decisions are being taken about war. 'Quite incapable of writing for the theatre. . . . At a time of deadlock like this I need either to do journalistic work or work in a theatre. Both impossible.'⁴

But he was not too enervated to appreciate the beauty of Marlebäk.

The streams which are full of fish and the lovely trees in the forests with their smells of berries and pines. . . . And just as the day vanishes during winter, the night vanishes during summer. Then the air is so potent and tasty, you scarcely need to eat. And what music fills these bright heavens! The wind is almost incessant, and as it meets many varied plants, grass, corn, shrubs and woods, a gentle sound of well-being emerges, swelling and ebbing, scarcely noticeable any longer, but always present.⁵

He was disinclined to resume the Caesar novel. He wrote short poems, and made notes for additions to *Der Messingkauf*, but it was hard to concentrate on work. 'It's not a matter of Hitler's current victories but entirely of my isolation as it affects productivity. If I listen to the morning news on the radio, reading at the same time Boswell's *Life of Johnson* and squinting out at the landscape of pines with mist from the river, the unnatural day is not beginning with a discord but with no sound at all.'⁶

Sometimes he was in a retrospective mood: 'People hesitate to describe writers like Hašek, Silone, (O'Casey) and me as bourgeois writers, but mistakenly. We want to concern ourselves with the affairs of the proletariat, want, for a certain time-span, to be the proletariat's writers. . . . This brings us into line with the bourgeois politicians who have concerned themselves with proletarian affairs.' From his viewpoint it was anomalous, even in wartime, that one class should be fighting on the same side as another: 'In England it's the gentry who are fighting the war, together with the City. They too are climbing into the big machines (Navy, Air Force) where the common man is not allowed.'⁷

It was Hella Wuolijoki who eased him into writing his next play. A folk play competition was organized by the Ministry of Education, with 120,000 Finnish marks as prize money, and she suggested they should collaborate. According to Brecht's note in the first published text (*Versuche 10*, 1951), it was 'based on the stories and a sketch [*Entwurf*] for a play by Hella Wuolijoki'. This is deliberately misleading. Her story 'A Finnish Bacchus' was written in the 1930s, but the play she based on it, *Sahanpuruprinsessa* (*The Sawdust Princess*) was complete. She had told him about it when he had told her about *Der gute Mensch*, and the split character of Shen Te reminded her of her uncle Roope, who had served as the model for her character Puntila in both the play and the screenplay she had based on it. An escapade of Roope's had caused a local scandal in the 1920s; Puntila, like Shen Te, has two sides to his nature, the sober man being unable to keep pace with the largesse of the drunk. On one alcoholic spree he becomes engaged to five women and gives away banknotes. (This is not to say that Brecht was unaffected by the drunken generosity and sober meanness of the millionaire in Chaplin's *City Lights*, a film he had reviewed.) In Wuolijoki's play, when Puntila's chauffeur, Kalle, helps him to dispose of his five fiancées, he promises, in return, to let the man marry his daughter, Eva, but it is only when Kalle reveals that his true identity is socially respectable – he is Dr Vuorinen – that he becomes acceptable to the rich farmer as a son-in-law.

Much more than tragedy, comedy had hinged on class distinctions. In the tradition that ran from Menander, through Terence and Plautus, through Shakespeare and Molière, to Oscar Wilde and Noël Coward, some characters had been ridiculed for trying to rise above their station, while others, who had shone by virtue of wit or wiliness or physical beauty, had turned out to be better born than they had seemed. Goodness was associated with nobility. Shaw had kicked against this tradition with his argument that given speech training, a flower-girl could be raised to the same level as a duchess, but Shaw never gravitated towards folk art – he was too addicted to reasoning – and it was one of the happiest accidents in Brecht's exile that this competition was for a folk play. Already, in *Der gute Mensch*, he had approximated to the naïvety of the old folk plays, avoiding sentimentality and aiming at objectivity, while achieving a theatrical poetry that depends less on verse or music than on distillation of action into a stylized simplicity.

In folk plays it had not been a premiss – as it had in traditional comedy – that social superiority implied moral superiority. In Brecht's reworking of Hella Wuolijoki's Puntila story, the chauffeur, being more of a man than the attaché, has a better claim to Eva. When drunk, Puntila is willing to shape his daughter's future accordingly; when sober he is less tolerant: 'When I paid for you to have a good education in Brussels, it wasn't so as you could fling yourself at the chauffeur but so as you could keep your distance from the servants, or else they'll get bolshy and trample all over you.' Both the tradition and the conventions of comedy are sharply contravened in the sequence showing that the existence of class barriers rules out the possibility of a happy ending. Instead of being united by a trick in the plotting to put them on the same social level, the lovers are forced to realize that they cannot bridge the differences between their life-styles, habits, manners, attitudes. Ruth Berlau has claimed that she gave Brecht the idea for this key sequence, in which Eva tries to prove that she could adapt herself to the routine of a hard-working chauffeur husband, but loses each round in the acting game Matti plays with her. He demonstrates the behaviour of a man who comes in tired after a hard day's work. Though eager to obey the orders he gives her, she forgets to use a darning-egg and mends his socks badly. She greets him with kisses and chatty sympathy, instead of holding out a towel for him to dry his hands. She fails to put the newspaper on the table for him and then, having put it there, interrupts his reading with more chatter. Finally she loses his job for him by shouting abuse from the window when he is woken up in the middle of the night to fetch his master from the station. Like Strindberg when he was writing *Frøken Julie*, Brecht inverted conventional assumptions about class: in both plays social superiority is a nuisance to a girl who is doing her best to please a socially inferior male, but proves inept and 'insensitive', as Eva is told by Matti (or Kalle, as the servant was called in Hella Wuolijoki's play and in Brecht's first version). Brecht may also have been thinking of Diderot's *Jacques le fataliste*, which he was reading: the fatalistic servant does not question his subordinate position; Matti does. There is also an affinity with Chekhov's *Cherry Orchard*, in which Ranevskaya is incapable of saving the estate because she is incapable of taking Lopakhin's proposals seriously. Brecht's more immediate model was Wuolijoki: unable to cope with her financial problems she was already on the point of selling her estate. Puntila is in financial trouble, and Matti, who understands machinery, is in some ways equivalent to Lopakhin. Like the failure of Ranevskaya's efforts to make Lopakhin marry her adopted daughter, Puntila's failure to win Matti as a son-in-law suggests that the decaying class's fuel tank was unsuitable for energy offered by the rising class. Matti is more realistic: he never assumes that Eva could be the right woman for him, or that Puntila would really let her marry him.

By 27 August 1940 Brecht had begun working on the play with Wuolijoki. Besides using her play, which she had quickly translated into German for him, he incorporated into the dialogue many of the stories she had told him about the estate. By 2 September this *Konversationskomödie* was half finished. 'What I have to do is elaborate the underlying farce, suppress the psychologizing speeches, making room for anecdotes about Finnish folk-life and for opinions, to realize the opposition of "master" and "servant" dramatically at the same time as restoring to the subject its poetry and comedy.' Thanks to Karl Valentin, he had learned how to filter ideas from Bavarian folk comedy into his one-act plays, and the unfamiliarity of Finnish folk life probably made it easier for him to deal with it. Though Wuolijoki had failed to realize the potential of her play, Brecht admired her vitality and her talent: 'What a charming epic poetess she is, sitting on her wooden stool and making coffee! Everything comes out with the simplicity and complexity of the Bible.'[8]

The Bible had appealed to all classes of all societies, and though literary critics had paid even less attention to the folk play than to the popular ballad, Brecht sensed a need for a new kind of theatre, 'naïve but not primitive, poetic but not romantic, close to reality but not topically political'. The new folk play could 'dispense with a unified and continuous story by presenting "numbers", i.e. loosely connected sketches. This form revives the "Pranks and Adventures" of the old folk epics, though they are almost unrecognizable.'[9]

Meyerhold had already been moving away from the well-made play towards episodic construction. Directing Ostrovsky's *The Forest* in 1924, he had taken Eisenstein's films as a model. 'The five acts of

Ostrovsky's play were split into 33 episodes, each one conflicting with the next. Clearly, this method makes it possible to wield a greater influence on the spectator.' But in Western Europe there was still, in the 1940s, no theatrical style which could have accommodated the poetry in the prose scenes of *Puntila*: in writing it Brecht was increasing the need for a new company like the Berliner Ensemble.

Brecht enjoyed working on the play, confident that German literature would be enriched by his comedies: 'Since the seventeenth century the Germans still didn't have any.' But in his diary the notes on the play alternate with war photographs clipped from newspapers and comments on news: 'It's 12.20. I just heard the announcer in blitzed London. He's sitting in an air raid shelter. The German bombers are once again over the "capital of the world".' He had to alternate between working on the play and reading about the Battle of Britain. 'Puntila means almost nothing to me, the war everything; about Puntila I can write almost everything, about the war nothing.... It's interesting how far removed literature is, as an activity, from the centre of all decisive events.'[10]

The tone of the play was, as he knew, 'not original, it's Hašek's tone in *Schweyk*, which I had also used already in *Courage*'. *Puntila* was easier to write than *Der gute Mensch*, and by 19 September he had finished it, keeping mainly to his outline, but introducing a visit to an employment market modelled on a local one. 'It's a fat little calf of a play. More landscape in it than in any of my plays, except perhaps *Baal*.' This is true, and one reason lies in his delighted response to Marlebäk. 'These bright nights are very beautiful,' he had written on his second day there. 'About three o'clock I got up, because of the flies, and went outside. The cocks were crowing but it hadn't been dark. And I do so like passing water in the open air.' Puntila and Matti pass water together in the courtyard at night: 'I could never live in the town,' says Puntila. 'Why? I like to go outside on to hard earth and make water in the open air under the stars. Otherwise what's the point?' When Hella Wuolijoki finally overcame her disappointment with Brecht's version – 'It's not dramatic, not funny, etc. Everyone talks in the same way.'[11] – and translated it into Finnish, she omitted this scene. The play was submitted for the folk play competition, but it was not one of the three prize-winners.

The tone of *Puntila* was still in Brecht's ears when, at the beginning of October 1940, he went back to the conversations he had started to write in Finland between two strangers at a station restaurant. He was prompted now partly by *Jacques le fataliste*, which retails Jacques's conversations with his master during their travels and adventures. Brecht saw that he could realize some of the ideas he had already planned for Ziffel by writing dialogue between him and Kalle. They discuss a wide range of subjects, and Brecht uses both of them as spokesmen for his own opinions. In Germany, says Ziffel, one could form the impression that there are only two kinds of men, priests and anti-priests: 'the representatives of this world, haggard and pale figures, familiar with all the various philosophies, the representatives of the other world, familiar with all the various wines'.[12]

As petrol became scarcer in Finland, it was growing harder for Hella Wuolijoki to run the estate: to transport milk by rail was extremely slow. When the Finnish government conceded to the Nazis the right of passage into Norway, the value of the land increased, and at the beginning of October she completed negotiations to sell it. Once again Brecht had to look for a new home. Back in Helsinki, in a modern house near the harbour, he found a flat with two whitewashed rooms and a kitchen. 'I look out on the sky, part of the harbour with little steamers and the wooden huts of a box factory.' He had one room and the children had the other, while Weigel slept in the kitchen.[13]

Invited to speak at the student theatre in the university, he offered the lecture on experimental theatre he had given eighteen months earlier in Stockholm, but he soon realized that the war was making theatre less experimental. 'To want the new is old-fashioned, to want the old is new.' He gave the lecture on 18 November to an audience of 'nice young people, with little apparent interest in either studying or theatre'.[14]

The closer America verged on involvement in the war, the more his hopes dwindled of being allowed to settle. The invitation to lecture at the New School for Social Research had been extended to September 1941, but on 6 November 1940, when Helene Weigel presented herself at the American consulate to argue her case, the consul, von Hellens, 'was icily ironic and cold. He said to Frau Brecht: "Possibly you speak English better than Swedish?" Frau Brecht speaks a broken Swedish and naturally her English is still worse.' When the President of the Finnish Refugee Committee, who made this entry in her diary, left the consulate with her, 'we felt somehow very close to one another'.[15] The Nazi informers in Finland were making Brecht's situation precarious, but in December, when an earlier application finally produced an entry visa to Mexico, he decided not to take advantage of it.

There is little in his diaries about his children, but on 4 December he reported on the sixteen-year-old Stefan, who had habitually listened to hours of jazz on the radio but now went every Saturday to performances of ancient church music. The turning-point, Brecht assumed, had been a visit to a musician, who played Mozart to them. 'Until recently he was very interested in morality. I had encouraged egoism, sharpened his distrust towards expectations of altruism.' At Stefan's age Brecht had profited from his cynicism, and now, wanting to enlighten his son, he explained that poverty precluded generosity: to survive, the little man had to be egoistic. The most important commandment was 'Be good to yourself'. Until two years ago Stefan 'had been stealing like a rat – gramophone records from shops, books from libraries. Without discussing private ownership, I tried to reform him by pointing to our abnormal situation and by appealing to his political insight.'[16]

Forced to stockpile the plays which said what he wanted to say, Brecht could not enjoy productions that seemed irrelevant to the current situation. Watching *Hamlet* in a touring Swedish version, he pronounced it to have the crudest plot Shakespeare had ever reworked, except for *Titus Andronicus*. 'Hamlet is simply an idealist who collides with the real world and gets knocked off course, an idealist who becomes a cynic. The question is not whether to act or not to act, but whether to keep silent or not keep silent, to be an accomplice or not to be.'

Brecht was inclined to think of Claudius's Denmark as if it were full of Nazi informers. Shakespeare's theatre was surrealistic, he went on, even if there were no shock effects in it: the camps of two enemy armies would still be pitched on one small stage. The ending of *Hamlet* had evolved from a bold compromise with the melodrama in Kyd's version of the play. 'All this thinking and planning, all this agony of conscience ends uncertainly, haphazardly, in a chaos of intrigue and accident.' Brecht's reactions were conditioned by Finnish attitudes to Hitler's advances: the Finns were 'keeping silent in two languages'.[17]

It was a bad winter for Margarete Steffin, who was growing visibly weaker, but in January 1941 she was well enough to collaborate with Brecht on finishing *Der gute Mensch*. 'The play is very long, so I'll add some poetry to it, a few verses and songs. It may then seem lighter and shorter.' She worked with him on 'Das Lied vom Rauch' ('The Song of the Smoke'), which ends the first scene. He now had six unperformed plays: *Die heilige Johanna*, *Furcht und Elend*, *Galileo*, *Mutter Courage*, *Puntila* and *Der gute Mensch*. He sent out copies of *Der gute Mensch* to friends in Switzerland, America and Sweden, but by the end of the third week in April he still had no reaction from any of them.[18]

In February the Norwegian newspapers were publishing recipes of a new kind: how to cook crows and seagulls. According to travellers, the German people were tired of the war. 'But this was like saying that workers in a factory were tired of work. The war has become an industry ... Hitler is trying to find a market for his products, a front.'[19]

Committed to the Marxist standpoint, Brecht keeps circling back to the image of production and consumption.

Though the formalities over the American entry visa would not be completed until May, Brecht was confident by March 1941 that he would be admitted to the States, together with his family and his two mistresses, Steffin and Berlau. And in April Wilhelm Dieterle, the film director, signed an affidavit supporting his application. Dieterle had been living in Hollywood since 1930, employed first by Warner Brothers and then by RKO. In 1939 he directed *The Hunchback of Notre Dame* with Charles Laughton. Many influential Americans were giving both money and time to help German colleagues who were in danger, but Dieterle was especially active and generous, sometimes writing crowd scenes into his films to provide jobs for non-English-speaking actors.[1]

Thinking about the American theatre, Brecht remembered an idea that had occurred to him in New York – 'to write a gangster-play which recalls certain events we all know'.[2] Between 10 and 28 March, though negotiating for the visa and planning to leave Finland, he wrote most of *Der aufhaltsame Aufstieg des Arturo Ui* (*The Resistible Rise of Arturo Ui*). His thesis was that the rise of Hitler had not been preordained or inevitable, and that there was nothing admirable or heroic in the criminal character. As in the schoolboy parable about the Balkan War, he is writing allegorically about contemporary history; as in *Dreigroschenroman* and *Die heilige Johanna*, he is at pains to show that trusts and market forces bulk larger than individuals; as in his treatment of Caesar and Iberin, he is arguing that an unhappy country's need for a hero may lead not to the emergence of a great leader but to the over-valuation of a mediocre one.

With a gangster story to tell, Brecht went back to the Chicago setting he had used before. The shooting of Ernst Röhm is presented in terms of Al Capone's St Valentine's Day Massacre, and like Capone, who attended the funeral of his victim O'Bannion, Ui goes to that of Dullfeet (Engelbert Dollfuss, the Austrian Chancellor). Charlie Chaplin had made a composite of Hitler and a Jewish barber in his 1940 film *The Great Dictator*; Brecht also wanted to make Hitler ludicrous but, unlike Chaplin, he was trying to expose the social and economic forces that had brought Hitler to the top. More obliquely, the hero-worship accorded to political gangsters is satirized by harnessing them to the blank verse we associate with the heroic mould. Here Brecht was repeating the stylistic trick he had used in *Die heilige Johanna*. In a bookmaker's office on 122nd Street, Ui bitterly complains:

> The city has no memory. Oh, short is the life
> Of local fame. No murder for two months
> And you're forgotten.

Direct allusion is made to Mark Antony's forum oratory when Ted Ragg, a journalist loosely based on Gregor Strasser, pretends to sympathize:

> And the loveliest scars
> Vanish with those who bear them. 'But can it be
> That in a world where good deeds go unnoticed
> No evidence remains of evil?' 'Yes.'
> 'Oh rotten world.'

The Mark Antony speech is used again when we see a down-at-heel tragedian tutoring Ui in the art of oratory. Brecht is sardonically placing Hitler's speech-making in a literary and theatrical perspective.

Like *Die heilige Johanna*, the play cantilevers out from the Wall Street crash of 1929, which had so many repercussions in Germany. No date is mentioned, but the vegetable market (like the meat market in the earlier play) is shown in the grip of the depression. The Prussian Junkers, who needed government loans and presented Hindenburg with a landed estate, are represented by the Cauliflower Trust, which sells a shipyard to Dogsborough, the Mayor of Chicago, at a give-away price. Brecht is again suggesting that crooked dealing necessarily entails violence: Dogsborough at first rejects Ui's offer of 'protection', but he is intimidated into accepting it when, at the official enquiry, a key witness is murdered; Hindenburg, who wanted to avoid a scandal about the estate, acquiesced in the appointment of Hitler as Chancellor in January 1933. Implicitly Brecht is overrating the importance of the Junkers' embarrassing gift, but historically he is accurate in his treatment of the Reichstag fire and its consequences. Germany was terrorized into accepting a myth of law and order imposed by thugs in uniform, just as the greengrocers accept Ui's offer of protection after a warehouse has been burned at his orders. Brecht also deals cleverly with Dogsborough's will: his condemnation of Ui is revised by Givola (Goebbels) just as Hindenburg's was edited before it was released to the press.

Brecht handles the annexation of Austria no less cleverly. Events, inevitably, are telescoped together: wanting to extend his commercial activities beyond Chicago, Ui experiments with the small town of Cicero, rather as the *Anschluss* was a dress rehearsal for the invasion of Poland and Czechoslovakia. Dollfuss's feeble successor, Kurt von Schuschnigg, tried to compromise with Germany, a policy caricatured in the behaviour of Dullfoot's widow, Betty, who repulses Ui's advances at the funeral but, as director of a wholesale greengrocery, does a deal with him. In the Austrian election of March 1938, 98 per cent of the terrorized electorate voted for Hitler; in the final scene of the play, Ciceronian vegetable dealers are told they are free to leave the meeting but are shot if they do so.

In *Rundköpfe* Brecht had ignored the role of the proletariat in helping Hitler to power; this time he ignored the racial issue he had treated in both *Rundköpfe* and in *Furcht und Elend*. But, as in both earlier plays, he helped to propagate the Marxist doctrine that the root of fascism was capitalism, and as in *Die heilige Johanna* he both oversimplified and overstressed the role of the monopolistic trusts. Nor was he prepared to recognize Hitler's personality as a factor in his rise to power: the man is represented as almost passive, a vulgar opportunist with no genius, only a flair for riding the crest of social forces, like a feeble swimmer on powerful waves. It is less damaging to the play that Goering is simplified into Giri, a cross between a dandyish clown and a mafia-type hit-man. Theatrically he is characterized by his habit of wearing the hat of his most recent victim.

While Brecht was still working on the play, the world première of *Mutter Courage* was being prepared in Switzerland. In the Zürich Schauspielhaus, Leopold Lindtberg was directing a cast headed by Therese Giehse, with a set by Teo Otto. The production, which was premièred on 19 April, roused the audience to an extraordinary pitch of enthusiasm; Brecht received a telegram from Lindtberg, Giehse and Otto, telling him of their success. 'It is bold of the theatre which consists mainly of emigrants, to put on something of mine; no Scandinavian theatre had the nerve to do it.'[3]

His own nerve is still more remarkable. It is extremely hard to go on writing plays without much hope of seeing them performed, and during his eight years of exile he had been prolific, resourceful and versatile. 'Biography, study of attitude, parable, comedy of character in a folkish tone, historical farce – the plays gravitate away from each other like stars in the physicists' new picture of the universe, as though some kind of dramatic atom had been exploded here.'[4] But they were recognizably the fruits of a tree that had been uprooted and planted in foreign soil. What made it possible for them to grow was the strength of his belief that they were all useful. In the fourth scene of *Mutter Courage*, Courage is waiting outside the captain's tent, to complain that her wagon has been damaged but, like a young soldier who arrives with a grievance, she ends by deciding not to wait. Their 'anger is not long enough'; Brecht's was.

On 2 May, when the American visas finally arrived for Brecht, Weigel, the children and Ruth Berlau, their Finnish friends urged them to leave immediately. More German motorized divisions were arriving, while Helsinki was full of German 'tourists'. But Brecht waited until Margarete Steffin's visa arrived on 12 May. On their last evening in Helsinki they were taken out to dinner in a restaurant with friends including Wuolijoki and Diktonius. While they were eating, the restaurant proprietor came over excitedly with the news that Rudolf Hess, head of the Nazi party's central office, had arrived in Scotland as a refugee.

If they had tried to leave from Petsamo, they might have been arrested, so they travelled on the trans-Siberian railway, leaving Finland on the 16th. Arriving in Moscow, they stayed for ten days at the Hotel Metropole. Margarete Steffin, the only member of the party to speak Russian, had to act as interpreter at meetings and in shops. Brecht was offered a job at the Moscow Art Theatre, but he did not want to stay in Russia. He saw Bernhard Reich, and Willi Bredel, who had been editing *Das Wort*.[5] To Lukács Brecht proposed an armistice. To the periodical *Internationale Literatur* he gave scenes from *Furcht und Elend*, which were published later.

The severe winter in Finland had told heavily on Margarete Steffin, as had the strain of the journey. In Leningrad, where Berlau had to share a bedroom with her, she coughed all night. Her weakness was exacerbated by her anxiety about Brecht's manuscripts, and she was all the more terrified of breaking down and delaying the others when the prospects were that neither Russia nor America would be at peace for much longer. But the strain was too much for her and, after collapsing, grey in the face, she was taken to a hospital. Brecht went with her and when they tried to settle her down with oxygen cushions, she insisted on having her Finnish mackintosh brought to her. Brecht discovered afterwards that she had saved up to £15 in sterling and smuggled the notes across the frontier in a mackintosh pocket. 'I loved her very much when I found that out.'[6]

He had, with some difficulty, booked tickets on a Swedish cargo steamer, the *Annie Johnson*, due to sail from Vladivostok. When he tried to change the tickets for a later sailing, he was told that the June ship might be the last before the Nazi troops marched in. His parting gift to Steffin was a ring and a small elephant; before leaving Moscow he arranged that if she died, a death mask would be made and kept for him, together with the elephant.[7] On 30 May he left for Vladivostok, but exchanged telegrams with her every day. She died on 4 June at nine in the morning. She was thirty-three.

The news reached him at ten in the evening, and the next day a telegram from her friend Maria Grasshohner, who had been looking after her, told him that she had

breakfasted quietly, read your telegram carefully and asked for champagne. Soon she felt ill and shivered and thought she was getting better. The doctor came at that moment. The next moment she repeated the word doctor three times. Died quietly. At the post mortem the doctor found both lungs in the final stage. Big cavities. Heart and liver greatly distended. The death mask was made for you.[8]

In a letter to her mother Brecht wrote: 'In her quiet, understanding way she has sacrificed herself as bravely and selflessly as if she had been fighting in a street battle. She is irreplaceable.' According to Berlau, he did not smile for four days after the news of her death.[9]

Part Four

BRECHT IN HOLLYWOOD

On 13 June 1941, nine days before the Germans invaded Russia, the Brechts left Vladivostok together with Ruth Berlau on the *Annie Johnson* and after stopping in Manila for five days, arrived on 21 July in San Pedro, the port of Los Angeles.[1]

They were met at the jetty by Martha Feuchtwanger and Alexander Granach, who drove them to the small flat in Argyle Avenue, Hollywood, which had been rented for them by William Dieterle's secretary. Of his old friends the first Brecht saw was Feuchtwanger, who had a big house, decorated in Mexican style, in Santa Monica. 'Essentially he is unchanged, but looks older.' He was working on a play about a charlatan German astrologer. He lost no time in advising Brecht to stay in Hollywood, where the cost of living was lower than in New York, and where the prospects of earning were greater. As usual Brecht took Feuchtwanger's advice, though it was soon apparent that he was not going to have an easy time. 'The house is too pretty, my profession here is gold-digging ... if I walk, I walk on clouds like a spinal patient. And here more than anywhere I miss Grete. It's like losing one's leader at the very moment of going into the desert.'[2]

As in Denmark, he made little effort to speak the language, though he had no difficulty in reading American thrillers. Resistance to speaking the language was partly a reaction against cultural pressure towards being a nice guy. He felt unsociable, isolated. At first he found nothing to replace the conversations in Lidingö about the Spanish Civil War or involvement in the amateur production of *Was kostet das Eisen*? Or the forest of birch trees surrounding the house in Marlebäk or the view of the harbour from his flat in Helsinki. 'Here one feels like Francis of Assisi in an aquarium or Lenin in the Prater (or at the carnival), a chrysanthemum in a mine or a sausage in a greenhouse.'

With the strain and anxiety of the long journey, Weigel had been losing weight, while their 11-year-old daughter, Barbara, had become tubercular: she spent her first American winter in bed. Brecht remained healthy, but 'I can't breathe in this climate. The air is totally tasteless, both in the morning and the evening, both in the house and the garden.

And there are no seasons. Everywhere it's been part of my morning routine to lean out of the window to taste the air; here I've given up this routine.' His output fell prodigiously: by the end of 1941 he had sketched out a new play *Die Gesichte der Simone Machard* (*The Visions of Simone Machard*) but he had not completed a first draft. Most of his working time was spent on revising and making additions to existing texts. Writing to H.R. Hays after six months in America, he complained that he had been 'paralysed to such a degree that in six months I've written only a few letters ... I couldn't even bring myself to thank the people who helped me to come over'.[3]

Early in August 1941 the Brechts moved from the flat to a small house in 25th Street, Santa Monica, twelve miles to the south-west of Hollywood. Brecht hated it. He worked in his bedroom, which was small and stuffy, with pink doors. He could take only three small paces while working, instead of roaming about freely as he liked to. One visitor noticed that there were few, if any, books in the room, but copies of *Freies Deutschland*, a communist magazine published in Mexico, were 'strewn about', while in the typewriter very thin paper was folded double. Gradually he imposed his personality on the room. 'With its scrubbed wooden floors, its walls bare except for Chinese prints, its upright piano and the ironstone ware Weigel collected from flea-markets, it became distinctively his.'[4]

Later in the month he learned that Walter Benjamin had poisoned himself on the Spanish border while trying to escape from the Nazis. 'The police stopped the small group to which he belonged. In the morning when his travelling companions went to tell him that they were allowed to go on, they found him dead.' The entry in Brecht's journal is terse and restrained, but about seven months later he wrote:

> I know of course: merely through luck
> I have survived so many friends. But last night in my dream,
> I heard these friends saying of me: 'The strongest survive.'
> And I hated myself.[5]

The death of Margarete Steffin was also weighing on him. 'I know I can't cure the pain of bereavement; at most I can keep it secret from myself. Often I've even swallowed a gulp of whisky when her image presented itself to me ... I can see no inner solution to this problem.'[6]

After responding so keenly to the scenic beauty of Marlebäk, he felt as though he had been

lifted out of the century. This is a metropolitan Tahiti. Right now I'm looking out on a garden with a lawn. Reddish blossoming bushes, a palm tree and white garden chairs.... They have nature here, because everything is so artificial.... 15,000 kilometres away, slanting right across Europe ... the slaughter which is continuing day and night, deciding our fate, produces nothing here except a faint echo in the hurly-burly of the art market.[7]

The American theatre struck him as equally unhealthy. 'Perhaps Ben Hecht comes into a bar and describes an idea for a play, i.e. he talks about the setting (the morgue) and produces a few gags. Immediately a colleague says: "Put me down with [*sic*] 1,000 dollars, Ben."' Everything had to be bought and sold: 'Reluctantly I look for a little price tag on this chain of hills or that lemon tree. You also look for the price tag on people.... Custom here demands that you try to "sell" everything, from a shrug to an idea, and so you're always a buyer or a seller. You even sell your piss to the urinal, so to speak.'[8]

Brecht was worse off than during the previous eight years of exile, not only financially but because his reputation had not spread across the Atlantic. Kurt Weill was famous. His new musical, *Lady in the Dark*, was a current Broadway hit, with Gertrude Lawrence and Danny Kaye. But most of the minority that knew Brecht by name knew him as the librettist for *The Threepenny Opera*, which had been produced on Broadway in 1933, to survive for less than a fortnight.

In Santa Monica his only income was about $120 a month from the 'European Film Fund', which had been established by William Dieterle's wife, Charlotte, and Liesl Frank. Spending $48.50 on rent, Brecht could not afford a car, while Weigel had to buy clothes for the children and furniture from Salvation Army and Good Will shops in Los Angeles. Fortunately a refugee doctor from Germany, Dr Schiff, provided free medical treatment for Barbara. Kurt Weill sent some money anonymously, but Brecht neither requested nor received help from the Committee for Exiled Writers, which had been set up by the left-wing League of American Writers.[9]

He had to decide whether to take the job Piscator was offering in New York. In the middle of September he wrote to ask how much it would cost to survive there, living simply and perhaps outside the city. Piscator wanted to stage *Der gute Mensch* or *Ui*, but Brecht's reaction was to ask whether the school could pay for him to be present during rehearsals.[10] With the teaching job he could have lived within reach of Broadway, but many refugees who had been writing in German – Franz Werfel, Vicki Baum and Erich Maria Remarque, for instance – were earning high incomes in Hollywood, and Brecht could not believe he would be less successful. If he had to sell himself, it must be for the highest possible price.

Scouring newspapers and magazines for ideas for new plays, as he had in Europe, he found a story in *Life* (15 September 1941). After a competition in Ohio, a family had been selected as the state's 'most typical farm family'. Given a model home at the Ohio State Fair, the parents and three children had tried to continue their normal routine for a week, while thousands of visitors watched them. In his outline story Brecht surmised what might have happened if the parents had quarrelled just before the fair opened.

Within less than three weeks he had started on his second film project, based partly on the *Joe Fleischhacker* fragment, and partly on his contempt for American bakers – 'There's no real bread in the States. I like bread, I eat my main meal at night, and it's bread and butter.' Fleischhacker, who had been modelled on a wheat tycoon, Curtis Jadwin, was now made into the 'bread king of Chicago'. Worked out in collaboration with Ferdinand Reyher, the story revolved around conflict between a ruthless tycoon and a working-class family. Reyher should have known the story would be unsaleable, but Brecht was forceful and experienced in dominating collaborative work. *The King's Bread* was finished on 4 October, and, three days later, Brecht took it to Max Reinhardt's son, Gottfried, who was assitant to the MGM producer Bernard Heyman. 'For an hour and a half, Brecht, his Augsburg accent still unadulterated, held me spellbound with a film story about the production, distribution and enjoyment of bread.'[11]

He was trying hard to tutor himself in the art of selling stories to what he considered to be 'the world narcotics trade'. He borrowed a treatment from Dieterle to use as a model, and by the end of 1941 he was collaborating with Fritz Kortner on an adaptation of Schnitzler's *Reigen* (*Round Dance*) intended for Charles Boyer.[12] Nine years later Max Ophuls would score a huge success with his verson of *Reigen*, *La Ronde*.

Brecht also worked with Robert Thoren on a comedy called *Bermuda Troubles*. Thoren had been an actor in Germany and was now writing for MGM. 'For relaxation he has a luxurious villa and a chicken farm. Between work sessions he telephones endlessly ... posing as charming husband and young father ... and incessantly shows off, without any object, but studiously avoiding all thinking.'[13] Brecht probably made little effort to conceal his contempt for Thoren and for others who were trading successfully.

In the middle of November 1941 the British launched their offensive in Libya. Brecht was pessimistic: 'No weapon can be new enough not to break down in the hands of a class as old as the English aristocracy.'

Five days later he was working with Kortner on another film story when Kortner's son came in with the news that Japanese planes had dropped bombs on Hawaii. 'As we switched the radio on, we knew that we were "in the world" once again. A gigantic nation roused itself, half drunk with sleep, to join in the war. In the street drivers listen to their radios in a strangely huddled pose.' Brecht had been following the news no less avidly than he had in Scandinavia, noting victories and defeats in his diary as if they were personal events. He was keeping a map of Europe on the wall behind his typewriter, and marking the advances of the German armies in a cancerous red. It had been a great strain to live in a neutral country. Now, feeling less isolated from reality, he could settle down within ten days to working on a play. His first intention was to call it *Jeanne d'Arc 1940*, but by 19 December, when he had completed nine scenes, he had changed the title to *Die Stimmen (The Voices)*.[14]

Heartening though it was, the American declaration of war made life more difficult. He was now an 'enemy alien'. He had a registration number – 7624464. Like other German immigrants in and around Hollywood, the Brechts came under suspicion. Some neighbours thought they were working for the Nazis; others thought it was for the Russians. Their movements were restricted to a five-mile radius of their home, and they were not allowed out of doors between eight in the evening and six in the morning – which meant that Brecht often had to stay the night with friends. Helene Weigel made black-out curtains.[15]

Playing chess with Oskar Homolka, and chatting to him about *Galileo*, Brecht felt 'reminded of a strange sunken theatre of the old days on submerged continents. Here there is nothing but the marketing of an evening's entertainment.' He spent New Year's Eve at the house of Elisabeth Bergner and her husband. The Feuchtwangers were there, and Alexander Granach. Erich Maria Remarque arrived, wearing a dinner jacket and accompanied by a Mexican film star, Lupe Velez.[16]

In 1933 Elisabeth Bergner had married the producer Paul Czinner, settled in England and made her West End debut. In the States she had been working only sporadically in plays and films. Despite her bad experience with *La dame aux camélias* in 1925, she liked Brecht and thought he might help her to make a comeback on the stage. They discussed Thomas Heywood's *A Woman Killed with Kindness* as a vehicle for her, and at one point he thought of asking Feuchtwanger to collaborate on adapting it.

Isolated and frustrated though he felt, Brecht was aware of his good fortune in having escaped. From an American newspaper he cut out a photograph of German soldiers – men of his own age, perhaps – dead in a snow-covered ditch on the Moscow front. Trying to identify with them, he could not hold back moral indignation:

> But I shall die in the prime of life
> Unloved, unmissed
> The reckless driver of a war machine
>
> Having learnt nothing, except at the end
> Having experienced nothing, except killing
> Not missed, except by the slaughterers.

Wanting this poem to be read in the country that had only just declared war, Brecht met the 25-year-old Eric Bentley, then a lecturer at the University of California at Los Angeles. After translating the poem, Bentley submitted it to *Partisan Review*, but Dwight Macdonald thought it was outrageous, and the translation finally appeared in *Rocky Mountain Review*.[17]

In the middle of January 1942 Elisabeth Bergner, who had found *Der gute Mensch* 'boring but excellent', produced a story idea which interested Brecht: a girl is hypnotized and then behaves as though in a trance, but she turns out to be faking. During February and March Brecht had regular meetings with the Czinners to build up the idea, but Czinner then sold it for $35,000. It was impossible to prove how much he had contributed, and Brecht felt as though he had been robbed.[18]

Being under forty-five, he was liable to be conscripted for military service. He registered in the middle of February, and in mid-March the government began to make its selection by drawing lots. To him it seemed like 'a gambling game between state and citizens'.[19]

Ruth Berlau had moved into a wooden cottage around the corner from the Brechts. He spent most of his afternoons with her, and she sometimes came to the house, but she was not *persona grata* when Weigel had guests. Resenting his unwillingness to champion her, Berlau surprised him by accepting an invitation to speak at a women's congress on democracy in Washington. She left Santa Monica in April or May, and she was then invited to New York by a Danish admirer, Ida Bachmann, head of a department in the Office of War Information, where she offered Berlau a job. To Brecht's dismay she accepted. He asked her to come back as soon as possible. 'No one here can take your place in any way.' 'In the afternoon if Eisler doesn't come, there's no alternative to Simenon.'[20]

*　　*　　*

Never slow to see how material intended for one medium could be adapted to another, Brecht had talked to Dieterle about Julius Caesar, and had gone on to write a 'treatment' under the title *Caesar's Last Days*. Alternating between two viewpoints – Caesar's and that of an old soldier who wanted to enlist in his army – the film would have made the same point as *Das Verhör des Lukullus*: the fame of an individual depends on the suffering of an anonymous group. A few historical films were being made, but Dieterle, who had quarrelled with Louis B. Mayer, head of MGM, was no longer in a strong position.[21]

After nine months in America, Brecht had won nothing at what he called 'the roulette game with the stories'. 'For the first time in ten years I'm not working properly ... I can't recall a single breath of fresh air in all these months. It's as if I was sitting a kilometre deep under the ground, unwashed, unshaven, waiting to hear the result of the battle for Smolensk.'[22]

It was through Max Reinhardt that he first sighted a chance of having a play on Broadway. He went with Feuchtwanger to have lunch at the 68-year-old director's big seaside villa, which was 'stuffed with his Berlin furniture and objets d'art'. Reinhardt had settled in Hollywood, where he had founded an acting school and a theatre workshop. 'The old magician, small, standing firmly on his legs, faded, like a drawing in Indian ink that had been attacked by blotting-paper, with his slow, effective movements, his deep voice, still with his tongue sensually in his cheek ... a weary, overworked angel of death.'[23]

A few days later they were discussing the possibility of producing *Furcht und Elend*. Reinhardt twice told Brecht that he considered Büchner's *Woyzeck* 'to be the strongest play in German literature and that the scenes reminded him of it'. Brecht had earlier entrusted the script to Reyher, who had reworked it between March and June 1939, using thirteen of Brecht's twenty-seven scenes, and structuring them into a three-act play with a plot-line involving a working-class boy called Eric. But Brecht never signed the contract.

Reinhardt gave no sign of annoyance when Brecht bombarded him with ideas for the production. German army lorries could appear four times, crowded with white-faced soldiers singing the Horst Wessel song, like Huns bringing a barbarous new order to Europe. Each scene could be prefaced by lorry noises. A voice could announce each scene. At the end the lorry could be seen near Smolensk, finally immobilized. As an epilogue the actors could climb across the footlights and tell the audience it must use force to stop the Nazi lorries.[24]

On 28 May four scenes from the play were presented in German, directed by Berthold Viertel with émigré actors and a black in white make-up (Brecht's idea). After seeing favourable reviews in German-language newspapers, he arranged for Reinhardt to be invited. He went on 14 June, when the four scenes were given a second performance, together with a fifth scene. Unfortunately the actress who was playing the Jewish wife recognized him in the middle of her scene, and, over-awed, was unable to go on.[25]

Although Harold Clurman and his actress wife Stella Adler would have helped to produce the whole play, with Reinhardt directing, the project came to nothing because Brecht refused to go ahead unless he could be personally involved in rehearsals.[26]

As Weigel was later to prove as director of the Berliner Ensemble, she had a strong capacity for leadership and formidable willpower. It was inevitable that she should have to abandon her acting career while in exile, but it was not inevitable that she should be so tolerant of infidelities and so dutiful as a housewife. Her personal loyalty was reinforced by an element of masochism, by lack of confidence in her femininity – a lack Brecht did little to remedy – and by total belief in the importance of his work. If he needed a woman for his writing, that woman must be tolerated.

His routine depended on her housekeeping, and it was irksome for him when some form of nettle-fever forced her to stay in bed: he made breakfast at eight for Barbara, but rather than prepare food for himself he ate his lunch in a drugstore, which he disliked, and took the children there for an evening meal at 6.30. He was also receiving incessant letters from Berlau, full of threats, reproaches and demands for reassurance. Why didn't he come to see her in New York? Perhaps they should break off their relationship. He did his best to persuade her that it did not have to be all or nothing.[1]

Badly though he needed to earn money, he was handicapped by hostility to the ethos. 'The spiritual isolation here is gruesome; in comparison with Hollywood, Svendborg was a metropolis.' Through Hanns Eisler, who brought Clifford Odets to Brecht's house and then arranged for the three of them to lunch with Fritz Lang, a chance emerged of launching *Furcht und Elend* as a film. Odets made several usable suggestions,[2] but Brecht's attitude to the project – like his attitude to Odets – was mainly negative.

On 1 June 1942 he appeared to have five chances of winning at the roulette game. It was possible that MGM would film *Dreigroschenoper*. Jean Renoir had expressed interest in collaborating on a film story. Anna May Wong, who had starred in the London production of Klabund's *Chalk Circle*, wanted to play Shen Te on Broadway. Reinhardt was still interested in *Furcht and Elend*, but the fifth possibility was more promising. Brecht had known Fritz Lang in Germany, and Helene Weigel had played a small part in his 1927 film *Metropolis*. Since the autumn they had been visiting him in his villa, and on 28 May, the day after Reinhard Heydrich, the notorious 'Reichsprotektor' of Bohemia and Moravia, had been assassinated, Lang and Brecht were on the beach together, talking about a 'hostage film'. Lang had been influenced by the *Lehrstücke*. He called his 1938 film *You and Me* 'a fairy tale inspired by Brecht'.[3]

Writing in German, they worked out a story. In fact it was British agents who killed Heydrich, but Brecht and Lang made the same assumption as the Nazis – that it was Czech resistance fighters – and their story was about the execution of hostages as the Nazis tried to hunt down Heydrich's killer. When Lang took the treatment to a producer, Arnold Pressburger, his reaction was positive. Throughout June Brecht and Lang, who was eight years his senior, worked together from nine in the morning till seven in the evening, though Brecht had misgivings. Apparently Lang was aiming to please an audience which would believe in 'the mastermind of the underground movement who hides behind a curtain when the Gestapo is searching houses' and in 'the corpse of a commissar falling out of a wardrobe'.[4] Writing to Berlau, Brecht complained that the 'manual labour' was exhausting. He was given a preliminary fee of $250, and when he asked for a total of $3,000, Lang promised $5,000, with a further $3,000 for extra work. At last Brecht could afford to move. The new house cost only $12.50 a month more in rent than the old one, and it was only one street away: they moved from 25th Street to 26th. Built about thirty years earlier, their Californian timber-house was one of the oldest buildings in the town. It was whitewashed, with an upper floor containing four bedrooms. Brecht's workroom was about 21 feet in length, and after whitewashing it they installed four tables. They moved in on 12 August.

By the 14th he was feeling sufficiently relaxed to resume work on *Der Messingkauf*, and to read Lucretius in the garden.[5]

Every morning at half past eight Brecht drove the twelve miles into Hollywood to work on scripting the hostage film in an office Pressburger had rented in the old Chaplin studios. Not breakfasting until one o'clock, he drank Californian white wine with the sandwiches he had brought. But the work bored him: 'This "technique" calls for an astonishing minimum of inventiveness, intelligence, humour and interest. One clambers from one situation to the next, introducing arbitrary characters. It's assumed that the actors can't act and the audience can't think.' He felt divorced from his earlier work. He learned from Feuchtwanger, who, since the curfew, had become very chatty in the evening over the telephone, that Thornton Wilder had seen *Mutter Courage* in Zürich, and been impressed.[6]

Instead of giving Brecht an assistant, Lang employed a highly experienced screenwriter, John Wexley, who was paid $1,500 a week, and may have been promised credit as sole author of the screenplay. At first, although he persisted in calling Brecht 'Bert' when even Weigel called him Brecht, Wexley seemed 'very left-wing and decent', but soon it became apparent that in preparation for a disagreement over credits, he was carefully accumulating written evidence to indicate that he was the sole author.[7]

The film, which Brecht wanted to call *Trust the People*, evolved into *Hangmen Also Die*, and during the filming he lost his residual respect for Lang. In the middle of October, when Brecht was working amicably with Wexley, Lang took the American into his office and insisted 'that what he wanted to make was a Hollywood picture. To hell with the scenes involving the crowd etc.' But until shooting began, Brecht had relatively little cause for complaint. On 18 October he said that if the *Versuche* series had been continuing, he would have included scenes from *Trust the People*, including the first, in which Heydrich shows Czech industrialists leaflets with the picture of a tortoise to persuade munitions factory workers into slowing down. He also liked the hostage scenes showing class differences in the camp. 'Five minutes before the Nazis take the hostages to be executed, there are outbreaks of anti-Semitism.' But because the industry did not wish to appear pro-Jewish there was a general reluctance to deal with anti-Semitism, and Lang did not want to show Jewish members of the Czech resistance being maltreated by Nazis.[8]

According to Brecht the film was constructed out of three stories, which give way to one another: 'the story of an assassin, that of a girl whose father is taken as a hostage, and that of something white – a quisling who is hunted down by an entire city'. This story must have appealed to Lang, who had done so well in 1931 with the film *M*, showing a whole city in the grip of fear until its criminals gang together in hunting down the child murderer. The main forces in the 1931 film are collective, and even the individual pervert, played by Peter Lorre, is shown to be more passive than active – gripped by drives he cannot master. In the original screenplay for *Hangmen Also Die* the main focus was on the group, not individuals, and one of Brecht's points was that 'the underground movement makes mistakes, which are corrected by the broad mass of people'.[9]

Early in October, with the script still unfinished, Pressburger told Lang that the schedule must be advanced by three weeks. The script was far too long, but instead of letting Brecht and Wexley cut it, another writer was hired – until Wexley discovered what was going on. He was then put in charge of scaling it down. For two weeks Brecht heard nothing from Lang, and Wexley looked like 'the incarnation of a bad conscience'. At the beginning of November Lang's secretary rang up to say that Brecht was 'invited, more than invited' to the shooting, which was about to start, and from then on he was progressively antagonized. The first scene to be shot was one that he and Wexley had scrapped – the heroine is arguing with her aunt about the décolletage of her wedding dress. The leading lady, Anna Lee, was 'a fifth-rate English actress, a smooth, characterless doll. The lord of the camera sits unapproachably in his machine. Next to me waits the German emigrant doctor who has to give him vitamin injections.' Beckoning Brecht to him, Lang said 'in a subdued and affected voice: "Hallo, Brecht. You'll get a script in the morning."' When he got it he was still more deeply dejected: Wexley had restored 'all the main stupidities' which during the previous ten weeks Brecht had worked so hard to eliminate. It was also depressing to watch the hairdresser and the wardrobe master trying to make the assassin immaculate, instead of looking as though he had been wandering around the streets for hours.[10]

Lang did not want Weigel in the small role of a vegetable woman. Repeating the stratagem he had used with Kattrin in *Mutter Courage*, Brecht had made the woman almost completely silent. Wexley had provided dialogue for her, and Lang – perhaps wanting an obstacle – insisted it was necessary. He gave Weigel a voice test, promised a full screen test, and then cast another actress in the part.[11]

Brecht at this time was far from immaculate. When Alexander Granach took him to a party at a Jewish Club, where one of his poems was recited and another sung in Yiddish, a tailor in the audience offered him a free suit and an optician offered a pair of new spectacles. He accepted the suit but not the spectacles.[12]

The shooting went on for fifty-two days, but Brecht stayed away more and more. Throughout his work in the German theatre he had gravitated towards a method that was more common in cinema, working collaboratively not only with other writers but with designers and composers, so that the verbal element could be fused with the visual and the musical. Text was something that could be cut or remoulded to fit the needs of the moment. But, thanks to the strength of his personality and of his faith in his infallibility, he had dominated most of the *ad hoc* committees that had discussed practical problems. Working on a Hollywood film without being fluent in English, he was in an unprecedentedly weak position.

Afterwards he was in no state for solitary labour in his workroom, and what could be more restorative than another collaboration with his old friend Feuchtwanger in a big house overlooking the mountains and the sea? Just before Christmas Brecht had been trying to sketch out the first scene of his play about a modern Jeanne d'Arc, but found it 'generally not theatrical yet, lacking in quality, dead'. Four days later he was reading a German draft of Feuchtwanger's memoir about his experiences in France during 1940. Interned outside Aix-en-Provence, he had escaped across the Pyrenees. This was 'probably his finest book. Remarkable epicureanism between pine trees, barbed wire and heaps of excrement.' It was nearly twenty years since they had collaborated on *Eduard II*, but with his personal knowledge of France in 1940, Feuchtwanger would be the ideal collaborator on what was now to be called *Die Gesichte der Simone Machard*. For Brecht the main point was that while the German army is advancing, the voices which prompt the young Frenchwoman are not *vox Dei* but *vox populi*. She saves France by paying attention to the blacksmith and the peasant. But Feuchtwanger 'wants nothing to do with anything technical or social (epic presentation, alienation effect, development of characters from social material instead of "biological", introduction of class conflicts into the story, etc.) and puts up with all that as just my personal style'. On the other hand, 'he has a feeling for construction, values linguistic refinements, also has poetic and dramaturgical ideas, knows a lot about literature, respects arguments and is a pleasant human being, a good friend'.[13]

At the beginning of January 1943 they were spending every morning enjoyably together but their routine was interrupted when Brecht learned that Pressburger and Lang were not intending to give him a credit for his work on the film. He had antagonized Pressburger by insisting on the same overtime bonus as Wexley. Though many of Brecht's contributions had been discarded, the film could not have come into existence without him, and plentiful evidence of his influence still exists in the end-product. One sequence in the hostage prison camp echoes an episode in *Furcht und Elend*. In the film a professor, shortly before his execution, dictates a letter enjoining his son to resist the Nazis; in the play a similar letter to a son has been smuggled out of prison by a man about to be executed.

Unlike Wexley, who was well-established, Brecht badly needed a credit, 'which would put me in a position to get a film job if the water gets up to my neck'. He telephoned the Screen Writers Guild to ask for arbitration, but Wexley was formidably forearmed. At the hearing on 20 January he 'sat in front of half a hundredweight of manuscripts and testified that he had scarcely ever spoken to me'. On their first day of working together, as soon as he had gone through a sequence, Wexley had dictated it in English to a secretary who made four copies on paper headed 'John Wexley'. In one scene, needing a German translation, he made manuscript additions to one copy and gave it to Brecht but then made an excuse for retrieving it. Brecht had been spasmodically suspicious that 'these tricks will be well paid', but had not been canny enough to accumulate documentary evidence to counter Wexley's. All he could submit was a written report on the discussions and working sessions, together with a few pages of dialogue. Though Eisler, who had written the music, gave evidence to support Brecht, and Lang pointed to dialogue and incidents that 'only Brecht could have written',[14] the decision went against him. The only credit he was given was as co-author (with Lang) of the original story.

Financially, though, he was already better off than he would have been if he had accepted Piscator's offer of a job in New York. With the money from the film he bought the house for $4,500, to be paid over a five-year period, and bought a second-hand Buick, while Weigel started to buy second-hand furniture.[15]

Die Gesichte der Simone Machard was completed during the first week in February. Intent on demonstrating once again that 'the Reich and the rich flock together', Brecht set the main action in and around a French hotel on one of the main roads from Paris to the south while the German army is advancing. The hotel has a garage and transport business attached to it; the owner is being pressured, rather half-heartedly, by the mayor to provide food for the retreating French soldiers and to put his lorries at the disposal of the refugees. A hotel proprietor is both a property owner and a tradesman: presenting the man as a type, Brecht makes self-interest incline him towards allying himself with the enemy. The spirit of patriotism is alive only in the lower classes, and especially in the girl, Simone, who works at the hotel. In a series of four dream sequences she identifies with Joan of Arc, and listens to the voice of an angel whom she associates with her soldier brother. The voice instructs her in resistance tactics. She coerces her boss into distributing food to the refugees, and ensures that his petrol is not given to the Germans by setting it alight. Instead of being martyred, like the saint, she is sent to an asylum which is run, brutally, by nuns. But the optimistic message is that actions like hers can be emulated. As the play ends, the sky is reddening: the refugees have set the village hall on fire.

Living on opposite coasts, Brecht and Piscator had little contact. Piscator still wanted to stage *Der gute Mensch*, but Brecht had been warned that New York critics had responded unfavourably to his first three productions at the Dramatic Workshop.[1] Nevertheless, Piscator was the likeliest source for an invitation to New York. As an 'enemy alien', Brecht was not allowed to travel without official permission, and, when Ruth Berlau transmitted his request, Piscator obliged with a friendly letter: Brecht was needed in New York to discuss a production of *Der gute Mensch* at the Dramatic Workshop's Studio Theatre and to give a lecture on the theatre's contribution to the war effort.[2]

On 8 February Brecht boarded a Southern Pacific train full of soldiers drinking lemonade and beer, playing cards, and listening to music on the radio but switching off whenever a news programme started. Seen through the windows of the train, Arizona and Texas reminded him of Siberia. 'The grey, two-storied timber farmhouses and the people look very poor.'[3]

After a four-day train journey he arrived in New York, where he stayed in Ruth Berlau's fourth-floor walk-up. He saw Karl Korsch, who was living on $100 a week from the Institute of Social Research, which had been founded by a Jewish businessman, Hermann Weil, who had made a fortune in wheat. It had been reconstituted by his son Felix as a self-financing institute for the study of Marxism and social reform. Brecht, who hated this capitalistic patronage of left-wing intellectuals, noted that Korsch was 'really changed in type ... stout, his eyes smaller, almost crafty'. But writing to him later in the year, Brecht said: 'I regard you as my teacher. Your works and your personal friendship mean a great deal to me, and all that matters is that you have patience with me.'[4]

Brecht also met Hans Langerhans, a friend who in 1933 had been leading a resistance group. He reported that in a Brandenburg prison he had heard a convict reciting Brecht's poem about the housepainter (Hitler).[5] Brecht also looked up Elisabeth Hauptmann.

Unlike Korsch, Georg Grosz had not changed much. Brecht went to an exhibition of his work, 'and the still-lifes impress me because they bring a superb materialistic sensual moment into German painting. But he's selling almost nothing.' Dozens of brilliant anti-Fascists and refugees from France had settled in New York; Wieland Herzfelde, the publisher, was there, and he arranged a Brecht evening. Brecht selected the material and rehearsed the performers. An Italian girl, Julia Charol, was due to perform a song from *Die heilige Johanna* with music by Paul Dessau, grandson of a Jewish cantor and composer of the music for the 1938 Paris production of *Furcht und Elend*. When Julia Charol backed out, Brecht encouraged Dessau to sing the song himself. Before he left New York, Brecht said: 'Come to Hollywood. We'll be able to work better there.'[6]

Held on 6 March 1943 in the studio theatre at the New School for Social Research, the Brecht evening was a success. Peter Lorre read several poems, including two on the subject of emigration. Two scenes from *Furcht und Elend* were read, and finally Elisabeth Bergner recited the poem about the Children's Crusade.[7] Piscator gave a party afterwards, and a repeat performance was arranged for 24 April. This time Brecht took part himself, reading unpublished poems.

With no immediate hope of screenwriting commissions, and with no better prospects on Broadway, he let himself be steered by Bergner and Czinner, despite his reasons for distrusting them, into adapting a Jacobean play – not *A Woman Killed with Kindness* but Webster's play *The Duchess of Malfi*. Bergner, who was now forty-two, had made a charismatic Broadway debut in 1935, playing the part she had created in London for C.B. Cochran – Gemma in *Escape Me Never* – and she was currently appearing in a thriller, but she had never established herself on Broadway as a serious actress, and the *Duchess* seemed like an excellent vehicle.

Needing a collaborator whose English was better than Feuchtwanger's, Brecht picked H.R. Hays, who, since helping over the affidavits, had translated *Mutter Courage* for the 1941 edition of *New Directions*, and translated *Arturo Ui* without any contract or remuneration. After a series of midnight meetings with Bergner, who preferred to discuss the project at the end of her evening performance, and after a meeting with Czinner and Ann Elmo, an agent who was acting for Brecht, the two writers signed a Dramatists Guild contract and received a small advance from Czinner.[8]

Digressing occasionally to translate each other's poems, they worked during April in Berlau's flat. Brecht wanted to tighten the play's construction and clarify motivation, bringing Ferdinand's incestuous desire for his sister into clear focus and activating the Cardinal with acquisitive designs on her property. According to Hays, 'I did all the writing, in the style of Webster, though Brecht and I discussed the scenes to be eliminated or added, and the content of scenes, and he sometimes contributed images.'[9] All the material Brecht produced in German was translated by Hays, mostly into blank verse. A few lines from Webster's 1612 play *The White Devil* were interpolated, and Brecht later introduced a prologue based on the first seventy-seven lines of Ford's *'Tis Pity She's a Whore*. Brecht told Hays that Bergner had failed in *La dame aux camélias* and was consequently scared of the death scene: it would be better if they could contrive to keep her vertical until the end. Hays did not want to sacrifice a scene that contained 'some of Webster's finest writing', and Brecht solved the problem by letting her die after kissing a poisoned prayer book. Cariola and the other ladies-in-waiting then march her up and down to counteract the effects of the poison. In Webster's play the Duchess and her children are strangled; it is Julia, the Cardinal's mistress, who dies after kissing a poisoned book. This sub-plot is cut out of the Brecht version.

Before he left New York at the end of May, they had completed two preliminary drafts and a final one, which was copyrighted by Hays. Brecht showed it to Eisler, who agreed to compose music for it.[10]

26 / Schweyk Resurrectus

On 3 April 1943, when Brecht attended the anti-fascist rally called *We Fight Back*, the performance included a comic sketch, 'Schweyk's Spirit Lives On', performed by two Czech actors, George Voskovec and Jan Werich. The sketch was described by a reviewer as 'a delightful, humorous portrayal of the Czech spirit of sabotage'.[1] Since he had worked on the adaptation for the Piscator production of *Schweyk* in 1927-8, it had been almost inevitable that Brecht would sooner or later return to this material, and as Piscator badly needed a large-scale American success, they had thought of collaborating on a new adaptation.

An alternative possibility emerged for Brecht: to collaborate with Weill on a Schweyk musical. Ernst Josef Aufricht was making money out of the *Dreigroschenoper* – recordings with Lenya were being sold – and he was eager to bring Brecht and Weill together again. Despite the success of *Lady in the Dark*, Weill seemed 'no longer so confident about his future here', and in May he invited Brecht to spend a week at his country house in New City on the Hudson. When Weill showed interest in musicalizing *Der gute Mensch*, Brecht, far from being unwilling to prostitute his prostitute, sat down to 'turn out a version of Setzuan for here'. Intending to do *Schweyk* with him on Broadway, Brecht wrote a complete story outline during the week in New City, and Weill composed some of the songs.[2]

Weill's name seemed like a solid guarantee of production on Broadway, but Brecht had several meetings with Piscator, who had managed to interest the Theatre Guild in a revival of this 1928 *Schweyk*. The translation was to be by the poet Alfred Kreymborg, and Brecht met him in May when he served as chairman for an anti-fascist event, a programme organized to commemorate the burning of books by the Nazis on 10 May 1933. Kreymborg's play *America America* had been one of the great left-wing successes of the early 1930s. Without mentioning the plans he was making with Weill, Brecht offered to collaborate with Piscator on a new adaptation of the text.[3] They even discussed actors, and Piscator introduced him to Zero Mostel.

Brecht's relationship with Berlau had improved during his stay in New

York. On the way back to Hollywood he wrote to her from Texas, reminding her to hide 'the white grandmotherish nightshirts' he had wanted her to wear in bed. 'I still keep seeing you in them.' But there would be trouble if Ida Bachmann found them. The urgent questions are: is she being realistic, happy, eager to learn new things, and faithful? In the summer she would come back to Santa Monica. After arriving there on the 26th, he became impatient at not hearing from her more often. She should write every day, even if it was only a line. And was she smoking too much? 'My last snack – the sandwich at night – I eat (in spirit) with you. Is that all right?'[4]

When he described some of his ideas for *Schweyk* to Stefan, his 18-year-old son immediately objected that Hašek's Schweyk would not have taken so many risks. Brecht agreed but decided to go against the grain of the 'unpolitical attitude' Hašek had given Schweyk.[5] The Nazis were more formidable than the Austro-Hungarian empire, so sharper counter-attacks were necessary.

Re-reading the novel in Grete Reiner's 1926 translation, Brecht had been overwhelmed by

the genuinely non-positive viewpoint of the people, which is itself the only positive value and therefore can't take a positive stand in relation to anything else. On no account must Schweyk become a shifty underhanded saboteur. He's just opportunistic with the tiny opportunities that are left. He righteously upholds the existing order, which is so destructive for him, in so far as he supports any principle of order, even the nationalistic, which he encounters only as an oppressive force. His wisdom is subversive. His indestructibility makes him into an inexhaustible object of abuse and, at the same time, into the soil where liberation can grow.[6]

This helps to explain why the novel fascinated Brecht. The premiss of what he called 'Aristotelian' drama was that the exceptional individual – heroic ruler, leader or nobleman – could validly be put on the stage as representative of the anonymous masses. Brecht's counter-thesis was that a superior wisdom was to be found among social inferiors, that morality, law and conventional art were all weapons of oppression; but however anxious he was to fight for the many against the few, theatre, even more than cinema, gave preferential treatment to individuals with a dominant personality, and Brecht had proved himself liable to win more sympathy than he wanted for his central figures – Galileo and Mutter Courage, for example. Unlike Pelagea Vlassova, Courage and Shen Te, Schweyk neither learned nor failed to learn from the experience of being a victim; unlike Kattrin, Frau Carrar, Simone and Johanna he was not willing to risk martyrdom. But like all seven heroines, he represented an attempt to portray the people, to distil the group into an individual. He had guile (like Galileo) coupled with subversive wisdom, expressed partly through digressive anecdotes (like Matti). He advises a dog that if it wants to survive the war, it should go on behaving just like other dogs – until it can bite. But Schweyk's genius for survival put him almost in line with Lindbergh's anonymous crew. Unlike any individual, he was unkillable. He was the archetypal little man whom any leader has reason to fear. This is established early on in the synopsis Brecht wrote for Weill in New City. The play was to begin with a prologue set in 'the higher regions', where a larger-than-life-size Hitler would ask for reassurance from his larger-than-life-size chiefs of staff: does the little man love him? The action would answer this question.

Within three days of arriving in Hollywood, Brecht was discussing the role with Peter Lorre, who, in the fourteen years since he had been cast as the village idiot, had become a big star, without ceasing to be a good actor. But he was nervous of the scene in which Schweyk, having slaughtered a stolen dog, gives it to Anna Kopecka so that she can cook a goulash for Baloun. Lorre contended that Schweyk was a dog-lover; 'of course Schweyk is not that, since he sells dogs'.[7]

The first act was finished on 9 June 1943, and the script was virtually ready by the 24th. Brecht called it 'a counter-play to *Mutter Courage*'.[8] The survival of Courage implies that war will continue so long as there are profits to be made out of it; the survival of Schweyk implies that despite war there will always be people. The emphasis is on the optimistic comedy. Weighed in the balance against an ostensibly great leader, Hitler, the little man is shown to be greater.

Though Brecht was writing a play with songs and aiming it at Broadway, he was also, as in the queue scene in *Die Mutter* and as in *Simone Machard*, incorporating hints on how to join in the fight against oppression. Whether the message would ever reach resistance workers was immaterial; Brecht could believe in the value of what he was doing. By spending time on the screenplay he had, as he saw it, financed three worthwhile projects: *Simone*, the Webster adaptation, and *Schweyk*.[9]

Survival had been a dominant theme in his anti-heroic plays from *Trommeln in der Nacht* onwards. What is new about *Schweyk* is that the attitude of a comically cynical survivor is combined with the achievements of a tragic martyr. Besides discouraging Baloun from enlisting, Schweyk succeeds with impunity in rescuing Anna from an importunate SS lieutenant, helps her to sap the morale of a Gestapo officer by telling his fortune and predicting death in the near future for him and twenty men, distracts a sentry at a vital moment so that a railway truck full of machine guns for Stalingrad is misrouted, and saves a Russian family from a brutal Nazi padre. The humour, though less saltily subtle than Hašek's, was more subtle than that of the average Broadway musical.

But Brecht was now in a weaker position and Weill in a stronger one than in 1933, when, collaborating in Paris, Brecht had refused to produce a mere scenario for a ballet. He now refused to provide a mere libretto for a musical comedy: 'I need a position which is semi-"influential", not one in which I fetch the beer. Besides, political questions are involved in this play, and I need to have a say in it.' Disagreements with Weill began in June when the casting of his musical, *One Touch of Venus*, brought him to Los Angeles. By the beginning of July Brecht had got far enough with revising his script to approach Kreymborg, and on 2 July Ruth Berlau was instructed to secure him as translator. 'If not Kreymborg, then Reyher, but let's not spend a year looking.'[10] In August Kreymborg accepted an advance of $100, provided by Peter Lorre. But after consulting Maxwell Anderson, Weill, who had received a revised text in July, decided it was too 'un-American' for Broadway, and Aufricht returned the $85,000 he had raised from backers.

Since February the Royal Air Force had been systematically bombing the European railway system, industrial plants in the Ruhr, and Berlin. 'The heart stands still', wrote Brecht, 'when one reads about the air raids on Berlin. They are unconnected with military operations, so the end of the war is not in prospect, only the end of Germany.' A week later the Secretary of the American Treasury boasted: 'We want to blast the city of Berlin off the face of the map.'[11] Outraged by the endemic idea that the German people was collectively responsible for the crimes of the Nazis – Fascism, he believed, had been imposed from above – and better disposed now towards the idea of a United Front, Brecht took an initiative to unite German émigrés in an anti-fascist proclamation. On 21 July a manifesto had been published in *Pravda*, printed in German and Russian, calling on German soldiers and workers to mutiny and sabotage the war effort. The signatories included politicians, trade unionists and writers. Wanting to issue a similar call from America, Brecht convened a meeting at the house of Berthold and Salka Viertel. He needed an impressive array of names, and none carried more weight than that of Thomas Mann, who was invited, though Brecht disliked him and disparaged him as 'that short-story writer'. Not that he had recently tried to read Mann's novels, though Eisler enthused about them at length.[12]

Mann came to the meeting on 1 August, and so did his brother Heinrich, together with Feuchtwanger, Ludwig Marcuse and the novelist Bruno Frank. The wives had coffee downstairs while the men worked in an upstairs bedroom. The resultant statement welcomed the *Pravda* manifesto, calling on the German people to 'force its oppressors to unconditional surrender and to fight for a vigorously democratic Germany'. They all signed it, but in the morning Thomas Mann telephoned Feuchtwanger to withdraw his signature: he did not want to become involved in anything that might be taken to be pro-communist. 'The stubborn absurdity of these "cultural ambassadors",' complained Brecht, 'momentarily paralysed even me. . . . They agree with Goebbels's equation between Hitler and Germany.'[13]

Piscator did not know that Brecht had completed an adaptation of *Schweyk* until Kreymborg wrote on 8 August, praising it as 'not only first rate but decidedly better than anything I could have done in an original form. . . . I have therefore decided to go ahead with Brecht, Weill and Aufricht.' Piscator, who had so often helped Brecht, was incredulous at his perfidy. He drafted a furious letter, denouncing the 'Brechtian swinishness' and threatening to knock him off his 'amoral Olympus'.[14] The letter he sent was a less impassioned warning that he would protect his legal rights, but he had failed to secure the American rights from Hašek's legal representative, who now sold them to Aufricht.

Christopher Isherwood was living in Hollywood at a Vedanta monastery. After meeting him a few times at the Viertels', Brecht, having designs on him as a translator, invited him to dinner, and he came on 20 September. Isherwood was 'small, gentle, wiry, patient and able to educe patience'. He complimented Brecht on *Der gute Mensch*, but seemed uneasy about the dilapidated gods. Brecht explained that they represented moral precepts which had become deadly, and had suffered accordingly on their tour of inspection. After Berthold Viertel arrived the conversation turned to Auden and Aldous Huxley. Isherwood was a Buddhist, Auden an Anglo-Catholic, and Huxley 'the vaguest kind of deist'. Brecht was allowed to mock Isherwood's 'witty, subtly nuanced, detailed descriptions of the spiritual agonies' of his two friends, 'but when I called him "bought", he looked at his watch and stood up'.[15]

Brecht, who had grown to expect a wide margin of tolerance even from new acquaintances, failed to understand how offensive he had been. 'I feel rather as a surgeon would if a patient stood up during the operation and went away. I had only wounded him.'[16] The letter of apology Isherwood afterwards received was not from Brecht but from Viertel. Weigel had reminded Isherwood of a Salvationist. Seeing that his commitment was religious, not political, they felt obliged to redeem him.

By September Berlau was again needing more reassurance than he could provide by letter. He had never wanted her to leave Hollywood, he said, and, on leaving Washington, she had promised to come back, though without seriously intending to. 'But I could see you'd been unhappy here, dissatisfied with the time I had etc. and I hoped I could come to New York as often as possible or permanently.' Their plans for the summer had fallen through, he said, because the $500 from Aufricht had failed to arrive, not because he was afraid she would destroy his domestic happiness. 'I no longer know what to do or what to say, because I do know what your oscillation between love and hate, between friendship and enmity have already cost us, Ruth.' But a week later he was more conciliatory, promising to write every day.[17]

Kreymborg had completed his *Schweyk* translation which, according to Brecht, had 'more errors that a dog has fleas', but he wrote to tell Kreymborg he was delighted. Realizing that Weill had lost interest, Brecht asked Eisler to set the songs, and hearing that Zero Mostel might accept the name part, he again thought about collaborating with Piscator. But, if Piscator was to be involved, 'I must have the last word over the production, i.e. co-direct with him officially.' With Mostel on the horizon, it should be easier to lever Peter Lorre into either committing himself to the part or backing the production.[18] Brecht would have been happy to have either of these highly dissimilar actors as Schweyk.

Through Lorre Brecht met Ernest Pascal, a London-born screenwriter who had been President of the Screenwriters' Guild in Hollywood. The contact renewed Brecht's hopes of making money through screenwriting. His June letters to Berlau mention an idea he would develop with Lorre in July and August. 'Something permanent could develop out of this – one or two films every year for United Artists. If that happened, I would bring you here.' To discuss ideas with Pascal he was invited to the lakeside house where Lorre was living with a millionairess, the daughter of a Chicago meat tycoon. 'The children bite Mummy's pearls to find out whether they're real, or to prove it to guests.' Lake Arrowhead was 'an artificial mountain lake under pine trees, 600 metres above sea level, property of a private company. On individual pines little red tags marked "Sold". Lorre rides, swims, drives a speedboat, shoots clay pipes and is nice – between patronage and discipleship.' 'A little girl asks me whether I'm a chauffeur, then whether I'm an actor, then whether I'm a writer. Her instinct is infallible – I must belong to the servant class.'[19]

There was a market for resistance stories, and in the morning the three men discussed Brecht's idea about a Marseilles museum curator who tries to make his peace with the Vichy government but, to save a seventeenth-century wooden statue from being exported to Germany, enlists the help of the underworld. Afterwards Brecht worked with Viertel on a treatment of the story, which he called *The Crouching Venus*.

Convinced of what he had told Stefan – that the most important commandment was 'Be good to yourself' – he felt entitled to be unscrupulous. Knowing that a new version of *The Duchess of Malfi* would be more commercially viable if W.H. Auden were involved in it, Brecht approached him, without admitting the extent of his commitment to H.R. Hays. The adaptation 'now exists in an English version ... I told Bergner no one could do it as well as you'. He also misled Auden about the extent of his deviation from the original. 'I have proceeded very cautiously with Webster's text, but had to interpolate a few new sequences and lines.' Auden agreed to collaborate but, like Piscator, Hays was kept in the dark about Brecht's double-dealing. It was at an agent's office in December that Czinner revealed their intention of using a 'British poet' to 'liven up the script'. Hays (in his own words) 'hit the roof and told them to take my name off the script'.[20]

In Brecht's plays guile is usually productive, but his own was often counter-productive, though his ruthlessness towards Piscator was not the decisive factor in making Weill and Aufricht withdraw. Working through Kreymborg's translation with Stefan, Brecht saw that the mistakes would be hard to rectify, and Lorre, after showing the translation to an American friend, expressed disappointment. Brecht turned to Berlau for advice. With help from Hans Viertel, Berthold's son, and then from Mordecai Gorelik, he translated a few sample pages himself, and then reviled Kreymborg's version as 'monstrously slovenly and irresponsible'.[21] When he went to New York in November they evolved a compromise: Berlau would collaborate with Kreymborg on a new version incorporating Brecht's corrections of errors in the earlier one.

In December Weill stated three conditions for collaborating. The play would have to be written by a top-class American author – someone like

Ben Hecht – and produced by a top-class American management. The part of Anna Kopecka must be played by Lenya. The script must be written for a 'musical play', with more openings for music than Brecht had provided: 'I do not under any circumstances wish to write incidental music'. Brecht had already tried to convince Weill that the part of Anna Kopecka had been written for Lenya, and he agreed that an American lyric-writer was needed for the songs, but what Weill wanted was a well-established author, 'who can find a way of rendering the humour of your script in American terms. ... Nor do I think the rights position clear enough to ensure the backing.'[22] Moss Hart was one of the backers who withdrew on hearing that there were two rival claims to the property.

Had Brecht dealt openly with Piscator, it might all have turned out differently; as it was, he had ruined a good chance of a Broadway production. At the same time, though, another hope was emerging. Eric Bentley, who was now teaching at Black Mountain College, used his Christmas holiday to work with Brecht at Elisabeth Hauptmann's flat in Riverside Drive on a new translation of *Furcht und Elend*, which Brecht wanted to title *The Private Life of the Master Race*. Together with her, Brecht could select the scenes for an American production, and supervise the shape of each sentence in the dialogue. In this translation the play would be his first to reach New York, and it would not be seen there until four years after his arrival in the United States.

He was incomparably more talented than most of the writers who were making big money in Hollywood, was an inveterate reader of thrillers, was hard-working, unscrupulous, eager to succeed and had no high-falutin ideas about refusing to prostitute his art. But he was as good at making enemies as he had once been at making friends.

Luise Rainer was a beautiful 33-year-old actress who had been born in Vienna, had worked with Reinhardt, had arrived in Hollywood at the age of twenty-five, had won Oscars two years running for her performances in *The Great Ziegfeld* (1936) and *The Good Earth* (1937), and had been married to Clifford Odets from 1937 to 1940. She lived in Los Angeles and met Brecht several times before he asked her, while walking with her on a beach, which role most appealed to her. When she mentioned the girl in Klabund's *Kreidekreis* – which he had seen, in 1925, with Elisabeth Bergner in the part – he claimed to have suggested the idea to Klabund, and he offered to make it into a Broadway vehicle for her. Since 1938 her career had disintegrated, but there was a Broadway backer, Jules Leventhal, who wanted to put on a show for her, and when Brecht went back to New York in the middle of November 1943 Leventhal commissioned him to write *The Caucasian Chalk Circle*, paying him an advance of $800.[1]

She was then performing to troops in the Mediterranean, and she returned to New York in February 1944, ill with jaundice and malaria. When she was better, he showed her a page of blank verse, and at their next meeting, using the same page, he introduced her to his style of acting by making her read it aloud and starting to rehearse her in it. She baulked. He roared at her: 'Do you know who I am?' 'Yes,' she answered coolly. 'You are Bertolt Brecht. And do you know who I am?' 'Yes. You are nothing. Nothing, I say.'[2] The contract did not stipulate that she was to play the lead, and though he would later send her a script, he may have engineered the quarrel partly in order to free himself from having to tailor the part of Grusche to the physique and the personality of this Viennese beauty. If she had played Grusche, she might have come close to repeating the performance she had given as the Chinese peasant wife in *The Good Earth*, which was based on a Pearl Buck novel.

Brecht started writing the play before he left New York, outlining the plot in detail and working on several scenes in collaboration with Ruth Berlau at her flat. The play *The Chalk Circle* was by the Yuan writer Li Hsing Tao. Klabund's version (which distorts the original, and has the two mothers pulling at a child of three months) enraged the German sinologist Alfred Forke, who published a translation of his own in 1926. Brecht was familiar with this, but vague about the source. One note of his refers to 'the ancient Chinese novel'. But he started off by calling his Grusche Hai Tang, the name of the prostitute heroine in Li Hsing Tao's play. During the early stages of writing he felt pulled in different directions by the demands of art and the demands of the contract. 'I write the play listlessly in this empty, severe room.'[3]

When collaborating on *Simone Machard*, Feuchtwanger and Brecht had agreed that the performance rights were at Brecht's disposal, while Feuchtwanger had the right to use the material in a novel. In 1943, when the playscript was submitted to Samuel Goldwyn, he returned it, saying he could not understand it. But after Feuchtwanger had written his novel, which was called *Simone*, Goldwyn bought the film rights for $50,000, and $20,000 went to Brecht. 'Buy new trousers' was Brecht's laconic diary entry,[4] but the payment eased all his financial anxieties, freeing him from the need to please Luise Rainer with *Der kaukasische Kreidekreis* (*The Caucasian Chalk Circle*).

It was soon after returning to Santa Monica in March that Brecht met Charles Laughton, who fell in love with him.[5] Though he had been married to Elsa Lanchester since 1929, Laughton was homosexual, and had deep feelings of personal inadequacy, which Brecht was able both to salve and to exploit. The actor had left England at the outbreak of war and, feeling guilty about this, haunted émigré circles in Hollywood. The two men met at the house of the Viertels, who entertained lavishly, and through them Brecht met Stravinsky, Chaplin, and John Houseman and many Hollywood actors.

Brecht had seen Laughton in *The Private Life of Henry VIII* (1933) and *Rembrandt* (1936), while Laughton, himself a frustrated writer, soon realized that Brecht had more understanding of acting technique than any other writer he had met. Still virtually unknown after nearly two years in America, Brecht had perhaps found a man who could help to bring him the fame he deserved. Laughton was fundamentally more serious than most film actors; there was even a streak of didacticism in him. When Brecht, who delighted in questions that were straightforward, basic and challenging, asked him why he acted, the answer was: 'Because people don't know what they're like and I think I can show them.'[6] This was almost identical with Brecht's boyhood boast to Ernestine Müller in 1917.

Immediately seeing Laughton as a possible Schweyk, Brecht gave him the revised translation, which he read overnight. He responded enthusiastically, and on 17 April read two acts of it to Brecht, Eisler and Hans Winge, an Austrian journalist who was working in a factory. 'We laughed uproariously, he understood *all* the jokes.' Laughton enjoyed reading aloud, and at the Brechts' house he read to them from *Measure for Measure*; at his own house from *The Tempest*. 'In front of a superb grandfather clock in the Bavarian baroque style, he squats on a white sofa, with legs crossed, so that only his Buddha-like stomach is visible, and reads the play out of a small book, in part like a scholar, in part like an actor. . . . He reads Caliban with compassion.' Later he read three acts of *King Lear*; he would spend up to a fortnight preparing himself for these readings.[7]

Brecht was working on *Der kaukasische Kreidekreis* and, for two weeks, had been wrestling unsuccessfully with the characterization of Azdak – a ribald combination of Baal and Schweyk elevated to the role of judge, so that once again, as in *Ausnahme und Regel*, *Rundköpfe* and *Furcht und Elend*, and as in his schoolboy parable on the Balkan War, Brecht would have a yardstick for measuring corrupt justice:

Azdak had to have the self-seeking, amoral, parasitical features of the lowest, most degenerate of judges. But I still needed an elementary cause of a social kind. I found it in his disappointment that, with the overthrow of the old masters, what ensued was not a new era but an era of new masters. So he goes on enforcing bourgeois law, only dilapidated, sabotaged, adapted to serve the unqualified self-interest of the judicature.[8]

As in Klabund's play, the judge is corrupt; as in Brecht's 'Der Augsburger Kreidekreis', justice is done by taking the child away from the mother who is unworthy of it.

He completed the play on 5 June and sent Luise Rainer a copy, but he was worried about Grusche. 'She should be artless, look like Brueghel's Dulle Griet, a beast of burden. She should be stubborn instead of rebellious, placid instead of good, dogged instead of incorruptible, etc., etc.' He spent three weeks on adjusting the characterization, making it more compatible with the reproductions of Dulle Griet that he glued to the title pages of the first copies, but Luise Rainer did not look like Dulle Griet. And having provided a backer, she was not likely to be pleased with a script in which her character disappeared from the action half way through the play, to reappear only in the closing scene. If she and Brecht had not quarrelled already, they would have quarrelled when she read it. He badly wanted a Broadway production, but he would not have written such a good play if his main object had been to produce a vehicle for Luise Rainer. 'I don't mind if she turns the play down,' he told Berlau,⁹ who was now pregnant, and in fact the play was oriented more to her than to the beautiful film star. There was no question of Berlau's playing the part, but he wanted to encourage her – as he had once wanted to encourage Marianne Zoff – to go ahead with the pregnancy. A message could be bottled in a play: maternity must be presented favourably. As with the instruction for resistance workers in *Simone Machard*, or the pacifist message in *Mutter Courage* to the population of Europe, success in communicating possibly mattered less to Brecht than the sense of doing as much as could be done. He also solicited detailed advice from Berlau; one question was whether another scene was needed to show how much the mother loved the child.

But if Berlau was influencing the play, so was Brueghel. The scene of the peasant wedding – a bed in a small space with neighbours crowding around the repulsive monk – is intensely theatrical but refreshingly remote from theatrical cliché. In *Kreidekreis*, as in *Puntila*, Brecht showed that he had learnt how ugly elements could be built into a beautiful stage picture. As Brecht describes it, *Dulle Griet* portrays 'the Fury defending her pathetic household goods with the sword. The world at the end of its tether.' *Kreidekreis* shows a world at the end of its tether, and the characteristics of the Fury are divided between Grusche and the governor's wife, while Brecht was, in effect, writing a new kind of folk play, 'naïve but not primitive, poetic but not romantic, close to reality but not topically political'. He may have believed he was writing for Broadway, but in Scandinavia he had habituated himself to writing for the future, and this play was as unlikely to reach Broadway as *The King's Bread* had been to please the Hollywood moguls. He was writing for a theatre that did not yet exist.

Responding as he did to the story of the chalk circle, he could draw more deeply on his resources than in any play since *Mutter Courage*, and this material had greater potential for epic treatment because it was not conducive to naturalistic writing; balladry could run through every artery in the organism. Villainous rulers, cruel soldiers, greedy peasants, a cowardly police officer, an opportunistic monk, a shrewish sister-in-law can be introduced like figures from a ballad, touched into three-dimensionality, while large hunks of human experience are absorbed as the narrative alternates between stylized action and poetic narration. The dramatic texture is extraordinarily rich, partly because the story-telling is so vigorous, partly because the language is so muscular.

The play reprises many themes Brecht had handled earlier. In *Trommeln in der Nacht* a soldier returned to find sordid obstacles in the way of reunion with his girl. In *Mutter Courage* characters had abruptly to change their image and their lifestyle as war gave way to peace, though none did this so comically as the ostensibly dying man in *Kreidekreis*, whose illness had been a stratagem to evade enlistment. Grusche's attempt to simulate the voice and the manners of a well-born lady is a reversal of the scene in *Puntila* where Eva tries to prove her downward social mobility; the final scene in *Dreigroschenoper* is echoed by the sequence in which Azdak is liberated after being dragged screaming to the gallows; the insistence that laws should be re-examined 'to see whether they are still valid' recalls the boy's attitude to customs in *Der Neinsager*; Azdak's line 'It would be easier for a judge's robe and hat to pass sentence than for a man without all that' makes the same point as the scene in *Galileo* showing how Cardinal Barberini's opinions change with his costume. And Brecht had often argued that a war is never lost by a prince or a profiteer: it is always the people who lose. But few of these points had previously been made with so much comic exuberance and robust optimism.

Whereas Shakespeare's rosiest comedies are set at an unspecified time in Illyria or the Forest of Arden, Brecht's is set (in the first version) on Sunday 7 June 1934 in a Caucasian village. In New York Brecht had spent time with the writer O. M. Graf, who in 1934 had visited the Caucasus with Tretiakov, but it may be more to the point that Stalin was Georgian and born with the name Djugashvili. In Brecht's play the tyrannous governor is Georgi Abashvili. But if this is a hostile reference to Stalin, it is balanced by an equally cryptic but much friendlier reference in a song Grusche sings. In Boris Souvarine's book *Staline, aperçu historique du bolshévisme* (Paris, 1935), which Brecht had been reading, the first chapter was titled 'Sosso', a Georgian diminutive of Joseph. Sosso was Stalin's nickname during boyhood and while working illegally for the party in Georgia. Grusche's song is about four generals who march to Iran and find different excuses for failing to attack the enemy. Then Sosso Robakidse marches to Iran, and, thanks to the soldiers' love for him, the enemy is defeated. 'Sosso Robakidse is our man.' When Hans Viertel recognized the allusion to Stalin, Brecht's only answer was: 'It's staying in.'[10] Five years in the States had made him less anti-Stalinist than during the show trials. When Brecht told Sidney Hook, apropos

Stalin's victims, 'The more innocent they are, the more they deserve to die', the joke touched the nerve of the same ambivalence that became visible in his dealings with Hanns Eisler's sister, Ruth Fischer, who had been secretary of the German Communist Party until Stalin had excommunicated her in 1926. When she showed Aufricht an article she had written under the title 'Bert Brecht, the Minstrel of the GPU', he was nervous that its publication might lead to Brecht's deportation, and he arranged for them to meet at the flat of Ruth Berlau, who fed them with scrambled eggs. The conversation took a nasty turn when Ruth Fischer said: 'Brecht, with your schoolboy political intelligence, you got interested in the Party when Stalin had already turned it upside down.' Instead of shouting at her, Brecht tried to be conciliatory, addressing her as 'comrade', but he failed to dissuade her from publishing the article. After it had appeared in the April 1944 issue of *Politics*, he more than once said: 'The swine must be shot. Ideological arguments between comrades can't be exposed to the police.'[11]

The Utopian prologue to *Kreidekreis* is as unrealistic as *Twelfth Night*. Delegates from two Kolkhoz villages, including a tractor driver and an agronomist, amiably debate whether a valley should be given to the goat-herding Kolkhoz or the fruit-growing Kolkhoz, and despite their legal claim to it, the goatherds give it away willingly. The difference between the prologue and the rest of the play is that in the Grusche and Azdak scenes the style, ostensibly dictated by the ballad-singer's narration, is suitable to fairy-tale material and fantasy. In the prologue the surface is realistic.

Of Brecht's previous plays, the closest to *Kreidekreis* is *Puntila*, which is also like a fairy story for adults. Both are rich in open-air scenes and natural images, while Azdak, like Matti, is a Schweykian character who briskly embroiders semi-relevant anecdotes into his racy dialogue. Both plays are balladesque, but the ballad element in *Kreidekreis* is stronger, and there is nothing in *Puntila* to compare with the sequence in which the narrator sings in verse the thoughts that Grusche cannot express in words, or with the ballad in which her role is sung by several musicians.

Though the Grusche episodes and the Azdak episodes are, effectively, plays-within-a-play, neither is comparable to Shakespearian plays-within-a-play because, in Brecht's case, the framework fades out of focus. But when the soldiers make the Fat Prince's nephew audition for the job of judge, the play-acting makes the audience glad to enter the game, especially when Azdak imitates the telegraphic style of the Grand

Duke. The nephew is not a formidable or convincing opponent – like the governor's wife, he is only a caricature – but he is solid enough to serve as a foil to Azdak.

Like *Der gute Mensch*, *Kreidekreis* was written slowly, over a period of nine to ten weeks. Before finishing it, Brecht made three attempts to secure Christopher Isherwood as translator, once visiting him in the Vedanta Centre, where he was living, once working through an intermediary. Resisting the pressure, Isherwood offered Brecht one or two hundred dollars if he needed money for a production. 'A lot because he has nothing, I know.' Brecht's next step was to have Ruth Berlau approach Auden about adapting the play for the American stage. But there was no prospect of a production. When Hans Winge outlined the idea to Mordecai Gorelik and George Auerbach, an American film producer, they criticized the construction. 'Where's the conflict, tension, flesh and blood, etc., etc.?' As they got into the car, they told Winge that Brecht would never be successful. He couldn't make an audience feel anything or even identify with his characters. 'And he makes a theory out of it. He's crazy and he's getting worse.'[12]

Brecht was not entirely immune to the hostile consensus of opinion, which made it harder to believe in the usefulness of his work. During his first eight years of exile he had produced six of his best plays; during his six years in America he would produce only one of his best plays – *Der kaukasische Kreidekreis* – together with another updating of the St Joan story, an updating of *Schweyk* and a rewrite of Webster's *The Duchess of Malfi*.

The Brechts were seeing a good deal of Oskar Homolka and his wife Florence; it was Homolka Brecht had in mind for Azdak. In May he started working with Homolka and Hans Viertel on a 'model translation' of the scene in which the soldiers maltreat Azdak. On 6 June, while he was playing chess with Homolka, Eisler telephoned with news of the Allied landings in Normandy. The cancerous red in the map of Europe on the wall behind Brecht's typewriter table no longer had to be extended. 'This army is breaking up like tinder. The generals are deserting.'[13]

Now that Germany's defeat was in prospect, Brecht could start planning where to live when the war ended. Rumours had been circulating that certain German refugees had been listed for 'custodial detention' after the war, and Brecht, who must have known that the FBI had a file on him – friends had been interviewed by agents – was saying that to escape from the US he would obtain a Czech passport through Bohus Benes, the Czech consul in San Francisco. Together with Hanns Eisler, Brecht approached Benes in June. FBI reports on him had been classified under 'alien control', but from 1944 he was regarded as a problem of 'internal security'.[14]

Behind Laughton's home on the Pacific coast, high above the ocean, was a magnificent garden with pre-Columbian statuary in it, a superb lawn, eucalyptus trees, oak trees and fuchsia bushes. But a subterranean stream had undermined the garden, and when one of its corners caved in, several Hollywood newspapers reported the incident. On 28 August, after telephoning to ask whether he could visit the Brechts, Laughton arrived, holding a coat over his head to hide his face. He was sorry to bring his troubles to people who had not had a proper home for ten years, he said, but what was happening to the garden symbolized what was happening to his career. He had been attacked as a ham, and had, out of anxiety, rejected several film offers. ' "It's only the beginning," he says. "It will get worse.... Quite honestly I don't want to see anyone now. I'm so ashamed." '[15] To cheer him up, Brecht showed him an unfinished poem about the garden.

The Brechts had been encouraging him to make recordings from the Bible, and he read them the story of David and Jonathan. 'He'd also brought a few volumes of Shakespeare with him, and read (or played) Osric from *Hamlet*, Jacques from *As You Like It* and the "clown bringing a basket" from the fifth act of *Antony and Cleopatra* – roles that should, in his opinion, be played as homosexual.'[16] It was a few days after this that Brecht showed him *Galileo*.

With Ruth Berlau in about the seventh month of her pregnancy, Brecht was himself in a highly emotional state. The diary entries are terse and cryptic: 'Remarkable how grief and anxiety make the shoulders droop forwards.' Since Brecht was not going to New York, Peter Lorre paid Berlau's air fare to Los Angeles and gave her the key to his Hollywood villa. The birth of the baby was to be kept secret from Weigel, and when Berlau was taken into the Cedars of Lebanon Hospital in Los Angeles for the removal of a tumour, the doctor was not told that Brecht was the father, though he was a frequent visitor to the hospital. The operation led to the premature birth of a boy, who was to be named Michael after the child in *Kreidekreis*, but he lived only for a few days. A note to Berlau which later found its way into Brecht's FBI file read: 'Love, I'm so glad you're fighting so courageously. Don't think I don't want to see you when you're ill. You're beautiful then, too. I'm coming tomorrow before noon.' But mostly he stuck to his working routine: 'Plan for day: get up at 7. Newspaper, radio. Make coffee in the small copper pot. Morning work. Light lunch at 12. Rest with detective novel. Afternoon work or pay visits. Supper 7 o'clock. Afterwards visitors. At night half a page of Shakespeare or Waley's collection of Chinese poems. Radio. Detective novel.'[17]

Charles Laughton's stomach, which had been described in Brecht's diary as 'Buddha-like', was soon to have a whole poem devoted to it. Other men carry their stomachs around like plunder to be hidden from those in pursuit of it,

> But the great Laughton recited his like a poem
> For his edification, detrimental to no one.
> Here it was: not unexpected, but not ordinary
> And built from foods, selected
> At leisure, as a pastime.

The admiration was genuine. Brecht had celebrated Galileo as a man whose thinking proceeded out of sensuality, but while he was capable of eating a box of chocolates in one evening, and while the number of cooks among his characters evidences an interest in food, generally, as Joseph Losey put it, 'he ate very little, drank very little and fornicated a great deal'. Without having any regrets about drinking so little or fornicating so much, he did crave for a bigger appetite. 'It struck me as naturally advantageous if people could eat a lot and with relish. . . . When I had what I'd wanted, I felt full so soon, that a plate of food soon began to give me discomfort. I couldn't finish it. My stomach was too small.'[18] So he was jealous of Laughton for scoring so often at the dinner-table.

Laughton could not read German, and the first English translation of *Galileo* Brecht showed him had been done, he said, by 'a secretary'. Laughton then commissioned two young MGM writers, Brainerd Duffield and Emerson Crocker, to produce a new translation. It may, as James K. Lyon suggests, have been chiefly to ensure Laughton's commitment to the play that Brecht proposed they should collaborate on revising and rewriting it for the American stage. Normally the only changes an actor can make to a text are by cutting, but, according to Brecht, Laughton 'showed that he had a wide range of opinions – all pressing for dissemination – about how people *really* behave when they're living together. . . . And he was so eager to show things as they really are that, in spite of his indifference to all political matters – or rather his timidity in them – he demanded or proposed changes in many passages, to sharpen them.'[19]

By 10 December they were collaborating systematically. They usually worked in Laughton's house, 'because the dictionaries of synonyms were too big to carry around. He consulted these volumes with inexhaustible patience, besides fishing out the most assorted literature to study various forms of behaviour or speech – Aesop, the Bible, Molière, Shakespeare.' Their conversation had to be in English, which Brecht found exhausting, but, like Laughton, he enjoyed exploring a passage's theatrical meaning by acting it. Brecht would perform it in German or bad English; Laughton would then 'play it back in correct English, trying any number of different ways until I could say "That's it" '.[20] This empirical method obviated the need for discussion and psychological analysis. As each crumb of text was tasted and tested, the problems of transition from point to point began to change. Laughton had a bad reputation in the film studios for building up his parts: directors diplomatically discouraged or rationed him. Now, for the first time, he had a playwright to encourage him and collaborate. In about 1942 Brecht had told Oskar Homolka that the part had been written for him;[21] now, like a tailor, he was altering it to fit Laughton.

Usually they worked during the mornings in the small library. 'But often L. would come out to meet me in the garden, running barefoot over the damp grass in shirt and trousers, and pointed out changes in the flowerbeds, for the garden preoccupied him constantly.' At libraries and museums Laughton ordered books and photocopies for background information and material to use on the set – Leonardo's technical drawings for instance – and they did careful research on costumes, studying Brueghel's paintings for information about class distinctions in dress. Determined to have fun during the preparatory work, Laughton said: 'Before you can entertain other people, you must entertain yourself' – a remark which might equally well have come from Brecht, who would later call the incubation of the production 'a piece of fun that lasts for two years'.[22]

In November 1941, after buying a little Chinese god of happiness in Los Angeles' Chinatown, Brecht had thought of writing a play, *Die Reisen des Glücksgotts* (*The God of Happiness's Travels*). After provoking excesses, the god of those who wish to be happy has to hide from the police, but when he is arrested and condemned to death, the executioners cannot harm him. In 1943 the idea came to serve as the basis for an opera, to be written with Paul Dessau. Brecht began on the libretto in January 1945, but never completed it, perhaps because it was carrying him closer than any play since *Baal* to the epicentre of his preoccupations. Baal was superhuman in his lust for life but not immortal, whereas the god can enjoy the poisons that the executioners give him. He can dance on the scaffold, and when his head is cut off, it grows like a plant, but immediately.[23] By translating the singular into the plural, Brecht could make this mean that: 'You can never quite kill humanity's appetite for happiness', but his own unquenchable appetite for happiness, which had made him identify with Baal, had subsequently made him identify with the people, project his own libido into the plural.

In February 1945 the work on *Galileo* had to stop for eight weeks while Laughton made the pirate film *Captain Kidd*. To occupy himself, Brecht decided to versify the Communist Manifesto. He had not forgotten the project he had abandoned in 1939 of writing a long didactic poem to refute the Lucretian assumption that the social order paralleled the natural order. Using dactylic hexameters, he wanted to make the Marx-Engels text appeal to a wider public. 'The manifesto is a work of art even as a pamphlet; but it seems to me possible to renew its propagandistic effect today, a hundred years later, and to endow it with reinforced authority by removing the pamphleteering quality.'[24]

Usually his verse made considerable impact when he recited it, but his friends' response to his hexameters was discouraging. His son, Stefan, was critical; Egon Breiner told him: 'You can't improve on Marx'; and Feuchtwanger 'told me the hexameters are bad. That means a lot of revision. Really I know too little about it.'[25] He was certainly the greatest twentieth-century German poet, but, unlike his predecessors and unlike Gottfried Benn, he had achieved his mastery over the language by resisting disciplines, including those of scholarship. This was for once proving disadvantageous.

In Hollywood he often met Chaplin – at Eisler's house, at the Viertels' and at parties. But the influence Chaplin had exerted on his formative years did not lead to any mutual understanding. At a party in March 1945 Chaplin imitated business with a handkerchief that Paul Muni performed as Chopin's teacher in the new Cornel Wilde film *A Song to Remember*. Chaplin claimed that he had already had that trick in his repertoire as an 8-year-old. Fritz Kortner said the imitation was typical of a character actor who was becoming senile, but to Brecht it meant that the character actor had survived in a form that was out of date.[26]

In the middle of February 1945 British troops reached the Rhine, and on 7 March Cologne was captured. Versifying the Manifesto, Brecht was distracted by 'the terrible newspaper reports from Germany. Ruins and no signs of life from the workers.' With the Nazis so close to surrender, there was little point in drumming up anti-Nazi sentiment, but he had to decide whether he wanted *The Private Life of the Master Race* to be seen in New York. A young producer, Ernest Roberts, wanted to present Eric Bentley's translation off-Broadway, directed by Piscator, with actors from his Dramatic Workshop; and when Brecht persisted in ignoring his letters, Bentley authorized the production himself. Discovering, through Ruth Berlau, what had happened, Brecht was nervous of getting second-rate actors in a second-rate production, and apprehensive about the political consequence. 'We must do nothing that might prevent the total overthrow of the whole German bourgeoisie (including the physicists, teachers, judges of *Furcht und Elend*). The workers *must* support each other.'[27] Emigré organizations such as the Council for a Democratic Germany wanted to prove that there was a core of goodness in the German people; Brecht wanted to prove that Nazism was only a facet of German imperialism, which was evil. But instead of vetoing the production, he countered Bentley's initiative by telegraphing an option on performance rights to Wolfgang Roth, the scene designer. 'Our friend Brecht has created a god-awful mess . . .', complained Bentley. 'I am now hectically trying to straighten things out.' And in another letter, 'He has neither good manners nor elementary decency. He lives out of his own theory that it is impossible to behave well in this society.'[28]

With his partner, Robert Reud, Leventhal had arranged for *Kreidekreis* to be translated by James and Tania Stern, and adapted by W. H. Auden, who contracted to deliver the adaptation by 1 February 1945. Brecht wrote to say how pleased he was, enclosing changes he had already made to the translation by the Sterns. They were working with Auden in a house on Fire Island. Brecht was sufficiently dazzled by Auden's name to depart from his usual policy of careful scrutiny and persistent procrastination over contracts: he empowered Samuel French and Company to negotiate a contract, which he and Auden signed on 12 March 1945. When he eventually read the English version, Brecht could find no Auden in anything but the lyrics, which he liked, and he listed changes he wanted in the prose dialogue. Auden was leaving for England at about the end of April, and Brecht would have liked him to rework the whole text before going, but he left the Sterns to make revisions.[29]

Before leaving Santa Monica in March 1945, Ruth Berlau succeeded in extracting a promise that may have been unprecedented – Brecht covenanted to be faithful. He would reassure her with the code phrase: 'Everything is all right.' The phrase is recurrent in his letters, but before the end of the year she had an affair with a Dane. Brecht wrote:

> What the child feels when the mother goes away with a strange man,
> What the carpenter feels when overcome by giddiness, the symptoms of age.
> What the painter feels when the model no longer arrives and the picture is unfinished.
> What the physicist feels when he discovers a mistake made early on in the series of experiments.
> What the flier feels when the oil pressure drops over the mountains.
> What the plane would feel, if it could feel, when the pilot got drunk.[30]

When Charles Laughton completed his filming, he was in no mood to resume the collaborative work on *Galileo*, but Brecht helped him to prepare for a gramophone recording of readings from Genesis. To develop his vocal flexibility, Brecht devised exercises. In a Cockney accent Laughton had to recite: 'At the beginning Mr Smith created the heaven and the earth', and, with the voice of a butler, 'In the beginning his lordship created ...'[31]

On 8 May Brecht was listening to the radio at six in the morning when Harry Truman, who had been President for less than a month, following Roosevelt's death, announced the unconditional surrender of Nazi Germany. 'Listening I look at the blossoming Californian gardens.' Roosevelt's death made Churchill the undisputed leader of the Western democracies, and without socialism, Brecht believed, it would be impossible to rebuild a democratic Europe; people would assume that the well-being of the workers depended on the prosperity of the entrepreneurs.[32] As a member of the Council for a Democratic Germany, he expressed his opinions in letters to the Protestant theologian Paul Tillich, who had accepted the presidency of the Council, which Thomas Mann had rejected. But now that Brecht seemed to be within reach of the large-scale theatrical success that had eluded him ever since he had sabotaged *Happy End*, he was anxious not to repeat what he had done then, sacrificing fame and money on the altar of political conviction.

Instead of planning his return to Europe, he resumed work on *Galileo* with Laughton, adding an argument with Ludovico, Virginia's rich suitor, in the scene about spots on the sun. But Brecht had to leave for New York, where *The Private Life of the Master Race* was due to open on 12 June.

When Brecht learned that Ernest Roberts's group was called 'The Theatre of All Nations', his response was: 'It's too many.' Nearly half the twenty-four actors were German or Austrian, with imperfect English; the Americans were mostly from Piscator's Dramatic Workshop, and several of them were inexperienced. 'Schoolchildren', Brecht called them.

For six days rehearsals were continuously interrupted by arguments between Piscator and Brecht. In an April letter to Berlau, Brecht had promised, ambiguously, not to 'take a position'; but the actors watched in embarrassment while author and director argued, and then on 29 May Piscator wrote a letter which started: 'Dear Mr Brecht', and continued in English. 'When I direct, I need the time for myself without your co-directing – and when you direct you need the time without me.... I suggest that you take over the directing, and I withdraw.'[33]

Brecht's first inclination was to cancel the production. His second, on discovering he was contractually committed, was to exclude the press. This, too, was impossible. In the next eighteen days he seems to have done his best to sabotage his own chances of success. He engaged Berthold Viertel as director, but told him what to do. Time was wasted on long theoretical discussions between Viertel and Brecht; confused, insulted, enervated, the actors had their confidence and their goodwill sapped. At the age of seventy-eight the great German actor Albert Bassermann had been cast as the father with his wife as the mother in the scene about the parents' fear that their son is spying on them; but when Brecht heard Bassermann speak English, he laughed. Full of contempt for the Austrian actress Vilma Kurer, who was playing the Jewish wife, Brecht cut her scene ruthlessly, and after the first night it was scrapped.[34] Except for Basserman, who was given private rehearsals, most of the actors were under-rehearsed, while Bassermann was given a wig that kept slipping.

When the play opened on 12 June the critics were almost unanimously antagonized by the difficulty of understanding the actors, by the slow pace and the lack of tension, by the unfamiliarity of Brecht's dramatic idiom. The *New York Times* suggested that some of the sequences 'would be more pointed if cut in half', while one reviewer forecast a brighter future for Brecht as a television writer than as a playwright. After forcing himself to sit through the production, Piscator wrote a long letter accusing Brecht of directing 'like every amateur. At different moments the other evening I wanted to jump over the footlights, come backstage and beat you. Not because I personally felt insulted when I saw the result of this work, but at the more objective harm you have done to yourself.'[35]

Brecht left New York in the middle of July 1945, having read only part of Piscator's letter.[1] On the way back to Santa Monica he stopped at Chicago to visit Stefan, who was in hospital because of persistent headaches. He was expecting to be discharged from national service.

The discomforts of the endless tug-of-war between artistic and political motivations are evident in a conversation Brecht had with Hans Winge. After reading the *Duchess of Malfi* adaptation, Winge quarrelled with Brecht's stress on the incest motive. Why not let feudal lust for landed property lead to the catastrophe? Brecht 'defended the poetic idea', and, arguing about *Galileo*, admitted both to having written it 'with no intention of proving anything', and to collaborating on it with a 'politically uninformed actor', but he defended the play as showing, at least, 'how the ruling class is aware about the totality of its ideology: it knows that the chain which holds down the oppressed is no stronger than its weakest link'.[2]

On 6 August the first atomic bomb was dropped on Hiroshima; three days later the second fell on Nagasaki. It seemed to Brecht that 'ordinary people' felt the bombs to be 'simply frightful. Though they are waiting impatiently for their husbands and sons to come home, the victory in Japan has turned sour.'[3]

Laughton was worried that science might now 'be so discredited that its birth – in Galileo – forfeited all sympathy. "The wrong kind of publicity, old man." ' But they were pleased when Churchill was defeated in the British elections. Laughton's immediate reaction was: 'Now I can play Galileo in London'.[4] Late in August he started on the film *Because of Him*, but continued his sessions with Brecht until the evening before shooting and fitted some in between bouts of filming. Refusing to feel that there was nothing he could do about the atom bomb, Brecht was intent on altering the balance of the play to condemn Galileo as a traitor. 'The atomic bomb has really made the relationship between society and science into a matter of life and death.'[5]

Blaming Galileo for Hiroshima was a naïve mistake which Marx would never have made, believing as he did, with Hegel, that individual virtues and vices never determine the course of history. Brecht's main revision to his play came in the penultimate scene. Originally he had wanted us to agree that Galileo did well to survive and write the *Discorsi*. In the new version he is given a long tirade of self-condemnation, and we are now meant to feel Andrea is wrong to argue that 'Science recognizes only one command: contribute to Science.' Galileo's retort is: 'Welcome to the gutter, brother in science and cousin in betrayal! You eat fish? I have fish. The smell isn't coming from the fish but from me.' He has failed to fulfil his duty to the ordinary people.

If scientists, intimidated by self-seeking rulers, are content to pile up knowledge for knowledge's sake, science can be crippled and all your new gadgets mean nothing but new hardships.... As a scientist I had a unique opportunity. In my lifetime astronomy reached the market-place. In this extraordinary situation the steadfastness of one man could have been like an earthquake. If I had held out, natural scientists could have evolved something like the Hippocratic oath of the doctors, a covenant to devote their knowledge exclusively to the good of mankind. As it is, the best we can hope for is a race of resourceful dwarfs who can be hired for anything.

This is an interesting piece of bad writing, not just because it becomes embarrassingly obvious that the dummy is voicing the ventriloquist's opinions, but because – atom bomb or no atom bomb – Brecht is repeating what he had done before with nearly all his best characters from Baal and Kragler to Mäckie Messer and Mutter Courage. Considerable sympathy is invested in a man or woman with a strong lust for living and then, after completing the play, Brecht turns against his character and produces a new version to make the audience sympathize less. It would be simplistic to suggest that Brecht is turning against himself, but an austere denial of the pleasure principle is clearly at work, and it complicated the final phase of Brecht's collaboration with Laughton. Expecting the actor's self-hatred to filter into the character's, Brecht was undismayed when Laughton, nervous of appearing propagandistic, seemed to be 'working relentlessly to eliminate the political elements'. Even Galileo's line 'Be careful when you go through Germany if you're smuggling the truth under your cloak' was reduced to 'Take care of yourself'. Laughton was also nervous of making the play look anti-Catholic. 'L's fear of offending the public (mostly on religious areas) often conflicted with his desire to correct the audience's fallacious ideas – usually the latter desire was victorious.' Having been despotic and unyielding with the vulnerable actors in *The Private Life of the Master Race*, Brecht was uncharacteristically tractable. Although his standpoint was closer to Winge's than to the film star's, he did not insist on sharpening the play's political points.[6]

The incongruity between the two collaborators may have accidentally added to the subtlety of the characterization. Eager to denigrate Galileo, Brecht was liable to eliminate ironies and ambiguities that had been present in the 1938 version; Laughton's inclination to be less censorious towards Galileo would be counterweighted by his censoriousness towards the self he projected into the character. He was depressed both about his career and about his personal cowardice. But he compensated with a perverse panache. 'Laughton is quite ready to throw his character to the wolves. He has a kind of Lucifer in his head, transforming self-contempt into empty pride – pride in the greatness of his crime etc. He insists on the full revelation of the degeneracy resulting from the crime which brought G's negative characteristics to fruition. Only the excellent brain remains intact, functioning in the void.'[7] The crack in Laughton's self-image came clearly into focus one October evening when, still filming in *Because of Him*, he walked past a picket-line during a ten-day strike at the studios. He was too insecure to jeopardize his work on the film, but when the picketers called him 'Scab'[8] he felt confirmed not only in his view of himself as a coward but also in the need to find strength in his weakness – and in Galileo's.

Like Brecht, Laughton enjoyed reading aloud to small circles of friends, and he even found opportunities of reading the translation to circles of strangers – in military hospitals for instance. Reactions were encouraging, and in December he read it to Orson Welles, who offered to direct the production. 'His attitude is agreeable,' wrote Brecht, 'his comments are intelligent. At least he won't be afraid of the audience. He understands when I tell him that what "can't be done in New York" mostly "can't be done" in Berlin either.' Brecht wanted the play to go on in the spring, but Welles said he could not find backing so quickly. Czinner, who would have liked to produce, had the money and had a theatre available, but Laughton 'hated the sight of that man'.[9]

When Laughton had a contract drawn up giving two thirds of the royalties to himself and a third to Brecht, Brecht reversed the proportioning, but agreed that the play should be billed as '*Galileo* by Bertolt Brecht. English version by Charles Laughton.' The contract was finally signed on 7 January 1946. In February Welles still wanted to direct and wanted his company, Mercury Productions, to present it. Brecht wanted Laughton as co-producer, and Welles did not object. Brecht went to Boston for the opening night of Cole Porter's *Around the World*, directed by Welles. Circus performers had been hired to train the cast and chorus; afterwards Brecht told Welles that the circus scene was 'the greatest thing I have seen in the American theatre'. Several meetings ensued, but soon Welles was complaining to Laughton: 'Brecht was very, very tiresome today until (I'm sorry to say) I was stern and a trifle shitty. Then he behaved. I hate working like that.'[10]

So far as Laughton knew, the text had been finalized, but during May Brecht was working intensively with Reyher, who, after their final working session, noted in his diary: 'Smacked the final scene into good shape and fixed ending to cut out his original bad final scene. Rewrote the big speech and others so that they say his meaning clearly for the first time. Really did a job of work on the play, and repaired it greatly.'[11]

The first letter to reach Brecht from Germany had arrived in October 1945. It was from the publisher Peter Suhrkamp, who had been one of the last people he saw before leaving Germany in 1933. Replying, he asked for news of Neher, Burri and Müllereisert. He had written a great deal, he said, which might be of interest to Suhrkamp, but none of his old work was to be published in its original form 'without my being able to state my present attitude to it. Everything needs to be changed.' But he gave Suhrkamp full power to represent him in Germany; in his second letter he offered to send food parcels and suggested that *Mutter Courage* was the play which should be performed there first. Seeing a chance to re-establish Weigel's career, he pretended that the name part had been written for her, and that 'in a few performances, given in exile, she has evolved a quite distinctive style for it'. Before the end of the month another, more exciting, letter had been written to Brecht: appointed as dramaturg at the Deutsches Theater in East Berlin, Herbert Ihering was interested in having productions there of *Mutter Courage* and *Galileo*.[12] Brecht was in no hurry to take advantage of this opening.

Since the loss of the baby, Ruth Berlau had grown increasingly unstable. She was still living with Ida Bachmann, who knew how ill she was, while Berlau herself did not. But Fritz Sternberg was in her flat one evening when Brecht telephoned from Los Angeles, and after speaking to him, she handed the receiver to Sternberg. Was it necessary for him to come, Brecht asked. 'Absolutely,' said Sternberg. And on 27 December 1945 she attacked both Bachmann and the doctor who was called. She was taken to Bellevue Hospital and, on New Year's Eve, transferred to a mental hospital in Amityville, Long Island, where she stayed for several weeks, receiving electro-convulsive therapy. Influenza and a high temperature kept Brecht in Santa Monica during January but, after a telephone conversation with her, he wrote to Reyher: 'They must allow her to call me here when she can. That, too, would help her.'[13]

In February 1946 he travelled to New York, arriving on the 10th. Hoping to arrange for her to be discharged from the hospital, he went to Amityville with Bergner and Czinner, but Berlau was not well enough to be released. When he told her he wanted to take her home, she said he would need enough cars for the thirty-two other patients, and she had the impression that he told Bergner no one was as crazy as a crazy communist. During his first week in New York he saw Berlau only once.[14]

Auden was there, and they worked together in February and March on the *Duchess of Malfi* adaptation. 'The discussions are interesting,' Brecht reported to Bergner, 'Auden very amiable and open. Let me know if you have any objections; I'm hoping that the love tragedy, one of the most beautiful in literature, is slowly coming out.'

Brecht disliked Auden's personal sloppiness and the untidiness of his desk, while Auden thought Brecht 'a most unpleasant man', one of the few people who deserved the death sentence. 'In fact I can imagine doing it to him myself.' The two men also disagreed about the play: Auden did not want to interfere so drastically with Webster's text. Brecht's instinct was to be explicit about Ferdinand's incestuous feelings towards his sister; to reduce the importance of Bosola, who was no more than 'a librarian, a frustrated scholar', while increasing the importance of Delio, Ferdinand's friend. Auden took the Duchess's relationship with Antonio to be no more than an escapade, while Brecht pounced on their scenes together as an opportunity to display the social consciousness of men 'too small to live with greatness'. He wanted to make Antonio into 'a kind of gigolo. Silk stockings and bombast are in order. Also he can show that he is cowardly and self-seeking.'[15] In Brecht's hands both the Duchess and her brothers become more class-conscious, as when she forbids Antonio to fight back. Brecht also added a scene in which Ferdinand kills the Cardinal.

In New York Brecht had several meetings with Bergner and Czinner, and with Wolfgang Roth, who built a model for the set. Bergner's enthusiasm for Jacobean drama made her greedy for the inclusion of passages from other plays by Webster (including *The Devil's Law Case*) and by Ford. The text dated 4 April 1946 has both Brecht's and Auden's name on it, but, without Auden's knowledge, Brecht, who could never regard a text as finished, went on working at it.

In March Ruth Berlau was discharged from the hospital. Brecht looked after her in her flat on 57th Street, which effectively became his flat. A draftsman's bench served as his desk, and the phrase 'The truth is concrete' was tacked in bold letters to the wall above. His bookcase was constructed of planks held with bricks, and a single Chinese scroll was hung on the wall. Curtains and covering for the couch were made of burlap. For six months during 1946 the young director Joseph Losey lived there with them. Brecht had met Losey in 1935 when they were both in Russia, and in 1936 Brecht had seen some of Losey's productions for the Federal Theatre Project, using cinema techniques to present current issues. Since then he had been directing short films and radio dramas.

On the telephone to Weigel Brecht threatened not to come back to her unless Berlau could live with them. To have her living in the same house would have been intolerable for Weigel, but characteristically she compromised, arranging for her to be given a room in the house of a friend, Anna Hagen Harrington. Once installed in Santa Monica, Berlau behaved with her usual lack of discretion, calling herself 'Brecht's backstreet wife'.[16] It was partly because of her – her breakdown, the time he devoted to her, the anxiety she caused him – that 1946 was Brecht's least productive year in America. He spent over half of it on the East Coast.

During the summer and autumn Charles Laughton was playing a Nazi in the film *Arch of Triumph*. Laughton wanted some of his scenes rewritten, and when the producer invited him 'to suggest a writer', he proposed Brecht, who was brought in as 'script doctor'.[17] He worked on several scenes and exchanges of dialogue, but none of his lines was used.

By this time the Brechts could have no doubt that the FBI was keeping watch on them and possibly tapping their telephone. According to their friend Rhoda Riker, Weigel once went up to the car from which an agent was watching the house and invited him to come inside. She also took pleasure in reading Polish recipes over the telephone.[18]

In June 1946 Orson Welles still wanted to produce and direct *Galileo*, but Brecht was trying to sell the script to a film studio which, in buying film rights, would have provided the money for a stage production; and when the 39-year-old Mike Todd, who had just entered the film business, offered better terms than Welles, Brecht and Laughton clinched a deal with him. Brecht now wanted it to be directed by the 36-year-old Elia Kazan, who had staged Wilder's *The Skin of Our Teeth* in 1942, but he would not have been free until November.[19]

It was not only Welles who felt Brecht had betrayed him: Reyher, after collaborating on what he took to be the final revisions, found that Brecht merely used them as a launching pad for another bout of rewriting with Laughton. 'He's a great worker,' Brecht explained to Reyher, 'so he knew how to appreciate your help.' When Reyher saw the new script, his response was: 'I think you and Laughton have gone mad with overwork and the California climate.... I pass over our efforts here, because virtually nothing of them is left.... I can only say refer to the German, refer to Laughton's earlier drafts.'[20]

Reyher was also frustrated in his championship of the director Harold Clurman. Eight years older than Kazan, Clurman had staged *Waiting for Lefty*. At first Brecht seemed interested, provided that Clurman was willing 'to understand that half his activity would consist of learning, of carefully assisting at first.... Does he know that I arrange and carefully control the groupings and movements, etc?' Clurman was undeterred, and Kazan was willing to co-produce with Clurman if Clurman directed. Clurman has described how Brecht rejected their offer when they met him at the Chelsea Hotel:

'I'd rather a circus director do it,' he went on. 'You are a Stanislavsky man and cannot possibly understand how to approach my play.'
At this I roared, 'My name is Clurman!'
But he roared back, if possible even louder, 'You don't understand, no one understands, even Piscator doesn't understand.... You will try to get "atmosphere"; I don't want atmosphere. You will establish a "mood"; I don't want a mood.'
I began to scream at the top of my voice ... 'Tell me what you're after, and I will follow your instructions.' ... Kazan never uttered a word.[21]

On the last day of March 1946 Herbert Ihering wrote a second letter from the Deutsches Theater, inviting Brecht to stage *Mutter Courage* there with Weigel, and holding out the prospect of a *Galileo* production with Walter Richter.[22] But Brecht went on procrastinating.

Another director who was considered – briefly, at least – for the Laughton *Galileo* was Alfred Lunt. Laughton sent him a script, and Brecht consulted Reyher about him. Finally Brecht settled on Joseph Losey, who was likely to be fairly submissive, but it soon became apparent that Mike Todd was not the right producer. At a meeting in his executive suite at Universal Pictures, Todd announced to Brecht,

Losey and the prospective designer, Howard Bray, that he was going to 'dress' the set with 'Renaissance furniture' from the Hollywood ware-houses. Brecht only giggled nervously, but from then on he was looking for another producer.[23]

It was easy to placate Reyher: he was persuaded into doing more work on the script in collaboration with Brecht, Laughton and Losey, who were simultaneously collecting visual material. Brecht was impatient to start working with Neher again. Neher had stayed in Germany through the war, designing in theatre and opera. He was now living with his wife in Zürich. Having discovered his address, Brecht had written to him in April. Meanwhile he went on using the methods they had evolved together. During the autumn of 1946 he and Laughton worked in the New York Public Library, looking through books on costume and on the art of the period. When Brecht and Laughton wanted Brainerd Duffield to play Lodovico they gave him a reproduction of Bronzino's *Portrait of a Young Man*, a picture of an arrogant courtier. Many of the costume ideas derived from Brueghel pictures, particularly in the Carnival scene, while the Prince would be dressed in a costume copied from a Renaissance portrait of a tailor.[24]

On 19 September, when Auden and Brecht signed the Dramatists Guild contract, *The Duchess of Malfi* had already had three weeks of rehearsal under the direction of a Cambridge don, George Rylands, and it was about to open on Rhode Island for the first of its four pre-Broadway try-out weeks. An old Etonian and a Fellow of King's College, Rylands had lectured on English Literature and directed a number of undergrad-uate productions before John Gielgud had enlisted him to direct *Hamlet* and *The Duchess of Malfi* for his Haymarket Theatre season of 1944-5. The production was such a success that, urged on by friends and backers, Czinner invited Rylands to direct the play in New York, without explain-ing that Webster's text had been subjected to radical surgery. When Bergner told him, the lecturer threatened to catch the next plane back to London Airport.[25] Rather than alienate both him and her husband's backers, she agreed to jettison the adaptation, while Rylands, in order not to appear unconciliatory, retained a few of the smaller changes Brecht and Auden had introduced. In Rhode Island, in Boston, the second stop on the tour, and in Hartford, Connecticut, the third, the play was billed as 'an adaptation by W. H. Auden and Bertold [*sic*] Brecht'.

After driving with Ruth Berlau in Charles Laughton's car from Santa

Monica to New York, Brecht went on to Boston, arriving in time to see the performance on 25 September. The letter he wrote may be phrased more politely than his verbal protest was, but the gist of his demands was no doubt the same. A new director should be engaged: Rylands seemed 'quite incapable of directing in such a way as to allow the audience to follow the plot'. The Brecht-Auden adaptation should be used, and no cuts made without their permission. Audibility should be improved by altering the blocking so that actors did not speak with their backs to the audience. And Ferdinand should be recast.[26]

Back in New York, Brecht asked Brainerd Duffield to take over as Ferdinand and started to rehearse him in Berlau's flat. But Czinner had no intention of meeting Brecht's demands, so he asked for his name to be withdrawn.[27] The odds against the production's success lengthened when McKay Morris, who was to have played Bosola, walked out. He was re-placed by a black actor, Canada Lee, who played the part in whiteface.

When the play opened on 15 October in New York at the Ethel Barrymore Theatre, Auden's name was on the programme as adapter, but not Brecht's. The reviews emphasized the length of the play and the dullness of the production. As soon as Rylands left New York, after a week of performances, Brecht accepted Bergner's invitation to rehearse the actors and rearrange parts of the play. He may have reinstated some of his own text. But the production survived only until 16 November.

By then his career on Broadway had received yet another setback: the opening of *Galileo* would have to be delayed considerably because Laughton, upset that it had been delayed so long already, had accepted a part in an Alfred Hitchcock film, *The Paradine Case*. Through his agent Laughton offered Brecht $5,000 'to defray part of the cost to you which the possible delay may occasion'. Interested in Azdak as a role that would show him off splendidly, Laughton had started on an English translation of *Kreidekreis*.[28]

But the delay encouraged Brecht to do what he would soon have to do anyway: set his sights on Europe. With his designs on the German-speaking stage, he needed to base himself in or near Germany. At the end of January 1946 Weigel had told Hella Wuolijoki they were 'waiting for the opportunity to return to Europe'. Without his permission, *Drei-groschenoper* had run for over a year in Moscow and had started a successful run at the Hebbel-Theater, Berlin, in July 1945. He was not intending to reject the opportunity of having *Galileo* produced at the Deutsches Theater, but he wanted to direct it, and he had no wish to settle in Berlin. He thought of living in Denmark, where some money had accumulated from pre-war royalties;[29] but in a letter to Neher, written at the end of October 1946, his proposal was that they should work together for a few years in Northern Italy or Switzerland, 'more or less theoretically and, among other things, preparing one production or another for Germany. If we make your designs obligatory, like the music, there would be more money for you. It would be nice, in Berlin for example, to have the Theater am Schiffbauerdamm at our disposal again. Geis must be running it, I think.' Meanwhile he wanted Neher to stay in Zürich: 'In Switzerland you can't so easily become involved in certain doctrinal battles.' 'I myself am convinced that we'll again build a theatre: only you and I can do that. It just has to be organized.' By December he had received 'offers from Berlin to use the Theater am Schiffbauerdamm for certain things', but he was planning to settle, temporarily, in Switzerland. He had been told that in northern Italy food was scarce. A letter to Weigel implies that if it had been a necessary prerequisite for living in Switzerland, he would even have been willing to apply for American citizenship. Stefan, who became an American citizen in December 1946, wanted to stay in the States; Swiss exit and re-entry visas arrived for the other three in March 1947, though they still needed transit visas.[30]

At the same time Brecht was making long-term plans for a return to Berlin, and trying to coax Piscator into forgetting his past behaviour and forging an alliance. 'Of all the people who have worked creatively in theatre during the last twenty years, none has been so close to me as you.' 'Without you', he persuaded, 'I can hardly imagine a successful battle for a mature political theatre and against provincialism, empty emotionalism, etc.' Not that Brecht wanted to share a theatre with him. They must have two theatres, two points of departure 'for establishing the ideas we share'. Brecht must first 'evolve a quite distinctive style' for his own plays.[31] But he needed first-class actors and if Piscator had committed himself to working in Berlin, together they would have exercised a more powerful magnetic pull on émigré actors (Kortner, Lorre, Homolka, Bois, for instance) than either of them separately.

In March 1947 Joseph Losey was rehearsing Arnold Sundgaard's *The Great Campaign* with a rich young friend, T. Edward Hambleton, as producer. The show was to open in New York at the end of the month. Laughton, who had gone on from *The Paradine Case* to another film, *The Big Clock*, was due to be free from the middle of April. Persuaded by Losey, Hambleton agreed to come in for half the production costs of *Galileo* at the small Coronet Theatre in Hollywood, if Laughton would put up the other half. By the end of April they had arranged that rehearsals would start at the end of May for the play to open on 1 July. But when Hambleton's lawyers tried to secure world stage rights, Brecht's answer was: 'I've held out against Hitler and I'm not going to give in to you.'[32]

Casting began in May: Laughton and four other actors were to be paid $40 a week for rehearsing and performing. Three others got $20, while the remainder of the cast – forty-two actors – received little or nothing. They were recruited from the film studios, from Laughton's acquaintances, and from ex-members of the Actors Lab in Hollywood, which had recently closed.

To control Brecht and Laughton it would have taken an Orson Welles or at least an Elia Kazan; Losey was willing to be not so much a director as a disciple. 'I'm learning,' he said, when asked whether he felt redundant. It was at his suggestion that Robert Davison, designer for *The Great Campaign*, and Anna Sokolow, who had choreographed it, were employed, but Weigel was effectively in control of costumes, and Sokolow, who was less tractable than Davison, walked out after Brecht had told her: 'We want none of your tawdry Broadway dances in the production.' She was replaced by Lotte Geislar. Losey did the casting,[33] but Brecht explained each scene to the actors, and gave them their moves.

According to Hambleton, Brecht 'did a great deal of screaming throughout rehearsals about the costumes, about the scenery and about everything'. But he had only one major quarrel with Losey, who threw his script at him, announcing that he was leaving. When Laughton telephoned, Losey said he would not go back unless Brecht apologized; Laughton rang again later with a message: Brecht wanted him to go back but never apologized. He went back.[34]

He also had to cope with a cast which had been trained to examine motivation. One actor raised this question when playing a monk who mocked Galileo by doing a mime to show that it is impossible to stand on a moving ball. Sitting next to Losey, Brecht whispered: 'Does the tightrope walker need a motive for not falling off the wire?' and burst into raucous laughter. To stay on his own tightrope, Losey had to accept humiliation after humiliation. When one actress took offence at his criticism and walked out, Brecht followed her and promised that Weigel would help her to understand the role. And when young actors baulked at the long speeches, it was Laughton who coached them.[35]

The presence of Losey may have conducted heat away from the tension between Brecht and Laughton. Some arguments could be ended by sidetracking Laughton into rewriting the lines, but he refused to produce the censorious characterization Brecht had come to want, or to reveal as much of his private self-contempt as Brecht had been counting on. After the recantation, according to Brecht, Laughton made Galileo look like an embarrassed boy, grinning after wetting his trousers.[36] And in the following scene Laughton was uneasy when he called Andrea his brother in science and cousin in treason.

The production had been due to open on 24 July, but Brecht, as in rehearsing *The Private Life of the Master Race*, had gone on making changes regardless of the deadline, and the opening had to be postponed until 31 July, though the run was due to end on 17 August. The final crisis occurred after a dress rehearsal at four o'clock in the morning of 31 July. The functional wooden set had been coated with shellac, which enraged Brecht because it 'destroyed the grain of the wood'. By throwing a tantrum he got his own way: the wood was stripped before the performance in the evening.[37]

Making his first appearance on stage for thirteen years, and knowing the first-night audience would be full of film-stars including Charlie Chaplin, Charles Boyer, Ingrid Bergman and Van Heflin (whose sister, Frances, was playing Virginia), Laughton was extremely nervous. In the previews he was so tense that during the opening scene, while stripped to the waist, with crepe hair stuck on to conceal the hairlessness of his chest, he put his hands in his trouser pockets and absent-mindedly played with his genitals. Brecht was apprehensive of mentioning this, and it was Weigel who tried to solve the problem by having the pockets of his trousers sewn up. Irately, Laughton insisted on having the stitches removed. At the opening performance he was not too unrelaxed to make a good impression, but it was a hot night, and Brecht later claimed that the actor 'insisted that lorries loaded with ice should be parked against the theatre and the fans turned on "so that the audience can think"'.[38]

Reviews were mixed. According to *Variety*, '*Galileo* in its present form is ponderous rather than powerful. There are fleeting moments that are exciting, but the peak level is not sustained and the overall impression is one of dullness.' But Brecht was satisfied both with the production and with 'the intellectual part of the audience'.[39] After six years in America he had at last had one of his plays staged as he wanted it to be.

The Coronet Theatre was packed for all seventeen performances, but when the production closed Hambleton was uncertain whether it would transfer to Broadway. By the end of August the American National

Theatre and Academy (ANTA) had agreed to present it in the late autumn. Brecht would have left by then. He had been planning to go in the middle of September, but he was delayed by difficulties over French transit visas and over selling the house. At the beginning of September he wrote: 'We want to leave for good from New York in mid-October, destination Zürich or Basel.'[40]

On 19 September a marshal arrived at the house with a subpoena to appear before the House Un-American Activities Committee in Washington. The committee had existed since 1938 but had not become infamous until 1946, when it started working on the assumption that Hollywood had been infiltrated by communists. Charlie Chaplin and Clifford Odets were summoned to appear in October, and Eisler, after being cross-questioned in September, was ordered not to leave the US.

The men under subpoena divided themselves into two groups, which became known as the friendly and unfriendly witnesses. The friendly group, which included Ronald Reagan, Walt Disney and Gary Cooper, were well disposed towards the committee; Brecht found himself listed in articles and petitions as one of nineteen-unfriendly witnesses', including the screenwriters Dalton Trumbo and Ring Lardner Jr. Brecht consulted a lawyer, Ben Margolis, but he did not attend strategy meetings before leaving Hollywood. Having never been a Party member he was in a different position from the others, who were advised neither to deny that they had joined nor to admit it, or they would have been left with a choice between answering questions about other communists or being cited for contempt of Congress. Nevertheless Brecht cautiously asked Eric Bentley to cut the prologue from his translation of *Der kaukasische Kreidekreis*.[41]

Before leaving Hollywood Brecht made a personal appearance on 15 October (together with seventeen of the other eighteen) at a rally sponsored by the Progressive Citizens of America, and staged by Losey with Gene Kelly as master of ceremonies. Brecht left by train the next day to arrive on the 20th in New York, where he saw Laughton, who was due to open in *Galileo* on 7 December, and where he met the Marxist journalist Hermann Budzilawski, who coached him for the performance he would have to give in front of the committee: 'rehearse' was his own word for what he did when he asked Budzilawski to cross-question him about his works. One idea to emerge from the rehearsal was that when confronted with English versions of his poems, he could argue that the translation was inaccurate. And although he did not need an interpreter at the hearing, he would be wise to use one: it would improve the possibilities of evading questions and creating confusion.[42]

The committee consisted of nine Representatives (including Richard Nixon) led by J. Parnell Thomas, with Robert Stripling as chief investigator. The week of 20–24 October was devoted to the 'friendly' witnesses. Robert Taylor was applauded for demanding that all communists should 'be sent back to Russia or some other unpleasant place'. Brecht arrived in Washington on 26 October with Losey and Hambleton, who, using his own name, had booked for Brecht a transatlantic air ticket for Friday 31 October. In case the hotel room was bugged, Brecht talked in the rose-garden with two lawyers, Robert W. Kenny and Bartley Crum. He said history was repeating itself in America: it had been an Un-German Activities Committee that had made him into a refugee from Europe.

The first 'witness' on 27 October was John Howard Lawson, who had attacked Brecht's 'discredited and thoroughly un-Marxist theories' in *Theatre Workshop*. Refusing to admit that he had joined the Party, Lawson shouted at Thomas, who had him removed from the room. Brecht listened to the hearings on the radio, but did not appear in the Old House Office Building until 30 October, when he had to answer questions. Nearly all the previous witnesses had become angry and abusive; one, Albert Maltz, had denounced the committee as anti-Semitic and Nazi. Wearing the suit he had been given by the Jewish tailor, and smoking cigars as he faced the three microphones, Brecht was scrupulously polite, but not scrupulously truthful, though he could have been sentenced to three years imprisonment if he had been found guilty of perjury. He was fortunate, too, in having as his interpreter David Baumgardt, who made Thomas complain: 'I cannot understand the interpreter any more than I can the witness'.

Asked whether he had worked in films, Brecht was able to say: 'I sold a story to a Hollywood firm, *Hangmen Also Die*, but I did not write the screenplay myself'. To the question other witnesses had refused to answer his reply was: 'I am a guest in this country and do not want to enter into any legal arguments, so I will answer your question fully as well as I can. I was not a member or am not a member of any Communist Party.' Asked whether he had written revolutionary poems and plays, he said that he had, in the fight against Hitler. They could be considered as revolutionary 'because I, of course, was for the overthrow of that government'. Had many of his writings been based on the philosophy of Lenin and Marx? 'No, I don't think that is quite correct but, of course, I studied, had to study as a playwright who wrote historical plays. I, of course, had to study Marx's ideas about history.' Was he familiar with the magazine *New Masses*? 'No.'

When Stripling cited the song 'Lob des Lernens', from *Die Mutter*, Brecht denied that 'Du musst die Führung übernehmen' meant: 'You must be ready to take over.' He made the interpreter say it meant: 'You must take the lead.' And when, after reading the poem 'Forward, We've Not Forgotten', Stripling asked: 'Did you write that, Mr Brecht?', he raised a laugh by answering: 'No. I wrote a German poem, but that is very different from this.'

Answering questions about *Die Massnahme*, he said it was 'the adaptation of an old religious Japanese play and is called Noh Play, and follows quite closely this old story which shows the devotion for an ideal until death'. Had Stripling been more familiar with Brecht's plays, he would not have been deceived by this confusion of *Die Massnahme* with *Der Jasager*. *Die Massnahme* had been discussed in some detail when Stripling had cross-questioned Eisler, but Brecht now got away with a misleading summary of the ending in which the young comrade is shot and thrown into a lime-pit. Realizing that he has done damage, said Brecht, the young man 'asks his comrades to help him, and all of them together help him to die. He jumps into an abyss and they lead him tenderly to that abyss ... they did not kill him – not in this story. He killed himself.' At the end Thomas said: 'Thank you very much Mr Brecht. You are a good example to the witnesses of Mr Kenny and Mr Crum.'

In the afternoon he was on the train back to New York with Losey and Hambleton, ready to use Hambleton's ticket the next day. Through Reyher's daughter, Brecht arranged for Weigel and Barbara to stay in New York until they could join him in Switzerland. He arranged for the Buick to be sold: the money would go to Stefan.[43]

When he left on 31 October he had in his pocket a microfilm of Ruth Berlau's *Galileo* photographs. It was not certain whether he would recover the bulk of his possessions, and he was not going to risk losing the record of his work.[44] He had been in America for two and a half years since the surrender of Nazi Germany.

Part Five

TOWARDS THE SCHIFFBAUERDAMM

Since the beginning of the 1920s Brecht had not only wanted a theatre of his own but needed one. Convinced, as he had been since childhood, that he could make practical suggestions to other people about how things should be done, and convinced, as he had been since his youth, that all the existing theatres should be closed down 'for artistic reasons', he needed a permanent base and a permanent company of actors, needed a long-term opportunity to work collaboratively with directors, designers, other writers and actors, testing his theories with practice, completing his plays by fleshing them into three-dimensionality, and developing his skill as a director. Retrospectively it can be said that he deserved a theatre. Before he died in 1956 the company he created, the Berliner Ensemble, was probably the finest in the world and certainly the finest in Europe. But though his company was formed six years before his death, he did not have a theatre of his own until 1954, and he did not succeed even then in establishing the contacts he wanted with German-speaking theatres outside East Germany. In 1949, negotiating for an Austrian passport, he wrote: 'I can't just sit myself down in one half of Germany and as a result be dead for the other half.' But that was the price he would need to pay for having a company and a theatre, and if he had resigned himself sooner to paying it, he might not have had to wait so long.

The transatlantic crossing was uneventful. At Le Bourget he met the writer Donald Ogden Stewart and his wife Ella Winter, who took him out to a 'fabulous meal'. Over a year had elapsed since Ihering's second letter, but before deciding whether to base his operations on East Berlin, Brecht had waited to see how the political situation would develop; learning that Anna Seghers was due from Berlin two days later to visit her children, he decided to wait for her. Her hair was now white, 'but the beautiful face fresh'. She was living in the American sector of Berlin, and she did not create a favourable impression of the city that was no longer a capital. 'Berlin a witches' sabbath, with a shortage of broomhandles.' Had she settled in East Berlin, she would have gained more of the 'privileges without which work is impossible', but would have been unable to keep her Mexican passport, and she 'would like her books to be read in the non-Russian zones too. She seems nervous of the intrigues, suspicions, espionage.' In 1933, after escaping from Berlin, Brecht had sounded out other people before deciding where to settle; doing the same again, he decided against Berlin. 'Alone or almost alone you can't exist there.' 'You need a home outside Germany.'[1]

On 5 November 1947 he took the train to Zürich and met Caspar Neher, who had come from Hamburg. After fourteen years of separation, Brecht struck him as 'fatter, more masculine, more reserved, and his gentleness was more apparent than it used to be.... Naturally all plans will change now. Various important things must be done.'[2] They were eager to work together in the theatre again. Three of Brecht's plays had been staged in Zürich during the war – *Mutter Courage*, *Der gute Mensch* and *Galileo* – and one of his reasons for settling there was that the theatre was the likeliest one to put his plays on while allowing him some control over production. He would then be able to use Weigel, who had arrived in Vienna with Barbara. Oskar Wälterlin, one of the theatre's directors, visited Brecht in his hotel, Zum Storchen, on the day of his arrival there. The next day Neher took him to the theatre, where he met another director, Kurt Hirschfeld, and the dramaturg Uz Oettinger. It was Hirschfeld who arranged a party in his flat, three days later, for Brecht to meet Max Frisch, Carl Zuckmayer, Erich Kästner and Werner Bergengruen. They drafted a manifesto addressed to the writers of all nations: 'Today we are no longer faced with the choice between peace and war but with the choice between peace and destruction. To the politicians, who do not yet know this, we decisively affirm that the people want peace.'

Brecht started translating the new version of *Galileo* into German. He stayed at the Hotel Urban in Stadelhoferstrasse until the middle of November, when Oettinger let him use a studio in Gartenstrasse. 'It is remarkable', wrote Neher, 'how the right things are proffered to him from all sides.'[3] He was intending to stay in Zürich for about a year. Weigel and Barbara arrived on 19 November.

The right flat was soon proffered. A man who had heard they were looking for one presented himself to them at the Odeon Café and arranged for them to move into the top floor of an old gardener's house which belonged to his parents. It struck Max Frisch as having 'something attic-like ... something excitingly temporary about it'. Even before he had gone into exile, Brecht's living spaces had created this impression.

His study had a pine floor and a large window with a view over the lake and the mountains, which, according to Frisch, Brecht did not notice: an environment which could not be altered was of little interest to him. 'The room is something like a studio: typewriter, paper, scissors, crates of books; newspapers are lying on an armchair, local, English, German, American. Now and then something is cut out and filed. On the big table I see glue with brushes, photographs.'[4]

On 24 November Brecht and Neher went to see Hans Curjel, who was running the Stadttheater in the small town of Chur in an Alpine valley. The three men discussed the possibility of staging either *Mutter Courage* or *Die heilige Johanna* in Chur, but they decided on an adaptation of *Antigone* co-directed by Brecht and Neher. Neher advised Brecht to work from Hölderlin's version of the Sophocles play, and he started towards the end of November.[5] Hoping to direct *Mutter Courage* in East Berlin, he wanted Weigel to play Antigone. She had not been on the stage since 1932, except for a few special performances in Copenhagen and Paris and, in 1946, an appearance in Vienna. Here was an obscure provincial theatre where she could regain her confidence.

Brecht worked rapidly on Hölderlin's text. 'I'm finding Swabian cadences and school Latin constructions and feeling at home. There's also something Hegelian in it.' (Hegel had seen the play as a dramatization of the dialectical process, with the *Weltgeist* split in a battle between political discipline and individual impulse.) On 29 November Brecht submitted the first scene to Curjel, who liked it, and by 12 December the script was finished. Brecht had amputated all the religious and tragic elements: '"Fate" eliminates itself automatically, so to speak, as one goes along. Of the gods the local sage, the god of happiness, remains. Bit by bit, as the adaptation of the scenes progresses, the highly realistic folk legend emerges out of the ideological fog.'[6]

Brecht failed to resist the temptation of making Creon into a Hitler figure. Set in Berlin during March 1945, the prologue shows two sisters waiting for Germany to surrender. Their brother has been hanged by the SS for deserting from the army. Hoping that he is still alive, one of the sisters goes to cut him down. When a gong sounds the two actresses change costumes, becoming Antigone and Ismene. In Brecht's version Kreon's war is not defensive but aggressive, motivated (like the war in *Die Horatier und die Kuriatier* and the one in *Rundköpfe*) by the need to distract the people from a valid grievance – in this case misgovernment by Kreon. In Sophocles's play the sympathy is divided between the ruler, who must preserve order, and the girl, who cannot let her brother's body be dishonoured. Sophocles's Polynices has raised an army in Argos to attack his native Thebes; Brecht's Polyneikes is a hero of the resistance against an egocentric tyrant, while Antigone's disobedience is neither wilful nor pious but exemplary. She is like Simone Machard but more self-conscious. After condemning Antigone to death, Sophocles' Creon undergoes a genuine change of heart when Tiresias tells him that the gods are displeased; Brecht's Tiresias is a pre-Marxist philosopher who explains the economic causes of the war; Kreon is prompted to revoke the execution order, not by contrition but by expediency: he needs the people's goodwill. In stripping Sophocles's play of its 'mythological veneer', Brecht had killed its resonance.[7] He retained a good deal of Hölderlin's text, but the verse he interpolated was uncharacteristically rhetorical.

With the return of Laughton to Broadway, and with a script that was the end-product of protracted collaborative work, Brecht had been hoping for a major success, but the New York reviewers were hostile to *Galileo*. Apart from Laughton's, all the parts had been recast, and there were changes in both production and script. Using Brecht's notes, and working with Laughton and George Tabori, Losey had revised the text and reblocked the moves. The play had some defenders, such as John Mason Brown in the *New York Post*, but in the *New York Times* Brooks Atkinson attacked it, and returned to the subject in several subsequent reviews. Drawn by Laughton, audiences poured in. Fifty to a hundred people were standing at each performance, and the run was extended for a week; but it was a non-profit production in which some actors received minimum salaries while others received none, and the only commercial theatre they could find for a transfer would guarantee no more than three weeks, which made it impossible to raise the backing. Brecht's conclusion was that 'the bourgeoisie is no longer at all prepared for this general, unspecialized thinking demanded by plays which concern themselves with it. . . . In short thinking is too difficult and therefore it is no longer a pleasure.'[8]

Neher brought his wife Erika to celebrate Christmas Eve with the Brechts. They tried to find something convivial on the radio, but the German-language stations seemed to be broadcasting nothing but the names of missing soldiers. Since the Nehers' son was missing in Russia, Brecht switched off, and settled down to working with his old friend on *Antigone*, their first production together since the ballet in Paris.[9]

Discussions on casting began before the end of the month. Neher had designed Oskar Wälterlin's staging of Goldoni's *The Liar*, and Brecht attended the dress rehearsal in Chur on 30 December before auditions for *Antigone* were held in Zürich on New Year's Eve. Early in January 1948 Brecht was meeting Neher to talk about masks and props, and about the possibility of staging *Puntila* in Chur.

None of the actors they wanted for Kreon was available, and it seemed possible that the production would be cancelled. Rehearsals started on 13 January, but both Kreon and Hamon were still uncast. The first day was devoted to the prologue and the second to the opening scene. After three days of rehearsing in Zürich it was obvious that it would be better to work in Chur, and on 16 January Weigel and Neher moved into the Hotel Sternen, ready to start rehearsals the next day, with the casting still unsettled.

As in some of Brecht's earlier collaborations with Neher, design, script and production seemed to emerge out of a single concept. The prologue was to be performed on a skeletal set, the classical stage already visible in the background, but with the traditional fluted columns replaced by four totem-poles hung with the skulls of horses. Horse-heads from a slaughterhouse were boiled in a bath-tub. Before rehearsals began, Brecht and Neher had wondered whether to mark out one acting area with the totem poles, symbolic of barbaric religion, and then move the actors out of this area to present a version of the play from which the gods had been excluded. The final decision was to use the four poles at the four corners of the main acting area, incorporating into the set a semicircle of benches to represent the auditorium, but the chorus, standing for the people, was kept out of this area. In Brecht's view, 'The whole of *Antigone* belongs on the plane of barbaric horse skulls. The play is by no means rationally thought out.'[10]

Hans Gaugler, a candidate for the role of Kreon, attended the rehearsal on 20 January, but two days later Brecht and Neher were still uncertain whether to abandon the production. On the 23rd, when Gaugler was still being tried out, Brecht quarrelled with Curjel. But the next day Gaugler was joining in discussions about re-scripting. Rehearsals were in full swing again, though they could not always work on the stage, since another production was also in rehearsal.

The production gave Brecht a better opportunity than *Galileo* to test ideas he would later crystallize in East Berlin, but he found that 'against the drrramatic [*sic*] style of acting which surrounds it, the epic style can only defend itself: it can't go over to the attack. Nor is there any middle ground for the actor to fall back on – any thoughtlessness and the curve is irreparably lost.'[11] He could not hope, in a single production, to restrain the other actors from 'acting' in the usual way.

When the first technical rehearsal was held on 3 February Neher protested at the shoddy decor, and the next day, after another technical rehearsal and a run-through, Curjel conceded that the opening, which had already been postponed once, could be postponed until 15 February. The dress rehearsal on the 5th showed that the second half of the play was still under-rehearsed, but when Brecht opened the rehearsals to the public, 'the audience surprised both us and itself with real applause'. He was delighted with Neher's costumes, props, basic groupings and ideas towards solving the chorus problem. The point was 'to find out what we could do for the old play and what it could do for us'.[12]

Ruth Berlau had arrived from New York in time to celebrate Brecht's fiftieth birthday on 10 February 1948, and his daughter Hanne, now an attractive girl of nearly twenty-five, was staying in Zürich for several weeks. Curjel arranged a celebratory evening in the town hall of Chur to introduce the production. The première on the 15th was so unsuccessful that only three more performances were given, and only one Sunday-morning guest performance in the Zürich Schauspielhaus. But at least Weigel proved that her talent had not deteriorated while in cold storage.

At the beginning of April Brecht saw a touring performance of Ferenc Molnár's play *Liliom* starring Hans Albers, 'a big, elegant fellow with vulgar charm, not without violence. We talked about doing a folk play with him, Eulenspiegel perhaps. Background: the Peasants' War. The great challenger to the cardinal vices of the Germans: obsequiousness, solitariness, over-subtlety, love of order.' Albers had been offered a portable theatre made of light metal alloy which could be toured, like a circus, all over Germany, and in Hollywood Brecht had become addicted to the idea of capitalizing on the popularity of star actors. He described Albers as 'probably the only folk actor there is. He is by no means young.' Later they planned a tour of *Dreigroschenoper* through West Germany with Albers as Macheath.[13] He played the part in Harry Buckwitz's 1949 Munich production, but the tour did not materialize.

In the spring of 1948 – Brecht's first spring in Europe for eight years – he proved that Max Frisch had been wrong to accuse him of not noticing the Alps: 'The colours of the vegetation, so much fresher and less crude than in California. The fruit trees on the railway track to Zürich. The landscaping is not mathematical like that of the zoos or plantations of California. And at least the country houses are signs of ancient sins.'[14]

Frisch would sometimes come to visit him; when they ate together it was in the kitchen. Besides writing, Frisch was practising as an architect, and when he showed Brecht around a building site Brecht was, of all his visitors there, 'by far the most appreciative, greedy for knowledge, expert in questioning'. But Ruth Berlau, who was with them, soon became bored. She was interested only in taking photographs of Brecht. In the Brechts' flat Frisch noticed that

reticent though he is, Brecht expresses himself forcefully through gestures. A slight, dismissive movement of the hand signals contempt, standing still at the decisive point of an emergent sentence, a question-mark, expressed with a harsh shrug of the left shoulder, irony, when with his lower lip he mimicks the blunt, down-to-earth seriousness of the right-minded man, or his abrupt, rather rasping laughter, shy but not cold, when a contradiction is driven to its extreme, but then his amazed and intimidated confusion, his defenceless face when he hears something that really touches, concerns or delights him.[15]

Working in Salzburg, Neher had become friendly with the composer Gottfried von Einem, a director of the Festival, who in February made overtures to Brecht. He liked the idea of involving himself in the Festival: Salzburg might be an excellent place to have a house, if only for use as a base.[16] But having no passport – only identity documents giving his name and place of birth – he was not allowed to travel there without permission from Bern.

Interrupted though it was by Neher's absences in Salzburg and in Milan, the collaboration had resumed almost as if the two friends had not been separated by the war. In the second half of April they discussed a new play about the return of the defeated Ares, god of war. Titled *Der Wagen des Ares* (*The Chariot of Ares*) it would have dealt with the post-war political situation as seen from the elevated viewpoint of the Swiss intellectuals.

Kurt Hirschfeld was eager to end the Zürich season with a production of *Puntila*, and Neher started on a series of drawings, but before the end of the month it was clear that he had too many other commitments. Teo Otto, who took over as designer, had worked on the 1941 production of *Mutter Courage*. Nominally Hirschfeld was the director of *Puntila*, but in practice it was Brecht; Leonard Steckel played Puntila, with Gustav Knuth as Matti, Regine Lutz as the dairymaid, and Therese Giehse (who had played Mrs Peachum in the 1929 production of *Dreigroschenoper* at the Munich Kammerspiele) as Emma. Brecht wrote the 'Pflaumenlied'

('Plum Song') specially for her. As a director Brecht had a delicacy, she discovered, which previously she had found only in Falckenberg and subsequently found only in Peter Stein.[17]

Retrospectively the production can be seen as an experiment to bridge the gap between the theoretical writings and the style that would be evolved for the Berliner Ensemble. Brecht once again used the half-height linen curtain which did not totally obscure scene-changes, and which could be used for projecting titles of scenes. Reprising Neher's idea for the moon in the Munich production of *Trommeln in der Nacht*, Brecht and Otto represented sun, moon and clouds emblematically on brass or lacquered wood, like the signboards outside shops. These were hung on the high wide screen of birchwood that formed the background to the set. Daylight, twilight and darkness were indicated by the intensity of light on the screen. Brecht wanted the acting area to be uniformly lit, but here he had to compromise, because the equipment at Zürich was inadequate. No coloured light was used, while blue, grey and white were almost the only colours used on the set; in the costumes black, blue, grey and white. Clothes and props were all made to look as though they had been in regular use. The four women from Kurgela, Puntila's fiancées, were not characterized as comic: they were given a sense of humour. There was no proper word in German for what English actors call 'business'. In the German theatre the word 'Kisten' (which had contemptuous associations) was generally used, but Brecht recognized that business was important. Significant points could be made silently, as when the four humble women are impressed by the butter, meat and beer being brought into the house of their fiancé.

Brecht was pleased with the production, in spite of the audience's unresponsiveness. 'Plays like this must be put on repeatedly until people get used to them as they got used to Schiller. This will take some years.'[18]

Since arriving in Zürich Brecht had been working on his *Kleines Organon für das Theater (Short Organum for the Theatre)*, modelling it on Francis Bacon's *Novum Organum*, which had been aimed against Aristotle's *Organum*. Eight years earlier, when Arnold Ljungdal had considered writing a book on his plays, Brecht had suggested that in form it should follow the *Novum Organum* 'with its short, summarizing chapters. This would make it possible to leave the work open-ended.' Deriving from the earlier *Messingkauf*, Brecht's manifesto was a theoretical counterpart to the *Puntila* production. Frisch had noticed Brecht's 'childlike talent for asking questions. An actor, what is that? What does he do?

What does he need that's special?' Brecht had 'a creative patience, willingness to start all over again from the beginning, to forget opinions, to collect experiences.' This is apparent in the *Organon*, which goes back to questions about what theatre is and how society has changed since 'a few people, in different countries, but keeping in touch, performed certain experiments in the hope of extricating Nature's secrets. ... They passed their discoveries on to people who exploited them practically, without expecting much more from the new sciences than personal profit.'[19] Brecht was making the same bald assumption he had made in *Galileo*: that science and its by-product, industrialism, would have evolved differently if only these individuals had not been egocentric.

The *Organon* reveals a childlike excitement in the progress science was still making: 'I can travel at a speed that was inconceivable to my grandfather; I can fly in the air, which my father could not.' But the bourgeoisie had stopped 'the new way of thinking and feeling from penetrating into the relationship people have with each other during the plundering and subjugation of Nature'. Brecht's language and his method of proceeding from point to point were subjective, unhistorical and unscientific, but the gist of his argument was that the 'scientific age' needed a new kind of theatre, unconcerned with relationships between human beings and gods. Both art and science should make human life easier, so theatre should provide 'workable representations of society which are then able to influence society'. Theatre should let itself be floated by the strongest currents in its society: it must move out into the suburbs and make itself available there to 'the broad masses of people who are productive and who are living uncomfortably'; though, before they can respond to 'the new form of entertainment', they 'must themselves develop a new science of society and put it into practice'.[20]

The quality of the writing and the cogency of the argument both improve when the essay turns to questions that bear directly on theatrical production. Discussing the alienation effect, Brecht claims it was basic to 'the variety of acting which was tried out between the First and Second World Wars at the Schiffbauerdamm-Theater in Berlin'. But, apart from the disastrous *Happy End*, he had been involved in only two productions there, *Dreigroschenoper* and Marieluise Fleisser's *Pioniere von Ingolstadt*: both were less relevant to the history of the alienation effect than the idea of whitening the soldiers 'faces in *Eduard II*. The *Organon* cites the use of masks in classical and medieval theatre, and the use of music and pantomime in Asiatic theatre. The object of 'alienation' was to encourage what Lenin called 'intelligent and conscious action', bringing out 'the content of the impulses' from 'the direct union of the subject with objectivity'. The undesirable alternative is 'quasi-instinctual action ... fragmented into endlessly complex material'. The contradistinction occurs in Lenin's *Zur Kritik der Hegelschen Wissenschaft der Logik* (*In Criticism of Hegel's Science of Logic*).[21] 'Alienation effect' is written in the margin of Brecht's copy against this passage, and he has marked Hegel's definition of the dialectic – 'the apprehension of opposed elements in their unity'. If theatre is to uncover the laws of motion that govern society, says Brecht in his *Organon*, each historical situation should be regarded as part of a process – should be studied in terms of its anomalies, the areas where it is in disharmony with itself. Presenting confrontations between human and non-human forces, as it had from *Oedipus* and *King Lear*, tragedy had been concerned neither with internal contradictions nor with variations in human nature. The assumption was that this never changed. Brecht was determined to present it as if it did, and, with the Charles Laughton experience fresh in his mind, he could confidently assert: 'It is an oversimplification if actions are made to fit character, and character to fit actions.' The director and the actor should look for anomalies, inconsistencies, areas of disharmony, both between the character and his behaviour, and between the actor and the performance. In *Galileo* Laughton had appeared 'on the stage as a dual figure, as Laughton and as Galileo'. He would have been unable to disappear completely into the character, while the audience would not, in any case, have wanted 'to be altogether deprived of his opinions and sensations'.[22] It had been paying to see him.

On 9 January 1948 Brecht had copied into his diary a passage from one of Schiller's letters to Goethe:

The dramatic plot moves before me; around the epic I myself move while it seems to stand still. .... If the event moves before me, then I am bound fast to the sensual event, my imagination loses all freedom ... I am pulled by an external force. If I move around the event ... I can vary my pace ... can step backwards or forwards. This fits in very well with the idea of the past, which can be conceived as static, and with the idea of *narrative*, for the narrator already knows the end when he is at the beginning or in the middle, and consequently each moment is of equal value to him, and so he maintains a quiet freedom throughout.[23]

The *Organon* demands that the actor should be a narrator in this sense – should retain this quiet freedom and share it with the audience. He need not pretend that the events taking place on stage have never been rehearsed. He may empathize with the character in rehearsal, but not in performance. Instead of trying to magnetize the attention of spectators, he should be prepared to let them withdraw now and then into their own thoughts. When studying the part he should memorize not just the lines but his own initial reactions to them – reservations, criticisms, astonishment – so that these can be worked into his performance. Whereas Stanislavsky, with his moralizing habit and his tendency to make the actor think of long-term motivation, was liable, especially in the earlier phase of his development, to push each performance towards homogeneity – for him coherence depended on consistency – for Brecht 'The coherence of a character will in fact materialize out of the contradictions between his individual qualities.'[24] This was already implicit in the plays of Chekhov, and it is formulated explicitly in Strindberg's preface to *Frøken Julie*. But in writing the *Organon* Brecht was reacting not so much against Stanislavsky as against current theatrical practice. After watching a rehearsal of Büchner's *Woyzeck*, directed by Steckel, he had written: 'Already, before I see the ruins of theatres, I get to see the ruins of acting.' Paying his first visit to post-war Germany in August, he had seen Heinz Hilpert's production of Frisch's *Santa Cruz* in Konstanz. He had made no comment until they were back in Switzerland. The outburst began with a cold snigger. 'Then he was screaming, white with rage. It was shameless, the way in which these survivors simply went on as if nothing but their houses had been destroyed. Then suddenly he was eager to go back. "Here we must start right from the beginning."'[25]

In the *Organon* he hit out at 'the current theatrical abuse of letting the leading actor, the star, "steal the limelight" by making all the other actors subservient to him: he makes his character formidable or wise by forcing his partners to make theirs frightened or attentive'. Always alert to dialectical elements in human interrelationships, Brecht made a proposal he would later use in the Ensemble: 'in rehearsal actors should exchange roles with their partners so that the characters get from each other what they need from each other. . . . The master is only the kind of master that his servant allows him to be.'[26] As a playwright Brecht had already capitalized on his awareness of the extent to which social roles are interdependent; later he would exploit it as a director.

His formulations and his example have strongly influenced many theatrical practitioners who share neither his political views nor even his interest in politics; and in practice he did not require actors or collaborators to be politically motivated, but it looked as though it would be advantageous for him to maintain, theoretically, that he did. In the *Organon* he contends that 'If the actor does not want to be a parrot or an ape, he must familiarize himself with today's knowledge of human relationships by joining in the class war. . . . No man can rise above the warring classes, for no man can stand above the human race.' He had just been working with the apolitical Laughton, but if *Galileo* had originally been intended to secure an American entry visa, he may have planned his manifesto for later use in impressing the East German authorities. This would explain why he had been at pains to associate the alienation effect with the Schiffbauerdamm, and it was now expedient to work from the simplistic premiss that non-political art is art that tacitly supports the dominant party.[27]

He had been trying since the spring to visit Salzburg, but at the end of August he was still waiting for a visa. He also wanted to visit Munich, where Erich Engel had taken over the Kammerspiele. Brecht failed to obtain a visa, but on 20 September he received Czech documents for the journey to Salzburg, Prague and East Berlin. On 17 October he and Weigel travelled to Salzburg, leaving Barbara in Zürich, where, together with Fritz Kortner's daughter, she was attending drama school. On the 18th, discussing the Festival with von Einem, Brecht made several proposals. 'Here', he wrote, '"everything can be had" i.e. on the black market. You pay more, and don't need ration books. Strict democracy for those without means, i.e. the workers. Everyone gets equally little. The city seems enfeebled, exhausted.'[28]

Arriving in Prague the next day, he found no exhaustion and no black market, 'at least none worth mentioning'. 'Once, when ration books were stolen in quantity, there were death sentences. The justice is undemocratic. If rich people are caught, they're punished more severely than the poor. Prices kept low. Apparently adequate supplies of potatoes and bread, despite the bad harvest last year. Little fat, milk only for children.'

On Friday 22 October he and Weigel left Prague in the early morning. By the middle of the day they were at the border of the Russian Zone of Germany.[29]

He was greeted like a man of importance. A car was waiting at the frontier to take him and Weigel to a Dresden restaurant, where a reception committee was waiting, together with photographers and radio reporters. Speeches were made. Ludwig Renn, Area President of the Kulturbund in Saxony, said that consciences now came before stomachs. The theatre people and Party officials in the delegation seemed 'very nice and very hungry'; the driver who took the Brechts to Berlin talked about shortages of food and clothes. His son had no shoes. For breakfast his family ate two slices of bread, for lunch potatoes, for dinner potatoes again.[1] He drove past blown-up bridges and armoured cars rusting in ditches. At the frontier between the Soviet zone and the city of Berlin he had trouble over the documents for the car, but when Brecht telephoned from a police station to the Deutsches Theater, two cars arrived. In one of them was Alexander Abusch, secretary of the Kulturbund, who conducted them to the headquarters, where Herbert Ihering, Slatan Dudow and Johannes Becher were waiting. Dudow was making a film, *Unser tägliches Brot (Our Daily Bread)*, for the East German Film Company DEFA; Becher, who had come back from Moscow in 1945, was now President of the Kulturbund. An official reception was to be given for Brecht in the afternoon.

He and Weigel were installed in the only part of the Hotel Adlon which had been rebuilt after the fire started by SS soldiers on the day following Hitler's death in the bunker. Having seen what remained of Friedrichstrasse only dimly in the dark, Brecht got up at 6.30 to look at the derelict streets. Fifty-seven per cent of Berlin's buildings had been wrecked, and three years after the end of the war there were still enormous stretches of rubble, especially in East Berlin and on both sides of the frontier that divided East from West, a space in which neither side wanted to invest. It was safer to walk in the middle of the road, for fear of falling debris. 'A few workmen, and women clearing the rubble. The ruins make less of an impression on me than the thought of what the people went through when the city was devastated.' In the next few months he would go on chatting to people in the street. One young student, the daughter of a sick mechanic, told him what she ate: 'for breakfast three dry pieces of bread, five more during the day; in the evening, soup – vegetables and potatoes'.[2]

At the reception there were speeches by Ihering and Wolfgang Langhoff, who had played Eilif in the 1941 production of *Mutter Courage* and was now Intendant (artistic director) of the Deutsches Theater. There was a speech by Alexander Dymschitz, the Soviet Officer for Cultural Affairs. Brecht struck him as 'very modest, silent, reserved, with a very workaday look and extraordinarily clever eyes, which gleamed in a special way'. There was a reason for Brecht's silence: 'I have arranged with Becher that I must say nothing.' But what he most wanted to say was said privately to Langhoff in answer to the question Ihering had raised over three years earlier: Brecht offered to direct *Mutter Courage* at the Deutsches Theater with Weigel in the part. In the evening he went to see the première of Julius Hay's play *Haben* (*Credit*) with Arnolt Bronnen's former friend Gerda Müller in it: 'miserable performance, hysterically constricted, totally unrealistic'.[3]

At a peace rally held by the Kulturbund on Sunday, Stefan Zweig made a speech, but Brecht again said nothing, 'determined to get my bearings and not to come forward'. In the evening he met Otto Müllereisert, who was practising as a doctor in Berlin. He 'looks as if he's been knocked about by the apocalyptic years'.[4]

Three and a half years had passed since the Russians had reached Berlin on 20 April 1945, but people were still talking about their brutality. 'After the battle drunken hordes made their way through the houses, fetched the women, shot down the men and women who resisted them, raping, with children watching, standing in queues in front of the houses, etc.' As assistant director Brecht had Heinz Kuckhahn, an old acquaintance who had written to him in California and had been sent a food parcel in reply. He told Brecht he had seen a woman of seventy shot after being raped, and seen a commissar shooting two soldiers who attacked him when he reprimanded them for plundering.[5]

The rape and plunder may have helped to frustrate Stalin's hopes of controlling Germany. If fascism was the most advanced phase of capitalism, a communist revolution should have ensued on its demise, and the Red Army was there to assist the insurrectionary workers in their bid for power. But looking at the posters proclaiming the friendship of the USSR towards a democratic Germany, people did not forget that Stalin had not only failed to restrain his troops: he was plundering himself, on a grand scale. In 1945 about eight million people were expelled from East Prussia, Silesia and Pomerania; scientists and skilled workers were transported to Russia; electronic equipment was roughly dismantled and transported to the Soviet Union in cattle trucks; telephones were uprooted and pitchforked into open lorries. Brecht went on asking questions about hunger and hardship, though without linking poverty to Soviet spoliation. But he must soon have become aware of the contempt in which so many Germans held the Russians. Joel Agee, the stepson of Bodo Uhse, chief editor of Aufbau Verlag, remembers watching an inoffensive soldier trying to buy groceries while sales-girls and other shoppers feigned incomprehension, sneering and winking behind the man's back. Generally the Russian soldiers were frustrated and unhappy: they were forbidden to fraternize with German girls, while only officers could bring their wives to Germany.[6]

This was the period of the Berlin airlifts. 'Above the totally silenced streets of ruins, the nightly throb of airlift cargo-planes.' Already, though not yet committed to living in East Berlin, Brecht sided with the Russians:

> Berlin, an etching by Churchill from an idea of Hitler's.
> Berlin, the rubbish dump near Potsdam.[7]

Brecht was not ignorant of the events that had led to the blockade. The division of Berlin into four sectors was an obstacle to the creation of a Soviet-style 'people's republic' in East Germany. While the other important cities – Leipzig, Dresden, Chemnitz (now rechristened Karl-Marx-Stadt) were easily controlled, Berlin, still the biggest industrial centre, could be tucked behind the curtain only if the Allies were ousted from the other three sectors of the city. In March 1946 members of the Social Democratic Party (SPD) were balloted about the possibility of a merger with the Communist Party (KPD) and 80 per cent of those who voted were hostile to the idea, which showed that democratic methods could not have been used to create what the Russians wanted. But in the Soviet zone there was no free vote, and on 21 April the merger was forcibly effected. Otto Grotewohl, a prominent member of the SPD, betrayed it by signing the agreement to dissolve it into the new Socialist Unity Party (SED).

The winter of 1947–48 was crucial for international communism. In October the Cominform had been established to co-ordinate the European communist parties, and it excommunicated Tito. Czechoslovakia, weakened by the death of Jan Masaryk, was forced into the Soviet bloc by the *coup d'état* of February. Determined to push the Allies out of West

Berlin, the Russians stopped coal deliveries, and on 24 January 1948 they detached the civilian coaches from the Allied military trains. Then on 23 June the bridge over the Elbe was 'temporarily closed for repairs', stopping all transport to West Germany. Within a week or so, Berlin could have been industrially paralysed and reduced to starvation. Within a week or so, Berlin could have been industrially paralysed and reduced to starvation if an air shuttle had not been started. Massive quantities of food, fuel and raw material were flown in at the initiative of the Americans, whose example was followed by the British and French. The Communists were to persist with the blockade until May 1949, but instead of winning Berlin they lost goodwill and increased the flow of refugees from East to West.

In East Germany hardships over food shortages were compounded by inefficiency in distributing supplies, but severe punishments were meted out for hoarding even such small quantities of potatoes as 10 lb. Brecht thought that groups of vigilante women should be organized to inspect lorries at control points.[8]

Within two weeks of his arrival in East Berlin Brecht was auditioning young actors for *Mutter Courage*, and on Monday 8 November Erich Engel arrived from Munich to co-direct. 'He has aged a great deal, but the eyes are still easy to recognize. The elegant, ribboned hat makes his head look like a skull.' Brecht wanted Neher to design the production, but to contact him in Salzburg it was necessary to cross over into the American sector and telephone Zürich, so that a telegram could be sent from there.[9] Things became easier from 4 November, when Brecht arranged to use the telephone of Gody Suter, Berlin correspondent of the Zürich *Tagesanzeiger*, who was living in the British zone. But Neher was entangled in other commitments, and instead of making a fresh beginning, as they would have done together, Brecht settled for the designs by Teo Otto which had been used in Leopold Lindtberg's Zürich production; Brecht kept the revolving stage and the cyclorama, but scrapped the canvas backdrops and the additional projections. Instead, signs were hung up with the name of the county or district in black letters. The new designer, Heinrich Kilger, changed the size of the screens that formed the permanent frame, and they were used only in the camp scenes, to differentiate them from the road scenes. Buildings such as the farmhouse and the parsonage were still set up three-dimensionally, but Kilger redesigned them. Hating the atmosphere generated by patches of semi-darkness, or coloured lighting, or both, Brecht flooded the stage with even white light.

The cyclorama at the Deutsches Theater had no entrance in it, so a stylized hovel was built to conceal the wagon at the opening of the play, while the stage, which had been empty during the prologue, sprouted a few wintry tufts of grass. Masks were used to give the recruiting officers grotesque faces. Afterwards Brecht wrote to Neher: 'The designs for *Courage* weren't good. We waited for you till the last minute and then had to improvise.'[10]

As Kattrin Brecht cast Angelika Hurwicz, a sturdy 26-year-old actress who had been with the Deutsches Theater since 1945. The cook was played by Paul Bildt, and the atheistic chaplain by Werner Hinz, who made it look 'as though he had lost his faith in the way another poor devil might lose his leg'. Bildt took the trouble to find a Dutchman who would tutor him in the accent.[11]

To alienate sympathy from Courage, Brecht made a number of textual changes. In Scene 5, for example, the original Courage had given away one of her officers' shirts, but not the 1948 Courage. More important, however, Brecht now had in Weigel a leading actress who, unlike Laughton, was generally in agreement with his intentions, though sometimes too emotional for his taste, and they had fierce arguments about how tearful Courage should become. In performance she was more emotional when Brecht was not in the theatre – taking Eilif in her arms, for instance. He could rely on her, though, not to play for sympathy: her characterization was 'hard and angry, which is not to say that Courage was angry, but she was, the actress'. She devised pieces of business to show how mercenary Courage was. For example she experimented with different ways of snapping her purse loudly shut at the end of a transaction. It could be done lightly, quickly and triumphantly, or sadly, absently, as when she handed over money to the peasants who were going to bury Kattrin. Effectively she sharpened Brecht's points. Kuckhahn was helpful: he suggested that Courage should lose 'her elder son because she becomes involved in a business deal, and added to this there is her sympathy with the superstitious sergeant major. This betokens a weakness which comes from the business and which she cannot afford.'[12]

Brecht was wary of introducing unfamiliar rehearsal methods, but, working with Gerda Müller and Erich Dunskus on the scene in which two old peasants say they can do nothing against the Catholics, he abruptly decided to make them interpolate the words 'he said' and 'she said'. 'Suddenly the scene was clear, and Müller discovered a realistic attitude.'[13]

The music for the Zürich production had been by Paul Burkhard, but in Hollywood Brecht had shown Paul Dessau a script, saying '"There are a few songs here to be composed." And he immediately started to read the poems, quietly, gently, with precise emphasis, and so musically that scarcely any poet can ever have read like that before.' He also showed Dessau a tune published in the appendix to *Hauspostille* – Brecht's own melody for the 'Ballade von den Seeräubern', which derived, apparently, from a French tune called 'L'Etandard de la pitié'. Dessau was 'really appalled at the banality of this tune and at Brecht's suggestion, polite though it was, that he wanted it used for his song. "It will take a lot of work to make that tolerable as the basis for an important song."' But he used it, and it was Dessau's score that was heard in Berlin.

With the production of *Mutter Courage* scheduled to open at the beginning of January 1949, Brecht had only a little over four weeks for rehearsals. Nevertheless, what struck Angelika Hurwicz – who had at first been nervous of working with him – was his patience. He encouraged actors to speak in their native dialect, which made them less declamatory and more expressive. And when a passage lacked the pressure it needed, 'he introduces a gesture to replace an emphasis, a pause to replace a gesture, a clearing of the throat to replace a glance, etc.'.[14]

At the beginning of December he approached Langhoff about opening a studio theatre within the Deutsches Theater. The first year would be devoted to attracting the best émigré actors as guest artists; the long-term objective would be to build up an ensemble. Three or four plays could be produced each season – initially perhaps *Galileo* with Kortner or *Schweyk* with Lorre, but only one play by Brecht. Perhaps Gorki's *Shelesnova* with Giehse and Steckel, and a play by O'Casey or Lorca. A children's theatre could be attached to the studio, and Margarete Steffin's children's plays – if they had not been lost – could be staged. His own plans were to write a play about Rosa Luxemburg and to complete the play he had started with Neher, *Der Wagen des Ares*.[15]

Introducing more alienation effects into the rehearsals, he found that they clarified the turning points. Paul Bildt quickly understood that Brecht's object was to stop the actors from identifying completely with the characters, while Kuckhahn suggested a refinement on making the actors interpolate such phrases as 'Courage said'. Instead they were to add: 'Courage is supposed to have said.'[16]

Rehearsals began at ten, but Brecht was getting up at 5.30 in the morning to make tea or coffee on the methylated spirit cooker he had in his hotel bedroom. 'If I look up, I see a large print of Brueghel's Peasant Dance on the wall. Walk up and down a bit on the red carpet and sit down to work. It does not get light outside until nearly eight. The ruins emerge. ... After eight Kuckhahn arrives. He orders my breakfast and we prepare for the *Courage* rehearsals. At nine I'm in my office in the theatre. Kasprowiak is waiting for me to dictate letters.'[17]

With the methods he was using he ideally needed not less than four months of rehearsal, but on 20 December, running the first eight scenes in sequence for the first time, he was pleased that Ihering noticed a volatility in Weigel's Courage that had not been apparent when the scenes were rehearsed separately. Paul Bildt recognized that he should have been working more pragmatically: he had been trying, prematurely, to present a character, instead of merely playing the situations, 'and now has a character with no development'.[18]

On 6 January Brecht was summoned to meet Friedrich Ebert, the son of the former President and now Oberbürgermeister of East Berlin. Langhoff was at the meeting, together with Fritz Wisten, Intendant of the Theater am Schiffbauerdamm, and representatives of the SED's Central Committee. 'The Herr Oberbürgermeister neither said "Guten Tag" to me nor goodbye, did not once speak to me, and uttered only one sceptical sentence about uncertain projects through which existing things could be destroyed.' Brecht's objective was to build up an independent ensemble dedicated to 'epic' acting, but in formulating his proposal he strategically emphasized the possibility of attracting émigré actors. Of those who had already returned, some had opted for West Germany; others were trying to divide their careers between East and West. It was possible that even without Piscator, Brecht's presence in the East would be magnetic, especially if he had long-term contracts to offer. Responding to his bait, the representatives of the SED suggested that if the Theater am Schiffbauerdamm was not available, the project might be accommodated in the Kammerspiele, and his company could give guest performances at Wisten's and Langhoff's theatres. 'There was also talk of economy and necessity. ... They have resumed the social democrat petty bourgeois ideal of a permanent stall in the theatre for each little man. ... For the first time here I feel the stinking breath of provinciality.'[19]

Mutter Courage opened at the Deutsches Theater on 11 January 1949, making an enormous impact. Despite the songs, the projections, and the captions which stayed in view all through a scene, the acting was quite different from what was familiar to the audience – less theatrical, more realistic. The only entry for the day in Brecht's diary is 'Helli's Courage character now superb. Great boldness in it.'[20] But the feeling of personal triumph must have been overwhelming. He had finally vindicated himself as a director – he had effectively directed productions which had been credited to other names, such as Joseph Losey's, but had had no major success in his own name since the *Mann ist Mann* of 1931.

Ideally the next step would be to arrange for productions of his plays in the West. To the actor Gustav Gründgens, who had supported the Nazis but was now Intendant of the theatre in Düsseldorf, he wrote: 'In 1932 you asked for permission to produce *Die heilige Johanna der Schlachthöfe*. My answer is yes.'[21] Unfortunately Gründgens was as unhurried in taking advantage of the permission as Brecht had been in granting it.

By the end of January 1949 Brecht was telling Neher they would have the Theater am Schiffbauerdamm for the next season. He would not, in fact, get it until 1954, but by the middle of February preparations could begin for the creation of the new company. Accepting Langhoff's invitation to use the Deutsches Theater as a base, Brecht promised not to press for the Schiffbauerdamm until other premises could be found for Fritz Wisten. Brecht did not want to be the Intendant of the new company, and after some little thought about who should be appointed to the position, he made a brilliant choice which only retrospectively seemed obvious: Weigel. She was given an office in Die Möwe (The Seagull), a cultural club in Luisenstrasse. Confident, at last, that he was to have a company of his own, he was in a stronger theatrical position than ever before: theorizing could give way to practice, and the term 'epic theatre' almost disappeared from his vocabulary.

Germany was no longer intact and no longer had a capital; nevertheless he was back in Berlin and as close as was possible to resuming the career that had been interrupted sixteen years earlier. He could relax. 'Have resumed the habit of leaning out of the window in the morning; the air here is so strong. And I have almost abandoned another habit: reading thrillers before I go to sleep. In all this time I've barely finished 2 or 3, I believe.'[1] But he had never been one to move in straight lines. He neither stayed in Berlin to consolidate his gains, nor planned to direct the new company's first production. Instead he made yet another conciliatory approach to Piscator. If he came to East Berlin, Brecht wrote, he could count on being offered the Volksbühne, and in the meantime would he like to direct a Berliner Ensemble production of *Nederlaget* (*The Defeat*), a play about the Paris commune of 1871 by Nordahl Grieg? Or a play by Lorca or O'Casey?[2]

Berlau had arrived from Copenhagen either late in 1948 or early in 1949, and she accompanied Brecht to Zürich when he went there on 23 February, mainly to renew his papers, leaving Weigel to prepare for the new company in Berlin. Before leaving Berlin he told Piscator he would be back within a few weeks, and told Reyher he would be back in April.

He would in fact stay away till the end of May. Within a few days he was able to inform Weigel that favourable reports on *Mutter Courage* had reached Zürich. 'The new enterprise is engaging real interest, especially as everything here is disintegrating. The bonds that tie Giehse and Steckel are wearing thin, Knuth is in Munich for most of the time. ...' He could bring both Giehse and Steckel to Berlin, though Steckel was holding out for $300 a month, while she was willing to work for $100.[3] Brecht also began to negotiate with Regine Lutz, who had played the dairymaid in the Zürich *Puntila*.

At the beginning of March he moved into a furnished room. He had been proposing *Nederlaget* without re-reading it, and when he did he found it 'astonishingly bad'. Instructing Weigel not to let anyone see a script, he set to work with Berlau on rewriting it. Still angling for Piscator, he wrote another letter, adopting the tone he had once used with Bronnen after sealing a pact for mutual careerist help: 'It would be a good opportunity for you to look around and survey the field. ... We couldn't do better than begin with your production. Besides, there's a heap of projects – one or another of them should be of interest to you. This is the right moment. It shouldn't be left much later. Everything's still fluid now.'[4]

To Berthold Viertel he wrote: 'Much is still fluid, but much is beginning to harden up. In production, places are becoming posts and positions. Rifts are deepening, scepticism is turning into suspicion, prejudices are solidifying, little men are getting big jobs and forming fierce cliques, etc.' He had chosen Gorki's *Vassa Shelesnova* for Viertel, he said, because from the beginning plans for it had been definite, and Giehse wanted to be directed by him. 'You *must* come. It's a matter of life and death for the project.'[5]

To Weigel he wrote: 'After Berlin it's extremely boring here.' But he did not hurry back: she could be trusted to nurse his infant company. She was anchored to East Berlin, anyway, by her role in *Mutter Courage*, while in Zürich he could revert to being a playwright. He worked on *Die Tage der Commune* (*The Days of the Commune*) and on a play for the Salzburg Festival. His plan was to establish moorings for the Berliner Ensemble in the major harbours of the German-speaking theatre. 'Perhaps we can name as associate members Viertel (Burgtheater, Vienna – haven't got his agreement yet), Hirschfeld (Zürich, is agreeable) Otto, Zürich, Neher, Salzburg. Would need someone in Munich and Hamburg.' *Die Tage der Commune* was to be the new company's opening production, while the Salzburg play was intended to secure him an Austrian passport, which would bring him freedom of movement. Writing to Gottfried von Einem, he said:

I now know of an alternative which would be worth more to me than any kind of advance payment, and that would be a refuge, in other words a passport. If this were possible, it should naturally be done without any publicity. And perhaps something like this would be best: Helli is by birth an Austrian (Viennese) and like me she has been stateless since 1933, and there is no German government now in existence. Could she again obtain an Austrian passport? And could I then, simply as her husband, get one?

As a postscript he wrote: 'Already the Swiss are making difficulties again. So again I can't get away from here.'[6] At the same time as setting limits on his commitment to the new society that Soviet communism was forming in Germany, he was concerning himself, as a playwright, with what Karl Marx had hailed as the start of a new age: the Commune, he said, had been a triumph of direct proletarian revolutionary action.[7] To Brecht it was obvious that no new age was dawning in East Germany, but he was unrealistic enough to believe he would be allowed to stage a play about the Commune, and that it could serve some educational purpose. If the political leaders were genuinely concerned for the well-being of the people, surely he could help them to learn, as Lenin had, from the example of the Commune.

Die Tage der Commune was not a counter-play to *Nederlaget* in the same sense that *Baal* had been to *Der Einsame*, but whereas Grieg had blamed the Commune's failure on lack of effective leadership, Brecht admired what had been a spontaneously collective uprising. The Central Committee called on the citizens to elect 'men of the people', and it was as responsible representatives of the collective will that Brecht saw the communards.

He reprises several themes from earlier plays. As in *Galileo*, but more ironically, he shows how it was possible to believe that a new age was dawning. As in *Simone Machard* it is assumed that only the proletariat is patriotic: the bourgeoisie inclines to support the enemy, who will prevent property and wealth from being redistributed: 'Now go and fetch Herr von Bismarck,' says Varlin at a meeting of the National Guard's Central Committee, 'so that he can protect your property from those who made it, the proletariat.' But *Die Tage der Commune* is unlike any of Brecht's previous plays in having no central character: the focus is spread evenly over a group of neighbours in Montmartre – a worker and his mother, a schoolmistress and a seamstress, a baker and his brother, a student priest – with some glimpses of Bismarck and Thiers, and several scenes showing delegates making speeches in the Commune. This time the history of the small fry is narrated more through samples than through representatives. The play is an ensemble play, close in style to those Piscator had chosen for production during the 1920s. The dialogue sometimes lapses into slogans and clichés, but this is compensated by Brecht's commitment in depicting his idea of a golden democratic age, however brief. More successfully than in the prologue to *Der kaukasische Kreidekreis*, he convinces us that rational discussion is leading to enlightened decision. He was probably using his memories of revolutionary Augsburg in 1918 to illuminate his reading of the Commune's *Journal officiel*, Prosper Lissagaray's eyewitness descriptions of events. Brecht also read Marx's pamphlets and Hermann Duncker's collection of documents.

He may also have been influenced by Büchner's *Dantons Tod*, which he was considering for the Berliner Ensemble. But it would have to be souped up: 'Danton really betrayed the revolution because he hobnobbed with the aristocracy, protected it, admired it, let it admire him, generally becomes a star, etc. Is therefore responsible for the Terror which was necessary (necessary against him), a Terror which then swallows up Robespierre too.'[8] Büchner had focused on a hero who refused to act; Brecht was focusing in *Die Tage der Commune* on a group of heroes who refused to act violently. The fair-minded leaders restrain the mob from marching on Versailles to unseat Thiers's government and from using force to take money from the Bank of France. This was another theme Brecht had often treated, but whereas Johanna Dark and Señora Carrar had been converted to violence, the Communards are not, and so they die on the barricades while Thiers and a group of bourgeois citizens watch from a safe distance, standing on a hill overlooking the city and staring through opera glasses.

Piscator was unresponsive to Brecht's overtures, so perhaps Engel could be inveigled into directing. He had been horrified when Brecht had spoken to him about *Nederlaget*, so Weigel was instructed to tell him that Brecht had discovered an old French play, which he was reworking.[9]

To his play for Salzburg Brecht did not devote much of his time in Zürich, but after a meeting on 5 March with Gottfried von Einem, who was there on a visit, Brecht left the next day with Ruth Berlau and his daughter Barbara to see the carnival in Basle, which made a great impression on him, as did Barbara's reaction to it: 'She had a great time, wearing an imperial costume at countless balls. The intolerable ennui, caused by laziness, seems to be on the wane.' But she did not like the idea of moving to Berlin. He asked Berlau to photograph the big papier mâché carnival heads and the masks. He also wrote some dialogue and notes for a new piece to be based partly on an abandoned idea for a play called *Der Pestkaufmann* (*The Plague Merchant*). The new play was to be called *Der Tod von Basel* (*The Basle Death*), but he soon saw that he could make it into a variant of *Everyman* which could be called *Der Salzburger Totentanz* (*The Salzburg Dance of Death*) and might possibly oust Hofmannsthal's *Jedermann* (*Everyman*) from the programme. As Brecht summarized the plot in a letter to von Einem, an emperor would make a contract with Death agreeing about the number of victims in the next war. The emperor and his entourage would be spared if they made a sign to Death, but Death would be too busy to remember the agreement.[10]

At the beginning of April 1949 Kurt Bork received news that the Politburo had decreed: 'A special ensemble will be formed under the direction of Helene Weigel. This ensemble begins its operations on 1 September 1949, and in the season 1949–50 produces three progressive works. The performances all take place in the Deutsches Theater or in the Kammerspiele in Berlin, and stay in the repertoires of these theatres for six months.' The budget of the Ensemble was to be a basic 340,000 marks for non-recurring expenses plus 1,125,500 for running costs.[11] On 18 May, when Bork passed this on to Weigel, he said that as soon as the new theatre had been built for the Volksbühne, the Ensemble would have the Theater am Schiffbauerdamm. Meanwhile the Ensemble would perform three times a week at the Deutsches Theater.

But on 20 April, using the forms von Einem had procured for him, Brecht applied formally for Austrian citizenship, writing to Dr Felix Hurdes, a minister in the Austrian government, and to Josef Rehrl, governor of the Salzburg district. One of the three references Brecht gave was Albert Einstein, Princeton. He claimed that his 'yearning for Austria', was 'in no way attributable to external circumstances'. Being fifty years old, he said, he wanted 'to do intellectual work in a country that offered the appropriate atmosphere for it'. 'Let me emphasize that I consider myself to be only a poet and do not wish to serve any definite political ideology. Nor do I wish to be regarded as the exponent of any such ideology. I repudiate the idea of repatriating myself in Germany.' Manœuvring simultaneously for an East German theatre and Austrian citizenship was in line with his double-dealing at the expense of Paula Banholzer and Marianne Zoff, or, more recently, of Hays and Piscator.

He always felt entitled to suck benefit from rival sources, as when he let Laughton revise Reyher's revisions. Directors and actors of stature – Fritz Kortner (who was in Zürich at the end of April), Peter Lorre and Oskar Homolka, for instance – could not be expected to join a company based in East Berlin, but might be interested in operations divided between Berlin and Salzburg. Brecht was being over-optimistic, but it had always been his habit to ask for a great deal. In America most of his demands had been refused; in East Germany, whatever the government's motives, he was being offered more scope for theatrical activity than he would have been given in the West.

Returning to East Berlin in time for Whit Monday, he found strong inducements for settling there. Weigel was proving herself as efficient in running a theatre as in running a household: while still playing Mutter Courage to packed houses, she had formed a company. Listening from the house they had been given in Weissensee to children's voices, radio music, the mixed sounds of trams, birds and rustling leaves, Brecht could begin to feel at home. The packing cases from Stockholm had arrived with most of his books, and the suitcases from Switzerland were on their way.[12]

In June, when the National Prizes for Literature were awarded, the first was divided between Heinrich Mann and Johannes Becher, while the second was awarded to Brecht, who refused it. 'They should have known I would regard such a classification as insulting.'[13]

He was in hospital for part of June and July with pyelitis, a kidney disease, and at the end of August he left to spend a week in Salzburg, Vienna, Munich and Augsburg. He talked with several officials about his passport, and after discussing his Salzburg play with Dr Hilbert of the Festspielhaus, he went to look at various courtyards where it might be staged. He met Neher in Vienna, and when Berthold Viertel arrived Brecht advised him to become an Austrian citizen, holding out some hope of employment during the winter season. In Munich he met Therese Giehse to discuss how she could come to Berlin, and he tried to engage the actress Maria Wimmer to play in the Gorki. With Jakob Geis he went to see Hans Albers, and at the Kammerspiele Brecht discussed a production of *Courage* in the spring. In the afternoon he went on to Augsburg, where he met his old friend Georg Pfanzelt. 'Augsburg rather ruined, strange, leaves me rather cold.'[14]

Back in Berlin, and confident that Weigel could deal with both the day-to-day administrative problems and with most of the casting, Brecht immersed himself in the artistic problems of preparing the first production. In devoting so many months of work to *Die Tage der Commune*, he had been underestimating the nervousness of the regime about revolutionary plays which might have made it look undemocratic, and this was not the moment for a production: *Die Tage der Commune* was later banned by the Party and not staged until after his death. He opted for *Puntila*, which had no direct bearing on current political issues but drew on folk stories to discredit the old class system. It was a safe play for the opening production, and Brecht made it still safer by writing in a servant who is a Party member. Surkkala's class-consciousness contrasts with Matti's.

Fortunately Neher was available to take charge of the designs. As with *Baal* thirty-one years ago, he would make detailed sketches, showing postures, costumes and groupings at particular moments, but this time, having complete control, Brecht could profit fully from their symbiotic working relationship. Wanting the four women of Kurgela to emerge as the most dignified figures in the play, Brecht hesitated for a long time over their clothes and make-up. How stylized should these be, and how attractive? When he was experimenting with false noses and clumsy boots, Neher, by making some beautiful sketches for the sixth and seventh scenes, found the right point of balance between naïvety and knowingness. He showed that they could play a kind of game with their rich fiancé, humorously challenging him to provide them with a cup of coffee. In his sketches Neher gave the four women garlands made with straw flowers, providing Matti with a broom which was to be used for sweeping the garlands away when the women, piqued at their cool reception, throw them on the ground. Their costumes were realistic in shape, but all four were made out of the same material, attractively deploying delicate colours.[15]

Each of the nine scenes had a title summarizing the action, but instead of projecting the titles on a screen, Brecht and Engel, who was again his co-director, made the cook – carrying kitchen utensils that indicated her various jobs throughout the day – step in front of the curtain to sing part of the Puntila song, accompanied by a guitar and an accordion. This put the story into a perspective based on the kitchen, while implying that the events had passed into the kind of folklore that might be sung about.[16]

Leonard Steckel, who had played Puntila in Zürich, introduced a piece of comic counterpoint during the tirade that comes when his daughter takes away his drink. Angrily buttoning his overcoat he kept getting buttons into the wrong holes. Generally, though, Brecht wanted to avoid 'the kind of gag that endeared the audience to humanity in a generalizing way'. His aim was to 'focus on class-relationships today'.[17] When Matti, for instance, obeying the whim of his drunken master, had to build an imaginary mountain on the billiard table, he did it angrily because Puntila, even in his drunken stupor, had not forgotten to sack Surkkala. As Matti malevolently demolished a grandfather clock and a rifle-stand, it was only with an effort that Puntila could smile.

Brecht also used facial caricature to conduct sympathy away from the socially superior characters. In Zürich Steckel had made Puntila paunchy but not unattractive. Using little make-up, he had come over as a fairly likeable man, though prone to fits of bad temper when sober. Being comic, they seemed venial. But in East Berlin Puntila was bald, and with, the aid of make-up, more repulsive. In the drunken scenes his charm appeared more reptilian. Through make-up or masks or a combination of the two, the attaché, the provost, his wife, the lawyer and the judge were all made to look more or less grotesque, as they moved 'in a majestic and inane way', while their social inferiors seemed likeable and moved in a normal way. Brecht's explanation for this was: 'The theatre is simply taking a position and catching up with certain features of reality – namely the deforming of physiognomy which afflicts parasites.'[18]

He was about half way through his rehearsals for the play when the Soviet zone of Germany was made into the German Democratic Republic. This happened on 12 October 1949, just after the Federal German Republic had been created in September, and Adenauer's government had been elected. There was no question of free elections in the East, but, not to be outdone, the Soviet authorities created a new state. This reduced Brecht's chances of using East Berlin as a base for operations that could extend to Salzburg, Zürich, Munich, Hamburg and Vienna. But he still wanted to be an Austrian citizen. Though he could easily have acquired a GDR passport, it would have been useless in the countries which did not 'recognize' the GDR. Trying to expedite the issue of his Austrian passport, he wrote to von Einem on the same day: 'I have no kind of official function or engagement in Berlin, and receive no salary at all. . . . Now, as before, it is my intention to regard Salzburg as my permanent place of residence.'[19] One advantage of having Weigel as head of the new company was that he could make statements like this one, but it was obvious by now that he would not be able to spend much time in Salzburg.

Weigel had, in any event, done extremely well for him and for the company, arranging for a rehearsal stage and a block of offices to be built. For actors and for members of the technical and administrative staff she had secured special privileges, which in this period of shortages would provide incentives for joining the company – travel facilities, flats, furniture and special meals.[20]

When Wilhelm Pieck took office on 2 November 1949 as the first President of the GDR, Brecht saluted him with the poem – 'An meine Landsleute' ('To my Compatriots') – enclosing a letter to express 'delight at your inauguration'.[21] The effective head of the new state was Walter Ulbricht, who had been the main organizer of Soviet communism in Germany since returning to Berlin from Russia in April 1945. Like Pieck, he had supported Stalin's alliance with Hitler: 'Socialism will be defended on the Rhine', he had said.

The production of *Puntila* opened on 12 November to a great deal of laughter and applause. The Russian authorities had reserved all the boxes level with the dress circle for members of the new government, and Brecht noticed that they joined in the laughter and applause. Some West Berlin reviewers gave signs of discomfort, but the press in the East was generally favourable. Brecht had been careful not to introduce more alienation effects than he could expect the audience to stomach. On the next day, after reading the newspapers, he was still asking himself: 'When will there be the genuine, radical epic theatre?'[22] But he was more interested in approximating to it himself than in having his plays performed at other theatres. He refused to give them a free hand with their productions of his plays: *Mutter Courage* was not to be staged at Wuppertal unless Ruth Berlau was invited to direct it. Nor was he more tolerant in East Germany: *Puntila* could not be done in Dresden unless it was directed by Heinz Kuckhahn.[23] Berlau's photographs of his productions were collected in *Modellbücher*, which could be sent out with the scripts. His contention was that the plays would misfire unless they were produced in an epic style, with the right grouping and blocking.[24]

Since Piscator would not work for him, the first outsider to direct a Berliner Ensemble production – under Brecht's supervision, no doubt – was Berthold Viertel, who went into rehearsal with Gorki's *Vassa Shelesnova*. The set was by Teo Otto and the cast was headed by Therese Giehse. Whereas Brecht and Engel had had thirteen preliminary rehearsals and forty-eight on the stage, Viertel had to make do with four preliminary rehearsals and twenty-nine on the stage, with some extra rehearsals for music and dancing. The production was to open on 23 December.

In December, still frustrated over *Die Tage der Commune*, Brecht hastily adapted Jakob Lenz's 1774 play *Der Hofmeister* (*The Private Tutor*). Lenz, 150 years before Brecht, had canvassed an anti-Aristotelian aesthetic in his *Anmerkungen übers Theater* (*Notes on the Theatre*, 1774), championing the episodic Shakespearian style. He also anticipated Hegel (and Brecht) in arguing that a specific attitude to the world must be implicit in any dramaturgy. 'Advantages of a Private Education' was his ironic subtitle for *Der Hofmeister*, which had, after a single performance, disappeared from the German repertoire. Lenz centres the play's thirty scenes on Läuffer, a drifting intellectual who lets himself be exploited by an unscrupulous major and his wife. Though they despise him, they employ him to tutor their daughter, who falls in love with him. Lenz had been employed as a tutor in 1770.

Läuffer's self-castration is both a desperate gesture of self-condemnation and a desperate bid for self-control. A tutor on an East Prussian estate had actually castrated himself after falling in love with an aristocratic girl. Ironically, Lenz shows that it does not prevent a country girl from marrying him: at least there will be no children to feed. Lenz wanted to expose the social forces that conditioned behaviour, but he did not believe that people could learn from experience.

Different though Brecht's outlook was, he had good reasons for staging the play. 'So far as I know, it's the earliest – and a very sharp – picture of the German misery [*deutsche Misere*]. Probably its only equivalent is [Schiller's] *Die Räuber*, in which man, to remain human, must become a robber. Here, to function in society, the male must emasculate himself.' Lenz's Läuffer, like Büchner's Woyzeck, is victimized by the dehumanizing pressures of a ruthless society, but Brecht's Läuffer becomes, like his Galileo, a figure at the crossroads, a man whose mistakes mortgage the future. Brecht had used the phrase 'neue deutsche Misere' on first seeing East Berlin: 'Noticeable all over this big city, where everything is constantly in motion, however small and provisional this may have become, is the new German misery, that nothing has been settled, though almost everything has been smashed.'[25] Just as he had once wanted to uncover the roots of the economic depression, he was bent on diagnosing the sources of the misery.

About seven months before he started on the adaptation, a re-reading of *Wilhelm Meister* had revived Brecht's animosity towards the Augsburg schoolteachers who had made Goethe's novel seem boring. 'The most sexless of all creatures', the literature teachers had 'with their long beards blocked our view of sensuality's only resting-place in German literature'.[26] Brecht now read the tutor's self-castration in Lenz's play as if it were a Book of Genesis explaining how the tradition of sexlessness had originated, and why Germany's pedagogues and intellectuals had proved impotent in the face of Nazism.

At the same time Lenz's play was refreshingly poetic when 'the theatres of the progressive countries are being mobilized for the cultivation of qualities desiderated by the state'. Looking at other productions in East Berlin, he had to gauge the risk of protesting against the endemic dullness of socialist realism: 'Recently we have often tended to disregard the poetic (artistic) side of works of art and to content ourselves with works that have no kind of poetic attraction, as we do with performances that have no kind of artistic attraction.' Theatre should not try to cut itself off from either Shakespeare or the German classics. Lenz pointed back to Shakespeare, and a new production of *Der Hofmeister* might serve as a preliminary study towards finding a new Shakespearian style.[27]

In adapting the play Brecht worked in collaboration with Berlau, Neher, Egon Monk and Benno Besson, a young Swiss director he had brought from Munich. They tightened Lenz's construction and sharpened the social focus. Tutors were treated like servants, but Läuffer tries to coax the major into providing him with a horse. Many of the points are expanded in discussions between students about love and philosophy, while certain objects, such as the knife used for the castration, become prominent.

Again Neher's influence extended far beyond the sets and costumes, as Brecht acknowledged by giving him a credit as co-director. Crucial postures and groupings were developed out of his sketches – Läuffer's obsequious obeisance, for instance, when he meets the major and his brother the privy councillor, who ignore him. This is what Brecht meant by *Gestus*: attitude crystallized into gesture or physical action. Lenz had made the privy councillor sympathetic, but Brecht, as usual, conducted sympathy away from every character in a superior social position.

Having cast Hans Gaugler as Läuffer, Brecht found his movement was excellent, but, until he was told to rehearse in Swiss dialect, his speech was expressionless. In the Swiss theatre he had been disciplined into speaking German with no sign of a Swiss accent. Stage German was 'only a feeble shorthand without overtones or undertones. People speak this language as if it were foreign.'

With forty-four preliminary rehearsals and forty on the stage, mostly lasting about five hours each, there was time for experiment. Wanting to check all temperamental self-indulgence and, in each situation, to subordinate psychological to social considerations, Brecht translated action into narrative by transposing dialogue into *oratio obliquà*.[28] But he was always at pains to avoid analytical arguments. It was calculated that throughout the rehearsals of *Der Hofmeister* (over 200 hours) there were not more than fifteen minutes of discussion between him and the actors. 'Don't tell me', he would say. 'Show me.'[29]

Neher was also designing the production of *Die Mutter* which Berlau was directing in Leipzig, using the detailed photographic record she had made from Brecht's production. 'How hard it is to reproduce humour and gracefulness. The model is still working like a straitjacket, which cramps the publicity department in its dealings with the public.' Brecht went to Leipzig, briefly, in the middle of January. He was trying to attract Peter Lorre to Berlin. Lorre was living in Partenkirchen in the Bavarian Alps, and Brecht wrote a letter to him in verse, reminiscent of the coaxing letters he had written in the 1920s to charm Bronnen or Neher.

> You are being summoned
> To a country that was wrecked,
> And we have nothing to offer you
> Beyond our need for you.

But for himself Brecht was simultaneously doing his best to leave escape routes open. To von Einem in Salzburg he wrote: 'Believe me, I'm as interested as ever, or still more. You must help me. So much depends on it for the artistic activity (and collaboration) since, without papers, so many countries, including West Germany, could become unreachable.'[30] Finally, despite a protest from the administration of the Salzburg district, Austrian citizenship was granted to Brecht and Weigel on 12 April 1950, three days before *Der Hofmeister* opened. Some reviewers called the play 'negative', but Brecht staunchly defended it: it satirized 'the period when the German bourgeoisie was erecting its educational system. . . . And the production could certainly be counted as a contribution to the great educational reforms which are currently being achieved.'[31]

Nor did his Austrian citizenship prevent him from enjoying the May Day demonstrations. He sat in the sun on a grandstand in the Lustgarten, watching the boys of the communist youth movement, the People's Policemen marching in military formation, the long procession of lorries displaying machines, trucks, clothes, with flags and placards. An American helicopter was cruising above the May Day parade on the other side of the Brandenburger Tor. On the East German side, during the speech by the Chinese delegate, a flight of doves was released. The Berliner

Ensemble had its own lorry, with the Courage wagon on display, and Barbara Brecht sitting on it waving a red flag. Weigel, who was also in the procession, was acclaimed by onlookers. Women held their children up to see her: 'Mother Courage!'[32]

Again at Whitsun, Brecht failed or refused to be reminded of the Hitler Jugend by the way that the Freie Deutsche Jugend was being organized. Recruits to the movement were given bright blue shirts with an emblematic sun rising on the left sleeve. According to an ex-member, Joel Agee, the Freie Deutsche Jugend recruited the most ambitious 'climbers into the bureaucracy. . . . Most of them developed unattractive symptoms of adulthood: humourless, in some cases fanatical purposiveness; philistine smugness masked (especially to themselves) as pious devotion to the principles of Marxism-Leninism.' What he disliked most of all was their relentless efforts 'to exemplify an idea of "forward-looking" youthfulness – pretending to be excited by the newest phony agitprop youth song, smacking their hands above their heads in rhythmic unison to celebrate the tedium inflicted by some politician at a mass rally'. Much that Brecht had denounced in *Furcht und Elend* was already repeating itself – children were being encouraged to spy on their parents – but he turned a blind eye to these sinister repetitions. To him the national rally of the youth movement seemed to be 'transforming the whole city completely. Like an abstemious old businesswoman who gets drunk, she becomes gay and unpredictable. In the evening the squares explode into a kind of Naples. They sit on the grass and watch films in the open air.'[33]

In August he took a summer holiday – his first since going into exile. He drove with Berlau while Weigel travelled separately with Barbara, but they all went to Ahrenshoop, a holiday resort on the Ostsee. 'There are some old fishermen's cottages, which look good, even painted dark blue, or dilapidated, or even renovated for the tourist trade.' The place had been fashionable during the Nazi period, 'and not much has happened since. Not much could happen. ... But in the summer, as territory belonging to Der Kulturbund, the district has a lot of visitors – mostly people who belong rather directly to the new government.'[34]

In the spring of 1947, deciding to settle in Switzerland, he had invited Reyher to come with him, and a year later he had mentioned the possibility of having a house near Salzburg with a room in it for Reyher. Since moving back to East Berlin he and Weigel had encouraged Reyher to believe they were interested in producing one of his plays and in helping him to get others staged at other Berlin theatres. Brecht also indicated that if he came to Berlin he could collaborate on a new project, perhaps a film. He arrived at the end of August to stay with them, having delayed the visit to finish a play.[35] They were still in Ahrenshoop when he arrived, and when they returned (Brecht on 28 August, Weigel three days later) Brecht had little time to spare for him.

In February Max Frisch had noticed a change in Brecht: he seemed more detached, more aloof. Reyher had the same feeling, and he was troubled that the Brechts' standard of living was so high – on a par with that of the bureaucratic elite – while the bulk of the population was suffering so much hardship. In 1948 the government had founded the Handelsorganisation (Trading Organization) or HO – a chain of shops offering food off the ration at much higher prices. A pound of butter, for instance, cost 35 marks – when an unskilled labourer could earn only 5 marks a day. But while Reyher was staying with them, Weigel was buying antique furniture in West Berlin. Reyher's verdict was: 'These are tough babies who do not hesitate to trouble a republic for a safety pin.'

Brecht stayed in Berlin for less than a week, leaving on September 2 to direct *Mutter Courage* at the Munich Kammerspiele with Therese Giehse in the part. Berlau was travelling with him, so there was no room in the car, he said, but Reyher was welcome to join them in Munich. Back in New York he told one friend that Brecht was now 'top dog' in East Berlin, and another that 'Brecht has too many people around him, too many women'.[36] The change must have seemed phenomenal. In Hollywood Brecht had not quite been a failure, but had never been a success; in Berlin he was a celebrity, a national culture-hero.

Reyher would have liked to be Brecht's friend, but Brecht devoted all his social energy to collaboration and sexual relationships. His relationship with Weigel was a partnership, and he was not generous either in the amount of time he spent with Stefan and Barbara, or in the amount of interest he took in Frank and Hanne. When Brecht learned of Frank's death in 1943, he made no reference to the event in his diary.

The friendships with Bronnen and Eisler had been based mainly on mutual professional need, and if Brecht was consistently friendly towards Laughton, it was because he needed a star to lead him to success. Even the symbiotic working relationship with Neher – closer than any working relationship with any other designer, composer, director or actor – was not enough to keep their youthful friendship alive. After the war they had little contact except over productions. With actors, including Busch, Brecht went on using the formal 'Sie' form (while Weigel used the 'Du' form) and even the ones who were invited to stay at his house could never draw him into talking about his childhood. According to Berlau, Müllereisert and Tombroch were the only male friends admitted to conversational intimacy.[37] Until the end of his life he went on enjoying the companionship of girls, but Berlau had become more of a long-distance personal assistant than a mistress, while his gregariousness was satisfied mainly by surrounding himself, as he always had, with disciples. Only now there was no chance that any of them would become close friends. He was isolated while surrounded by people.

Directing *Mutter Courage* in Munich he could refer to the *Modellbuch*. He did not follow it slavishly, but he consulted it for information about groupings and distances. Without asking the Munich actors to copy postures or gestures, he used the photographs to evaluate the new solutions he was being offered to problems that had already been solved. He kept the sequence of positions he had used for the wagon, but everything else was variable, and Giehse's reactions to emotional pressures were quite different from Weigel's. After throwing the cook's possessions out of the wagon, for instance, both Weigel and Giehse said: 'The stupid man', with great affection for him. Weigel stood still, her arms hanging loosely, looking at his things; Giehse spread her hands almost ceremonially above the bundle of possessions as if at a burial service. For Kattrin's sake she was burying her love for the man.

At the beginning of October Brecht, together with Jakob Geis, Emil Burri and Ruth Berlau, again went to visit Peter Lorre in Partenkirchen.[38] Brecht wanted to work with Geis and Burri on a film adaptation of Gogol's *Overcoat* – Brecht had sketched out an idea for it in Hollywood and now he offered Lorre the leading part, also inviting him to play Hamlet at the Berliner Ensemble. Lorre was forty-six. During his seven years of working with the Ensemble, Brecht would help several actors, including Weigel, to build international reputations, but the only star he would ever succeed in attracting into the Ensemble would be Curt Bois, the comedy actor and cabaret performer who returned to Berlin in 1950 after playing character parts in Hollywood and on the New York stage. Brecht had not yet abandoned the hope of a base in Salzburg, and while he was in Munich he had meetings with Gottfried von Einem to discuss the *Salzburger Totentanz*, and with Oskar Homolka to offer him the role of Azdak if *Der kaukasische Kreidekreis* were to be produced in Salzburg. But neither plan matured.

On 8 October the Munich production of *Mutter Courage* opened triumphantly. 'Giehse succeeds astonishingly well in reorganizing the performance she gave with so much success in Zürich and Vienna.' But he may have felt (retrospectively, at least) that her performance was too tragic. It was after it that he made Courage end the play with a new line: 'I must get back into business', and a note in *Theaterarbeit* explains: 'Experience shows that for many actresses it is easier to play this final scene as simply tragic.' The playwright did not want 'to remove the tragic elements but to add a warning: that Courage has learnt *nothing*'.[39]

Back in Berlin, he started work on directing *Die Mutter* with Weigel – now nearly nineteen years older than when she had created the part, and closer to the character's age. The decor was by Neher again, and the music by Eisler. They had twenty-two preliminary rehearsals and forty on the stage.

In Berliner Ensemble rehearsals neither Brecht nor any of the other directors referred to his theoretical works, and probably few of the actors read them. But one phrase which often recurred was: 'It should be demonstrated that. ...' A play was an argument. Instead of impersonating individuals in a particular set of circumstances, the actors were required to state a case about a social situation and to make the audience take sides. Weigel, in spite of their disagreement about emotionality in the theatre, could find her way to a most expressive physical realization of his intentions, whether they were spelt out in the script or not. Her Pelagea was deeply touching. The gentleness in her gait and manner had developed from the idea of giving her a drooping left shoulder. 'Someone who grows like that is not very pushing.' In the first scene, by handling the pot of lard lovingly, she was making a statement that was partly about a mother's concern with feeding her son, but mainly about the reverential attitude towards food of those who live close to starvation. She was also helping to prepare for the moment when the pot would be smashed during the Tsarist militia's vandalizing search for evidence, and it was characteristic of her acting, as it was of Brecht's direction, that objects relevant to eating, drinking, working or money should be handled in such a way as to make what Brecht called a historical statement. Sometimes an hour of rehearsal time was invested in exploring such questions as how Galileo would handle a telescope. How would Grusche pick up a baby? Or a bottle? How would Eilif drink in the presence of his captain? So far as possible, the whole story of the play should be told through actions, so that an audience would be able to understand without hearing. Brecht held what he called a 'marking' rehearsal after the final dress rehearsal. The actors had to go through the whole play speaking the words rapidly and perfunctorily, but keeping rhythms, pauses, and movements intact.[40]

In his 1932 production of *Die Mutter* Brecht had been concerned mainly with agitprop; in his 1950 production he retained such agitprop techniques as direct address to the audience while trying to give a more accurate picture of life in pre-revolutionary Russia. In all acting there is a mixture of particularization (deriving from situation and individuality of character and actor) and generalization (based mainly on ideas about type, class and society). What the Berliner Ensemble developed more scrupulously and systematically than any previous company was a system for imbuing the generalization with political significance. Weigel had a passionate, quasi-religious faith in communism and in Brecht; he had a passionate, quasi-religious faith in collaborative work and in the weighting of significant detail. Together with the ability to recognize acting talent and to inspire devotion, this combination of passions at the core of the company's work would have given it tremendous advantages, even if it had not been so generously funded by a new-born state, which, eager to establish its identity, set a high value on cultural propaganda. The funding made it possible to scrap sets or even whole productions after great quantities of time and money had been spent on them. A production of Pirandello's *Liola*, for instance, would later be dropped after the adaptation had been completed and the rehearsals started: the social content was found to be too slight.[41]

Brecht had always wanted to build a counter-world, an alternative reality. In his early poems, gangs of tough males find freedom and danger by venturing into unknown places or pitting their strength against natural forces. In many of his plays an individual or a group goes against the law or sets up new laws. Now, for the first time, he had a chance to build a miniature society of his own, and to anyone who saw the company in the early 1950s it was striking that the actors looked so unlike actors. Brecht has possibly done more than anyone else to dislodge conventional good looks from the theatre. He was unambivalently hostile to the 'criteria of beauty and character' used in what he took to be a tradition which had passed from the German court theatres to Hollywood. 'The paintings of the great artists exemplify very different criteria of beauty and character.'[42] This note in *Theaterarbeit* is followed by full-page reproductions of two portraits by Holbein and Dürer. At the same time, fuelled, as always, by the kind of perversity that impelled him to inhibit spontaneous reactions out of suspicion that they might only be stock responses, he hit out hard against theatrical clichés in casting and in characterization. Why should all statesmen be stately, all princes princely?[43]

The alienation effect – one of his strongest weapons against romanticism and rhetoric – had always depended on introducing a dialectic of dissonance and discrepancies: captions in a realistic set, songs punctuating realistic action, Chaplinesque comedy in a play about Nazism. In casting, too, contrasts and contradictions could be valuable. In the Berliner Ensemble version of Synge's *Playboy*, Christy Mahon was played by the same short, plump, unglamorous actor, Heinz Schubert, who had taken over as the second son in *Mutter Courage*. Satirically, and not unrealistically, this stressed the way in which a man's sex appeal can emanate from his reputation as a killer. Later, in Moscow, protesting against the pretty girls and good-looking boys recruited for the drama school attached to the Art Theatre, Brecht said: 'In the Berliner Ensemble we're more interested in the young people who find it hard to get a job because they deviate from the norm.'[44]

He believed that while some individuals were habitually gentler or noisier than others, everyone had a heterogeneous mixture of temperamental traits – especially good actors. Directors should help them to develop by casting them in roles that would bring hidden qualities to the fore. And with his love of ambivalence and ambiguity, Brecht wanted to focus contradictory tendencies in behaviour: 'The actor should cultivate all temperamental elements, for his characters come to life only through their own contradictoriness.'[45] What he had learnt from Hegel and Marx had been confirmed by theatrical experience.

He also encouraged actors to emphasize disjunction and discontinuity, playing one thing after another, rather than one thing out of another. On the other hand Brecht was like Beckett in his distaste for what actors call 'taking the stage', i.e. wandering all over it. 'To indulge the desire for variation is to devalue all stage movements: the audience no longer looks for a specific meaning in each one.' In the first sequence of *Mutter Courage* he made the two soldiers stay close together in one spot until the wagon rolled on;[46] their stillness was all the more theatrical for being theatrically unconventional, and it helped them to show how cold they were by stamping and slapping themselves: had they been striding about, each additional movement would have counted for less.

He also turned his perversity in on himself, challenging his own inclinations, and proceeding in the rehearsal room by applying dialectical theory to theatrical practice. The basic trick was to diagnose or to provoke disagreements, conflicts or counter-tendencies, and then accommodate them within the structure. The lifelong habit of working colla-boratively had taught Brecht that anything could be improved through alterations based on other people's suggestions. As a writer he had always benefited from having disciples and collaborators; as a director he had assistants, and not only they but actors, technicians and cleaners were encouraged to interrupt. Manfred Wekwerth, later an assistant director, had barely introduced himself to Weigel when she sent him into a rehearsal. Stopping to shake hands, Brecht said: 'Watch this and write down everything you disagree with.'[47]

He was expert at developing an internal dialectic into a dramatic conflict. He could internalize dialogue with other people so that their contribution was wholly integrated, and then, with or without more help from them, look at his work as critically as if he had had nothing to do with it. Like his scripts, his productions were constantly subject to revision, and if photographs bulked large in the Berliner Ensemble's work, it was not so much in order to preserve poses, gestures and groupings as to improve them. Like Galileo, looking at the pendulum as if he did not understand why it was swinging, Brecht looked at the photographs as if he could not understand how he had arrived at that action or that false nose. Pushing his spectacles up onto his forehead he would stare, frowning, at the irrefutable evidence: 'Do you understand that?'[48] An inveterate iconoclast, he never felt happier or more self-confident or more entitled to indulge his solipsism than when piloting a group of people in forming first an antithesis to his own thesis, and then a synthesis that could be fleshed solidly in actors' performances. Moves, business and lines would all be revised ruthlessly.

His awareness of his tendency towards solipsism put him on his guard against narcissism and inwardness, both in himself and in others: it was partly to counter self-indulgence of this kind that he encouraged friends and the most casual acquaintances to sit in on rehearsals, and partly to involve the actors in interaction with an audience from the earliest possible moment. Most directors insist on the privacy of rehearsals; Brecht insisted on giving the actor the kind of stimulation that he most responded to himself – feedback, resistance, counter-proposals that could be absorbed. If truth is concrete, acting must tell enough truth to withstand scrutiny from the first moment.

In many ways an intensely private man, shy and sexy, Brecht distrusted the behaviour that privacy inculcated. Even his durable but in so many ways unsatisfactory relationship with Weigel gained from being put into a company context: in 1950, on the morning of her fiftieth birthday, the whole company met outside her window to serenade her. The company formed a surrogate family which benefited from her zeal and efficiency as a housewife. The actors' canteen and shopping facilities were matters of personal concern to her, and when she was off-stage, during performances, she was available to chat with actors, technicians and staff. But she was excluded from all directorial discussions, and Brecht became abusive if she persisted in trying to intervene when he was in conference with his assistants. As at home, he rigidly separated her concerns from his: sometimes she had to write, pleading for an hour of his time to discuss theatre business.[49]

Every morning at nine o'clock, when he stopped writing, he conferred with his assistants until the rehearsal started at ten. Outside rehearsals and conferences he preferred them to submit ideas to him in writing. He told them that the quality of their suggestions interested him more than their practical value, and that speech was always action. 'A thought is as good as its visual counterpart.'[50] It was a directors' theatre. Actors were free to make suggestions during rehearsals, but the answer, after a whispered consultation between directors and assistants, was an unexplained yes or no. Once a show had opened, actors were liable to find notes on their dressing-room tables with new lines or instructions about changes in a performance, or they might be issued by the make-up man with a new wig at the demand of the directors.[51] (As in most German theatres, actors did not do their own make-up.) On the other hand, between directors, assistant directors and designers, there was more collaboration than was usual in the 1950s.

The part of the servant girl in *Die Mutter*, which Margarete Steffin had played in 1932, was now played by Käthe Reichel, a girl who had dangerous affinities with her predecessor in the role. She was not consumptive, but had suffered severely from bronchitis; she wrote stories and poems. One day during rehearsal, Brecht drew her aside to ask: 'Are you getting anything out of this?' Soon they were lovers, and he was giving her 'more skilful legs'.[52]

In the theatre, one of the directors or assistant directors sat in on each performance, and they went on making changes not only to the production but to the script. When *Die Mutter* opened at the Deutsches Theater on 10 January 1951, the emphasis in Scene 8 was on lack of unity between workers and peasants. The butcher cooked only for the strike-breakers and one of the strikers, Jegor Luschin, went away without accepting any of the revolutionary newspapers Pelagea Vlassova brought for them from Rostov. During the run, the text was changed: he accepted as many as she would give him, but she kept some back to distribute at the butcher's shop, in the bakery and in the dairy, where the workers were not on strike.[53] Dramatically the first version was more forceful, but the second was more 'positive', and the Berliner Ensemble was coming under criticism for being 'negative'.

Having previously called Hans Albers the only folk actor, Brecht now applied the phrase to the 51-year-old Ernst Busch, whom he had known since 1927, and who was now, as Semion Lapkin, giving 'the first great characterization on the German stage of a class-conscious proletarian'. But he incorporated 'something of Mark Antony's attitude into the strike scene, and something of Mephistopheles's into the scene with his school-teacher brother'. No middle-class actor would have been capable of playing the scenes with the revolutionaries so knowingly: 'a brief glance, understanding and contemptuous, when Pavel says he did not tell his mother about his joining the movement. And when Pavel obstinately remains seated after the Commissar's shouted order to stand, a quiet and kindly "Get up".'[54]

Brecht's desire that even ugliness should be portrayed beautifully was not so easy to realize in *Die Mutter* as in *Der Hofmeister*. Grey had to be the predominant colour, and the costumes had to denote poverty, but both Neher's colour sense and his *modus operandi* were helpful. First he sketched episodes – perhaps six figures grouped around a remonstrating proletarian woman. Unlike almost any other director, then or now, Brecht would often start rehearsals without knowing what the set was going to look like. Ideas would evolve through rehearsing the actors with the designer present as co-director for virtually all the visual elements, including postures and gestures: as in the early work on *Baal*, Neher's sketches stimulated Brecht, who used them to stimulate the actors.[55]

Neher took tremendous care over the details that mattered. His choice of a low chair and a high table, for instance, would affect the movements of the people eating. Like Brecht, he was meticulously realistic over props relevant to eating, working and money – purses, cutlery, weapons, for instance – but he stylized other details to make generalizing statements about social conditions. A doorway might be unrealistically low, a yard impossibly cramped. And by eliminating or streamlining details which had little narrative value, he made the important ones stand out. The distinctive visual style of Berliner Ensemble productions had roots in the personal relationship between Brecht and Neher. The interaction between them during their formative years had sharpened the perceptions and profoundly affected the taste of both men.

In Hollywood, when Paul Dessau was working on the *Mutter Courage* music, Brecht had read him parts of *Das Verhör des Lukullus*. He obviously wanted it set as an opera, but Dessau did not volunteer, and eventually Brecht asked him to approach Stravinsky, who was living in Los Angeles. Stravinsky said he was too busy. In Berlin, during preparations for *Mutter Courage*, Brecht one day saw Dessau in Die Möwe and shouted that the director who was with him wanted to do *Lukullus* as a radio opera on Nordwestdeutsche Rundfunk. 'Dessau, you can get a contract for an opera.'[1] Dessau accepted the commission, which led to more conversations with Brecht about staging it in an opera-house. Some material had to be discarded, some new material added, but Brecht always enjoyed restructuring.

The communist authorities may already have been putting pressure on him to write in a more 'positive' way; it was with the opera that the conflict came into the open. The Korean war had started in June 1950, when communist forces from the north invaded the non-communist south. United Nations troops were sent in to defend the south, and China joined in to help the north, but to the communists the south Koreans were the aggressors. It was no time for an outright condemnation of war, and Dessau's score was open to charges of 'formalism': it involved nine kinds of percussion instruments, a piano tricked out with drawing-pins, and no violins. The vocal writing ranged between atonality and melody verging on folk-song. The People's Education Ministry may have tried to coerce Dessau into making changes, for in January 1951, when the chorus was already in rehearsal, he was in favour of postponing the production till the autumn. Brecht maintained that 'the material is important right now, while the American threats are so hysterical'.[2]

Some Party officials wanted to ban the production, but with Hermann Scherchen as conductor considerable expenses had been incurred, considerable publicity attracted. By way of compromise, three performances were authorized, and tickets channelled to safe bureaucrats and members of youth organizations. But until the Berlin Wall was built in 1961, West

Berliners had easy access to East Berlin, and tickets for this opera were in such demand that a black market formed. In the sharply divided first-night audience the Westerners were all the more demonstratively enthusiastic for sensing that their enthusiasm was not shared. The other two performances were cancelled. The official newspaper *Neues Deutschland*, condemning Brecht for 'relapsing into doubt and weakness', attacked his message, 'especially when, by the style of production, it is being put forward as an authoritative comment on the current situation'.[3]

Writing to Walter Ulbricht before the première, which was scheduled for 17 March, he pretended that the libretto had been written in 1937, and defended it as 'a condemnation of predatory wars', relevant to the 'shameless enlistment of the old generals for the purpose of a new aggressive war in West Germany'. But on the same day as the performance the central committee of the Party had engaged itself to 'fight against formalism in art and literature for a progressive German culture'. Shortly after the performance Brecht and Dessau were summoned to meet Pieck and Grotewohl, who had both seen the performance. Afterwards Brecht said that if Grotewohl had not been Minister President, he would have wanted to employ him as chief dramaturg at the Ensemble. Writing to Anton Ackermann, Secretary of State and a leading functionary in the Ministry of Culture, Brecht promised to make the text less pacifistic. 'Our artists are prepared to change and with complete devotion to support you in the battle for a great new art.' A fortnight later he wrote to tell Pieck he had added three arias 'positive in content'.[4] The demands of Pieck and Grotewohl can best be gauged from changes made before the opera was brought back into the repertoire, seven months later, under the new title *Die Verurteilung des Lukullus* (*The Condemnation of Lucullus*). The Roman general is contrasted with the king on the frieze, who is lauded for conducting only defensive wars. It is also revealed that Lucullus was sent to Asia not in the name of Rome's masons, bakers, weavers and peasants, but as a tool of the tax-farmers, silversmiths, slave-dealers and bankers. At the beginning of April Brecht sent copies of the changes to Pieck, Grotewohl, Anton Ackermann, the editor-in-chief of *Neues Deutschland*, the head of the cultural department in the central committee, and the head of the literature office. But Brecht would not attend the première of the new version at the Opera House.

Even with Weigel to take charge of the company he had been overworking and, since the end of December, had been feeling unwell. On 17

January 1951 he had gone back into St Hedwig's hospital for an investigation, and stayed there several days. The next production after *Die-Mutter* was to be an adaptation of two full-length plays by Hauptmann: *Der Biberpelz* (*The Fur Coat*) and *Roter Hahn* (*Red Rooster*), pruning enough away to make them into a double bill, while converting *Der Biberpelz* from tragedy into a tragi-comedy. This was at the suggestion of Therese Giehse, who played the thievish washerwoman. The rewriting was done by a dramaturgical collective, headed by Brecht, the other members being Monk, Peter Palitsch, the actor Ernst Kahler and three other young disciples. Brecht said that the working-class movement, which Hauptmann had virtually ignored, must come into the picture, so a new character, a socialist, was introduced, and Dr Fleischer, Hauptmann's spokesman for liberalism, was made to look slightly absurd, while Giehse's character was contrasted with a more exemplary member of her class. At the same time both plays became more episodic. Keen to have Berthold Viertel direct another production, Brecht offered him a choice of the double bill, Hauptmann's *Die Ratten* (*The Rats*), a Lorca play and an Ostrovsky.[5] When even this failed to tempt him, Brecht decided to go ahead with the double bill; Weigel and Hurwicz both agreed with him that the 24-year-old Egon Monk could direct. It was not his fault that when the double bill opened in March, it had to close after fourteen performances: the controllers of Hauptmann's literary estate objected to the adaptation.

Brecht's next experiment in adaptation was with Shakespeare's *Coriolanus*, and here too he cut back on the tragedy. Coriolanus's pride was readjusted to centre on the belief that he was irreplaceable.[6] But unlike Brecht's variation on *Measure for Measure*, *Coriolan* stays respectfully close to its original, though Brecht still believed it was only an unhappy land that needed a hero. In this play it is the function of the populace and the tribunes to transform society so that such individuals as Coriolanus become redundant. Shakespeare's mob was already more Elizabethan than Roman, but Brecht gives it a class-consciousness that pulls it into the twentieth century. Solidarity and organization are within its reach. Shakespeare obviously shared at least some of his hero's contempt for the mob, which is not only gullible and volatile but cowardly, eager to 'steal away' when war is in the offing; Brecht's mob is more courageous.

One of the play's attractions for him was that it provided a blatantly aristocratic role in which, perversely, he wanted to cast the proletarian

Ernst Busch;[7] at the same time Shakespeare's text pushed him back into exploring the contentious differentiation between just and unjust. There had been irony - as well as flattery - in the remark about wanting Grotewohl as a dramaturg, but there was ambivalence under the irony, and in principle he was as willing to accept guidance from politicians as from stage technicians. In *Coriolan* he wanted the audience to side with the tribunes when they advise the people to fight for Rome. This is a just war which may help to spread democracy. And it is the rise of democracy that has robbed Coriolan of grounds for believing himself to be indispensable. Unlike Shakespeare's Volumnia, Brecht's dissuades her son from attacking Rome by arguing that history is moving against him. In comparison with the many, the one no longer matters.

The daily flow of refugees from East to West was still high, and when Paul Bildt and Werner Hinz decided to join it, Brecht had to find a new cook and a new chaplain.[8] Rather than just recast the two parts, he decided to overhaul the whole production. Movements, groupings, stage business had all become familiar; it was time to look at them critically. Scheduling himself forty-six days of rehearsal, he started work on 26 June, with Ernst Busch as the cook, Erwin Geschonneck as the chaplain and Regine Lutz as Yvette.

Political considerations were prominent in the discussions Brecht held with his assistants about making changes. As the only representative of 'the class that was making money out of the war', the captain had been played as loutish and surly. But now, believing West Germany to be swarming with warmongers who were all the more dangerous for looking *soigné* and sophisticated, Brecht made the captain aristocratically elegant. With paternal condescension, he now rewarded Eilif for his bravery by letting the boy drink from his tankard and smoke his pipe.[9]

During the cook's first scene with Courage, Busch introduced an old Dutch song in praise of pipe-smoking, 'Nit Betteres als de Piep', pulling her down on his knee as he sang, and reaching for her breast. She slipped the capon into his groping hand, but at the end of the song he whispered the figure 'thirty' lyrically into her ear. As the chaplain, Geshonneck introduced several telling moments. In the sixth scene, after losing at draughts, he sidled up to the blackboard by the bar and wiped off one of the chalk lines showing how much he owed for drinks. Both in selecting from ideas proffered by the actors and in interpolating details of his own, Brecht would work for internal variety and contradiction in each sequence. He no more liked a scene to sit still than he liked sitting still himself while writing or thinking. 'The stiffness or heaviness which usually predominates in Germany during sad sequences derives from the way that in tragedy – for no reason – the body is forgotten and so muscular cramp seems to set in. What nonsense.'[10] Though the political thinking behind the productions was simplistic, the blending of contradictory impulses made the resultant performances subtler than any others to be seen in Berlin. While the working-class audience stayed away, intellectuals from East and West flocked to his productions.

By the beginning of July 1951 Brecht had completed the text for a political cantata, *Der Herrnburger Bericht* (*The Herrnburg Report*), written for the third summer festival organized by the Freie Deutsche Jugend. The previous year a group of young communists from West Germany, crossing the border at Herrnburg, had their names taken by West German police. The cantata comprised ten poems based on the story as told by three girls who were present at the round-up. The poems were written in agitprop doggerel with lines like:

> Adenauer, Adenauer show us your hand
> For thirty silver pieces you'll sell our land.

Illustrated with two clips of film, the poems, each introduced by a short commentary, had such titles as 'The policeman asks the young people how they got on in the German Democratic Republic' and 'The Police warn the Free German Youth that they must not sing while marching through Lübeck'. The music required was very different from what Dessau had written for the opera.

But in the summer, when the secret of Brecht's Austrian citizenship was revealed, it caused such a scandal that Gottfried von Einem resigned from the Festival directorate. Brecht would later sympathize: 'Do write to me at once if you need any kind of testimony or letters from me. Should I send you a few pages of the *Salzburger Totentanz*, which is now fully planned? I don't understand how you, as an artist, can be blamed for having helped another artist – at that time I had no papers at all.'[11]

He was now back in the habit of taking his summer holiday in the same place. On 10 July he went back to Ahrenshoop, but he could not relax. He had to prepare for the Ensemble's second season. He was still hoping that it would be feasible to stage *Die Tage der Commune*, but he needed to make a more definite expression of solidarity with the regime than he had during his first season. In 1948 the government had introduced into the factories a system of 'technically substantiated' norms, and in October the Stakhanovite system was introduced: a coalminer who 'fulfilled his norm with 380 per cent' was awarded the National Prize, first class. Soon there were other 'heroes of labour', and factory shifts were organized into 'brigades', so that productivity could be stepped up by means of competition and cash incentives. The 'hero of labour' who attracted Brecht's attention was a stove-fitter, Hans Garbe, who in 1949 had rebuilt an anular brick kiln at a factory without any loss of production. Taking a production assistant with him to make notes during their three sessions with the man, Brecht encouraged him to talk about his life. The intention was to make him the subject of a new didactic play in verse written in 'large rough chunks'. 'This work-man sets himself up by producing. Subject for investigation: what changes for him and in him when instead of being the object of history he becomes its subject – with the proviso that this is not a merely personal matter, for it does concern the class.'[12]

Apart from this play and *Die Tage der Commune*, the new season was to include *Galileo* with Steckel in the part, and Brecht had tried until at least April 1951 to persuade him. His second choice for the role (in May 1951) had been Fritz Kortner. His third (June–July 1951) was Oskar Homolka. He also wanted to stage *Coriolan* with Ernst Busch in the part.[13] But the season was harder to plan than the first had been. Few scripts of topical plays had been submitted, and 'their authors – not all of them young – have not yet escaped from the blueprint of the natur-alistic drama, while the political shaping of the material is mostly blunt'.[14] Reviving one of his old ideas, Brecht set his dramaturgical department to work on a play presenting several trials, but the project came to nothing.

On 16 August he returned to Berlin. The cantata was to have been given daily performances throughout the youth festival, but it had been cancelled by the Party. Brecht arranged a private performance, inviting Pieck and other members of the government. Brecht could not under-stand why they objected to his carefully calculated condemnation of the West German authorities for blocking freedom of movement between the two halves of Germany. He could not know – and they could not tell him – that they were themselves working out ideas for blocking freedom of movement in order to reduce the flow of refugees. Early in 1952 they were to announce that the State Security Ministry was taking control of frontier police and customs officials and, after a newspaper campaign to foment fears of invasion from the West, they inaugurated 'emergency arrangements' at the frontier. Without special permits there would be no entry to a strip of territory three miles wide and stretching the whole length of the border with West Germany. All 'unreliable inhabitants' were to be evacuated from this belt, while in Berlin fences and barbed wire entanglements were erected, brick walls were built, the number of open roads into the free sectors was reduced from 227 to 47, and West Berliners were suddenly forbidden entry into the Soviet zone.[15] Though the wall was not built until 1961, Brecht's *Herrnburger Bericht* coincided with draconian measures to enforce what he was attacking the West for wanting.

Nevertheless the government was sufficiently pleased to award him the National Prize, first class, in October. But besides staying away from the première of the revised *Verurteilung des Lukullus* on 12 October, he had been negotiating for a West German première of the original version, which would have its first truly public performance at Frankfurt in January 1952.

In November and December 1951 he was still working with his collaborators on *Coriolan*, but it would not be staged until after his death. Once again ideological expediency was the determining factor: with trouble in other communist countries over the 'cult of personality', it was the wrong moment for a production pivoting on a leader's belief that he was irreplaceable. The next production by the Berliner Ensemble was of Kleist's 1808 verse comedy *Der zerbrochene Krug* (*The Broken Jug*) with Therese Giehse as director and leading actress. This provoked acrimonious arguments between her and Brecht, who said she was putting too much beauty into the dialogue of 'that Prussian Junker'. Unable to watch Brecht shouting at Giehse, one actress rushed out of the rehearsal room, but Giehse stood her ground. In her opinion he was jealous of Kleist's talent.[16] The production opened on 23 January 1952 with Geschonneck as the village judge.

Puntila continued in the repertoire with Curt Bois in the part. At the same time another actor was given a chance to direct: Ernst Busch was entrusted with a turgid Soviet play about the October Revolution by Nikolai Fyodorovich Pogodin, *Kremlyovskie Kuranti* (*Kremlin Chimes*). Dating from 1940, the play had Lenin and Stalin among its characters. The Berlin première was on 28 March 1952, followed, four weeks later, by Egon Monk's production of Goethe's *Urfaust*, which was rehearsed after Monk and some young actors had taken the initiative, preparing a few scenes from the play and then performing them for Brecht.

In February, wanting to organize a country retreat for himself, Brecht went to look at houses in Buckow, an hour's drive to the east of Berlin.

'Find on a beautiful property on Lake Scharmützel under huge old trees a small house, old, not lacking in nobility, with another, roomier house next to it, equally simple, about 50 paces away. Something of this kind would be within one's means, including maintenance. In the larger house people could be invited.' He arranged a workroom in the small house, where he had a view of the lake and the hills. The notice on the door of his workroom was different in style from the notice that had been nailed to the door of his attic room in his father's Augsburg house:

Considering that I can work for myself during only a few weeks in the year, considering that when working I must pay attention to my health, considering that during the writing of plays or the reading of thrillers, any human voice in the house or from the house constitutes a welcome excuse for breaking off, I have decided to make myself an isolated area and for this I use the floor with my workroom in it and the small space in front of the house bounded by the wash-house and the summerhouse. I do not wish this rule to be taken as binding. Principles are kept alive by violating them.

But he counted on getting a lot of work done. He considered Buckow to be 'peaceful and boring enough for work'.[17]

In the last week of February he went with Weigel to Warsaw, where the Ensemble had been invited to give guest performances. He noticed how the Nazis had systematically blown up beautiful buildings in the old part of the city, and he looked uncritically at new buildings 'more habitable than the old ones'. Jack Lindsay, who was also staying at the Hotel Bristol, used to breakfast with the Brechts and show them around. He was told that the Poles wanted some cultural contacts with East Germany, and Brecht was the only living German writer who would not have been unpopular. He questioned Lindsay about what was going on among English writers and what effect they were having on the Cold War. He was unwilling to believe any political situation could be impermeable to the influence of writers.[18]

During March, when both the Pogodin play and *Urfaust* were in rehearsal, Brecht went only occasionally to the Pogodin rehearsals and almost every day to the *Urfaust*, where some of the actors felt he was giving Käthe Reichel preferential treatment. In Denmark he had summed up *Faust* as the story of a scholar who would have been unable, without help from the Devil, to seduce a German girl. Now he wanted to show how love was 'totally deformed by the pact with the Devil'. Caspar Neher, who was to design the costumes, suggested the period of *Werther*, but Brecht was in favour of a medieval setting, with costumes in the style of Dürer, 'so that the Devil, the magic and all the nonsense of the old marionette play could emerge naïvely, while what is "modern" in Goethe, the Gretchen tragedy and the Auerbach students, seem distanced'. As in *Galileo*, Brecht wanted to bring out a contrast between two cultures, two ages. 'So Earth-spirit as squawling, crouching beast à la Bosch, and the Devil as folk-devil with horns and cloven hoof.' He enjoyed the rehearsals, laughing a great deal.[19] A guest performance was given in Potsdam before the decision was taken to introduce another classic into the Ensemble's repertoire.

After the Berlin première on 23 April, East German reactions were unfavourable. Brecht was accused of encouraging irreverence towards Germany's cultural heritage. The productions of Lenz, Kleist and Goethe were 'fatalistic and pessimistic pictures of static conditions; they had only one hero: "German misery". ... We have never previously seen such mockery of the German folk-song on our stage.'[20]

The relationship with Weigel was worse than ever, and it seemed likely they would divorce. They were living separately, and in the summer she went to Ahrenshoop, while Brecht spent most of the time at Buckow, where he was relaxed enough to read Horace, though this time he was irritated by the poet's self-satisfaction. But it was pleasant to be in the country: 'In front of my door is a corner formed by a demolished wash-house and another wall. There are grass and pine trees, wild rose-trees on the wall. I have a thin garden table and I have picked up the right bench for it, with iron legs and the rest of it painted white, very elegant.'[21]

Through serving on the governing committee for a drama competition, Brecht discovered *Katzgraben*, a play by Erwin Strittmatter about collective farming. It had been rejected by the jury selecting plays for the World Youth Festival in Berlin. Brecht still believed that 'the most infallible sign that something is not art, or that someone does not understand art is boredom'.[22] Even when directed by Brecht, *Katzgraben* was boring, but he understood the art of survival: if the play about the stove-fitter was not going to materialize, he must make an alternative gesture of support for the regime.

Katzgraben presented an optimistic view of East Germany's agriculture when it was not easy to be optimistic. Collectivization was introduced at the second SED conference in July 1952, when Ulbricht proclaimed even higher priority for heavy industry, more nationalization, new measures against the middle class and the Church, together with a series of administrative reforms to 'bring government closer to the people'. During his six-hour speech he also announced that three model producer-cooperatives had been formed in Germany by progressive farmers who had been invited to visit collective farms in the Soviet Union. Collectivization had begun there in 1929, when the state nationalized the property of at least a hundred million peasants. In Germany, Ulbricht promised, collectivization would be entirely voluntary. But owners of large farms soon found themselves blamed for shortages and persecuted by 'quota enforcement officers'. Many were accused of anti-state offences, many were imprisoned. They were not allowed to sell their property and, as capitalists, they were not free to join co-operatives. In the first four months of 1952, 22,852 farmers arrived in West Berlin refugee camps, while the 'new' farmers who joined collectives found themselves harnessed to extortionate delivery quotas. Short of both livestock and machinery, they were committed to working with inefficient or inexperienced colleagues. Though Brecht visited a village in Lausitz with Strittmatter and members of the Ensemble, looking at relevant farms, they both turned their backs on the prevalent social reality – just as Brecht ignored the suffering when he wrote about the Soviet collectivization, and he wrote about it only obliquely in his *Me-ti: Buch der Wendungen* (*Me-ti: The Book of Changes*) which purported to be a translation from the Chinese. It consists of texts accumulated between 1934 and the last years of his life. In them he would write cryptically about Marxism–Leninism and developments in the Soviet Union, using Chinese-sounding names. Ni-en is Stalin, To-tsi Trotsky.[23] Needing a designer for *Katzgraben*, he studied sketches submitted by designers in other theatres. Karl von Appen's were astonishing for their precision and detail. Even the characters' faces were carefully painted. The assistant directors were scornful, but Brecht was reminded of Velazquez's portraits.

Back in Berlin he worked with his assistants on an adaptation of a radio play by Anna Seghers, *Der Prozess der Jeanne d'Arc zu Rouen, 1431* (*The Trial of Jeanne d'Arc in Rouen, 1431*). Directed by Benno Besson, it went into rehearsal simultaneously with a new production of *Die Gewehre der Frau Carrar*, directed by Egon Monk, who had proved his competence. Käthe Reichel played Joan of Arc and Weigel again played Señora Carrar. Before the two productions opened in the second half of November Brecht went to Frankfurt, in West Germany, where Harry Buckwitz was directing *Der gute Mensch*, with designs by Teo Otto. Brecht spent three days there, returning in time for the première on 16

November of *Die Gewehre der Frau Carrar*, followed a week later by the Jeanne d'Arc play. November was also the month of the Berliner Ensemble's first foreign tour. The productions of *Die Mutter* and *Der zerbrochene Krug* were successfully taken to Krakow, Lodz and Warsaw.

In December a conversation with the critic Ernst Schumacher, who was writing about Brecht's plays from 1918 to 1933, prompted him to look back once again at his early work. *Im Dickicht* he now described as dealing 'with the impossibility of conflict, which is here optimistically regarded as sport. (In capitalism what does not come out, i.e. what gets overlooked.)' It was in line, he now claimed, with *Galileo*, which dealt with the impossibility of unlimited research, and with *Kreidekreis*, which dealt with the harm done by maternal possessiveness – in which capitalism has not been hidden.[24]

At the end of the year he was still working on *Coriolan*, though not without misgivings about the scenes he had altered. He thought of including translations of them in the published text. Eventually, he maintained, when the people had developed a stronger feeling for history and a greater self-confidence, it would be possible to perform the play as Shakespeare wrote it.[25]

33 / Whitewashing

The first half of 1953 was a depressing and dangerous period for Brecht and the Ensemble. 'Our performances in Berlin no longer have much resonance,' he wrote in his diary. 'In the newspapers reviews come out months after the first night, and there's nothing in them except a bit of wretched sociological analysis. The audience is the petty bourgeois audience of the Volksbühne; workers make up scarcely 7 per cent. So our efforts are totally pointless unless the style of acting is later taken up, i.e. if its didactic value is one day realized.'[1]

On 5 March, the day after he wrote this, Stalin died. In the German Democratic Republic schools closed and gloomy people conversed in subdued voices. Day after day the newspapers published black-bordered photographs of Stalin, while even humorous magazines were filled with encomiastic tributes to 'the greatest son of the working class'. Radio stations sustained a flow of mournful music, punctuated with grave reminders of 'the world's deep sorrow and gratitude'. Johannes Becher wrote a fulsome verse panegyric, but Brecht, contributing to a symposium in the periodical *Sinn und Form*, made only a stonewallingly ambiguous comment: 'When they heard that Stalin was dead, it must have stopped the heartbeats of the oppressed in five continents – those who have already been liberated, and those who fight for world peace. He was the incarnation of their hopes. But the intellectual and material weapons he created are still there, and there is the teaching to be recreated.'[2] This was neither too critical of Stalin to be safe nor so laudatory that it might have to be repudiated later.

He was equally cautious when a Stanislavsky Conference was held on 17–19 April in East Berlin. The Party's line, strongly canvassed in *Neues Deutschland*, was that acting and production should follow the Soviet example. If socialist realism was to triumph in the German theatre 'formalism' and 'cosmopolitanism' must be firmly resisted. And was it not true that in certain theatres 'formalism and its twin brother schematism look out from every hole and corner, starting from the selection of plays, right down to the adaptation, the basic concept for the staging, the staging itself, the design and the acting?' Aware of being at the centre of the target area, Brecht and Weigel attended the conference and declared that they were not totally opposed to Stanislavsky's theories. What Brecht said was almost pleonastic: that actors and directors should take from Stanislavsky what helped them and did not hinder them. Weigel claimed that there were common factors between Brecht's approach and Stanislavsky's, but *Neues Deutschland* hit back at them: in so far as the Ensemble tried to put Brecht's theories into practice, it was 'undeniably in opposition to everything that Stanislavsky's name stands for'.[3] If it had not been for the thaw which ensued on Stalin's death, the history of the Berliner Ensemble might have been short and obscure.

Tensions in East Berlin were extremely high. In March 1953 there were 58,605 refugees to West Berlin, compared with 11,528 the previous December. The administrative reforms were causing enormous confusion, as drastic changes were made both to district boundaries and to the responsibilities of officials. Food shortages were worsening as more farms were collectivized, while the distribution of supplies became more inefficient. A panic government measure of April withdrew ration cards from house owners, private employers, businessmen and independent tradesmen, leaving them no legal means of buying food, except at the expensive HO shops designed for the privileged, while another governmental decree raised the prices there.

Brecht tried to immerse himself in rehearsals of *Katzgraben*, which was to open in May, but enervation surfaced in bursts of autocratic behaviour. At five o'clock one evening, reminded that the stage had to be prepared for *Mutter Courage*, he asked for ten more minutes of rehearsal. Thirty minutes later, when the chief technician told him what the time was, he shouted: 'I'll go on rehearsing till it's all been put right.' At the next interruption there was a row. The evening performance was cancelled, the audience was turned away and the rehearsal went on.[4]

After Stalin's death the future of the satellite countries was uncertain. To protect himself, Brecht proposed at the beginning of May that 'brigades' should be formed to help the artistic and ideological development of his theatre. He would start a brigade which would organize discussions about play rehearsals and related problems, artistic and social.[5] Soon it began to look as though liberalization was coming. One early sympton was an offer from the state to grant independence to the Protestant Church. A more positive sign followed on 11 June, when the Politburo of the SED issued the text of a resolution acknowledging 'a series of errors on the part of the SED and the government over the rationing system and the emergency measures for collecting farm produce. . . . The Politburo proposes a shift of emphasis from heavy industry to the needs of workers, farmers, the intelligentsia and all members of the middle class.' Ration cards were restored to those who had forfeited them, and farmers who had left the country were offered incentives to return, while all other refugees were offered exoneration and either full restitution of property which had been confiscated, or compensation.

In the next few days 'economic criminals' were released from prisons, and the slogan 'Construction of socialism' was dropped. But the concessions were nearly all in favour of the farmers and the middle classes. The workers, overstrained by arduous norms, had been disgruntled even before the resolution of 14 May imposed a general 10 per cent rise in norms. On 5 June building workers in East Berlin found their wages had been reduced without notice, and on 12 June, when they were informed that wages would be calculated according to new norms with retrospective effect from 1 June, there were shouts for a mass meeting. Encouraged by the signs of thaw, the editor of *Neues Deutschland* published a surprisingly objective account of the dispute, and on 15 June building workers, marching to protest outside the government building, were joined by other workers until over 2,000 people were marching. They were refused admission. After a mass meeting in the street, with shouted demands for lower norms and a free election, a procession formed to march down Friedrichstrasse. A police loudspeaker van was sent out to disperse it with the promise that the norms would be reconsidered, but soon the demonstrators had their own loudspeaker, and they were using it to demand the resignation of the government, the release of political prisoners and a general strike. As the procession was passing the Police Praesidium on the way back to Alexanderplatz, it was announced over the loudspeaker that two hostages had been seized by the police, but when the crowd threatened to storm the building, the two men were released.

Brecht was in Buckow on 15 June, but with his sensitivity to political change and his need to protect his position, he would have kept himself informed of developments in Berlin. Knowing that the new theatre for the Volksbühne was ready, which meant that a decision would soon have to be taken about the future of the Theater am Schiffbauerdamm, he decided to remind the government that it needed his support. Since the beginning of the year his relationship with the Party had been uneasy, and rumours of friction had leaked into West German newspapers. June 15 was the day on which he wrote to Grotewohl suggesting that an excellent way of quelling 'these nonsensical rumours of discord' would be to announce that the theatre was to be taken over by the Berliner Ensemble.[6]

On 17 June, holding mass meetings all over East Berlin, workers voted to support the builders who had planned to march from the Strausberger Platz. People were assembling there in tens of thousands, but Red Army troop carriers and armoured cars were stationed in side streets, waiting for orders, while Soviet armoured divisions on training manœuvres outside Berlin had already begun to close in. When the marching strikers arrived at the government building, police swarmed out to cordon off the entrance, while police lorries drove around a corner, and the men who jumped off formed a line across the street. As the marchers, pushed from behind, surged forward, the police attacked with truncheons before the Russian armoured vehicles arrived. Driving slowly, they divided the crowd.

Trams and trains came to a halt as transport workers joined the strike. At the sports stadium Ulbricht's portrait was burned. The word went around that the Lustgarten was to be the assembly point, and by noon about 50,000 people were massing there. Speeches were made from a tribune until half a dozen Red Army tanks drove into the crowd, which stampeded to escape, while some strikers threw stones at the tanks. Part of the crowd ran down Unter den Linden, pursued by a tank. Three boys tore down the red flag from the top of the Brandenburger Tor. In the Leipziger Strasse the Russians machine-gunned strikers when stones were thrown at the police. At the Police Praesidium, when sentries were disarmed, the police counter-attacked with fire-hoses. Police trucks were overturned and set on fire. Methodically the Russians cleared the Lustgarten, the Alexanderplatz, Unter den Linden. Sixteen people had been killed, and the rising had been crushed. Eager to blame agitators from the West, the communists announced that Willi Gottling, a West Berliner, had been sentenced and shot. Gottling had been taking a short cut through East Berlin to collect the dole.

Brecht had come back to Berlin on the 16th. On the morning of the 17th there should have been a rehearsal for a new production of *Don Juan* in an adaptation by Brecht, Besson and Elisabeth Hauptmann, but it was broken off. In theory Brecht must decide whether to side with the Party leaders or to express solidarity with East German workers, whose rising was no less spontaneous than the one he had depicted in his Commune play. Even if he had not just written to Grotewohl about the theatre, he might have felt he could not afford the risk of losing it. What he said, according to Wekwerth, was that he considered the question of norms to be 'a subject for discussion, not grounds for strike action'. Before the day was over he dictated letters to Ulbricht, Grotewohl and Vladimir Semionov, political adviser in the Soviet central commission. To Ulbricht he wrote: 'History will pay its respect to the revolutionary impatience of the Socialist Unity Party of Germany. The great discussion with the masses about the tempo of socialist construction will cause the socialist achievements to be sifted and secured. It is necessary for me at this moment to express to you my allegiance to the Socialist Unity Party of Germany.' The letter also offered practical help: if Ulbricht wanted to speak on the radio, the programme could begin and end with songs and recitations by Ernst Busch and other performers.[7]

But on 21 June Brecht was furious to find that of these three cautiously worded sentences to Ulbricht, only the last was quoted in *Neues Deutschland*. Gody Suter wrote: 'That was the only time I have seen him helpless, almost small, as he pulled out of his pocket the original – obviously well thumbed and produced many times – of that letter.' Events during the rising had been confused, motives muddled; even if he had spent the day in the streets, trying to observe objectively, he could not have told the whole truth about what had happened, though he could have tried to tell nothing but the truth. He did not try. In a fuller letter, which *Neues Deutschland* published on 23 June, he said the demonstration had evidenced

the dissatisfaction of an appreciable section of Berlin's workers with a series of economic measures that had miscarried. Organized fascist elements tried to abuse this dissatisfaction for their bloody purpose. For several hours Berlin was standing on the verge of a third world war. It is only thanks to the swift and accurate intervention of Soviet troops that these attempts were frustrated. It was obvious that the intervention of the Soviet troops was in no way directed against the workers' demonstrations. It was perfectly evident that it was directed exclusively against the attempt to start a new holocaust. . . . I now hope that the agitators have been isolated and their network of contacts destroyed.[8]

Even in a letter to Peter Suhrkamp Brecht knowingly or unknowingly muddled facts with surmises based on unreliable reports: 'All kinds of *déclassé* young people', he said, had 'poured in columns through the Brandenburger Tor, over the Potsdamer Platz and the Warschauer Brücke.' No doubt a number of West Berliners did come over to watch what was going on, and some of them may have shouted encouragement to the crowd, but Brecht had no evidence for assuming that 'a fascistic and war-mongering rabble' was attacking the Party. As in his letter to *Neues Deutschland*, he tried to justify the action of the Soviet army by asserting that 'for several hours, until the intervention of the occupying forces, Berlin stood on the verge of a third world war'.⁹ Like the churchmen and courtiers he pilloried in *Galileo* for refusing to look at the evidence, he was rushing to express blind support for the dogmas of orthodoxy.

But if the apriorism was at variance with what he had preached, it was not inconsistent with his previous practice. Of all his plays, the one which feeds most directly on contemporary events, *Furcht und Elend*, depended entirely on second-hand information. He absorbed news avidly from other people, from newspapers and radio, but seldom from observation. In one of Brecht's stories about Herr Keuner, the question is put: 'What do you do when you are fond of someone?' ' "I make a sketch of him," said Herr K, "and take care that he looks like it." "That it looks like him?" "No," said Herr K, "that he looks like it." ' Brecht had reached the point where his perceptions were inseparable from his prejudices, and his thinking was conditioned by clichés. In October he said that the 'historic achievements' of the SED had been threatened on 17 June by 'fascistic and war-mongering riff-raff'.¹⁰

He spent most of the summer in Buckow, where he wrote *Turandot oder der Kongress der Weisswäscher* (*Turandot or the Congress of Whitewashers*). The whitewashers are Western intellectuals who whitewash capitalism; one of the impulses behind the play may have sprouted from a grain of unease at the need to whitewash actions committed in the name of communism. In so far as he was still capable of sincerity, Brecht was sincere in believing more genuine freedom was to be had in the Soviet-dominated countries than in the West. He argued that in capitalist countries people had to live within limits determined by their jobs: a 'cook was merely a cook, not a whole human being'. He cannot have believed that the gunners in the Soviet tanks had aimed away from the workers. On the premiss that the means could justify the end, he took lies to be justifiable. What is harder to assess is the extent to which he was telling them cynically, wanting the Party leaders to reward him with a theatre, or committedly, wanting to counteract the damage done to the communist cause by the new bout of Soviet brutality. More urgent still was his fear that the Russian bullets might have punctured the loyalty of his most stalwart collaborators. Already Viertel, Neher and Engel had drifted westwards, and after the rising had been crushed Therese Giehse never wanted to act again.¹¹

The difference between good lying and bad lying is one of the main themes in *Turandot*. The perverted princess is sensually titillated by skilful whitewashing, but clumsy lying costs a suitor his head. Brecht had planned a play about *Turandot* in the 1930s, when he had 'Carola Neher in mind for the part', and now he was writing it for Regine Lutz. The chances that he would ever write his 'Tui' novel had receded almost to vanishing point, but before coming back to Berlin he had thought of combining the Turandot material with the Tui material he had collected for his projected satire on intellectuals – Walter Benjamin had noted in 1934 that Brecht might set part of the novel in China.

The new play picks up several old themes. The conflict in *Im Dickicht der Städte* starts with Shlink's insulting attempt to buy an opinion from Garga; the hallmark of the Tuis is that they live by selling the produce of their brains. 'In our day their brains feed them better when they hatch out something that harms a great many people.'[12] The play is savagely satirical, and perhaps the savagery was partly directed against the Tui who was now in control of Brecht.

One question he was asking himself was whether intellectuals and artists were necessarily parasites, sycophantic and venal. Was he, as a servant of the regime, any different from the court Tui who flatters the emperor? Instead of equating bourgeois businessmen with the criminal, he now wants to equate criminal and intellectual. If the ruling class in a capitalist economy could count on its intelligentsia to whitewash the crimes committed in raising prices by withholding supplies from a hungry people, what were the intellectuals doing in a communist country? The question is implicit when the emperor's brother, who is keeping cotton off the market, asks him: 'What do you have your 200,000 whitewashers for?' Some of the satire is unsubtle: the highwayman Gogher Gogh is studying to qualify as a Tui, and Nu Shan tells the princess that his only reason for becoming a highwayman was to make himself into a Tui. It is during a sequence in the school for Tuis that the play touches most directly on the issue that had provoked the building workers' strike. The teacher, Nu Shan, is guiding his pupil, Shi Meh, by operating a pulley which raises a breadbasket in front of the pupil's eyes whenever he is in error, lowering it when he is not. The pupil is delivering a practice speech on the question: 'Why is Kai Ho in the wrong?' (Kai Ho is a Marx-like redeemer who never appears on stage.)

Kai Ho speaks of liberty. *The basket moves.* But in reality he wants to enslave the ferrymen, cottagers and weavers. *The basket sinks.* It is said that the ferrymen, cottagers and weavers do not earn enough – *the basket rises* – for their families – for them to live in luxury and over-abundance with their families

– *the basket sinks* – and that they have to work too hard – *the basket rises again* – for they want to spend their lives in idleness – *the basket stays still* – which is indeed natural. *The basket moves.* The dissatisfaction of many people – *the basket rises* – of a few people – *the basket stays still* – is exploited by Kai Ho, who is therefore an exploiter. *The basket sinks rapidly*

Brecht was too practised in the art of ambiguity to be unaware that this could be interpreted as referring to the Berlin rising, and he knew that satire directed against one side might rebound on the other. He was not so much taking advantage of this as expressing his lifelong contempt for intellectuals, which was in line with his boyhood sense of superiority to teachers. To survive indefinitely in a communist state, an intellectual needs to be an opportunist. He had proved his superiority to other opportunists when he wrote so guardedly about the death of Stalin, but possibly he would not have exempted himself wholly from the charges he was laying against the Tuis, and there is more specific self-accusation in some of the poems he wrote in Buckow. One was about a nightmare:

> Last night in a dream I saw fingers pointing at me
> As a leper. They were work-worn and
> They were broken.

Another poem was called 'Die Lösung', which means either 'The Solution' or 'The Dissolution'. It started with a reference to the leaflets distributed in the Stalinallee after the uprising, stating that the people

> Had forfeited the government's confidence
> And could win it back only
> By working twice as hard. Wouldn't it
> Be simpler if the government
> Dissolved the people and
> Elected another?

After going for over five months without, apparently, writing in his diary, he made an entry on 20 August which contradicted his letter to *Neues Deutschland*: 'The 17 June has alienated the whole of existence. In all their directionlessness and wretched helplessness, the demonstrations of the working class still show that here is the rising class. It is not the petty bourgeois who take action but the workers.'[13]

But after so many years of writing in the interstices between good lying and bad lying, he could no longer take refuge in the confessional mode, as he had when writing his diary during the triangular relationship with Marianne Zoff and Recht. 'Back in Buckow alone with a cold, the

Weissensee house half empty and unheatable.' Lonely, Brecht offered a glass of red wine to a plumber working in the house:

An apprentice he sacked for stealing and stupidity is now in the People's Police. Has applied for training as an officer. It's said in the town that Nazis condemned to ten years' imprisonment for crimes 'against human rights' are being recruited into the People's Police. Under Hitler the bureaucracy was also overblown, but then there was more money around. The Russians were trying to foist their Asiatic culture on to Europe.... What we needed was free elections. I said: 'Then the Nazis will be elected'.

Fundamentally Brecht was still afraid of the German people. The demonstrations of 17 June had reminded him of Nazi demonstrations in the 1930s, while most of the faces he saw every day were faces that had watched the resistible rise of Adolf Hitler. Even members of the Ensemble looked like potential enemies: 'The country is still sinister. Recently, after driving to Buckow with young people from the script department, I sat in the pavilion during the evening, while they were working or chatting in their room. It suddenly struck me that ten years ago all three of them, whatever they had read of what I'd written, would immediately have handed me over to the Gestapo if they'd got hold of me.'[14] If fascism could be kept at bay only by restraint, then restraint was admissible, and free elections were not. Brecht would not have wanted to calculate how many of the charges he had laid against the Third Reich could equally well be laid against the GDR.

Writing about elections in February 1954 he argued that bourgeois societies kept the voter in ignorance about his situation, so that his freedom was illusory. He disregarded the question of why so many citizens were leaving the Democratic Republic; in April 1953 nearly 60,000 had gone in one month.[15] Since 1951 there had been discussions about using West German forces in the NATO army, and Adenauer had been pressing for rearmament. Theoretically there was no East German army, only armed troops of People's Policemen housed in barracks, and a paramilitary youth organization which was euphemistically called 'The Society for Sport and Technology'. Nevertheless Adenauer, in Brecht's view, was the aggressor, and his counter-measure was the revival of *Die Gewehre der Frau Carrar*, which was premièred in the middle of November 1952.

During the first half of October he was rehearsing changes in *Katzgraben*, which had opened in May. At the same time he was planning to move into a house not far from the theatre, in Chausseestrasse. It had a view over the cemetery where Hegel was buried. One of the scene-painters was moving out of the house, and it would be available from the beginning of August. It had been built in the 1930s and it contained a huge room with big windows – an ideal workroom for Brecht, who took the top floor, leaving the first for Weigel. The kitchen was on the ground floor. There was a lavatory half-way up the stairs, and a garage underneath.[16] They had separate doorbells, one marked B.B., one H.W.B. Brecht's rooms were austerely furnished, with few objects on display that did not originate from China or Japan. In the library a portrait of Confucius was hung underneath a scroll of a poem by Mao Tse-tung. A picture of a Kabuki actor stood on the bookcase opposite, with three Noh masks hanging on the wall above it. In the bedroom was the picture he called The Doubter, a scroll of a Chinese philosopher pondering.

Later in the month Brecht left for Vienna to direct the last two weeks of rehearsals for *Die Mutter* at the new Theater an der Scala with Weigel and Busch in their old parts, but with most of the company new to the play. The earlier rehearsals had been taken by the 24-year-old Manfred Wekwerth, who had worked as his assistant director on *Katzgraben*.

With Eisler, who was there, Brecht discussed the play about the stove-fitter Garbe. They were planning to collaborate on it in March and April, writing it in the style of *Die Massnahme*, and introducing a complete act about the rising of 17 June. This proves that Brecht was intending to adopt a public attitude acceptable to the Party. He ate a cassata at the Hotel Sacher, but he stayed at a pension in the Karlsplatz. He went to see the Brueghels in the Kunsthistorisches Museum, and he appreciated the Viennese cuisine, though 'like every art it cannot survive without constant praise'.[17]

In November rehearsals started for *Der kaukasische Kreidekreis*, which, like *Puntila*, could not have received the production it needed from any other company. Brecht was directing, with Wekwerth as his assistant and von Appen as designer. Over ten months were to elapse between the first rehearsal and the first night, but in Brecht's view this was not enough. 'Characters like Azdak and Grusche cannot be created by directing actors. It would take five years at the BE to give the extraordinary Angelika Hurwicz the right presuppositions. And this Azdak is the product of Busch's whole life, including his childhood in proletarian Hamburg, his struggles in the Weimar Republic and in the Spanish Civil War, and his bitter experiences after 1945.'[18]

Despite the leaflets distributed in the Stalinallee, a degree of liberalization was to be expected, and Brecht was concerned about the rigid cultural policy of the Staatliche Kunstkommission (State Commission of the Arts). Less than a fortnight after 17 June the German Academy of Arts, which had Brecht as one of its most active members, published a protocol demanding greater independence for publishers and artistic directors of theatres. The state should not 'interfere in questions of artistic production and style. Criticism should be left to the public.' On 11 and 15 July 1953 Brecht also published two poems in the *Berliner Zeitung*, attacking the commission. One of them makes the point:

> The Office for Literature licenses only one book
> For each idea in the newspapers ...
> So that
> For the works of many a master
> No paper is available.

Writing for *Neues Deutschland* in August 1953, he was even more outspoken, attacking the commission's 'poverty of argument', its 'inartistic administrative measures' and ' "vulgar-Marxist" language'. Brecht had powerful supporters, including Wolfgang Harich, a convert to communism who had been appointed, at the age of twenty-five, as Professor of Marxist Philosophy at the Humboldt University. The commission collapsed under the attack; it was replaced at the beginning of 1954 by a new Ministry of Culture, with the friendly Johannes Becher as Minister. Brecht had won a major public battle, while privately he triumphed in dispossessing Harich of his pretty wife, Isot Kilian, an actress playing small parts for the Ensemble. 'Divorce her now,' was Brecht's advice. 'You can marry her again in about two years' time.'[19]

Knowing that she was likely to be his last love, he found it gratifying that she so strongly resembled his first. Both easily became emotional; both surprised him with the depth of their feelings. 'These women weep when they're scolded, whether rightly or wrongly – simply because they're being scolded. They have a sensuality which no one needs to arouse and is of little help to anyone. They try to please everyone, but don't like everyone who likes them. Like my first girl-friend, my present one is most loving when she is enjoying herself. And with neither of them do I know whether I am loved.'[20]

Wanting to give the frustrated Isot more to do, he made her one of his assistants. One day, walking into his work-room, he found her sitting on the sofa next to a young man, who was lying there

rather sleepily. With forced joviality she made a remark about 'situations liable to serious misinterpretation' and she stood up. During the work that followed she was rather embarrassed, indeed frightened. It was not until two days later, after we had been working side by side more or less in silence and without the usual signs of affection, that she asked whether I was angry with her. I told her she'd been spreading herself around with the nearest man in the place where she was supposed to be working. She said that without thinking she'd sat down for a few minutes with the young man, but nothing had happened. I laughed.

I find that I've lost respect for her: she strikes me as vulgar. Not without relief I notice the complete disappearance of my love. But she's still nonplussed, doesn't defend herself, behaves exactly as if she'd just been caught having a silly, unnecessary affair, and she tries only one thing: to ask for my advice at every opportunity. I can neither refuse advice nor keep it to myself.[21]

Brecht was so possessive towards his girl-friends that he used to check up on them by telephoning twice every evening, once early and once late, but they had no chance to be possessive with him.

The relationship with Käthe Reichel continued, not without turbulence. The only firm understanding between them was that she would tell him if she became involved with someone else. But she hated to be questioned, even when he tried to turn suspicions into a joke. In the summer of 1955, in Leipzig, he met Käthe Rülicke, and immediately offered her a job as assistant, taking her fully into his confidence, even about the Berlau problem. In the autumn of 1953 he had still been trying to reassure Berlau that he needed her as much as ever, but he saw less of her and she felt increasingly neglected, living an isolated life, drinking heavily. In the spring of 1955 Brecht, often going for more than a week without seeing her, would be shocked by her appearance when he did.[22] She was becoming increasingly aggressive, liable to slap faces, scream abuse, throw stones at windows. Her place was being taken mainly by Käthe Rülicke, who was jealous of Reichel, and could not always keep her jealousy out of critical comments on the actress. Reichel was making excessive demands on the director's time. But the actress was safe: unlike the assistant, she ran no risk of being banished from rehearsal for several days.

Weigel went on behaving with enormous tact and self-restraint, protecting the interests of her husband and her company. When a visiting Pole, a potential assistant, Konrad Swinarski, started to flirt with Isot Kilian, Weigel took him aside to explain that it upset Brecht if other men paid too much attention to women he loved.[23]

Harich had already started on the hopeless course he was to continue after Brecht's death, trying to liberalize the regime from within, while laying plans, in discussion with colleagues from Poland and Hungary, for a less doctrinaire Marxism. Weigel attended some of the meetings he organized but Brecht stayed away, though he did make sporadic attempts of his own at improving the system. To the population as a whole, he told Grotewohl, the *Volkskammer* (parliament) looked like 'a gigantic façade.... Couldn't we pump more life into the *Volkskammer* too?'[24]

That he was no longer out of favour with the Party leaders was confirmed in March 1954 when the Theater am Schiffbauerdamm was finally given to the Berliner Ensemble, over four years after the company had made its debut with *Puntila* in the Deutsches Theater – years of increasingly strained relations between Brecht and Langhoff, who quarrelled constantly. It is never easy for two companies to share one theatre, and Brecht was expert in the art of appearing to lose his temper in order to get his own way. Sometimes he would yell abuse, then whisper: 'Let's see how that works', then yell again.[25] He was conscious of himself as a performer, and the actors formed an appreciative audience.

On 19 March 1954 Besson's production of *Don Juan* launched the Ensemble's first season in its own building. Brecht was simultaneously preoccupied with a task that had a bearing on the future of his theatre: the first volume of his plays had been published in 1953 by the East German Aufbau Verlag, and it was due for republication. Not content to leave the plays, even in their revised form, to speak for themselves, he prepared a commentary: 'Bei Durchsicht meiner ersten Stücke' ('On Rereading My First Plays'), which is dated March 1954. Adopting the self-critical stance that orthodoxy required, he denounced *Baal* as 'lacking in wisdom' and liable to present numerous difficulties to readers 'who have not learnt how to think dialectically'. Perhaps they would take it as no more than an apologia for uninhibited egotism. But for Baal 'the art of living is conditioned by the same restrictions as all art under capitalism'. Dealing with *Trommeln in der Nacht*, he had to explain what he called the 'faint suspicion of approval on the author's part' for Kragler's refusal to fight on the barricades. The rebels 'were the tragic figures; he was comic'. But since the playwright had not had the technique of alienation at his disposal, 'it must be left to readers or audiences, with no help from the alienation, to alter their attitude to the play's hero from sympathy to a certain antipathy'. What Brecht was condemning was his earlier self, but most of his life had prepared him for this moment.

On 1 April an adaptation of a Chinese folk play was introduced into the repertoire, *Hirse für die Achte* (*Millet for the Eighth Army*). Manfred Wekwerth, who directed, had adapted it with Elisabeth Hauptmann. At the centre of the action is a village where the harvest is diverted from the occupying Japanese army to the revolutionary Eighth Army. Wekworth wanted the mayor to be played by an actor who seemed cunning, but Brecht resisted this type-casting. Why shouldn't the mayor be 'a simple, wise man? His enemies force him to be devious.'[26]

Brecht was a wise man who had found it necessary, from boyhood onwards, to be devious.

In the summer of 1954, just over three months after acquiring its own theatre, the Berliner Ensemble made guest appearances in Bruges, in Amsterdam and in Paris, where it appeared at the international festival, Théâtre des Nations, and won first prize for best play (*Mutter Courage*) and best direction (Brecht and Engel). But on the first night Brecht was not available for the curtain-call: after buying a batch of thrillers and visiting a dog cemetery, he fell asleep before the performance was over. Since 1953 Roland Barthes had been championing him in the magazine *Théâtre populaire*, preparing the ground for him, rather as Kenneth Tynan did in England, but it was the three performances at the Théâtre Sarah-Bernhardt that made the decisive breakthrough.

In Berlin Brecht worked hard at bringing *Der kaukasische Kreidekreis* to three-dimensional life, evolving stage pictures to replace the mental pictures he had formed when he wrote it. He had worked only once before with von Appen, who had been making preliminary designs for the production since November 1953, but, though his style was quite unlike Neher's, Brecht, with his genius for collaboration, knew how to set a designer's imagination on the right track. 'A manger,' he said. 'Nativity figurines.'[1] This made von Appen think of Christmas displays in the Catholic south of Germany and in Italy.

Selecting the right materials for decor and costumes involved them in historical and ethnographic research centred on ancient Caucasian history. They chose copper, silver, steel and silk for the nobility, and woven linen for the ordinary folk, with some articles for both made of leather and wood; no other materials were used. Brecht encouraged von Appen to start work by sketching groupings, and they experimented together on a model set with small figures. It was Brecht's idea that the stylized scenic backgrounds should be painted on silk, like Chinese watercolours or flags, and while working with the models and figures, he went on reducing the space for the wedding guests till von Appen almost protested; but rehearsal showed how comedy could be extracted from the manœuvrings of each guest for more elbow-room.[2]

The collaboration with Paul Dessau was less successful. The actors and musicians found it difficult to perform what he had composed, while Brecht became impatient. After several quarrels, Dessau stayed away from rehearsals. To Brecht it seemed that he was not doing enough; to Dessau it seemed that not enough was being done for the music.[3] The result was that a great deal of it was cut, and what remained contributed less than it could have done to the production.

As in *Mutter Courage*, the revolving stage was used skilfully. Grusche plodded intrepidly onwards against the movement of the revolve, which brought fragmentary cut-out sets towards her, and then came to a halt for the scene to be played. Afterwards, as she plodded further, the revolve would move the set away to be concealed behind a flag of scenery and removed from the revolve. The use of masks and the stylized crossing of the abyss in Scene 3 were characteristic of Chinese theatre; Brecht is said to have given a satisfied smile when Chinese students told him that the play reminded them of their own drama.[4]

It was the first of Brecht's own plays to be given a new production in the building. Angelika Hurwicz noticed that he used the word *Verfremdung* only once during the months of rehearsal: when the scene between Grusche, her brother and her sister-in-law struck him as too emotional, he made the actors rehearse with interpolations of 'said the man' or 'said the woman'. One advantage of having so much time was that cliché could be avoided by dint of developing internal contradictions. The peasant, for instance, who sells milk at an extortionate price, afterwards helps Grusche to pick up the baby: the man is both avaricious and kindly. Brecht would ask questions, theoretical or practical, which needed practical answers, and which elicited collaborative help not merely from other actors in the rehearsal room but from technicians and visitors. He might say, for instance: 'I'd like the servants, in spite of their haste when packing the governor's wife's things, to give indications of insubordination. How can this be done?' But moments of autocracy would intrude on democratic proceedings, especially now that his health was failing. If he felt too exhausted to go on rehearsing, he would simply dismiss the actors and refresh himself by making arrangements about music or costumes or the set.[5]

A November telephone call from Moscow informed him that he had been awarded the 'Lenin Prize for Peace and for Understanding between the Peoples'. Having been known as the Stalin Prize, it had just had its name changed. Two days later the news was confirmed in *Neues Deutschland*. In an interview he told *Izvestia*: 'We are living in very dark times in Germany, and friendship with the Soviet Union is enormously important to us.'⁶ He was echoing the phrase he had used to describe the Nazi period.

He was rehearsing Johannes Becher's 1941 play *Winterschlacht* (*Winter Battle*), a story about a middle-class Nazi soldier who, after being decorated for bravery, refuses to kill Soviet partisans. He prefers to die with them. Wanting E.F. Burian, who was in Prague, to direct, Brecht stressed the play's timeliness when 'the West German bourgeoisie is staking everything on rearmament to carry out their plans against us and the Soviet Union, which is making them reach progressively back to Nazism'. The scene depicting the rout of the *Wehrmacht* could be particularly instructive: 'You still hear people saying: "If it's a matter of fighting the Russians, I don't mind taking a rifle on my shoulder once again." '⁷ The production was finally directed by Brecht himself, assisted by Wekwerth, with music by Eisler.

When it had been suggested in December 1953 that an East–West committee of writers should be formed, Brecht had been one of the scheme's most enthusiastic advocates: 'Such a committee could counteract cultural tension', he told Ulbricht, 'while providing the opportunity to discuss really humanistic principles with West German writers and scientists.' But at the end of 1954, participating in a West Berlin symposium, he took an uncompromising stance: 'You can't have discussions with warmongers and war criminals. They're enemies of humanity and they must be annihilated. In the interests of humanity.'⁸ But he went on working inside the GDR for a relaxation of tension in relations with the West. The letters he wrote to various ministries include proposals for greater freedom of cultural exchange and for buses with sleeping accommodation to be permitted between Berlin and Munich.

Once the production of *Winterschlacht* had opened on 12 January 1955, he would have liked to start work on a revival of *Galileo* but neither Ernst Busch, whom he now wanted for the part, nor Erich Engel, whom he needed as co-director, had accepted. Brecht began working, together with Elisabeth Hauptmann and Benno Besson, on adapting George Farquhar's 1706 play *The Recruiting Officer*. In October 1954 Britain, France, the US and the Soviet Union had agreed to end the occupation of Germany, and a nine-power agreement on Western European Union was signed. One of Brecht's two main objects was to comment obliquely on rearmament in Western Germany, and he made the play's action contemporaneous with the American War of Independence in order to put recruiting in the perspective of British imperialism. The difficulties of the recruiting officers are increased by leaflets containing the Declaration of Independence in draft form and subversive statements by Benjamin Franklin. After his experience with the *Herrnburg Cantata* he was prepared for difficulties with the government, which would soon have to take a decision about enlistment for the Volksarmee.[9] But he was allowed to go ahead, and von Appen painted houses, furniture and trees in the style of copperplate engravings on hanging pieces of scenery, which could be flown rapidly in and out. The play's title was changed to *Pauken und Trompeten* (*Drums and Trumpets*). Another motive, as in *Turandot*, was to provide a part for Regine Lutz. Sylvia, the heroine, disguises herself as a soldier, and the resulting entanglements would show off Lutz's talent for comedy.

Even before Brecht was fifty-seven his heart was weakening, but this was not yet diagnosed; the doctor he trusted, Dr Hüdepohl, was a kidney specialist attached to St Hedwig's hospital, and it is possible that Brecht would have survived longer had he consulted a heart specialist sooner. Any writer is liable to be trapped into describing symptoms instead of treating them as signals for quick action. 'The first unmistakable signs of age', Brecht wrote, 'are given to us, I think, by the eyes. It's nothing more than the feeling that the eyes just aren't young any longer.' He felt that his talent was dwindling. 'Of course I too was gifted, especially forty years ago. Younger people are mostly gifted; it's a matter of sexual diseases.' His face now had a slightly bloated look, and he used a stick for walking; on car journeys he would lean back in the seat. But it was fear of flying that induced him, before he left for Moscow to receive the Peace Prize, to instruct Rudi Engel, General Director of the Academy of Arts: 'In the event of my death I do not wish to lie in state or be put on show. There should be no speeches at my grave. I should like to be buried in the graveyard beside the house in which I live, in Chaussees-trasse.'[10]

On the way to Moscow with Weigel and Käthe Rülicke, who could speak Russian, he stopped in Warsaw, where the annual Book Fair was in progress. Intending to write a play about Einstein, he had arranged to meet the physicist Leopold Infeld, but the conversation was demoralizing: 'Today we must talk quietly. My wife is dying in the next room. ... Einstein is no good for a play. He has no partner. With whom do you want to make him talk?'[11]

Going on to Moscow he invited Bernhard Reich and Asja Lacis to meet him there. Arriving at the Hotel Sovietskaya, he and Weigel were shown into a huge room with an enormous double bed; shyly she asked for a smaller room. Reich found him 'outwardly very different: the face broad ... the body stocky'. He invited Reich to direct a production for the Ensemble, and tried to expedite proceedings for his rehabilitation with the Soviet authorities, as well as trying to find out what had become of Carola Neher. He also appealed to the director Nikolai Okhlopkov for help in arranging for the Ensemble to visit Russia, and he tried to interest the actress Faina Ranevskaia in *Mutter Courage*, but the play was not to receive its Moscow première until 1960. It had its first English production shortly after his visit to Moscow, when Joan Littlewood directed the play at Barnstaple, taking the lead herself, and chafing against the presence of Brecht's assistant, Carl Weber, in the rehearsal room.[12]

On 25 May, in the Kremlin, the Lenin Prize was presented to him. In his speech – translated into Russian for him by Boris Pasternak – he called it 'the highest and most desirable of all the prizes that could be awarded today'. He spoke emotionally but misleadingly about his youthful feelings towards Soviet communism:

I was nineteen years old when I heard about your great revolution, twenty when I glimpsed the reflection of the great conflagration in my home town. I was a medical orderly in an Augsburg barracks. The camps and even the barracks emptied, the old town was suddenly full of new people coming in great waves out of the suburbs, with a vivacity that was unknown in the streets of the rich, the officials, and the businessmen. For some days working-class women spoke in the quickly improvised soviets and changed the thinking of young workers in soldier's overalls, and the factories carried out the orders of workers.[13]

At the Moscow Art Theatre he saw a production he liked of Ostrovsky's *Among Thieves and Robbers:* 'The whole of Stanislavsky's greatness is visible.' He also saw a Shakespeare play produced by the drama school of the Moscow Art Theatre and directed by 'a student of Stanislavsky, "traditional" (in the bad traditions of the eighties) with hollow pathos, petty bourgeois passion, caricature comedy and the usual crude mockery of the steward who believes he is permitted to fall in love with his mistress'. According to Brecht's diary this was *Much Ado About Nothing*, but obviously it was *Twelfth Night*. He went to a production of Mayakovsky's 1930 play *The Bath-house*, 'a vivid chamber mystery play, very vivaciously performed with excellent actors. Realistic acting, alienation effects everywhere, comic pathos.' Hearing that Nikolai Akimov was going to produce *Die Gesichte der Simone Machard* in Leningrad, Brecht asked for an 11-year-old girl to be cast as Simone.[14] This is inconsistent with the adult thinking behind her dialogue, but consistent with his previous attempts to downgrade Galileo, Courage and Grusche. He may also have been thinking of Eisler's advice that Simone should be less like a saint and more like a sacrifice.

At the beginning of June he went back, exhausted, to Buckow, only to leave again in the middle of the month with Weigel for Paris, where the Ensemble was returning to the Théâtre des Nations with *Der kaukasische Kreidekreis*. When the company was on tour Brecht habitually stayed away from first-night performances. 'In the evenings', writes Vladimir Pozner, who was acting as his interpreter in Paris, 'we made ourselves comfortable on the terrace of the café on the corner next to the theatre and waited for the performance to end. In the crowd that overflowed from the pavement to the boulevard, no one guessed that the man with the fringe, who in the fifteenth century might have modelled for any primitive painter, for any Augsburg master, this peasant with his grey jacket buttoned up to his neck, was a poet of genius.'[15]

But he was surprisingly image-conscious. Newspaper photographers had to submit contact prints for him to decide which ones to authorize. 'If you studied the rejected photographs and compared them with the others, perhaps you could to some extent reconstruct Brecht's image as he liked himself, or, we can assume, least disliked himself. ... When I one day discussed this with him, he smilingly told me: "I know that I look stupid, but why should I admit that to other people?" '[16]

Mostly the Brechts ate at a restaurant on the Boulevard Sébastopol. 'I thought Parmentier meant Parmesan,' Brecht told Pozner, 'and now I've got to eat a potato pancake.' Once, at a small bar-restaurant near Notre Dame where recherché cheeses were served on wooden plates, Pozner made him try a strong goat's-milk cheese. 'He smiled without parting his lips, which made him look embarrassed, almost shy. His smile became more pronounced, his small eyes began to twinkle. "I'd like to exhibit this platter of cheeses in the foyer of my theatre," he said, "to teach the Germans what culture is." '[17]

Back in Berlin at the end of June he worked with his old friend Emil Burri and the film director Wolfgang Staudte, who was preparing to direct *Mutter Courage* for DEFA with Weigel as Courage, Simone Signoret as Yvette, and Ekkehard Schall, who had played the conscience-stricken German soldier in *Winterschlacht*, as Eilif. The casting was aimed partly at French cinema audiences. As in the filming of *Dreigroschenoper*, Brecht quarrelled with the director, and shooting, which began on 18 August, had to stop.

He was hostile to the rapidly growing relationship between Schall and Barbara, whom he still regarded as a child. When she became pregnant, he was incredulous. 'How can the child have a child?' Weigel answered: 'If you don't know by now ...'.[18]

Pauken und Trompeten opened in the Theater am Schiffbauerdamm on 19 September, followed on 9 November by an adaptation of an old Chinese play, *Der Tag des grossen Gelehrten Wu* (*The Day of the Great Sage Wu*). Brecht's main contribution to the production was pressure for a more demonstrative style of acting. At the beginning of December he was supervising Angelika Hurwicz's direction of Ostrovsky's *The Stepdaughter*: 'These plays look easy but they're difficult because the storyline disappears for long stretches, like a desert stream.'[19] The production opened on 12 December.

He had been trying to take an active part in preparations for the new production of *Galileo*. Ernst Busch had agreed to play the part; but Brecht had little stamina left, and his temperature was often above normal. He was being treated with digitalis and courses of injections.[20] But *Galileo* rehearsals started in the middle of December, with Engel as co-director and Neher as designer. Eisler was doubtful of whether Busch, who came from North German Protestant working-class stock, could play a Renaissance Italian: he lacked not only Laughton's embonpoint but most of the other outward symptoms of pleasure-loving. Busch was almost Puritanic in his compulsion to work. But this stood him in good stead. He researched thoroughly, reading books about astronomy and physics, classical and modern; soon he was accusing Brecht of understanding nothing about science. Brecht may have been sly enough to seem more ignorant than he was; certainly he encouraged Busch to lecture him in the rehearsal room, for this made the actor more authoritative, more accustomed to relishing his knowledge. Astronomical terms crept unobtrusively into his everyday vocabulary. 'At this period his postures and gestures were changing. He worked during his leisure. All these months his friends did not have an easy time of it.'[21] Busch also researched into Galileo's life. In December, when he asked Brecht whether Virginia was the only daughter, the answer was 'Yes', but Busch discovered that Galileo had three daughters, all illegitimate.

Between the middle of December 1955 and the end of March 1956, Brecht took fifty-nine rehearsals, trying never to direct for more than two hours in a day. According to Käthe Rülicke, who was working as his production assistant, he talked more and demonstrated less than formerly. He wanted Busch to show Galileo being torn between two great vices, science and gluttony. Brecht laughed a great deal at his own suggestion of how Galileo should react when Andrea brings the news that Descartes has stopped writing: 'Busch, it would be nice if we had here a nerve-shattering pause. ... What the audience doesn't know and will find it hard to understand is that it's a blow for Galileo when a rival stops working.' Sometimes Busch tried to make the performance more naturalistic than Brecht wanted; when he argued, Brecht kept interrupting him, talking loudly and emphatically. To make Heinz Schubert more relaxed as the little monk Brecht asked him to rehearse in a Berlin accent, which irritated Busch, who started answering in a Berlin accent.[22]

In February 1956 Brecht went to Milan with Weigel, Barbara and Elisabeth Hauptmann for Giorgio Strehler's production of *Dreigroschenoper* in the Piccolo Teatro. Berlau was told that the production was 'brilliant in conception and in detail and very aggressive'. Using Teo Otto as designer, Strehler had updated the action to 1914, setting the wedding scene in a garage instead of a stable. 'That is very good, and after the third world war it could be transposed to 19...' Brecht had told Pozner that there were only two directors – Chaplin and himself. Now he named Strehler as 'probably the best director in Europe'. While in Milan Brecht succumbed to a virus influenza with cardiac complications.[23]

Back in Berlin, he resumed work on *Galileo* and participated in the adaptation of J. M. Synge's *The Playboy of the Western World*. Seeing the play at the Théâtre des Nations with Cyril Cusack as Christy Mahon, Brecht had wanted to build a Berliner Ensemble production around an unromantic casting of the central role. Wekwerth was told he could direct if he fulfilled two conditions: he must prepare a rough translation within a fortnight, and must use Barbara as Pegeen Mike. She had already fulfilled the two conditions her father had imposed. She must score a success at another theatre and cook a good beef broth.[24]

Brecht had said that the Irish people were 'expressionism mixed with Schiller', and, taking this seriously, Wekwerth tried to evolve an appropriate style. Brecht was at first too ill to sit in on rehearsals, and when he did come, he was appalled. Wekwerth had to change tack. In the new version the play was called *Der Held der westlichen Welt* (*The Hero of the Western World*) to suggest that a cult of violence was endemic in the West, together with a general admiration for crimes like the patricide Christy Mahon boasts about. Synge's title had referred to the west of Ireland, but the production aimed a broadside at Western capitalism.

Blow-ups of American comic strips featuring Micky Spillane-like violence (which Brecht secretly enjoyed) were featured on the drop-curtain.

At the beginning of April Engel took ten rehearsals of *Galileo*, but
they were suspended when it became obvious that Brecht was too ill to
resume. 'The postponement is worst of all for you,' he wrote to Busch,
'especially the hiatus in May–June. I'm really troubled about this, I start
sweating when I think about it. But the break can also be a bit useful
with the possibility of building up strength for me *and for you*.' Nor was
he well enough to complete the revision he had begun of Beckett's
Waiting for Godot, presumably for production at the Ensemble. His
annotations stop at page 33 of the German translation. The main change
is to make the Pozzo-Lucky sequence into a dream of Vladimir's, giving
many of his lines, while he is asleep, to Estragon.[25]

Suffering again from a virus influenza, Brecht went into the Charité
hospital. While he was there he wrote a poem which uses the blackbird's
song, as he had used it before, semi-symbolically, to represent the work
of the artist.

> For a long time already
> I had felt no fear of death. For there is nothing
> I can miss, provided that I myself
> Am missing. Now
> I managed to be pleased
> With the blackbirds after me, too.

After coming out of hospital he felt so weak that he agreed to accom-
pany Peter Suhrkamp (whom he had visited in a West Berlin clinic early
in February) to Johann Ludwig Schmitt's private clinic in Munich for
the second half of August and the first half of September. Weigel was in
favour of this, and she asked Therese Giehse to persuade him to see
another specialist.[26]

Brecht spent most of June and July in Buckow. Through Ruth Berlau
he was arranging to buy a country house in Denmark, at Humdebaek in
Zealand. But probably it was his intention to instal her in it, spending
little time there himself. Though his temperature was still high, he tried
to work between eight and eleven in the morning, preparing his plays
about Einstein and the stove-fitter Garbe, but he knew he would not be
able to go on working in the theatre. 'You can do that', he told Wekwerth. 'What do I have pupils for?'

He was feeling too weak to supervise preparations for bringing *Mutter
Courage*, *Der kaukasische Kreidekreis* and *Pauken und Trompeten* to
London, but he left a message on the notice-board: the acting needed to

be 'quick, light and strong. This is not a matter of haste but of speed, not just of quick acting but quick thinking. We must preserve the tempo of a run-through, and infect it with quiet strength, with our own fun. The dialogue must not be spoken grudgingly, as if giving away your last pair of boots, but must be tossed in the air like balls.'

He had been intending to leave for Munich in the evening of 14 August, but after he had left the rehearsal in the morning, the doctors found that he had sustained a serious heart attack, which had probably occurred three days ago. From six o'clock in the evening he was unconscious; he died at 11.45.[27]

He had asked for a stiletto to be put through his heart as soon as the doctors were sure he was dead, and then to be buried in a steel coffin so that the worms would not be able to get at him. Both instructions were obeyed, but his will was not. He had left the proceeds of *Dreigroschenoper* to Elisabeth Hauptmann, of *Kreidekreis* to Berlau, of *Die Mutter* to Rülicke, of certain poems to Kilian. The will was typed and signed, but not witnessed by a notary because Kilian, who had been given the job of taking it to one, had found too many people in the waiting-room.[28]

Inheriting the whole of his fortune, Weigel paid comparatively small amounts of money to the other women, but, when Peter Suhrkamp intervened, acted more generously towards Elisabeth Hauptmann.[29] Weigel survived her husband for fifteen years and went on running the Ensemble until she died in 1971. Schall married Barbara and went on working at the Theater am Schiffbauerdamm, where he is now the leading actor, with Galileo and Puntila among his parts. The company is run by Manfred Wekwerth; the square outside is called Bertolt-Brecht-Platz. Elisabeth Hauptmann survived until 1973 and Ruth Berlau, with deteriorating health, until 1974. Walter Brecht, Marianne Zoff and Paula Banholzer are still alive and in 1981 both women contributed to a book which was published under the title *So viel wie eine Liebe. Der unbekannte Brecht. (So Much Like Love. The Unknown Brecht.)*

Notes

Abbreviations

TB, AA	*Tagebücher 1920–22, Auto-biographische Aufzeich-nungen*	GG	*Gesammelte Gedichte*
		GW	*Gesammelte Werke*
		SzLuK	*Schriften zur Literatur und Kunst*
AJ	Arbeitsjournal		
BBA	Bertolt Brecht Archives	SzPuG	*Schriften zur Politik und Gesellschaft*
'Durchsicht'	'Bei Durchsicht meiner ersten Stücke'		
		SzT	*Schriften zum Theater*
F/O	Frisch and Obermeyer, *Brecht in Augsburg*		

1 The One and the Many

1 Münsterer, p. 12.

2 *Flüchtlingsgespräche* in *Prosa*, p. 1402; letter to H. Ihering, 10.22.

3 F/O pp. 15–16.

4 'Durchsicht', pp. 12–13; Münsterer, p. 7.

5 Walter Brecht interview; Fanny Brecht (cousin), F/O p. 23.

6 F/O pp. 19, 23.

7 Fanny Brecht, F/O p. 23; Heiner Hagg, F/O pp. 21, 22.

8 Walter Brecht interview; Franz Kroher, F/O p. 31; letter to Ihering, 10.22; Kroher, F/O p. 33.

9 Hagg, F/O p. 22; obituary by Brecht in the *Augsburger Neueste Nachrichten*; *Flüchtlingsgespräche* in *Prosa*, pp. 1402, 1403.

10 *Prosa*, ibid.

11 Ibid., pp. 1403–4.

12 Fanny Brecht, F/O p. 24.

13 Bronnen (1960), p. 113; Jahresbericht (annual school report), 1911–12, F/O p. 24.

14 Walter Brecht interview; F. X. Schiller, F/O p. 44.

15 *Flüchtlingsgespräche* in *Prosa*, pp. 1402, 1403.

16 Schiller, F/O p. 45.

17 Franz Reiter, F/O p. 47; 'Die Bekenntnisse eines Erst-Kommunikanten', *Gedichte* 1920–3, unpubl.

18 Heinrich Scheuffelhur, F/O pp. 51–2.

19 Stephan Bürzle, F/O p. 56.

20 Münsterer, p. 65.

21 Völker (1976), p. 14.

22 Wilhelm Brüstle, 'Wie ich Bert Brecht entdeckte' in Schumacher (1978); Schuhmann, pp. 31ff.; 'Turmwacht' in *Augsburger Neueste Nachrichten*, 8.8.14.

23 'Notizen über unsere Zeit' in *Augsburger Neueste Nachrichten* (*Der Erzähler*) (literary supplement).

24 Brüstle, ibid.

25 Walter Groos, F/O p. 69; letter to Caspar Neher, 10.11.14.

26 'Der Freiwillige', *Prosa*, pp. 11–12.

Brecht's *Kleines Organon für das Theater* is included in the *Schriften zum Theater*.

27 'Augsburger Kriegsbrief',
    Augsburger Neueste Nachrichten,
    14.8.14.
28 GG p. 9.
29 Münsterer, p. 68.
30 *Flüchtlingsgespräche* in *Prosa*,
    pp. 1414–15; Maiberger in F/O.
31 F/O pp. 55–7, Ledermann, F/O p. 79.
32 Max Knoblach, F/O p. 80; Karl
    Seidelmann, F/O p. 84; Franz
    Feuchtmayr, F/O pp. 80–2.
33 R. M. Aman, F/O p. 92; Frieda Held,
    F/O p. 123; H. Hagg, F/O p. 125.
34 Paula Banholzer, F/O p. 125.
35 R. M. Aman, F/O pp. 91–2.
36 Letter to Neher, 13.12.17.
37 H. W. Sorgel, F/O p. 109; Walter
    Groos, F/O pp. 88, 90.
38 Högel, F/O p. 16.
39 H. Kasack, 'Der Augsburger Bert
    Brecht', *Schwäbische Landeszeitung*,
    3.1.47.
40 GG p. 54; 'Ballade von den
    Abenteurern', GG p. 217.
41 'Wo ich gelernt habe', SzLuK
    pp. 502–7.
42 Max Hohenester in Högel, p. 19.
43 Hedda Kuhn, F/O p. 60; Rudolf
    Prestel, F/O pp. 131–2.
44 E. Müller, F/O p. 98.
45 Johann Harre, F/O pp. 110, 111.
46 Letter to H. Hagg, n.d.; H. Hagg,
    F/O p. 100.
47 Eisler in Bunge (1970), p. 94.
48 Bürzle, F/O p. 56; *Der Marquis von
    Keith*, Act Two; Münsterer in Witt,
    p. 23.
49 Letter to Neher, 9.17; Conrad Kopp,
    F/O p. 114.

2   Apprentice Swindler

1   Münsterer, p. 30; E. Müller, F/O p. 98;
    Münsterer, p. 30.
2   Letters to Neher, 8.11.17; 18.12.17;
    beginning of 2.18.
3   Ibid., 15.12.17.
4   Ibid., 30.12.17.
5   Hedda Kuhn, F/O p. 161; letter to
    H. Hagg, 23.11.17; letter to Neher,
    23.11.17.
6   Hedda Kuhn, F/O p. 159; Münsterer,
    p. 20.
7   Letter to Neher, 29.12.17.
8   Letter to Neher, 5.18; H. Kuhn, F/O
    p. 119; p. 158.
9   Hedda Kuhn, F/O p. 161.
10 Ibid.; Münsterer, pp. 42, 43.
11 Münsterer, p. 42; E. Emmerich in
    Schwäbische Landeszeitung,
    Augsburg edn, 24.8.56; obituary by
    Brecht in *Augsburger Neueste
    Nachrichten*; letter to Neher,
    mid-3.18.
12 Letter to Neher, mid-3.18.
13 Letters to Neher, 3.18; 29.12.17;
    mid-3.18.
14 Schumacher (1978), p. 31.
15 M. H. Siegel, F/O pp. 120–1.
16 Münsterer, p. 90; memoir written
    eight years later by a student
    member of the seminar, BBA
    474/120.
17 Schmidt, p. 63; Münsterer, p. 21.
18 Letter to Paula Banholzer, 5.18.
19 'Durchsicht'.
20 F. Mayer, F/O p. 135.
21 Letters to Neher, 24.2.18; 10.4.18;
    4.18; beginning of 7.18.
22 Letter to Neher, 1.6.18; Harrer, F/O
    p. 112; Schmidt, p. 13.
23 Otto Bezold's diary, 21.5.18;
    Schmidt, p. 65.
24 Letter to Neher, mid-6.18; Völker
    (1971), p. 28.
25 Letters to Neher, 22.7.18; beginning
    of 9.18.
26 Ibid. 11.5.18; 17.5.18; 26.8.18.
27 'Vom Klettern in Bäumen', 'Vom
    Schwimmen in Seen und Flüssen', GG
    pp. 209–10.
28 'Vom dem Gras und
    Pfefferminzkraut', GG p. 84; 'Die
    Geburt im Baum', GG p. 85; 'Von

der Freundlichkeit der Welt', GG
p. 205.

3   The Marching Corpse

1   Münsterer, p. 95; Tretiakov in Witt,
    p. 73.
2   Münsterer, p. 97; Hagg, F/O p. 140.
3   Kessler, *Tagebücher*, 10.11.18.
4   Münsterer, pp. 96–7; Bunge interview
    14.6.82.
5   Kessler, *Tagebücher*, 17.12.18.
6   Hagg, F/O p. 143; Münsterer, p. 99;
    GW, vol. 20, p. 25.
7   E. Lauermann, F/O p. 147.
8   Völker (1976), p. 38; Münsterer,
    p. 103; Fischer, p. 93.
9   GW, vol. 20, pp. 6–7.
10 GG p. 22; note on p. 524 of *Poems
    1913–56*.
11 'Ballade von dem toten Soldaten',
    GG p. 258; *Die Pleite* 4.19; Beth
    Irwin Lewis, *Georg Grosz: Art
    and Politics in the Weimar Republic*
    (Milwaukee and London, 1971);
    Kesting, p. 14.
12 Münsterer, p. 100; Neher diary in
    Völker (1971), p. 13.
13 Neher diary 13.2.19, op. cit., p. 14.
14 Ibid., 22.2.19, p. 14.
15 Feuchtwanger in Witt, pp. 11, 13;
    Völker, p. 12.
16 Münsterer, p. 105; letter to Jakob
    Geis, 28.4.19.
17 Münsterer, p. 105.
18 Ibid., pp. 131–2.
19 Ibid., pp. 107–9.
20 H. Kuhn, F/O p. 161; Münsterer,
    p. 91.
21 Tretiakov in Witt, p. 74.
22 V. Baur, F/O p. 164; R. M. Aman,
    F/O p. 166.
23 Münsterer, p. 96; Neher's diary in
    Völker, p. 15; Münsterer, p. 126;
    Frieda Held, F/O p. 172.
24 Neher's diary 9.5.19, F/O p. 173;
    Knoblach, F/O pp. 174–6.

25 Feuchtwanger, *Success* (London,
    1930), p. 223.
26 H. Kuhn, F/O p. 176.
27 Neher's diary in Völker, p. 18.
28 Hecht, Insel edn, p. 48.
29 TB, 18.8.20.
30 SzT p. 161.
31 Ibid.
32 Letter to Ruth Berlau, summer 1942.
33 F/O p. 193.
34 F/O pp. 104–5, p. 56; Münsterer,
    p. 145.
35 'Ballade von den Abenteurern', GG
    p. 217.
36 'Bargan lässt es sein', *Prosa*, p. 36.
37 Neher diary, 1.1.20 in Völker, p. 20.
38 Ibid.; letters to Hanns Johst
    12–19.1.20.
39 Neher diary in Völker, pp. 21–2.
40 Interview with Marianne Zoff in
    Banholzer.
41 H. Kuhn, F/O p. 162; letter to Neher,
    end of 2.20.
42 Zuckmayer, pp. 311–12.
43 Stefan Zweig, *Die Welt von gestern*
    (Stockholm, 1947), pp. 286–7.
44 Letter to Dora Mannheim, end of
    3.20.
45 Ibid., 24.3.20; end of 3.20.
46 TB 20.6.20; GW, vol. 8, p. 23.
47 *Volkswille*, 15.4.20; 'Eine
    Abrechnung', *Volkswille* 14.5.20,
    both in SzT, vol. 1, p. 21.
48 GG p. 88; AA p. 197; 'Lied von
    meiner Mutter', GG p. 79; AA
    p. 197.
49 GG p. 76.
50 AA p. 196.
51 TB 18.6.20.
52 TB 16.6.20.
53 AA pp. 197–8.
54 AA p. 195; TB 17, 20.6.20.
55 TB 21–6.6.20.
56 TB 21–27.6.20.
57 TB 27, 30.6.20; 1.7.20.
58 TB 1.7.20.
59 TB 7.7.20.

60 TB 8.7.20.
61 TB 14, 4.7.20; 22.8.20.
62 TB 16.7. 20; GG p. 236.
63 TB 15, 27, 28.7.20.
64 TB 30.7.20.
65 TB 4.8.20; 18.7.20.
66 TB 17, 7.8.20.
67 TB 1.9.20.
68 TB 3.9.20; AA p. 193; TB 3, 12.9.20.
69 TB 5, 8, 9.9.20.
70 TB 12, 15.9.20.
71 TB 16–21.9.20.
72 Ibid.
73 TB 22.9.20; 30.8.20.
74 TB 24, 26.9.20.
75 SzT p. 23; review of *Tasso*, 13.10.20, p. 28.
76 GW, vol. 15, pp. 20–1.
77 Review of *Alt-Heidelberg*, 15.10.20; SzT p. 30; SzT p. 47; SzT p. 34; 'Querulanterei' 22.12.20, SzT p. 52, 55.
78 *Volkswille*, 13.1.21.

4 Love and Anti-Love

1 TB 9.2.21.
2 TB 21.5.21; 13.2.21.
3 TB 14.2.21.
4 TB 15.2.21; Neher's diary 13 and 25.2.21 Völker in (1971), p. 26; TB 7.21.
5 TB 25.2.21.
6 Ibid.
7 TB 28.2.21.
8 TB 20, 27.2.21; M. Zoff interview in Banholzer.
9 TB 26.2.21.
10 Zoff interview cit.; TB 8.3.21.
11 TB 8, 9.3.21.
12 TB 9, 10, 11, 12, 13.3.21.
13 TB 16, 17, 21.3.21.
14 TB 22, 23.3.21.
15 TB 25, 26, 27.3.21.
16 TB 29–31.3.21.
17 TB 1–3, 4.4.21.
18 TB 5–11.4.21.

19 TB 12.4.21.
20 TB 13.4.21.
21 Ibid.
22 TB 14, 15, 16, 17.4.21.
23 TB 18, 19, 20–23.4.21.
24 Bunge interview 14.6.82.
25 TB 28.4.21.
26 TB 30.4.21; 2.5.21.
27 TB 3–6.5.21.
28 TB 7.5.21.
29 TB 9.5.21; 9.4.21.
30 TB 10–14.5.21.
31 TB 15, 16, 19, 21.5.21.
32 TB 25.5.21.
33 TB 14, 19, 14.6.21.
34 TB 17.6.21.

5 Urban Jungle

1 TB 25.8.21; 4.9.21.
2 TB 15.9.21; 16.6.21; 'Durchsicht', p. 13; TB 16, 18, 30.9.21.
3 TB 5.3.21.
4 TB 5.10.21; Rimbaud, *Une saison en enfer* – Adieu.
5 Gisela E. Bahr (ed.), *Im Dickicht – Erstfassung und Materiallin* (Frankfurt, 1968), pp. 134–7.
6 TB 6.10.21.
7 Bahr, op. cit., pp. 9–10.
8 TB 6, 26.10.21.
9 TB 26, 15.10.21.
10 TB 25, 28, 29.10.21.
11 TB 7.11.21; 30, 31.10.21.

6 Bertolt and Arnolt

1 TB 9.10.21.
2 7, 12.11.21.
3 TB 12.11.21; letter to Paula Banholzer, beginning of 12.21; Hauptmann, p. 187.
4 Letter to Paula Banholzer cit.; G.E. Bahr (ed.), *Im Dickicht* (Frankfurt, 1968) pp. 134–7.
5 Letter to Paula Banholzer beginning of 12.21; TB 16.11.21; 10, 11.2.22; AJ 1.11.43.

6   TB 19.12.21.
7   TB 25.12.21.
8   Bronnen (1960), p. 16.
9   Zuckmayer, pp. 375, 236; Bronnen (1960), p. 20.
10 TB 31.1.22; 10.2.22; H. Kuhn, F/O p. 221.
11 Bronnen (1960), pp. 27, 32–3.
12 Ibid., pp. 35, 36.
13 Bronnen (1954), p. 99.
14 Bronnen (1960), pp. 50, p. 41; Neher quoted by Bentley, p. 56.
15 TB 24.11.21; Bronnen (1960), p. 41.
16 Bronnen (1960), pp. 45–6, 53.
17 Ibid., p. 58; letter to Neher, 12.21; Bronnen (1960), p. 58.
18 Fleisser in GW (Frankfurt, 1972), vol. 2, p. 297; Reich p. 264; Bronnen (1960), p. 62.
19 Bronnen (1960), p. 63.
20 Ibid.; Carl Weber.
21 *Theaterarbeit*, pp. 163–6.
22 Alfred Kantorowicz, *Deutsches Tagebuch* 2 (Munich, 1961) p. 302; Reich, p. 234.
23 *Börsen-Courier*, reprinted in Witt, pp. 32–5.
24 Alfred Kerr's review reprinted in *Die Welt im Drama*; Engel, pp. 164–6.
25 Letter to Bronnen, 23.1.23.
26 Letter to Ihering, in Völker (1971), p. 33.
27 Bronnen (1960), p. 96; letter to Bronnen, c. 2.23.
28 Ibid., p. 105; letter to Bronnen, 3.23; Fleisser, op. cit., p. 299; AA p. 201.
29 Bronnen (1960), p. 115; letter to Barret [sic] O. Clark 26.4.23; Reich, pp. 239–40; AA p. 201.
30 Bronnen (1960), pp. 113, 114; Berlau in Bunge, *Brechts Lai-Tu*.
31 Bronnen (1960), p. 116.
32 Ibid., pp. 120–1, 123, 124; Alfred Döblin in Völker (1971) p. 34; Bronnen (1960), p. 125.
33 Wolfgang Pintzka in Engel, pp. 254–5; Engel's notes of 1923, p. 77.
34 Josef Stolzing, *Völkischer Beobachter*, 12.5.23; Thomas Mann, 'Briefe aus Deutschland' GW (Frankfurt, 1974), vol. 13, pp. 289–90.
35 Fleisser, op. cit., p. 301.
36 Bronnen (1960), pp. 126, 128–31.
37 Berlau in Bunge, op. cit.
38 Letter to Marianne and Hanne 9–10.23.
39 Letter to Weigel, end of 1923.

7   Cheese-white Faces

1   Zuckmayer in Engel, p. 251; Reich, p. 237.
2   Reich in Witt; Reich, pp. 236–8.
3   'Durchsicht', p. 14.
4   Zuckmayer, p. 378.
5   Story told by Brecht to Otto Gelsted, Engberg, p. 92; Bronnen, p. 82.
6   Reich, p. 239; Lacis, p. 38.
7   Reich in Witt; Lacis, p. 37.
8   Letter to Ihering end of 2/beginning of 3.24; Fleisser GWII p. 301; Lacis, p. 37.
9   Hans Braun, *Münchener Zeitung*, 20.3.24.
10 Reich, p. 70; Lacis, *passim*.
11 Ihering (1948).
12 Zuckmayer.
13 Reich, pp. 251–2.
14 Reich in Völker (1971), p. 35.
15 Ihering, *Börsen-Courier*, 9.12.23.
16 Braun, *Münchener Zeitung*, 20.3.24; Roda-Roda, *Berliner Zeitung*, 22.3.24; Reich, pp. 262–3.
17 Reich, pp. 272–8; Völker (1976), p. 68; letters to Weigel, 6.7.24.

8   Berlin Attic

1   Reich in Witt; Lotte Lenya in Witt; Elisabeth Hauptmann diary, 1.2.26, BBA 151/03; Reich in Witt.
2   Sternberg, p. 20; Völker (1971) p. 36; Reich, p. 281; letter from Rimbaud to G. Izambard, 13.5.1871; note dated 21.5.25, GW, vol. 15, p. 57.

3 Lines added in 1974 to Begbick's interlude speech; 'Ballade vom armen BB', GG p. 263; interlude speech.
4 Broadcast speech, SzT p. 976.
5 Reich, pp. 289, 287; Völker (1976) pp. 120–1.
6 Elisabeth Hauptmann's tribute to Engel, Engel, pp. 222–3; Aristotle, *Poetics*, Section 9.
7 Reich in Witt.
8 *Vorrede*, SzT pp. 976–8.
9 *Der Hitler-Prozess* (report, Munich, 1924); Taylor, pp. 22–3.
10 'Entdeckungen einer jungen Frau', GG p. 161.
11 Völker (1971), p. 37; AA pp. 204–5.
12 'Brief über eine Dogge', *Prosa*, p. 114; p. 115; Fischer, p. 205.
13 Reich, pp. 297, 299.
14 AA p. 205.
15 'Ballade vom armen BB', GG p. 262.
16 'Was arbeiten Sie?' 1926 interview in *Brecht im Gespräch*, pp. 187–90.
17 SzT pp. 61–2.
18 SzT p. 63; interview cited by E. Hauptmann in Witt.
19 E. Hauptmann's diary, 3.1.26, in Witt.
20 'Was arbeiten Sie?' cit.; *Prosa*, pp. 120, 134.
21 *Prosa*, p. 143.
22 'Das Urbild Baals', *Die Szene*, 1.26; SzT p. 955; and see E. Hauptmann's diary 18.1.26 in Witt.
23 E. Hauptmann's diary, 18.1.26, in Witt.
24 Ibid., 7.2.26.
25 H. H. Jahnn, 'Vom armen B. B.', *Sinn und Form*, II, pp. 424–5.
26 Hugo von Hofmannsthal, *Das Theater des Neuen* (Vienna, 1947).
27 'Matinée in Dresden', *Prosa*, p. 158.
28 Note made by E. Hauptmann on 23.3.26 and copied into her diary on 26.7.26, in Witt; *Leipziger Tageblatt*, 5.6.24, reprinted in Alfred Döblin, *Griffe ins Leben* (Berlin, 1974); TB 20.5.21.
29 Reich, p. 294.
30 E. Hauptmann's diary, 29.4.26 in Witt.
31 Guillemin interview cit.
32 'Glossen über Kriminalromane', SzLuK pp. 41–2; Eisler in Bunge (1970), *passim*; Hauptmann, p. 173.

9 Boxing-Ring and Corn Exchange

1 Völker (1976), pp. 123–4.
2 E. Hauptmann's diary, 26.7.26, in Witt.
3 Ibid.; Eisler in Bunge (1970), p. 149.
4 Marx and Engels, *Werke* (Berlin, 1956–68), XX, p. 498.
5 Bunge (1970), p. 146; 'Kurzer Bericht über 400 junge Lyriker', SzLuK p. 69.
6 Weill in *Der deutsche Rundfunk*, 13 and 27.3.27; Nicholas Nabokov, 'Time in Reverie', BBC talk 11.6.58; Weill, 'Anmerkungen zu meiner Oper Mahagonny', *Die Musik*, 30.3.27, reprinted in Drew.
7 Conversation with Stephen Paul. Insert to Deutsche Grammophon Gesellschaft issue of Weill's works.
8 'Über die Verwendung von Musik für ein episches Theater', SzT; Sanders, p. 67.
9 Sternberg, pp. 7, 8, 9–11, 12.
10 SzT p. 181; 'Sollen wir nicht die Aesthetik liquidieren?', *Börsen-Courier*, 2.6.27, reprinted in SzT pp. 95–9; pp. 98–9; *Proletarisches Theater*, 1920–1, cited by Schumacher in Demetz.
11 Sanders, p. 91; 'Lotte Lenya remembers *Mahagonny*', booklet in Philips album of the recording.
12 Lenya in Witt.
13 'Lotte Lenya remembers *Mahagonny*'.
14 Sternberg, pp. 19–20; Erwin Piscator, *The Political Theatre* (tr. Hugh

Rorrison) (New York, 1978); letter
to Piscator, beginning of 8.27;
Willett (1978), p. 72.
15 B. Diebold, 'Das Piscator Drama',
Der Querschnitt, 1.28.

10 **Dreigroschenoper**

1 Aufricht.
2 Lenya in Witt.
3 Aufricht, p. 68.
4 Ibid., p. 70.
5 Sternberg, p. 21.
6 Aufricht, p. 72.
7 Zuckmayer, p. 267.
8 Aufricht, p. 78.
9 Heinrich Fischer,
Fassmann, pp. 50–1; *Berliner
Tageblatt*, 1.9.28;
Börsen-Courier, 1.9.28.
10 Kessler, *Tagebücher*, 27.9.28.

11 **Didactic Drama**

1 Letter to B. von Brentano, 9.10.28;
Sternberg, pp. 30–1; SzT p. 153.
2 Sternberg, pp. 36–7.
3 Aufricht, pp. 92–3.
4 'Über alltägliches Theater', GG
p. 768; GG pp. 766, 769.
5 Berlau interviewed in Bunge, *Brechts
Lai-Tu*.
6 *Bertolt Brecht: Leben und Werk im
Bild* (Insel), p. 181; Frisch (1972);
Encore 7–8.58, p. 26.
7 Kuckhahn interview; GW, vol. 8,
p. 100.
8 Sanders, p. 137.
9 Reich, p. 301.
10 *Unter dem Banner des Marxismus*,
III, vol. 5, Oct. 1929.
11 Eisler in Bunge (1970), pp. 96–7.
12 BBA 449/37.
13 Letter to Paul Hindemith end
1934/beginning 1935.
14 Lingen, pp. 43–5; letter to
Hauptmann 27.7.29.
15 *Versuche*, I, pp. 23, 24.

16 Letter to Weigel autumn 1928.
17 BBA 827/10.
18 Aufricht, p. 100.
19 Engel, pp. 81–4.
20 To Manfred Wekwerth and to the
singer Bettina Jonic, for instance.
21 Alfred Kerr, *Berliner Tageblatt*,
3.9.29.
22 Aufricht, p. 101.

12 **City of Nets**

1 Eisler in Bunge (1970), p. 256;
Howard Taubmann, 'From Long
Hair to Short', *New York Times*,
28.1.49; Sanders, p. 149.
2 'Lotte Lenya remembers
Mahagonny' (Philips album
booklet); H. H. Stuckenschmidt,
'City of Nets', in Philips album;
Alfred Polgar, 'Krach in Leipzig', in
Das Tagebuch, repr. in *Ja und Nein:
Darstellungen von Darstellungen*
(Hamburg, 1956).
3 Herbert F. Peyser, 'Berlin hears
Mahagonny', *New York Times*,
10.1.32; 'Lotte Lenya Remembers
Mahagonny'.
4 Drew, p. 20.
5 *Versuche*, vol. 2, pp. 102–3.
6 Ibid., p. 104.
7 Simone de Beauvoir, *The Prime of
Life* (London, 1965); John Oser
interview with G. Bachmann,
Cinémages, 3; 'Six Talks on G. W.
Pabst'.
8 Tatlow, p. 228.
9 Sanders, p. 159.
10 Hauptmann, pp. 176–7; BBA 158/44.
The dating is by Hertha Ramthun.
See Tatlow, p. 253.
11 Otto Hopf, *Musik und Gesellschaft*
(Wolfenbüttel, 1930), pp. 118–19;
review in *Die Weltbühne*, reprinted in
Der Jasager und der Neinsager, ed.
Peter Szondi (Frankfurt, 1966).
12 Eisler in Bunge (1970), p. 256.

13 Ibid., p. 157.
14 Ronald Hayman, 'A Last Interview with Brecht', *London Magazine*, 11.56.
15 Kessler, *Tagebücher*, 13.10.30.
16 Lotte H. Eisner, *The Haunted Screen* (tr. Roger Greaves) (Berkeley, 1973), pp. 343–5.
17 Ihering (1961), p. 136.

13 Change the World

1 Brecht quoted by Reich, p. 287.
2 Mayer (1961), p. 41; Engels, *Ludwig Feuerbach und der Ausgang der klassischen Philosophie* (1927), p. 98.
3 Note by Brecht cited by Willett (1959), p. 62.
4 Gisela Bahr (ed.), *Die heilige Johanna* (Frankfurt, 1973), pp. 212–13.
5 Letter to Lukács end 1930/beginning 1931.
6 Interview 3.34, *Brecht im Gespräch*, p. 191.
7 Walter Benjamin, Gershom Scholem, *Briefwechsel 1933–40*, ed. Scholem (Frankfurt, 1980), *passim*.
8 Benjamin, 'Ein Familiendrama auf dem epischen Theater' in *Versuche über Brecht*.
9 Weigel interview in Hecht (ed.), *Materialien zu Bertolt Brechts 'Die Mutter'*, p. 28.
10 BBA 1386/27; E. Preobrazhensky, *The ABC of Communism*, p. 245; Dickson, pp. 169–71.
11 Schacht's evidence at the Nuremberg trials, cited by Dickson, p. 169; Wolfgang Schäfer, *Entwicklung und Struktur der Staatspartei des Dritten Reiches* (Marburg, 1957), p. 17.
12 Tretiakov in Witt.
13 Aufricht, pp. 123–8, 127.
14 'Sonnet', BBA 152/67.
15 Weigel interview in Hecht, *Materialien*, op. cit., pp. 28–30.

16 Hecht and Unseld, pp. 17, 18; *Börsen-Courier*, 18.1.32; *Weltbühne*, 26.1.32.
17 Letter to Weigel, 1932; Berlau in Bunge, *Brechts Lai-Tu*; letter to Weigel end of 1932/beginning 1933.
18 Frisch (1972), pp. 26–7.
19 'Als der Faschismus immer stärker wurde', GG p. 205.
20 AA p. 217.
21 Ibid.; conversation reprinted in Benjamin, *Tagebücher*, 23.7.32.
22 AA p. 218.
23 Sanders, p. 189.
24 Sternberg, p. 37; Natalya Rosenel, 'Brecht und Lunatcharsky', *Neues Deutschland*, East Berlin 8.2.58.
25 Walter Hofer and Christoph Graf, 'Neue Quellen zur Reichstagsbrand Geschichte' in *Wissenschaft und Unterricht* 27, part 2, 1976.
26 Letter to Suhrkamp, 10.45.

14 Deadly Sins and Denmark

1 Engberg, p. 86.
2 Letter to Weigel 3.–4.33; 'Unpolitische Briefe', SzPuG p. 184.
3 Kesting, p. 70; letter from Brentano, Völker (1976), ch. 15; letter to Weigel, March–April 1933.
4 Barbara Brecht-Schall interview, 24.5.82.
5 Engberg, p. 72.
6 Letter from Weill to Hans and Rita Weill, 23.7.33.
7 Engberg, p. 79; letters to Margot van Brentano, 4.33; to Johannes Becher, 6.33.
8 Berlau in Bunge, *Brechts Lai-Tu*.
9 Hermann Kesten, 'Wiedergefundene Briefe', *Süddeutsche Zeitung*, 19/20.5.73.
10 Renoir, *Les filmes de ma vie*, tr. as *My Life and My Films* (London, 1974); letter to K. Korsch, end 12.33.
11 Letter from Benjamin to G. Scholem, 31.12.33; letter to Benjamin,

beginning of 1934; letter to Weigel, 12.33.

12 Letter to Benjamin, 22.12.33.
13 Engberg, p. 72.
14 Berlau in Bunge, op. cit.
15 Ibid.
16 Ibid.
17 Letter to Tretiakov, 4.33.
18 SzT, vol. 3, pp. 7–13.
19 Letter to G. Grosz 2.9.34; Mari Ohm in Engberg, p. 75.
20 Berlau in Bunge, op. cit.; Engberg, p. 90.
21 Interview 3.34, *Brecht im Gespräch*, pp. 192, 193.
22 Letter to Benjamin, 6.2.34.
23 Letter to Verlag Allert de Lange, 13.1.34; letter to Robert Storm Petersen, 1.35.
24 Benjamin, *Understanding Brecht*, pp. 108, 81.
25 'Lob des Zweifels', GG p. 626.
26 Letter to Verlag Allert de Lange, 23.6.34; letter to Margot von Brentano, 23.6.34; *Understanding Brecht*, pp. 93, 105, 106.
27 *Understanding Brecht*, p. 107; Yeats, 'A General Introduction for my Work', *Essays and Introductions* (London, 1961).
28 Letter to Georg Grosz, 2.9.34; *Understanding Brecht*, p. 112.
29 Draft of letter to his father, mid-1935.
30 AA 1934.
31 *Understanding Brecht*, p. 114.

15 **London and Moscow**

1 Postcard to Weigel, 13.10.34.
2 'Die Hölle der Enttäuschten', GG p. 532; letter to Weigel, 11.34.
3 Letter to Princess Bibesco, end of 1934; letter to Margot von Brentano, 12.34.
4 Letter from Piscator, 27.1.35, BBA.
5 Letter to Weigel, spring 35.

6 Letter to Weigel, 3.35; *Deutsche Zentral Zeitung* (Moscow), 23.5.35.
7 Reich, pp. 370–1.
8 'Verfremdungseffekte in chinesischer Schauspielkunst', SzT.
9 'Kritik der ch(inesichen) Sch(auspiel) k(unst)', BBA 61/25.
10 Ibid.
11 *Organon*, Section 44; 'Verfremdungseffekte'.
12 Ibid.
13 *Deutscher Reichsanzeiger u. Preussischer Staatsanzeiger*, 11.6.35, Ausbürgerungsliste.

16 **Anger in New York and Copenhagen**

1 Letter to Paula (Banholzer) Gross, 29.5.35.
2 *Berlinske Tidende*, 14.6.35; Engberg, p. 141; letter to Benjamin, 13.6.35; Gide, *Journal 1889–1939* (Paris, 1948), p. 1229.
3 Hecht, *Bertolt Brecht* (Insel edn), p. 119; Völker (1971), p. 63; letter to K. Korsch, late June or early July 1935; letter to G. Grosz, *c.* 7.35.
4 Letter to P. Peters, end of 8.35.
5 Witt, p. 122.
6 Ibid., p. 124.
7 'Rede an die dänischen Arbeiterschauspieler über die Kunst der Beobachtung', GG p. 763; GG pp. 1164, 1165; Minutes of the Executive Board of the Theatre Union, Baxandall, p. 70; GG pp. 559–60; Baxandall, p. 73.
8 Baxandall, pp. 74, 75, 74.
9 Letter to Weigel, 11.35; Baxandall, p. 75; Bunge (1970), p. 233.
10 Baxandall, p. 76.
11 Ibid., p. 77; Gorelik in *Theatre Arts Monthly*, 3.57.
12 Baxandall, p. 76; Sklar quoted by Baxandall, p. 76.
13 *New York Times*, 21.11.35; letter to Piscator, 8.12.35; Willett (1978), p. 83.

14 Letter to V. Jerome, 2.36.
15 Bunge (1970), p. 233; letter to Weigel end 1935/beginning 1936.
16 Baxandall, p. 81.
17 Ibid; letter to Gorki, 18.12.35.
18 Letter to Piscator, 7.36.
19 Bunge (1970), pp. 63–7.
20 BBA 2112/49–50; GG p. 565.
21 Engberg, p. 118.
22 SzT p. 102.
23 *Berlinske Tidende*; Völker (1976), p. 246.
24 Harald Lander, in Engberg, p. 175; letter to K. Korsch, late 1936 or early 1937.
25 Letters to Piscator, Jean Renoir and Max Gorelik, 16., 17. and 19.3.37.

17 Civil War in Spain

1 Note at end of play.
2 GW, vol. 17, pp. 987–8.
3 S. Spender, *World within World* (London, 1951), p. 240.
4 Gide, *Journal* 1889–1939 (Paris, 1948), p. 1126; Gide, *Retour de l'U.R.S.S.*
5 Spender, op. cit., p. 241.
6 GW, vol. 8, pp. 247–50.
7 Berlau in Bunge, *Brechts Lai-Tu*; 'Morgens und abends zu lesen', GG p. 586; 'Als er sie abholen kam', GG p. 782.
8 Letter to Weigel, beginning of 11.37.
9 Letter to K.Korsch, *c.* 10.37; 'Beschreibung des Spiels der H.W.', GG p. 782.
10 Letters to Weigel, 4.11.37; 11.37.
11 'Rede eines sterbenden Römischen Vaters an seinen Sohn', GG pp. 573–4.
12 GG pp. 697, 637, 638.
13 GG pp. 718, 719.

18 Caesar and Galileo: Businessman and Rebel

1 Letter to Martin Andersen Nexö, 25.3.38; letter from M. Steffin to Benjamin, Völker (1971), p. 70; letter to the American Guild for German Cultural Freedom, 9.38; to K. Korsch, Völker, p. 70.
2 Engberg, p. 196; letter to K. Korsch, 4.38; letter to S. Dudow, 4.38.
3 AJ 15.8.38.
4 GG p. 634.
5 Letter to Piscator, 3/4.38; to S. Dudow, 4.38; to Weigel, 5.38.
6 Benjamin, pp. 46–7; *Das Schwarze Korps* (Munich), 7.7.38.
7 *Das Wort*, 6.38.
8 'Die Strassenszene', *Versuche* 10, 1950.
9 Letter from Benjamin to Kitty Marx-Steinschneider, Völker (1971), p. 72.
10 Letter to K. Korsch, 11.37; Benjamin, *Understanding Brecht*, p. 116; letter to Feuchtwanger, end of 11.37; *Understanding Brecht*, pp. 115, 114–15, 119, 115.
11 SzPuG pp. 111–14.
12 AJ 23.7.38.
13 *Understanding Brecht*, p. 117.
14 GG pp. 683–4.
15 *Understanding Brecht*, pp. 117–18.
16 Ibid., pp. 119, 120.
17 Ibid.
18 AJ 16.8.38.
19 AJ 25.7.38, 7.38. Draft of 'Weite und Vielfalt der realistischen Schreibweise', article for *Das Wort* in Willett, *Brecht on Theatre*, pp. 114, 109, 112; *Understanding Brecht*, p. 121.
20 *Understanding Brecht*, AJ 18.8.38.
21 AJ 25.9.38; 7.10.38.
22 Lyon (1978), p. 55; Berlau interview with Lyon, 23.10.70, Lyon (1980), pp. 55, 56.
23 Völker (1971), p. 74; AJ 23.11.38; Bunge (1970), p. 249; Lyon (1978), p. 57.
24 Leonard Olschki, *Galileo und seine Zeit* (Halle, 1927), cited by Dickson, p. 471.

25 GG p. 641; note on *Galileo*, Demetz, p. 118.
26 Demetz, p. 117; written answer to a question posed in 1955 at a Darmstadt Theatre conference.
27 Schumacher (1968), p. 24.
28 GW, vol. 17, p. 1110.
29 Marx and Engels, *Über Kunst und Literatur*, ed. M. Kliem (Berlin 1967–8), vol. I, p. 398; Marx-Engels, *Werke* (Berlin 1956–68), vol. XX, p. 457; *Galileo*, Scene 1.
30 Letter to Christina di Lorena, Granduchessa di Toscana (written 1615; publ. 1637).
31 Letter to Hans Tombrock, BBA 1940/1.
32 *Berlinske Tidende*, 6.1.39.
33 Berlau in *Brechts Lai-Tu*; 1934 interview in Hecht, *Brecht im Gespräch*, p. 196; AJ 25.2.39.
34 AJ 1.39; GG p. 743.
35 *Versuche* 2.
36 BBA 125/21; 127/42; 124/58.
37 AJ 15.3.39; Berlau in *Brechts Lai-Tu*, AJ 15.3.39.

19 **History of the Small Fry**

1 AJ 15.3.39; letter to H. P. Matthis, 11.4.39.
2 Letter to Matthis, 11.4.39.
3 AJ 15.7.39.
4 *Texte für Filme*, II, pp. 356–65.
5 Letters to Tombrock. *Bilder und Graphiken zu Werken von Bertolt Brecht*, catalogue IV, Neue Münchener Galerie 64.
6 AJ 5.39 Whitsun.
7 AJ 9.9.39; 1.9.39.
8 AJ 3, 4.9.39.
9 AJ 4, 11.9.39.
10 AJ 11, 21.9.39.
11 'Note for Scandinavian audiences'; BBA 2112/217–19.
12 Hecht (ed.), *Materialien zu Brechts*

'*Mutter Courage*'; GW, vol. 17, p. 1138.
13 'Verfremdungseffekte in den erzählenden Bildern des älteren Brueghels', *Bildende Kunst* 1957, no. 4.
14 Berlau in *Brechts Lai-Tu*.
15 Gerda Lindner quoted in Jan Olson, *Bertolt Brechts schwedisches Exil* (Lund, 1969), p. 68.
16 AJ 7, 14.12.39.
17 AJ 14.1.40.
18 *Prosa*, pp. 330, 336.

20 **Near the Finland Station**

1 AJ 6.5.40; letter to H. P. Matthis, 5.40; Schumacher (1978), p. 152.
2 AJ 6.5.40; *Prosa*, pp. 1383, 1389.
3 Letter to Tombrock, 4.5.40.
4 AJ 11.6.40.
5 AJ 14. 20.6.40.
6 AJ 6.5.40; Prologue to *Der gute Mensch von Sezuan*.
7 Tatlow, pp. 268–9.
8 AJ 29, 30.6.40.
9 AJ 1.7.40.

21 **Puntila and the Sawdust Princess**

1 AJ 5, 30.7.40.
2 Letter to Hella Wuolijoki, n.d., Völker (1976), pp. 297–8; Berlau in *Brechts Lai-Tu*; letter to Hella Wuolijoki, 1940/41.
3 Letter to Berlau, 7.7.40.
4 AJ 15.9.40; 30.7.40.
5 AJ 8.7.40.
6 'Über Lyrik', p. 89; AJ 19.8.40.
7 AJ 5.8.40; 16.7.40.
8 AJ 27.8.40; 2.9.40.
9 'Anmerkungen zum Volksstück', *Versuche* 10, pp. 117–18, 121–2.
10 AJ 6, 10, 16.9.40.
11 AJ 19.9.40; 6.7.40; 24.9.40.
12 *Prosa*, p. 394.
13 AJ 7.10.40; Barbara Brecht-Schall interview, 24.5.82.
14 AJ 16.10.40; 18.11.40.

15 Diary of Sylvie Kylliki-Kilpi, 6.11.40.
16 AJ 4.12.40; 20.6.40.
17 AJ 11.12.40; 'Finnische Landschaft', GG p. 822.
18 AJ 25, 30.1.41; 20.4.41.
19 AJ 18.2.42.

22 Hit Man

1 Lyon (1980), p. 27.
2 AJ 10.3.41.
3 Bernard Kissel, *Tages-Anzeiger* (Zürich), 21.4.41, and Bernard Diebold in *Die Tat* (Zürich), 22.2.41; AJ 20.4.41.
4 AJ 24.4.41.
5 Letter from A. Granach to Lotte Lieven-Stiegel, 16.7.41, and postscript 22.7.41, both in Granach Archiv, Akademie der Künste, Berlin.
6 AJ 16.3.42.
7 Letter to Mikhail Apletin, 30.5.41.
8 AJ 13.7.41.
9 Letter to Frau Steffin, Schumacher (1978), p. 160; Berlau in *Brechts Lai-Tu.*

23 Suffocating in the States

1 AJ 13.7.41.
2 AJ 13.7.41; 1.8.41.
3 AJ 23.3.42; 21.1.42; letter to H. R. Hays, end of 1.42.
4 AJ 16.7.42; Eric Bentley, intro. to Brecht, *Parables for the Theatre* (Oxford 1948); Losey, p. 12.
5 AJ 8.41; 'Ich der Überlebende', GG p. 182.
6 AA p. 232.
7 AJ 9.8.41.
8 AJ 22.10.41; 21.1.42.
9 Lyon (1980), p. 45; Baxandall, p. 85.
10 Letters to Piscator, 14.9.41; 8–9.41; 9.41.
11 AJ 4.10.41; Gottfried Reinhardt, *Der Liebhaber* (Munich 1973), p. 268.
12 Letter to Benjamin, 'Brecht in der Emigration', *Neue deutsche Literatur*

II (1963), p. 182; AJ 27.7.42; Lyon (1980), p. 51.
13 AJ 2.12.41.
14 AJ 3, 8.12.41; 14.8.44; 17.12.41.
15 Lyon (1980), p. 38.
16 AJ 27, 31.12.41.
17 AJ 9.1.41; GG p. 841; Bentley intro. to *Parables.*
18 AJ 16.1.42; 11.4.42; Cp. 'Die Schande', GG p. 858.
19 AJ 18.3.42.
20 Völker (1976), p. 331.
21 AJ 8.4.42; Lyon (1980), pp. 53–4.
22 AJ 21.4.42.
23 AJ 8.41.
24 Lyon (1978), pp. 59–61, 63; letter to Max Reinhardt, end of 5.42.
25 Eisler in Bunge (1970), p. 237; letter to Berlau end of 5/beginning of 6.42; Lyon (1980), p. 103.
26 Lyon (1980), pp. 94, 362.

24 Sour Smell of Success

1 Letters to Berlau, end of 5.42, beginning of 6.42, and 6.42.
2 Letter to K. Korsch, 10.42; Bunge (1970), p. 235.
3 AJ 21.10.42; Peter Bogdanovich, *Fritz Lang in America* (London 1967), p. 38.
4 AJ 27, 29.6.42.
5 Letter to Berlau, n.d.; AJ 20.7.42; 12, 14, 17.8.42.
6 Letter to K. Korsch, 10.42; AJ 19, 20, 22.8.42.
7 AJ 5.8.42; Lyon (1980), p. 60; AJ 5.8.42.
8 AJ 16, 18.10.42; Lyon (1980), p. 61.
9 AJ 18.10.42.
10 Lyon (1980), p. 64; AJ 2, 4.11.42.
11 AJ 24.11.42.
12 Lyon (1980), p. 207.
13 AJ 20, 24.12.42; 25.11.42; 3.1.43.
14 AJ 3, 20.1.43; Lyon (1980), p. 87; AJ 20.1.43; 5.8.42; Lyon (1980), p. 67.
15 Lyon (1980), p. 103.

25 Old Friends in New York

1   Letters from Piscator, 23.9.41 and 21.1.42; letter from Hays, n.d.
2   Letters from Piscator, 1.12.42.
3   AJ 12.2.43.
4   AJ 14.2.43; letter to K. Korsch, end of 1942.
5   AJ 16.2.43.
6   AJ 3, 4 and 5.43; Witt, pp. 129, 176–8.
7   Lyon (1980), p. 364.
8   Note by Hays in Brecht, *Collected Plays*, vol. 7, p. 334; Lyon (1980), pp. 110–11.
9   Note by Hays, op. cit.
10 Letter to Hays, 6.43.

26 Schweyk Resurrectus

1   *Aufbau* 9.4.43.
2   AJ 3, 4, 5.43; Knust (ed.), *Materialien zu Schweyk* (Frankfurt, 1974).
3   Willett, see Lyon (1980), p. 365.
4   Letters to Berlau, 26.5.43; 3, 4, 11.6.43.
5   AJ 27.5.43.
6   Ibid.
7   AJ 29.5.43.
8   AJ 9, 24.6.43.
9   AJ 24.6.43.
10 Letters to Berlau 23.6.43; 2.7.43.
11 AJ 29.8.43; news-clipping stuck into AJ 7.9.43.
12 Eisler in Bunge (1970), p. 61.
13 Lyon (1980), p. 261; AJ 1.8.43.
14 Knust, p. 295.
15 AJ 20.9.43.
16 Ibid.
17 Letters to Berlau 7, 14.9.43.
18 Ibid.; two letters to Kreymborg, n.d. (9.43); letter to Berlau 18.9.43; Lyon (1980), p. 117.
19 Letters to Berlau 28.6.43; 5.7.43; AJ 3–6.7.43; letter to Berlau, n.d.
20 Letters to W. H. Auden, n.d. (12.43);

beginning of 12.43; note by Hays in *Collected Plays* vol. 7.
21 Letters to Berlau 9.43; 27.9.43.
22 Letter from Weill 5.12.43.

27 New Kind of Folk Play

1   Supplement to Dramatists' Guild Contract, 7.12.44.
2   Letter from Luise Rainer, 24.1.44; Lyon (1980), p. 124.
3   Lyon (1980), p. 125; letter to Berlau, 2.4.44; Tatlow, p. 294; GW, vol. 17, p. 1205; BBA 128/6; AJ 10.4.44.
4   Lyon (1980), p. 78; contracts dated 27.3.44; mid-11.43 to mid-3.44.
5   Joseph Losey interview, 27.11.81.
6   'Aufbau einer Rolle', GW, vol. 17, p. 1118.
7   Letters to Berlau 2, 18.4.44; AJ 29.4.44; 30.7.44; 'Aufbau einer Rolle'.
8   AJ 8.5.44.
9   Letter to Berlau, 7/8.6.44.
10 AJ 19.7.44; Lyon (1980), p. 297.
11 Aufricht, pp. 258–9, 260.
12 AJ 17, 28.5.44.
13 AJ 14.8.44.
14 Lyon (1980), pp. 309, 314.
15 AJ 28.8.44.
16 Ibid.
17 AJ 1.9.44; Lyon (1980), p. 224; AJ 5.9.44.
18 'Der Bauch Laughtons', GG p. 775; Barbara Brecht-Schall interview, 14.1.81; Guy Flatley, 'Remembrances of Joseph Losey's Productions', *Los Angeles Times*, 9.3.75; AA p. 214.
19 Lyon (1980), p. 171; 'Aufbau einer Rolle'.
20 AJ 10.12.44; 'Aufbau einer Rolle'; letter to Berlau n.d. (7.45); AJ 10.12.44.
21 'Aufbau einer Rolle'; Lyon (1980) p. 173.
22 'Aufbau einer Rolle'; Willett, *Brecht on Theatre*, p. 168.

23 AJ 20.7.43; GW, vol. 17, pp. 947-8.
24 AJ 11.2.44.
25 Lyon (1980), p. 285; AJ 3.3.44.
26 AJ 4, 5.3.44.
27 AJ 10.3.44; letter to B. Viertel, 3.45.
28 Letter from E. Bentley to James Laughlin, 2.4.45; to B. Viertel, n.d.
29 Letter to Auden, 1.45; to Berlau, late 3.45 or early 4.45; AJ, end of 4.45.
30 Lyon (1980), p. 226; GG p. 938.
31 AJ, end of 4.45; 3.5.34.
32 Letter to Berlau, 4.45; to P. Tillich, 8.45.
33 Lyon (1980), p. 134; letter to Berlau, mid-4.45; letter from Piscator, 29.5.45.
34 Lyon (1980), p. 137; K. Phelan, 'The Private Life of the Master Race', *Commonweal*, 29.6.45.
35 L. Nichols, *New York Times*, 13.6.45; B. Rascoe, *New York World Telegram*, 13.6.45.

28 Galileo and Hiroshima

1 Letter to Berlau, 7.45.
2 AJ 30.7.45.
3 AJ 10.9.45.
4 Ibid.; letter to Berlau, 7/8.45.
5 Letter to Berlau, late 9.45 or early 10.45; AJ 20.9.45.
6 AJ 10.10.45; 10.12.45.
7 AJ 10.10.45.
8 Ibid.
9 AJ 20.9.45; 10, 17.12.45.
10 BBA 582/13-15; 582/16-19; letter from Welles, 23.2.46; from the Berg-Allenberg Agency, 16.4.46; Lyon (1980), p. 179; letter from Welles to Laughton, late 4.46 or early 5.46.
11 F. Reyher diary, 7.5.46.
12 Letters to Peter Suhrkamp, 10.45; end of 1945/beginning of 1946; BBA 211/28.
13 Sternberg, p. 54; letter to Reyher, 1.46.
14 Lyon (1980), p. 222; letter to E. Bergner, 16.2.46.
15 Letter to Bergner, ibid.; Lyon (1980), p. 237; SzT, vol. 4, pp. 194-6; letter to Bergner, 16.2.46; *Duchess* (Brecht's version), Act III, Sc. 1; letter to Bergner, 16.2.46.
16 Lyon (1980), pp. 227, 225.
17 H. Winge, 'Brecht and the Cinema', *Sight and Sound*, Winter 1947.
18 Lyon (1980), pp. 314-15.
19 Letter from R. A. Wilson to Laughton, 25.6.46; letter to Reyher, mid 7.46.
20 Letter to Reyher, ibid.; letter from Reyher, 15.8.46.
21 Letter to Reyher, n.d. (7.46); H. Clurman, *All People Are Famous* (New York 1974), pp. 140-41.
22 BBA 211/29.
23 Lyon (1980), pp. 179-81; Losey (1961).
24 Lyon (1980), p. 182; *Losey on Losey* (London 1967), p. 170.
25 Hayman, *John Gielgud* (London 1971), p. 148; Lyon (1980), p. 145.
26 Letter to P. Czinner, 26.9.46.
27 Lyon (1980), p. 146; letter from Ann Elmo and Richard Rodgers, 22.10.46.
28 Letter from the Berg-Allenberg Agency, 16.10.46; letter to E. Bentley, 7-8.46.
29 Letter from Weigel to Wuolijoki, 27.1.46; Sternberg, p. 45; AJ 25.9.45; letter to Berlau, late 9.46 or early 10.46; letter to Bergner, n.d.
30 Letters to Neher, 10.46; 1.11.46; 12.46; to Reyher 3.47; Lyon (1980), p. 313.
31 Letters to Piscator, 3.47; 2.47.
32 Letter from Losey to Reyher, 27.4.47; Lyon (1980), p. 184.
33 Lyon (1980), p. 185, 186; Berlau in Bunge's *Brechts Lai-Tu*.
34 Losey interview, 27.11.81.
35 Lyon (1980), p. 197; 'Aufbau einer Rolle', GW, vol. 17, p. 1118.
36 Hecht, *Materialien zu Galileo*, p. 76.

37 Losey, p. 10.

38 Berlau in *Brechts Lai-Tu*; 'Aufbau
einer Rolle'.

39 Letter to Reyher, 15.9.47.

40 Letter to Reyher, early 9.47.

41 Bentley, intro. to Brecht, *Parables for
the Theatre* (Oxford 1948).

42 Lyon (1980), p. 323.

43 Letter to Stefan Brecht, 12.47.

44 Schumacher interview, 22.5.82.

29 **A Home Outside Germany**

1 AJ 1, 4.11.47; letters to Berlau,
5.11.47; 3.11.47.

2 Neher diary, 5.11.47.

3 Ibid.

4 Witt, p. 143.

5 AJ 16.12.47.

6 Ibid.

7 Hecht, *Materialien zur Antigone*,
p. 126.

8 Losey interview, 27.11.81; *Losey on
Losey* (London, 1967), pp. 168–9; AJ
22.12.47.

9 AJ 25.12.47.

10 Berlau in Bunge, *Brechts Lai-Tu*; AJ
4, 18.1.48.

11 Letter to Hans Curjel, 7.2.48.

12 Letters to Reyher, 7.2.48; 4.48.

13 AJ 2.4.48; letter to Weill, 6.12.48.

14 AJ 12.4.48.

15 Witt, pp. 146, 144.

16 Letter to Reyher, 4.48.

17 Giehse, pp. 92–3, 173.

18 'Notizen über die Zürcher
Erstaufführung', *Versuche* 22–4,
p. 110; AJ 10.6.48; 'Notizen', p. 111.

19 Letter to Arnold Ljungdal, 6.40;
Witt, p. 144; *Organon*, section 15.

20 *Organon*, sections 16, 17, 2, 20, 24,
23.

21 Lenin, *Zur Kritik der Hegelschen
Wissenschaft der Logik*, ed. V.
Adoratski (Vienna and Berlin, 1932).

22 *Organon*, sections 45, 52, 49.

23 Letter from Schiller to Goethe,
26.12.1797.

24 *Organon*, sections 50, 53, 49, 57, 53.

25 AJ 15.4.48; Frisch (1972).

26 *Organon*, section 59.

27 *Organon*, section 55.

28 AJ 18.10.48.

29 AJ 19, 22.10.48.

30 **East Berlin**

1 AJ 22.10.48.

2 Kuckhahn interview, 18.5.82; AJ
23.10.48; 3.2.49.

3 Dymschitz, 'Ein gewöhnliches Genie',
Theater der Zeit, Berlin 1966, vol.
XIV, p. 14; AJ 23.10.48.

4 AJ 24.10.48.

5 AJ 25.10.48; letter to H. Kuckhahn,
4.47; AJ 25.10.48.

6 Agee.

7 AJ 27.10.48.

8 AJ 31.10.48; 3.11.48.

9 AJ 8.11.48; 3.11.48.

10 Letter to Neher, 25.1.49.

11 'Anmerkungen', p. 19.

12 Ernst Kahler interview, 18.5.82; SzT,
vol. 6, pp. 160–1; Weigel interview in
Theaterarbeit; AJ 25.11.48.

13 AJ 10.12.48.

14 Witt, pp. 179, 172–5.

15 AJ 12.1.49.

16 Ibid.

17 AJ 18.12.48; Frisch (1972).

18 AJ 21.12.48; 20.12.48.

19 AJ 6.1.49.

20 AJ 11.1.49.

21 Letter to G. Gründgens, 18.1.49.

31 **The Berliner Ensemble**

1 Letter to Neher, 25.1.49; AJ 20.2.49.

2 Letter to Piscator, 9.2.49.

3 Letter to Piscator, 9.2.49; to Reyher,
21.2.49; to Weigel, end 2.49.

4 Letter to Piscator, 5.3.49.

5 Letter to Viertel, 3/4.49.

6   Letters to Weigel, 5.3.49; 3.3.49; to von Einem, beginning of 4.49.
7   Marx, pamphlet later titled 'The Civil War in France'.
8   Letter to Weigel, 6.3.49.
9   Ibid., end of 2.49; beginning of 3.49.
10   Ibid., 6.3.49; letter to von Einem, beginning of 4.49.
11   Schumacher (1978), p. 235.
12   AJ Whit Monday 1949.
13   18.6.49.
14   AJ 28.8–4.9.49.
15   *Theaterarbeit*, pp. 22–8.
16   Ibid., p. 20.
17   Ibid., pp. 21, 42.
18   Ibid., pp. 22, 45.
19   Letter to von Einem, 12.10.49.
20   AJ 13.11.49.
21   Letter to Pieck, 2.11.49.
22   AJ 13.11.49.
23   Letter to Städtische Bühnen, Wuppertal, 26.8.49; to Staatstheater Dresden, end of 1949/beginning of 1950; to Städtische Bühnen, Wuppertal, 26.8.49.
24   AJ 14.11.49.
25   AJ 9.12.48.
26   AJ Whitsun 1949.
27   AJ 14.11.49; 22.12.49; 5.3.50.
28   AJ 5, 8.3.50.
29   *Theaterarbeit*, p. 131.
30   AJ 8.3.50; 'An den Schauspieler P.L. im Exil', GG p. 967; letter to von Einem, 2.3.50.
31   *Theaterarbeit*, p. 120.
32   AJ 1.5.50.
33   Agee, p. 118; AJ 26.5.50.
34   AJ beginning of 8.50.
35   Letters to Reyher, 3.47; 4.48; Lyon (1980), pp. 142–3.
36   Frisch (1966), p. 18; Brant, p. 24; Lyon (1978), pp. 148–9, 146.
37   Berlau in Bunge *Brechts Lai-Tu*.
38   AJ 10.50.
39   AJ 8.10.50; *Theaterarbeit*, p. 299.
40   *Theaterarbeit*, p. 412; Michael Mellinger, 'Goodbye to Berlin',

Encore, 9–10.60; Weigel interview in *Theaterarbeit*; C. Weber, pp. 102, 104.
41   Wekwerth, p. 244; Mellinger, op. cit.
42   *Theaterarbeit*, p. 387.
43   *Messingkauf*, 4th night.
44   Reich, p. 383.
45   *Messingkauf*, 4th night.
46   *Theaterarbeit*, p. 387; *Mutter Courage*, Anmerkungen, p. 14.
47   Wekwerth, p. 13.
48   Ibid., p. 83.
49   Mellinger, op. cit.; Bunge interview, 21.5.82; BBA 1340/19.
50   Bunge interview, 21.5.82.
51   Schubert interview, 9.5.82; Mellinger, op. cit.
52   AJ 21.5.51; letter to K. Reichel, end of 1954 or beginning of 1955.
53   *Theaterarbeit*, pp. 134–5.
54   Ibid., pp. 156, 151.
55   Ibid., p. 151; *Messingkauf*, 4th night.

32   Setbacks

1   Witt, pp. 180–1.
2   AJ 15.1.51.
3   *Neues Deutschland*, 22.3.51.
4   Letter to W. Ulbricht, 12.3.51; to Anton Ackermann, 25.3.51; to W. Pieck, 6.4.51.
5   GW, vol. 7, p. 1269; letter to B. Viertel, 11.50.
6   AJ 20.5.51.
7   Wekwerth, p. 201.
8   AJ 26.5.51.
9   Wekwerth, pp. 83–4.
10   'Anmerkungen', p. 19, and Wekwerth, p. 84; 'Anmerkungen', pp. 37, 48.
11   Letter to von Einem, 18.10.51.
12   AJ 11.7.51.
13   Letter to Neher, mid-1950; to Leonard Steckel, 4.51; to B. Viertel, 6–7.51; to Neher, mid-1950.
14   *Theaterarbeit*, p. 146.
15   AJ 21.8.51; Brant, pp. 32–3.

16 Giehse, pp. 95–100.
17 AJ 14.2.52; AA pp. 197–8; letter to Reich, 26.6.56.
18 AJ 25.2.52; letters from Jack Lindsay to the author 25.7.81 and 6.8.81.
19 Völker (1971), p. 143; SzL, vol. 2, p. 249; AJ 6.4.52; 2.2.52; Wekwerth, p. 99.
20 'Weitere Bemerkungen zum Faust Problem', *Neues Deutschland*, 27.5.52.
21 AJ 15.7.52; 30.8.52.
22 Witt, p. 240; AJ 28.12.52.
23 Brant, p. 37; *Prosa*, vol. 2, p. 450.
24 AJ 6.12.52.
25 AJ 27.12.52; Einstein, *Mein Weltbild* (Berlin, 1955), pp. 22–3.

33 **Whitewashing**

1 AJ 4.3.53.
2 Agee, pp. 82–3; GW, vol. 7, p. 881.
3 'Für den Sieg des sozialistischen Realismus auf der Bühne', *Neues Deutschland*, 17.4.53; *Berliner Stimme*, 6.6.53.
4 Witt, p. 226.
5 GW, vol. 7, p. 727.
6 Letter to Grotewohl, 15.6.53.
7 Wekwerth, p. 64; letter to Ulbricht, 17.6.53.
8 *Neues Deutschland*, 23.6.53.
9 Letter to P. Suhrkamp, 1.7.53.
10 *Prosa*, vol. 2, p. 386; Leiser, 'Brecht, Grass und der 17. Juni', *Weltwoche* (Zürich), 11.2.66.
11 Hayman (1956); Völker (1976), p. 381.
12 Völker (1976), p. 398; Benjamin diary 9.34; *Me-Ti*, *Prosa*, pp. 419–585.
13 'Böser Morgen', GG, p. 1010; 'Die Lösung', p. 1009; AJ 20.8.53.
14 AJ 12.9.53; 7.7.54.
15 22.2.54 SzPuG p. 328; Koenigswald.
16 Letter to Weigel, mid-1953.
17 AJ 15–30.10.53.
18 AJ 7.2.54.

19 *Neues Deutschland*, 12.8.53; Völker (1976), p. 388.
20 AA p. 237.
21 AA pp. 237–8.
22 Letters to Berlau, BBA 676/07; 799/48; 3.4.55.
23 Völker (1976), pp. 387–8.
24 Letter to Grotewohl, 19.7.54.
25 Ekkehard Schall interview, 14.5.82.
26 BBA 92/43.

34 **Schiffbauerdamm**

1 Berlau in Bunge, *Brechts Lai-Tu*.
2 Hecht, *Materialien zu Brechts 'Der kaukasische Kreidekreis'*, pp. 95, 97, 98.
3 Letter from Dessau, no date.
4 *Brecht im Gespräch*, pp. 158 ff.
5 *Materialien*, p. 62; Rülicke-Weiler, p. 58; Hurwicz in *Materialien*, pp. 57, 60.
6 Rülicke-Weiler, Witt, p. 209.
7 Letter to E. F. Burian, 20.9.54; AJ 10–11.54.
8 Letter to Ulbricht, 2.12.54; Völker (1971), p. 151.
9 Reich, p. 385.
10 AA p. 238; Schumacher (1978), p. 105.
11 AJ 5.55.
12 Reich, pp. 381, 380–7, 387; letter to N. Okhlopkov, 21.5.55; to Faina Ranevskaia, 25.5.55; to Joan Littlewood, 22.6.55.
13 SzPuG pp. 343–4.
14 AJ 5.55.
15 Schumacher (1978), p. 286; Pozner in Witt, p. 270.
16 Witt, p. 269.
17 Ibid., pp. 270, 268.
18 Interviews with Ekkehard Schall and Barbara Brecht-Schall 14 and 24.5.82.
19 Schumacher (1978), p. 304; Völker (1971), p. 154.
20 Witt, pp. 270–1.

21 'Aufbau einer Rolle – Busch', GW, vol. 17, p. 1118.
22 Schumacher (1978), p. 306; BBA 1134/01-136.
23 Letter to Berlau, 11.2.56; Witt, p. 278; letter to Berlau, 11.2.56; Reich, p. 388.
24 Wekwerth interview, 21.5.82; Barbara Brecht-Schall interview, 24.5.82.
25 Letter to E. Busch, 30.4.56; BBA 1061.
26 'Als ich im weissen Krankenzimmer war', GG, vol. 2, p. 451; Giehse, p. 79.
27 Wekwerth, pp. 76–8.
28 Wekwerth interview, 21.5.82.
29 Völker (1976), p. 388.

Bibliography

Brecht in German

Gesammelte Werke, 20 vols ('Werkausgabe'), Frankfurt, 1967
Arbeitsjournal, 2 vols, Frankfurt, 1973
Versuche 1–15, Frankfurt, 1957–9
Briefe, 2 vols, Frankfurt, 1981
Prosa, 4 vols, Frankfurt, 1980
Gesammelte Gedichte, 4 vols, Frankfurt, 1967
Tagebücher 1920–22, Autobiographische Aufzeichnungen 1920–54, Frankfurt, 1978
Schriften zur Politik und Gesellschaft 1919–1956, Frankfurt, 1967
Schriften zur Literatur und Kunst, Frankfurt, 1967
Schriften zum Theater, Frankfurt, 1963
Texte für Filme, Frankfurt, 1969
Über Lyrik, Frankfurt, 1964
'Bei Durchsicht meiner ersten Stücke' (introduction to vol. 1 of plays), March, 1954
Brecht im Gespräch. Diskussionen, Dialoge, Interviews (ed. Werner Hecht), Frankfurt, 1975
Theaterarbeit: 6 Aufführungen des Berliner Ensembles, Dresden, no date
Materialien zu Bertolt Brechts 'Die Mutter', ed. Werner Hecht, Frankfurt, 1969
Materialien zu Brechts 'Leben des Galilei', ed. Werner Hecht, Frankfurt, 1963
Materialien zu Brechts 'Mutter Courage und ihre Kinder', ed. Werner Hecht, Frankfurt, 1964
Materialien zu Brechts 'Der kaukasische Kreidekreis', ed. Werner Hecht, Frankfurt, 1966
Materialien zu Brechts 'Der Gute Mensch von Sezuan', ed. Werner Hecht, Frankfurt, 1968
Materialien zur Antigone, ed. Werner Hecht, Frankfurt, 1965

Works by Brecht available in English

Collected Plays, ED. JOHN WILLETT AND RALPH MANHEIM

1	*Baal, Drums in the Night, In the Jungle of Cities, The Life of Edward II of England, A Respectable Wedding, The Beggar, Driving Out a Devil, Lux in Tenebris, The Catch*
2.i	*Man equals Man, The Elephant Calf*
2.ii	*The Threepenny Opera*
2.iii	*The Rise and Fall of the City of Mahagonny* and *The Seven Deadly Sins*
5.i	*Life of Galileo*
5.ii	*Mother Courage and her Children*
6.ii	*The Resistible Rise of Arturo Ui*

7   *The Visions of Simone Machard, Schweyk in the Second World War, The Caucasian Chalk Circle, The Duchess of Malfi*

INDIVIDUAL PLAYS

Baal (tr. Peter Tegel)
The Caucasian Chalk Circle (tr. James and Tania Stern with W. H. Auden)
The Days of the Commune (tr. Clive Barker and Arno Reinfrank)
Drums in the Night (tr. John Willett)
The Good Person of Szechwan (tr. John Willett)
In the Jungle of Cities (tr. Gerhard Nellhaus)
Life of Galileo (tr. John Willett)
The Life of Galileo (tr. Howard Brenton – National Theatre version)
Man equals Man and *The Elephant Calf* (tr. Gerhard Nellhaus)
The Measures Taken and other *Lehrstücke* (various translators)
The Mother (tr. Steve Gooch)
Mother Courage and her Children (tr. John Willett)
Mr Puntila and his Man Matti (tr. John Willett)
The Resistible Rise of Arturo Ui (tr. Ralph Manheim)
A Respectable Wedding and other one-act plays (various translators)
The Rise and Fall of the City of Mahagonny and *The Seven Deadly Sins*(tr. W. H. Auden and Chester Kallman)
St Joan of the Stockyards (tr. Frank Jones)
The Threepenny Opera (tr. Ralph Manheim and John Willett)

POETRY

Poems 1913–1956 (ed. John Willett and Ralph Manheim), also available without the notes in 3 volumes (1913–28, 1929–38, 1938–56), 1976

CRITICISM

Brecht on Theatre (tr. and ed. John Willett)
The Messingkauf Dialogues (tr. John Willett)

FICTION

Short Stories 1921–1946 (ed. John Willett and Ralph Manheim)
The Threepenny Novel (tr. Desmond I. Vesey) (available in Penguin)

DIARIES 1920–22 (tr. John Willett)

All the above are published by Eyre Methuen.

Political and Social Background

Agee, Joel *Twelve Years: An American Boyhood in East Germany*, New York, 1981
Benjamin, Walter *Briefe*, 2 vols, Frankfurt, 1966
    Tagebücher, Frankfurt, 1980
Brant, Stefan *Der Aufstand*; tr. by Charles Wheeler as *The East German Rising*, Nijmegen, 1955

Craig, Gordon A. *Germany 1866-45*, Oxford, 1978
Fischer, Ernst *An Opposing Man* (tr. P. and B. Ross), London, 1974
Kessler, Harry Graf *Tagebücher 1918-37*, Frankfurt, 1961
Koenigswald, Harold von *The Soviet Zone of Germany*, Esslingen, 1959
Mander, John *Berlin: The Eagle and the Bear*, London, 1959
Mann, Thomas *Betrachtungen eines Unpolitischen*, 1918
Milosz, Czeslaw *The Captive Mind* (tr. Jane Zielonka), London, 1953
Taylor, Ronald *Literature and Society in Germany 1918-1945*, London, 1980
Weber, Hermann, and Pertinax, Lothar *Schein und Wirklichkeit in der DDR*, Stuttgart, 1978

Biographical, Critical and Interpretative

Anders, Günter *Bert Brecht: Gespräche und Erinnerungen*, Zürich, 1962
Aufricht, Ernst Josef *Erzähle damit du dein Recht erweist*, Berlin, 1966
Banholzer, Paula *So viel wie eine Liebe. Der unbekannte Brecht* (ed. A. Poldner and W. Esen), Munich, 1981
Baxandall, Lee 'Brecht in America, 1935', *Tulane Drama Review*, Autumn 1967
Benjamin, Walter *Versuche über Brecht*, Frankfurt, 1966. (Tr. by Anna Bostock as *Understanding Brecht*, London, 1973.)
Bentley, Eric *The Brecht Commentaries 1943-1980*, London, 1981
Bergner, Elisabeth *Bewundert viel und viel gescholten. Unordentliche Erinnerungen*, Munich, 1978
Boie-Grotz, Kirsten *Brecht - der unbekannte Erzähler: Die Prosa 1913-1934*, Stuttgart, 1978
Bronnen, Arnolt *Arnolt Bronnen gibt zu Protokoll*, Hamburg, 1954
   Tage mit Brecht: Geschichte einer unvollendeten Freundschaft, Munich, 1960; Berlin, 1974
Bunge, Hans *Fragen Sie mehr über Brecht: Hanns Eisler im Gespräch*, Munich, 1970
   Brechts Lai-Tu; Ruth Berlau erzählt (to be published in East Germany)
Demetz, Peter (ed.) *Brecht: a Collection of Critical Essays*, Englewood Cliffs, 1962
Dessau, Paul *Notizen zu Noten* (ed. F. Hennenberg), Leipzig, 1974
Dickson, Keith *Towards Utopia*, Oxford, 1978
Döblin, Alfred *Aufsätze zur Literatur*, Freiburg, 1963
Drew, David (ed.) *Kurt Weill. Ausgewählte Schriften*, Frankfurt, 1976
Dymschitz, Alexander *Ein unvergesslicher Frühling*, Berlin, 1970
Eisler, Hanns *Musik und Politik. Schriften 1924-1948* (ed. G. Mayer), Leipzig, 1973
Engberg, Harald *Brecht auf Fünen* (tr. Heinz Kulas), Wuppertal, 1974
Engel, Erich *Schriften über Theater und Film*, Berlin, 1951
Esslin, Martin *Brecht: a Choice of Evils*, London, 1959
   Mediations: Essays on Brecht, Beckett and the Media, London, 1980
Fassmann, Kurt *Brecht: eine Bildbiographie*, Munich, 1958
Fleisser, Marieluise 'Avantgarde', in *Gesammelte Werke*, Frankfurt, 1972
Fradkin, Ilja *Bertolt Brecht*, Leipzig, 1974
Frisch, Max 'Erinnerungen an Brecht', *Kursbuch* No. 7, Frankfurt, 1966
   Tagebuch 1946-1949, Zürich, 1967
   Tagebuch 1966-1971, Frankfurt, 1972
Frisch, Werner, and Obermeyer, K. W. *Brecht in Augsburg*, Frankfurt, 1976

Gersch, Wolfgang *Film bei Brecht*, Munich, 1976
Giehse, Therese *Ich habe nichts zu sagen. Gespräche mit Monika Sperr*, Munich, 1973
Gorelik, Mordecai *New Theatres for Old*, New York, 1940
Gray, Ronald *Brecht the Dramatist*, Cambridge, 1976
Grimm, Reinhold *Brecht und Nietzsche oder Geständnisse eines Dichters*, Frankfurt, 1979
    Bertolt Brecht und die Weltliteratur, Nuremberg, 1961
Grosz, Georg *Ein kleines Ja und ein grosses Nein*, Hamburg, 1955
Hauptmann, Elisabeth *Julia ohne Romeo*, Berlin, 1981
Hayman, Ronald 'A Last Interview with Brecht', *London Magazine*, vol. III no. 11
    (November 1956), pp. 47–52.
Hecht, Werner *Brechts Weg zum epischen Theater*, Berlin, 1962
    Aufsätze über Brecht, Berlin, 1970
    Sieben Studien über Brecht, Frankfurt, 1972
    Bertolt Brecht, Sein Leben in Bildern und Texten (ed.), Frankfurt, 1978
Hecht, Werner, and Unseld, Siegfried (eds) *Helene Weigel zu Ehren*, Frankfurt, 1970
Herzfelde, Wieland *Zur Sache*, Berlin, 1976
Högel, Max *Bertolt Brecht: Ein Porträt*, Augsburg, 1962
Ihering, Herbert *Die zwanziger Jahre*, Berlin, 1948
    Bertolt Brecht und das Theater, Berlin, 1960
    Von Reinhardt bis Brecht, Berlin, 1961
Innes, C. D. *Erwin Piscator's Political Theatre*, Cambridge, 1972
Karasek, Hellmuth *Bertolt Brecht*, Munich, 1977
Kesting, Marianne *Bertolt Brecht in Selbstzeugnissen und Bilddokumenten*, Hamburg,
    1959
Kortner, Fritz *Alle Tage Abend*, Munich, 1959
Lacis, Asja *Revolutionär im Beruf* (ed. H. Brenner), Munich, 1971
Lingen, Theo *Ich über mich*, Velber (Hanover), 1963
Losey, Joseph 'The Individual Eye', *Encore*, March–April 1961
Lyon, James K. *Bertolt Brecht and Rudyard Kipling*, The Hague, 1975
    Bertolt Brecht's American Cicerone, Bonn, 1978
    Brecht in America, Princeton, 1980
Mayer, Hans *Bertolt Brecht und die Tradition*, Pfullingen, 1961
    Anmerkungen zu Brecht, Frankfurt, 1965
    Brecht in der Geschichte, Frankfurt, 1971
Melchinger, Siegfried Introduction to *Caspar Neher*, Velber (Hanover), 1966
Mittenzwei, Werner *Bertolt Brecht: Von der 'Massnahme' zu 'Leben des Galilei'*, Berlin,
    1962
    Brechts Verhältnis zur Tradition, Berlin, 1972
    Wer war Brecht? (ed.), Berlin, 1977
Münsterer, Hans Otto *Bertolt Brecht: Erinnerungen aus den Jahren 1917–1922*, Weimar,
    1966
Needle, Jan, and Thomson, Peter *Brecht*, Oxford, 1981
Parmalee, Patty Lee *Brecht's America*, Columbus, Ohio, 1980
Pike, David *German Writers in Soviet Exile 1935–1945*, Chapel Hill, 1982
Piscator, Erwin *Schriften* (ed. L. Hoffmann, 2 vols), Berlin, 1968
Rasch, Wolfdietrich 'Bertolt Brechts marxistischer Lehrer', *Merkur*, August 1963
Reich, Bernhard *Im Wettlauf mit der Zeit*, Berlin, 1970

Rülicke-Weiler, Käthe *Die Dramaturgie Brechts*, Berlin, 1966
Sanders, Ronald *The Days Grow Short: The Life and Music of Kurt Weill*, London, 1980
Schmidt, Dieter *'Baal' und der junge Brecht*, Stuttgart, 1966
Schuhmann, Klaus *Der Lyriker Brecht 1913–1933*, Berlin, 1964
Schumacher, Ernst *Drama und Geschichte in Brechts 'Leben des Galilei'*, Berlin, 1968
Schumacher, Ernst and Renate *Leben Brechts in Wort und Bild*, Berlin, 1978
Spalter, Max *Brecht's Tradition*, Baltimore, 1967
Steinweg, Reiner (ed.) *Brechts Modell der Lehrstücke*, Frankfurt, 1976
Sternberg, Fritz *Der Dichter und die Ratio*, Göttingen, 1963
Tatlow, Anthony *The Mask of Evil*, Berne, 1977
Viertel, Berthold *Schriften zum Theater*, Berlin, 1970
Viertel, Salka *The Kindness of Strangers*, New York, 1969
Voigts, Manfred (ed.) *100 Texte zu Brecht*, Munich, 1980
Völker, Klaus *Brecht-Chronik: Daten zu Leben und Werk*, Munich, 1971
    Bertolt Brecht: Eine Biographie, Munich, 1976
Weber, Betty Nance, and Heinen, Hubert (eds) *Bertolt Brecht: Political Theory and Literary Practice*, Manchester, 1980
Weber, Carl 'Brecht as Director', *Tulane Drama Review*, Autumn 1967
Wekwerth, Manfred *Schriften. Arbeit mit Brecht* (ed. L. Hoffmann), Berlin, 1975
Willett, John *The Theatre of Bertolt Brecht*, London, 1959
    The Theatre of Erwin Piscator, London, 1978
Witt, Herbert (ed.) *Erinnerungen an Brecht*, Leipzig, 1964
Zuckmayer, Carl *Als wär's ein Stück von mir*, Frankfurt, 1966

Index